CA

INTERACTIVE TEXT

Advanced
Paper 5

Managing People and Systems

BPP is the **official provider** of training materials for the ACCA's CAT qualification. This Interactive Text forms part of a suite of learning tools, which also includes CD-ROMs for tuition and computer based assessment, and the innovative, Internet-based 'virtual campus'.

In this June 2004 edition

- Clear language and presentation

- Plenty of activities, examples and quizzes to demonstrate and practise techniques

- Syllabus and teaching guide

- Question and answer bank, including questions from the Pilot paper

FOR DECEMBER 2004 AND JUNE 2005 EXAMS

First edition 2003
Second edition June 2004

ISBN 0 7517 1651 0 (Previous edition 0 7517 1171 3)

British Library Cataloguing-in-Publication Data
A catalogue record for this book
is available from the British Library

Published by

BPP Professional Education
Aldine House, Aldine Place
London W12 8AW

www.bpp.com

Printed in Great Britain by W M Print
45-47 Frederick Street
Walsall, West Midlands
WS2 9NE

All our rights reserved. No part of this publication may be reproduced, stored in a retrieval system or transmitted, in any form or by any means, electronic, mechanical, photocopying, recording or otherwise, without the prior written permission of BPP Professional Education.

We are grateful to the Association of Chartered Certified Accountants for permission to reproduce the syllabus, teaching guide and questions of which the Association holds the copyright. The Answer Bank has been prepared by BPP Professional Education.

©

BPP Professional Education
2004

Contents

Page

INTRODUCTION
How to use this Interactive Text - Syllabus – Study sessions – Approach to examining the syllabus (iv)

PART A: THE BUSINESS AND ACCOUNTING ENVIRONMENT

1	The business environment	3
2	Organisational structure	20
3	Business planning and control	48
4	The accounting function	56

PART B: EFFECTIVE MANAGEMENT OF BUSINESS AND ACCOUNTING SYSTEMS

5	Monitoring business and accounting systems	69
6	Identifying and preventing fraud	85
7	Improving control procedures	100
8	Management information and reporting systems	116

PART C: MANAGEMENT THEORY, PRINCIPLES AND TECHNIQUES

9	Leadership, management and supervision	129
10	Individual and group behaviour	154
11	Team management	170
12	Motivation	187

PART D: INDIVIDUAL EFFECTIVENESS AT WORK

13	Planning and organising personal work	209
14	Constructive relationships	233
15	Performance appraisal	266
16	Training and development	285

PART E: HEALTH, SAFETY AND SECURITY IN THE WORKING ENVIRONMENT

17	Health and safety in the workplace	309
18	Security in the workplace	341

QUESTION BANK 363

ANSWER BANK 371

LIST OF KEY TERMS 405

INDEX 407

REVIEW FORM AND FREE PRIZE DRAW

ORDER FORM

How to use this Interactive Text

HOW TO USE THIS INTERACTIVE TEXT

Aim of this Interactive Text

> To provide the knowledge and practice to help you succeed in the examination for Paper 5 *Managing People and Systems*

To pass the examination you need a thorough understanding in all areas covered by the syllabus and teaching guide.

Recommended approach

(a) To pass you need to be able to answer questions on **everything** specified by the syllabus and teaching guide. Read the text very carefully and do not skip any of it.

(b) Learning is an **active** process. Do **all** the activities as you work through the text so you can be sure you really understand what you have read.

(c) After you have covered the material in the Interactive Text, work through the **Question Bank**, checking your answers carefully against the **Answer Bank**.

(d) Before you take the exam, check that you still remember the material using the following quick revision plan.

    (i) Read through the **chapter topic list** at the beginning of each chapter. Are there any gaps in your knowledge? If so, study the section again.

    (ii) Read and learn the **key terms**.

    (iii) Look at the **exam alerts**. These show the ways in which topics might be examined.

    (iv) Read and learn the **key learning points**, which are a summary of each chapter.

    (v) Do the **quick quizzes** again. If you know what you're doing, they shouldn't take long.

This approach is only a suggestion. You or your college may well adapt it to suit your needs.

Remember this is a **practical** course.

(a) Try to relate the material to your experience in the workplace or any other work experience you may have had.

(b) Try to make as many links as you can to other papers.

SYLLABUS

Managing People and Systems

AIMS
To develop knowledge and understanding of the role of a manager in an effective, efficient, safe and secure accounting environment. This includes the coordination of work activities, the maintenance of an effective accounting system, people management, personal effectiveness, health and safety and security issues within the workplace.

OBJECTIVES
On completion of this paper, candidates should be able to:

- develop an overview of the overall business organisation and its critical external relationships and identify the key external regulations and relationships affecting accounting and business
- understand how accounting systems are affected by organisational structure and the overall management information system
- describe methods for resource planning and coordinating work
- explain the purpose, structure and organisation of the accounting function and its relationships with other organisational functions
- identify systems and procedures for effective functional management
- describe principles of management leadership, delegation, motivation and communication
- explain principles of effective working relationships and teamwork
- understand the need for effective performance appraisal, development and training to enhance personal and organisational effectiveness
- understand the importance of a safe and secure working environment.

POSITION OF THE PAPER IN THE OVERALL SYLLABUS
No prior knowledge is required before commencing study for Paper 5. This paper provides the basic techniques required to fulfil the role of a manager in the accounting environment.

SYLLABUS CONTENT

1 **The business and accounting environment**
   (a) Environmental influences on the organisation
      (i) political, economic, social and technological
      (ii) external regulations affecting accounting and business practice
      (iii) external relationships (stakeholder interests)
   (b) The organisation
      (i) the structure of business functions
      (ii) sources of management information
      (iii) the nature of policies, systems and procedures
      (iv) types of business transactions
      (v) methods of planning and control
         - business planning and control
         - information management and control
         - human resources planning and control
   (c) The accounting function
      (i) purpose
      (ii) structure
      (iii) position within the organisation
      (iv) types of accounting system
         - manual
         - computerised

2 **Effective management of business and accounting systems**
   (a) Monitoring business and accounting system
      (i) the role of internal auditors
      (ii) the role of external auditors
      (iii) the role of management
   (b) Recognising potential weaknesses in the accounting system
      (i) weaknesses of controls
      (ii) potential areas for error and fraud
   (c) Fraud
      (i) common types of fraud
      (ii) the implications of fraud
      (iii) detecting fraud in the accounting system
      (iv) preventing fraud
   (d) Internal controls
      (i) the importance of internal controls
      (ii) the control mechanisms in the accounting system
   (e) Management information and reporting systems
      (i) features of a management information system
      (ii) information flows within an accounting system
      (iii) processing and storage of data and transactions

Managing People and Systems

3 Management theory, principles and techniques
  (a) Managing people for effective working relationships
    (i) principles of leadership, management supervision and delegation, including consideration of:
      – communication
      – resolving problems and queries
    (ii) principles of authority
      – differing styles of management
      – taking corrective action
  (b) Individual and group behaviour
    (i) organisational culture
    (ii) contribution of individuals and groups to organisational success
  (c) Team management
    (i) team formation
    (ii) team development
    (iii) team evaluation and rewards
  (d) Motivation
    (i) key theories of motivation
    (ii) the function of sanctions and rewards in motivation

4 Individual effectiveness at work
  (a) Planning and organising personal work
    (i) understanding roles and responsibilities
      – effective work methods and practices in the organisation
      – reporting procedures
    (ii) work planning and planning aids (diaries, schedules, action plans)
    (iii) prioritising and time management, including unforeseen situations
  (b) Constructive relationships
    (i) methods of communication
    (ii) influencing, negotiating and coordinating
    (iii) procedures for dealing with disagreement and conflict arising from:
      – personality
      – working style
      – status
      – work demands
  (c) Improving individual performance
    (i) personal performance and appraisal
      – setting objectives
      – assessing progress
    (ii) identifying areas for individual learning

5 Health, safety and security in the working environment
  (a) The importance of health and safety
    (i) health and safety in the working environment
      – legislation
      – regulations
      – record keeping
      – keeping up-to-date with requirements
    (ii) common hazards and how to deal with them
    (iii) using equipment and behaving safely at work
    (iv) emergency procedures
      – illness
      – accidents
      – fires
      – security breaches
    (v) recommending improvements to health and safety
  (b) Recognising security risks
    (i) physical breaches of security
      – unauthorised physical intrusion
      – security of hardware and equipment
      – security of systems data and software
    (ii) methods of reducing or avoiding security risks.

EXCLUDED TOPICS

The syllabus does not require knowledge of specific computing hardware systems or their specifications, or how software systems are designed, developed, tested and implemented.

KEY AREAS OF THE SYLLABUS

All areas of the syllabus are equally important.

APPROACH TO EXAMINING THE SYLLABUS

The paper is constructed in such a way that it provides a broad assessment of the main issues involved in managing systems and people. In general terms, the paper is divided into five parts:

Managing People and Systems

1 The business and accounting environment
2 Effective management of business and accounting systems
3 Management theory, principles and techniques
4 Individual effectiveness at work
5 Health, safety and security in the working environment

Note that although the syllabus is sub-divided into five main parts, each part has a different number of teaching and learning sessions allocated to it. The number of sessions in each area reflects the number of learning outcomes identified within that area and this in turn determines the associated teaching and learning time required. For example, although health, safety and security in the working environment contains only two teaching and learning sessions it is still considered to be as important as any other area within the syllabus in terms of assessment. It should also be noted that although the course follows this structure, the nature of the syllabus means that there will often be some overlap between the individual topics.

Structure of the examination:
The examination is a two-hour written paper.

	No. of marks
5 compulsory questions (20 marks each)	100

As indicated above, a question will normally be set in each of the five syllabus areas detailed in the approach to examining the syllabus. Candidates therefore need to ensure that they have a broad knowledge of all aspects of the five key areas of the syllabus.

Managing People and Systems

STUDY SESSIONS
THE BUSINESS AND ACCOUNTING ENVIRONMENT

1 **The organisation's environment and external relationships**
   (a) Define an organisation and its environment
   (b) Identify the main stakeholders within and outside the organisation
   (c) Describe general political, economic, social and technological factors affecting the organisation and its stakeholders
   (d) Identify the authorities to whom businesses are accountable in financial terms
   (e) Identify what financial information businesses need to provide for government agencies
   (f) Describe the role of external auditors
   (g) Outline the role of accounting standards setting bodies
   (h) Outline the role of corporate governance with respect to accountability
   (i) Describe the overall role and purpose of employment, health and safety and data protection legislation within the business

2 **Organisational structure**
   (a) Identify the purpose and objectives of an organisation
   (b) Recognise the stages needed to establish an organisation
   (c) Explain what influences the structure of an organisation, with reference to the work of Fayol.
   (d) Describe the business as a system with clearly defined functional areas
       (i) explain the role of production or direct service provision
       (ii) explain the roles of sales and marketing
       (iii) explain the role of accounting and finance
       (iv) explain the role of human resource planning
   (e) Identify organisational levels and spans of control
   (f) Recognise how departments within an organisation are structured
       (i) describe the hierarchical structure and functional divisionalisation
       (ii) describe the matrix or task based structure of business
       (iii) explain geographical divisionalisation
       (iv) explain product or service divisionalisation

3 **Business and resource planning and co-ordination**
   (a) Outline the purpose of an overall business plan
       (i) identify the objectives of long-range planning
       (ii) outline the role of short-range planning
   (b) Identify elements of resource planning and control
       (i) describe the elements of the organisational plan
       (ii) describe the elements of the human resource plan
   (c) Explain the need for co-ordination in the planning process

4 **General systems and clerical procedures in business**
   (a) Explain the purpose of systems, policies and procedures in a general business context
   (b) Describe the principles of effective systems and procedures
   (c) Identify and explain general office procedures and systems using flowcharting techniques
   (d) Review the effectiveness of office procedures and identify weaknesses
   (e) Review the effectiveness of financial control procedures and identify potential weaknesses

5 **Accounting systems and procedures**
   (a) Outline the function and purpose of the accounting system within an organisation
   (b) Identify key elements of the accounting system and procedures and how they are structured
   (c) Explain how the accounting department integrates and co-ordinates with other functional areas
   (d) Explain the difference between manual and computerised accounting systems

EFFECTIVE MANAGEMENT OF BUSINESS AND ACCOUNTING SYSTEMS

6 **Internal control and auditing**
   (a) Explain the importance of internal controls in an organisation
   (b) Describe the responsibilities of management with respect to internal control
   (c) Describe the different roles of the internal and external auditors
   (d) Recognise the weaknesses of controls and the features of effective control procedures

Managing People and Systems

7 Identifying and preventing fraud in an accounting system
- (a) Describe the three prerequisites for fraud, eg dishonesty, opportunity and motivation
- (b) Identify common types of fraud
- (c) Explain the implications of fraud for an organisation
- (d) Identify the scope for fraud using manual as against computer systems
- (e) Describe systems and procedures to discover and prevent fraud
- (f) Understand the role of the auditor in dealing with fraud
- (g) Identify the duty and responsibilities of management in the prevention and detection of fraud

8 Improving control procedures within the accounting system
- (a) Describe the payroll system and appropriate controls
- (b) Describe the main stages of the purchases cycle and appropriate controls
- (c) Describe the main stages of the sales cycle and appropriate controls
- (d) Describe the cash system and appropriate controls
- (e) Explain how controls are more effective if systems are integrated

9 Management information and reporting systems
- (a) Describe the main features of a management information system
- (b) Describe the information flows within the accounting system
- (c) Draft examples of relevant management reports from an accounting system
- (d) Understand how data and transactions are processed and stored within the accounting system

MANAGEMENT THEORY, PRINCIPLES AND TECHNIQUES

10 Effective leadership, management and supervision
- (a) Describe the process of determining authority and responsibility with reference to Contingency Theory, and the work of Woodward, Burns and Stalker, Fayol, Mintzberg, Weber
- (b) Describe the skills, traits and characteristics of a leader, with reference to Blake and Mouton, Handy, Hersey, Blanchard and Likert
- (c) Explain the role of management, with reference to the work of Drucker, Kanter, Ouchi, Peters
- (d) Explain the role of the supervisor in achieving tasks, building the team and developing individuals
- (e) Describe the principles of effective delegation
- (f) Compare and contrast the terms 'leadership', 'management', 'supervision' and delegation

11 Individual and group behaviour
- (a) Explain the concept of organisational culture and discuss its limitations, with reference to the work of Anthony and Handy
- (b) Discuss the differences between individual and group behaviour
- (c) Outline the contribution of individuals and teams to organisational success
- (d) Identify work that benefits from either an individual or team approach
- (e) Recognise behaviour facilitating and inhibiting organisational success

12 Team Management
- (a) Define the purpose of a team
- (b) Outline the composition of successful teams, with reference to the work of Belbin, Peters and Waterman
- (c) Explain the stages in the development of a team using Tuckman's "Forming, Storming, Norming, Performing and Dorming"
- (d) Identify and explain key team building blocks and blockages, with reference to the work of Woodcock
- (e) Describe the main ways of rewarding a team
- (f) Identify appropriate methods to evaluate team performance

13 Motivation, concepts and models
- (a) Outline the key theories of motivation: Maslow, Herzberg, Handy, Equity Theory, Argyris, McLelland, Vroom, McGregor's Theories X and Y and Ouchi's Theory Z
- (b) Outline the difference between content and process theories of motivation
- (c) Describe ways in which management can motivate staff

Managing People and Systems

　　(d) Explain the importance of the reward system in the process of motivation
　　(e) Explain the importance of feedback

INDIVIDUAL EFFECTIVENESS

14 Work effectiveness
　　(a) Explain the benefits of planning and organising personal work in the context of:
　　　　(i) understanding roles and responsibilities
　　　　(ii) using effective work methods and practices in the organisation
　　　　(iii) identifying appropriate reporting procedures
　　　　(iv) using work planning and planning aids (diaries, schedules, action plans)
　　　　(v) prioritising work and time management, including unforeseen situations

15 Effective communication and interpersonal skills
　　(a) Recognise the importance of good communication, both formal and informal, in the workplace
　　(b) Identify and describe the main methods and attributes of effective personal communication and the effects of poor communication
　　(c) Distinguish between verbal and non-verbal forms of personal communication
　　(d) Define the term 'interpersonal skills' in the context of effective management practice
　　(e) Explain the importance of developing effective personal working relationships
　　(f) Identify appropriate ways of gaining commitment from individual staff members
　　(g) Describe appropriate methods for dealing with conflict in a work environment

16 Effective training and development
　　(a) Distinguish between training and development
　　(b) Explain the importance of training and development to the organisation and the individual
　　(c) Explain the roles and responsibilities of a training manager
　　(d) Explain the methods used to analyse training needs
　　(e) Suggest ways in which training needs can be met
　　(f) Compare and contrast the various methods used in developing individuals in the workplace
　　(g) Describe methods of staff evaluation and follow-up

17 Appraisal of competence and individual development
　　(a) Explain the process of competence assessment
　　(b) Outline the purpose and benefits of the staff appraisal process
　　(c) Describe the barriers to effective staff appraisal
　　(d) Identify the management skills involved in the appraisal process
　　(e) Describe the roles of the appraisor and appraisee in the appraisal process
　　(f) Explain the process of preparation for an appraisal interview, including location of interview and pre-interview correspondence
　　(g) Recognise the importance of feedback from the appraisal interview
　　(h) Explain the link between the appraisal process and effective employee development

18 The individual learning process
　　(a) Explain the process of learning in the workplace
　　(b) Describe the ways in which individuals learn
　　(c) Explain the effect of individual differences on learning
　　(d) Outline the barriers to learning
　　(e) Describe the role of management in the learning process
　　(f) Suggest appropriate ways in which the organisation can motivate individuals to learn

HEALTH, SAFETY AND SECURITY IN THE WORKING ENVIRONMENT

19 Health and safety in the workplace
　　(a) Outline the main provisions of relevant legislation on health and safety
　　(b) Identify possible sources of danger to health and safety of individuals within the workplace
　　(c) Suggest appropriate preventative and protective measures
　　(d) Discuss the role of training in raising awareness of safety issues

Managing People and Systems

(e) Describe safe working conditions and identify potential hazards

(f) Outline the role and responsibility of management in promoting health and safety

20 Security in the workplace

(a) Describe possible sources of security breaches within the workplace
  (i) identify means of physical intrusion
  (ii) describe threats related to hardware and equipment security
  (iii) explain hazards from internal and external software security breaches

(b) Outline measures for preventing security breaches
  (i) describe methods of preventing physical intrusion
  (ii) explain measures of protecting hardware and equipment
  (iii) identify strategies for reducing the risk of software security breaches

PAGE 9

Approach to examining the syllabus

APPROACH TO EXAMINING THE SYLLABUS

Paper 5 is a two-hour written paper.

The written examination consists of one section, as follows:

	No of marks
5 compulsory questions of 20 marks each	100

Analysis of Pilot paper

Pilot paper

1. Different types of management structures
2. Fraud
3. Managerial roles and qualities
4. Training and personal development
5. Data protection and security

Part A
The business and accounting environment

Chapter 1   The business environment

Chapter topic list

1. What is an organisation?
2. The organisation as an open system
3. Environmental influences on organisations
4. Organisational stakeholders
5. Financial accountability
6. Legislation and business practice

The following study sessions are covered in this chapter:

		Syllabus reference
1(a)	Define an organisation and its environment	1(a)
1(b)	Identify the main stakeholders within and outside the organisation	1(a)(iii)
1(c)	Describe environmental factors affecting the organisation	1(a)(i)
1(d)	Identify the authorities to whom businesses are financially accountable	1(a)(ii)
1(e)	Identify what financial information businesses need to provide for government agencies	1(a)(ii)
1(f), (g)	Describe the role of external auditors and regulatory bodies	1(a)(ii)
1(h)	Outline the role of corporate governance with respect to accountability	1(a)(ii)
1(i)	Describe the impact of legislation on business practice	1(a)(ii)

Part A: The business and accounting environment

1 WHAT IS AN ORGANISATION?

1.1 Here are some examples of organisations.

- A multinational car manufacturer (eg Ford)
- An accountancy firm (eg Ernst and Young)
- A charity (eg Oxfam)
- A local authority
- A trade union (eg Unison)
- An army

What organisations have in common

1.2 The definition below states what all organisations have in common.

KEY TERM

An **organisation** is: 'a *social arrangement* which pursues collective *goals*, which *controls* its own performance and which has a *boundary* separating it from its environment'.

1.3 Here is how this definition applies to two of the organisations listed in Paragraph 1.1.

Characteristic	Car manufacturer (eg Ford)	Army
Social arrangement: individuals gathered together for a purpose	People work in different divisions, making different cars	Soldiers are in different regiments, and there is a chain of command from the top to the bottom
Collective goals: the organisation has goals over and above the goals of the people within it	Sell cars, make money	Defend the country, defeat the enemy, international peace keeping
Controls performance: performance is monitored against the goals and adjusted if necessary to ensure the goals are accomplished	Costs and quality are reviewed and controlled. Standards are constantly improved	Strict disciplinary procedures, training
Boundary: the organisation is distinct from its environment	Physical: factory gates Social: employment status	Physical: barracks Social: different rules than for civilians

(a) Organisations are preoccupied with **performance**, and meeting or improving their standards.

(b) Organisations contain formal, documented **systems and procedures** which enable them to control what they do.

(c) Different people do different things, or **specialise** in one activity.

(d) Organisations pursue a **variety of objectives** and goals.

(e) Most organisations obtain **inputs** (eg materials), and **process** them into **outputs** (eg for others to buy).

1: The business environment

Why do organisations exist?

1.4 Organisations achieve results which individuals cannot achieve by themselves. They enable people to be **more productive**.

(a) **Overcoming people's individual limitations**, whether physical or intellectual.

(b) **Enabling people to specialise** in what they do best.

(c) **Saving time**, because people can work together or do two aspects of a different task at the same time.

(d) **Accumulating** and sharing **knowledge** (eg about how best to build cars).

(e) Enabling people to **pool their expertise**.

(f) Enabling **synergy**: by bringing together two individuals their combined output will exceed their individual output.

How organisations differ

1.5 The enormous variety of organisations was hinted at in Paragraph 1.1. Here are some possible differences between them.

Factor	Example
Ownership (public vs private)	Private sector: owned by private owners/shareholders. Public sector: owned by the government
Control	By the owners themselves, by people working on their behalf, or indirectly by government-sponsored regulators
Activity (ie what they do)	Manufacturing, healthcare
Profit or non-profit **orientation**	Business exists to make a profit. The army, on the other hand, is not profit orientated
Legal status/size	Limited company or partnership
Sources of **finance**	Borrowing, government funding, share issues
Technology	High use of technology (eg computer firms) vs low use (eg corner shop)

Two key differences in the list above are **what the organisation does** and whether or not it is **profit orientated**.

1.6 **Within** a typical organisation, there are many different types of activity being carried out.

- **Purchasing materials** and components
- Carrying out **operations** on purchased materials and components
- **Accounting and record keeping**, eg keeping track of costs
- **Research and development** of new products or technologies
- Taking **orders** from customers
- **Planning** and implementing marketing strategies to obtain new customers
- **Employing** people and paying them
- **Co-ordinating** all the above to ensure the organisation reaches its goals

Part A: The business and accounting environment

2 THE ORGANISATION AS AN OPEN SYSTEM

Systems theory

> **KEY TERM**
>
> A **system** is a collection of interrelated parts which taken together forms a whole such that:
>
> (a) The collection has some purpose
>
> (b) A change in any of the parts leads to (or results from) a change in some other part or parts.

2.1 An organisation is a type of system.

Open and closed systems

2.2 **General systems theory** makes a distinction between open, closed and semi-closed systems.

(a) **A closed system is isolated from its environment and independent of it**, so that no environmental influences affect the behaviour of the system, nor does the system exert any influence on its environment.

Closed:
Shut off from its environment

(b) **An open system is connected to and interacts with its environment.** It takes in influences from its environment and also influences this environment by its behaviour. An open system is a stable system which is nevertheless continually changing or evolving.

Controllable inputs
Uncontrollable inputs ▸
Unexpected inputs

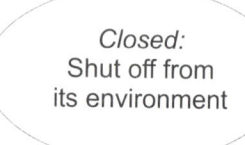

▸ Both predictable
▸ and unpredictable
▸ outputs

(c) **Few systems are entirely closed.** Many are **semi-closed**, in that their relationship with the environment is in some degree restricted.

Predicted/controlled
inputs from the ▸
environment

Semi-closed:
Relating to its environment in a controlled prescribed manner

▸ Predictable /
controllable
outputs

2.3 **Social organisations, such as businesses and government departments, are by definition open systems.** Organisations have a variety of interchanges with the environment, obtaining inputs from it, and generating outputs to it.

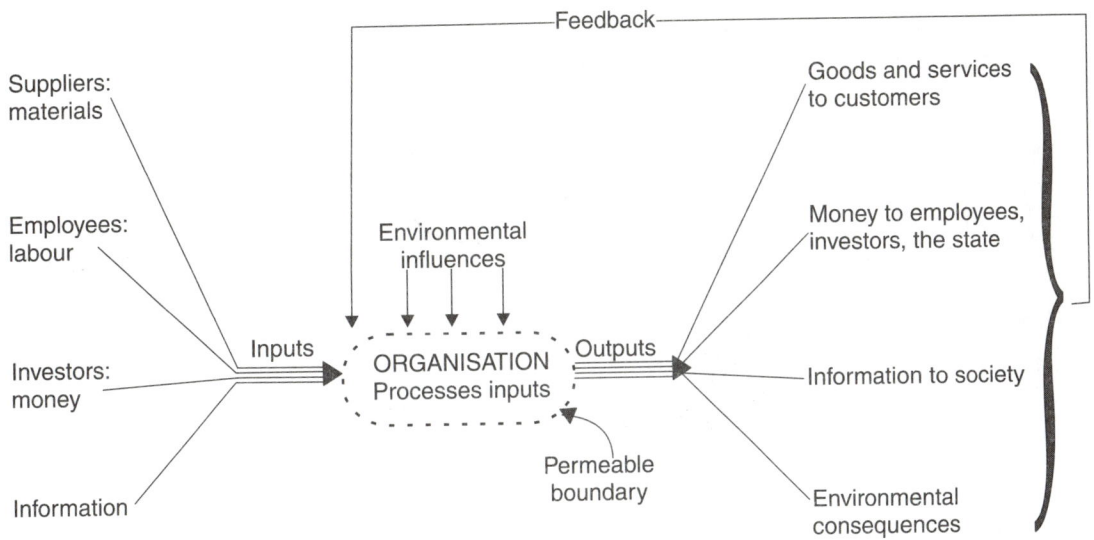

Environmental uncertainty

2.4 A large part of business strategy consists of making the organisation's interaction with its environment as efficient as possible. An organisation needs to 'fit' comfortably with its environment. In the context of strategic management, therefore, the degree of **uncertainty** in the environment is of great importance. The greater the uncertainty, the greater the strategic challenge.

2.5 Uncertainty depends on **complexity** and **stability**: the more complex or dynamic the environment is, the more uncertain it is.

(a) An **uncomplicated, stable** environment can be dealt with as a matter of routine. Since the future is likely to resemble the past, extrapolation from history is a satisfactory way of preparing for future events.

(b) Where the environment is **dynamic**, the management approach must emphasise response to rapid change.

(c) **Complexity** makes an environment difficult to understand. Diversity of operations and technological advance contribute to complexity.

3 ENVIRONMENTAL INFLUENCES ON ORGANISATIONS

3.1 As we have seen, an organisation is an **open system**, so it interacts with its environment. A large part of strategic planning for any organisation is concerned with managing its **relationship with the environment**.

3.2 The environment of an organisation is **everything outside its boundaries**. Its immediate (or **micro**) environment consists of its suppliers, customers, competitors and **stakeholders**. Stakeholders are explained further in Section 4.

3.3 Moving further out from the organisation is the **macro environment**. This consists of factors over which the organisation itself has less control, but which can seriously affect its business practices and profitability.

Part A: The business and accounting environment

3.4 A useful model for this type of environmental analysis uses the acronym **PEST**. The environmental influences are analysed under four categories:

- Political/legal
- Economic
- Social
- Technological

3.5 We will look at each of these in turn.

Political/legal

3.6 Legal factors affecting all companies

Factor	Example
General legal framework: contract, tort, agency	Basic ways of doing business; negligence proceedings; ownership; rights and responsibilities, property
Criminal law	Theft; insider dealing; bribery; deception
Company law	Directors and their duties; reporting requirements; takeover proceedings; shareholders' rights; insolvency
Employment law	Trade Union recognition; Social Chapter provisions; minimum wage; unfair dismissal; redundancy; maternity; Equal Opportunities
Health and Safety	Fire precautions; safety procedures
Data protection	Use of information about employees and customers
Marketing and sales	Laws to protect consumers (eg refunds and replacement, 'cooling off' period after credit agreements); advertising standards
Environment	Pollution control; waste disposal
Tax law	Corporation tax payment; Collection of income tax (PAYE) and National Insurance contributions; VAT
Competition law	General illegality of cartels; price fixing

3.7 Some legal and regulatory factors affect **particular industries**, if the public interest is served. This is for either of two reasons.

- The industries are, effectively, monopolies.
- Large sums of public money are involved (eg in subsidies to rail companies).

For example, electricity, gas, telecommunications, water and rail transport are subject to **regulators** (Offer, Ofgas, Oftel, Ofwat, Ofrail) who have influence over market access, competition and pricing policy.

Political risk and political change

3.8 The political environment is not simply limited to legal factors. Government policy affects the whole **economy**, and governments are responsible for enforcing and creating a **stable framework** in which business can be done. The quality of **government policy is important in providing** three things.

- Physical infrastructure (eg transport)
- Social infrastructure (education, a welfare safety net, law enforcement, equal opportunities)
- Market infrastructure (enforceable contracts, policing corruption)

Political risk

3.9 The political risk in a decision is the risk that political factors will **invalidate the strategy** and perhaps severely damage the firm. Examples are wars, political chaos, corruption and nationalisation.

3.10 Companies should ask the following six questions.

1	How **stable** is the host country's political system?
2	How **strong** is the host government's commitment to specific rules of the game, such as ownership or contractual rights, given its ideology and power position?
3	How **long** is the government likely to remain in **power**?
4	If the present government is **succeeded**, how would the specific rules of the game change?
5	What would be the effects of any expected **changes** in the specific rules of the game?
6	In light of those effects, what **decisions and actions should be taken now**?

The economic environment

3.11 The economic environment is an important influence at local and national level.

Factor	Impact
Overall growth or fall in Gross Domestic Product	Increased/decreased demand for goods and services.
Local economic trends	Type of industry in the area. Office/factory rents. Labour rates. House prices.
Inflation	Distorts business decisions. Wage inflation compensates for price inflation.
Interest rates	How much it costs to borrow money affects **cash flow**. Some businesses carry a high level of debt. Rises in interest rates affect customers' mortgage payments.
Tax levels	Corporation tax affects how much firms can invest or return to shareholders. Income tax and VAT affect how much consumers have to spend.
Government spending	Suppliers to the government (eg construction firms) are affected by spending.
The business cycle	Economic activity is always punctuated by periods of growth followed by decline, simply because of the nature of trade. The UK economy has been characterised by periods of boom and bust. Government policy can cause, exacerbate or mitigate such trends, but cannot abolish the business cycle.

3.12 The **forecast state of the economy** will influence the planning process for organisations which operate within it. In times of boom and increased demand and consumption, the overall planning problem will be to **identify** the demand. Conversely, in times of recession, the emphasis will be on cost-effectiveness, continuing profitability, survival and competition.

Part A: The business and accounting environment

The social environment

Demography

> **KEY TERM**
>
> **Demography** is the study of human population and population trends.

3.13 **Factors of importance to organisational planners**

Factor	Comment
Growth	The rate of growth or decline in a national population and in regional populations.
Age	Changes in the age distribution of the population. In the UK, there will be an increasing proportion of the national population over retirement age. In developing countries there are very large numbers of young people.
Geography	The concentration of population into certain geographical areas.
Ethnicity	A population might contain groups with different ethnic origins from the majority. In the UK, about 5% come from ethnic minorities, although most of these live in London and the South East.
Household and family structure	A household is the basic social unit and its size might be determined by the number of children, whether elderly parents live at home etc. In the UK, there has been an increase in single-person households and lone parent families.
Social structure	The population of a society can be broken down into a number of subgroups, with different attitudes and access to economic resources. Social class, however, is hard to measure as people's subjective perceptions vary.
Employment	In part, this is related to changes in the workplace. Many people believe that there is a move to a casual flexible workforce. Some research indicates a 'two-tier' society split between '**work-rich**' (with two wage-earners) and '**work-poor**'. However, **most employees are in permanent, full-time employment.**
Wealth	Rising standards of living lead to increased demand for certain types of consumer good. This is why developing countries are attractive as markets.

3.14 **Implications of demographic change**

(a) **Changes in patterns of demand**: an ageing population suggests increased demand for health care services. A young growing population demands schools, housing and work.

(b) **Location of demand**: people move to the suburbs and small towns.

(c) **Recruitment policies**: there are relatively fewer young people, so firms will have to recruit from less familiar sources of labour.

(d) **Wealth and tax.** Patterns of poverty, and hence the need for welfare provisions may change. The tax base may alter.

Activity 1.1

How should a company selling package holidays for the 18-30 age group be expected to deal with the following long-term developments?

(a) Falling numbers of school leavers
(b) More young people going to university
(c) Greater disposable income among the 18-30 age group
(d) More people choosing independent holidays rather than packages

Technological factors

3.15 **Technology contributes to overall economic growth**. There are three ways in which technology can increase total output.

- Gains in **productivity** (more output per units of input)
- **Reduced costs** (eg transportation technology, labour-saving, time-saving)
- New **types** of product

3.16 **Effects of technological change on organisations**

(a) **The type of products or services that are made and sold.**

(b) **The way in which products are made** (eg robots, new raw materials)

(c) **The way in which services are provided.** For example companies selling easily transportable goods - for instance, books and CDs - are enjoying considerable success over the Internet.

(d) **The way in which markets are identified.** Database systems make it much easier to analyse the market place.

(e) **The way in which firms are managed.** IT encourages 'delayering' of organisational hierarchies, homeworking, and better communication.

(f) **The means and extent of communications with external clients.** The financial sector is rapidly going electronic - call centres are now essential to stay in business, PC banking is here, and the Internet is highly significant.

3.17 The impact of recent technological change also has important social consequences, which in turn have an impact on business.

(a) **Homeworking.** Whereas people were once collected together to work in factories, home working will become more important.

(b) **Intellective skills.** Certain sorts of skill, related to interpretation of data and information processes, are likely to become more valued than manual or physical skills.

(c) **Services.** Technology increases manufacturing productivity, releasing human resources for service jobs. These jobs require **greater interpersonal skills** (eg in dealing with customers).

Activity 1.2

The term 'global village' illustrates the 'shrinking' of the world due to globalisation. Differences still exist, however. What environmental factors might account for the variability of consumer demand in different countries?

Part A: The business and accounting environment

4   ORGANISATIONAL STAKEHOLDERS

KEY TERM

Stakeholders: groups or individuals whose interests are directly affected by the activities of a firm or organisation

4.1 Some of these stakeholders will be internal – such as shareholders and employees – and some of them will be external – such as banks and the government. All of them will want information about the organisation and its financial results.

4.2 These will be the main stakeholders for a large, listed company.

(a) **Managers of the company** appointed by the company's owners to supervise the day-to-day activities of the company. They need information about the company's financial situation currently, and in the future to enable them to manage the business efficiently and make effective decisions.

(b) **Shareholders of the company**, ie the company's owners, want to assess how well the management is performing. They want to know how profitable are the company's operations.

(c) **Trade contacts** include suppliers who provide goods to the company on credit and customers who purchase the goods or services provided by the company. **Suppliers** want to know about the company's ability to pay its debts. **Customers** need to know that the company is a secure source of supply.

(d) **Providers of finance to the company** might include a bank which allows the company to operate an overdraft, or provides longer-term finance by granting a loan. The bank wants to ensure that the company is able to keep up interest payments, and to repay the amounts advanced.

(e) **The taxation authorities** want to know about business profits in order to assess the tax payable by the company.

(f) **Employees of the company** are interested in information about the company's financial situation, because their future careers and salaries depend on it.

(g) **Financial analysts and advisers** need information for their clients or audience. Stockbrokers need information to advise investors; credit agencies want information to advise potential suppliers of goods to the company; journalists need information for their readers.

(h) **Governments and their agencies** are interested in the allocation of resources and the activities of enterprises. They also require information for national statistics.

(i) **The public.** Enterprises affect the public in a variety of ways. They may make a substantial contribution to the local economy by providing employment and using local suppliers. Another important factor is the possible polluting effect of an enterprise on the physical environment.

Activity 1.3

Identify the stakeholders in a private family-run company.

5 FINANCIAL ACCOUNTABILITY

Financial accounting regulations

5.1 For an unincorporated business, any form of accounting information is adequate if it gives the owner(s) of the business a basis for planning and control, and satisfies the requirements of external users such as the Inland Revenue.

5.2 Limited companies are more closely regulated. The regulations on accounts come from a number of sources.

- **Company law** enacted by the UK Parliament, and also EU law
- **Financial Reporting Standards** issued by the Financial Reporting Council
- The requirements of the **Stock Exchange**
- **Tax law** may have an impact

Company law

5.3 Limited companies are required by law to publish **accounts annually** for distribution to their shareholders.

- A copy of these accounts must be lodged with the Registrar of Companies and is available for inspection by any member of the public.
- The published accounts should show a '**true and fair view**'.
- The Companies Act also contains set **formats** for company accounts and states what information must be disclosed.

Non-statutory regulations

5.4 The **Financial Reporting Council** (FRC) is independent of the accountancy profession and draws its membership from a wide spectrum of accounts preparers and users. Its chairman is appointed by the Government. The FRC guides the standard setting process. The **Accounting Standards Board** (ASB) is responsible for the issue of **Financial Reporting Standards** (FRSs). FRSs lay down prescribed accounting treatments in areas where a variety of approaches might be taken. The aim is to ensure that users can compare the accounts of different companies. Some **Statements of Standard Accounting Practice** (SSAPs) issued by the ASB's predecessor are still in force.

5.5 The **Urgent Issues Task Force** (UITF) is an offshoot of the ASB. Its role is to assist the ASB in areas where an accounting standard or Companies Act provision already exists, but where unsatisfactory or conflicting interpretations have developed.

International accounting standards

5.6 The International Accounting Standards Committee (IASC) attempts to co-ordinate the development of international accounting standards. It includes representatives from many countries throughout the world, including the USA and the UK.

5.7 International standards are not intended to override local regulations. In the UK, however, the ASB will support international standards by incorporating them within the UK standards, although not every IAS has so far been incorporated in this way.

Part A: The business and accounting environment

The Stock Exchange regulations

5.8 The Stock Exchange is a market for stocks and shares, and a company whose securities are traded in this market is known as a 'quoted' or 'listed' company.

Such a company commits itself to certain procedures and standards, including matters concerning the disclosure of accounting information, which are more extensive than the disclosure requirements of the Companies Acts.

Auditing regulations

5.9 Company legislation also requires that the accounts of a limited company must be **audited**.

> **KEY TERM**
>
> An **audit** may be defined as an 'independent examination of, and expression of opinion on, the financial statements of an enterprise'.

In practice, a limited company must engage a firm of chartered or chartered certified accountants to examine its accounting records and its financial statements in order to form an opinion as to whether the accounts present a 'true and fair view' and comply with the Companies Act. At the conclusion of their audit work, the auditors issue a report addressed to the owners of the company (its **members** or **shareholders**) which is published as part of the accounts. Audit work is governed by Auditing Standards which are issued by the Auditing Practices Board.

Taxation regulations

5.10 Taxation regulations will affect the work of the accounts department of any organisation that runs a PAYE system or is registered for VAT.

   (a) A substantial amount of payroll work consists of keeping records (P11s) and submitting returns (P11D, P14, P35 and so on) to the Inland Revenue and the DSS.

   (b) VAT returns must be submitted at regular intervals and can also involve considerable administrative effort.

5.11 Regulations such as these have a significant impact on the **timing** of accounting work, since returns are required every month for payroll and every three months for VAT, and the **information must be ready in time** to comply with these requirements.

5.12 **Corporate governance**

> **KEY TERM**
>
> The **Cadbury Report** defines **corporate governance** as 'the system by which companies are directed and controlled'.

5.13 Corporate governance is a topical issue. A number of high profile scandals and frauds exposed the fact that shareholders in listed companies often have insufficient influence over the activities of the directors, and in many cases have insufficient knowledge of how the company is being run. The Enron and Barings Bank scandals are notable examples.

5.14 The Cadbury Committee on corporate governance was appointed by the government and reported in 1992. Its recommendations took the form of a Code of Best Practice (the Cadbury Code).

5.15 The main provisions of the code are:

- Separation of the posts of Chairman and Chief Executive
- **Audit committees** to be established by all listed companies. These should consist of non-executive directors (directors not involved in the day-to-day running of the company). The audit committee reviews points arising from the audit and deals directly with the auditors.
- **Non-executive directors** should be financially independent of the company
- Executive directors service contracts should not exceed three years
- Directors emoluments to be disclosed in the accounts
- Directors' pay to be decided by a remuneration committee of non-executive directors

5.16 You can see that these provisions are mainly concerned with limiting the powers of executive directors and making them more accountable to the shareholders.

5.17 Since the Cadbury report there have been several other committees which have produced similar recommendations. In 1998 the key guidance from all of them was re-issued by the Stock Exchange in the form of the **Combined Code**.

5.18 The stock exchange rules require that, as part of its annual report, a company must include a statement of whether, and how, it has applied the principles of the combined code. This statement must be reviewed by the auditors before it is published.

6 LEGISLATION AND BUSINESS PRACTICE

6.1 Organisations operate within a framework of laws which is very broad in scope, and deals with a range of specific issues.

How an organisation does business	- **Contract law**: what constitutes a valid, enforceable contract - **Selling and advertising practices**: fair and truthful claims - **Safety and product labelling**: protecting consumers - **Data protection**: what personal data organisations can hold and use
How an organisation treats its employees	- **Employment protection**: fair dismissal and redundancy procedures - **Employee representation**: rights of consultation, participation in decision making, involvement of trade unions - **Health and safety**: protection of employees at work - **Pay and benefits**: minimum rights and obligations - **Equal opportunity**: protection against discrimination in access to jobs, promotion, training and rewards

Part A: The business and accounting environment

How an organisation deals with its owners	• **Duties of directors** • **Reporting of results** • **Constitution of formal meetings**
How an organisation complies with criminal law	• **Avoiding or reporting civil crimes** such as extortion, theft, assault, invasion of privacy and so on
How an organisation discharges its responsibilities to government	• Collection and payment of **taxes** • Provision of **reports and returns**

6.2 Organisations are affected by legislation in the following areas.

Area of law	Requirements cover	Source of requirements (in the UK)
Health and safety at work	• Health and safety procedures • Personal responsibility for self and others	• Health and Safety at Work Act • Specific Regulations under the Act
Intellectual property and copyright	• Reproduction (eg by photocopying) of others' work • Using others' work (words, images) in your own	• Copyright, Designs and Patents Act 1988
Data protection	• Obtaining, storing, disclosing and using any 'personal data' (about individuals) • Responding to requests by individuals to access data held about them	• Data Protection Act 1998 • Criminal Justice and Public Order Act • Related Code of Practice
Discrimination and equal opportunities	• Administration of recruitment, selection, promotion, training and pay policies • Interpersonal behaviours implying racial vilification or sexual harassment	• Sex Discrimination Act 1986 • Race Relations Act 1996 • Disability Discrimination Act 1995 • Legislation on 'Article 13' covering sexual orientation and religion and age • Related Codes of Conduct

Area of law	Requirements cover	Source of requirements (in the UK)
Company law	• Keeping accounting records and statutory registers • Making annual returns to the Registrar of Companies • Preparing and circulating annual reports and accounts • Preparing and auditing financial statements	• Companies Acts

6.3 Regulatory control

In addition to legislation, there has been an increase in recent years in the guidance, monitoring and control of organisational practices through 'watchdog' bodies, voluntary Codes of Practice and industry Standards.

- **Regulatory bodies** oversee the activities of businesses in areas such as competition and compliance: examples include the Accounting Standards Board (ASB), the Auditing Practices Board (APB) or the Health and Safety Executive.

- **Codes of Practice** may be agreed by industry representative bodies, or published by other bodies, like the Arbitration, Conciliation and Advisory Service (ACAS). They allow monitoring bodies (such as the Commission for Racial Equality or the Advertising Standards Authority) to measure the behaviour of organisations against defined standards.

    There is a complex body of **regulations and standards** covering the reporting of the financial performance of organisations and the verification of reports by auditors: eg Financial Reporting Standards (FRSs).

- **Professional bodies** such as ACCA and CIMA monitor and enforce (through the granting or withdrawal of membership status and privileges) their own standards of competence, ethical conduct and continuing professional education.

Part A: The business and accounting environment

Key learning points

- Businesses are **open** systems – they interact with the environment.
- **PEST** is a useful model for analysing the business environment.
- **Political risk** is an important factor to consider when looking at new markets.
- Business planning must take into account the forecast state of the **economy**.
- **Demographic change** will alter patterns of demand.
- Public companies have a number of external **stakeholders**.
    - Companies are regulated by:
    - Company law
    - Financial Reporting Standards
    - Stock Exchange requirements
    - Tax law and regulations
- **Corporate governance** refers to how the company is managed.
- The **Combined Code** on corporate governance is intended to reduce the possibility of managerial fraud.
- Organisations must comply with Employment, Health and Safety and Data Protection legislation.

Quick quiz

1. What are the some of the advantages of people working together in organisations?
2. What management approach is needed in a dynamic environment?
3. How would you differentiate the micro and macro environments of a business?
4. How does Data Protection law relate to organisations?
5. What areas are covered by Employment law?
6. What is political risk?
7. How do interest rates affect business operations?
8. How does IT affect the way in which firms are managed?

Answers to quick quiz

1. Some of the advantages you could have mentioned are:
    - enable people to specialise
    - save time
    - accumulate and share knowledge
    - enable people to pool their expertise
    - enable synergy

2. In this environment management needs to be prepared to react rapidly to change.

3. The micro environment is directly around the business – its customers, suppliers, competitors etc. The macro environment is further away and cannot be directly controlled. It can be categorised as political/legal, economic, social and technological factors.

4. Data protection law regulates what personal data organisations can hold and use. This is most obviously applicable to data held about employees.

5. Minimum pay, equal opportunities, dismissal and redundancy procedures, trade union rights.

6. The risk that political factors will invalidate the strategy and maybe even damage the firm.

7   Higher interest rates will make it harder for the company to borrow any funds needed for expansion and will also make it harder for its customers to obtain funds, which may have an adverse effect on sales.

8   IT encourages 'delayering', homeworking and better communication.

Answers to activities

Answer 1.1

Declining numbers of school leavers means that the overall market is declining, and more young people going on to university leads to a further decline, as it can be assumed that they will have to repay student loans and will have little disposable income left for holidays.

The greater disposable income among the 18-30 age group suggests, however, that those who are not impoverished students have more money to spend. Perhaps the increase is concentrated more at the age 30 end. And this would fit in with more sophisticated tastes in foreign travel – less interest in cheap packages.

The holiday company will have to formulate a strategy to deal with this change in the market. It needs to do some research and discover what destinations are now of interest to the travelling members of this age group. Then it should look at how it can offer holidays which, for a slightly higher price, offer some of the benefits of independent travel.

Answer 1.2

Economic factors During times of recession, consumers will spend less on a variety of goods, but the precise effects in different countries will depend upon how deeply each one falls into recession.

Social factors Spending habits are always likely to be socially or culturally defined.

Technology Demands for technological products will vary from country to country, depending on the level of technological advancement and consumer sophistication. The use of technology itself (eg Internet) to sell goods to customers will also vary.

Answer 1.3

The principal stakeholders in a private family company will be:

- Employees and family
- Suppliers
- Customers
- Banks or other lending agencies
- Tax authorities
- Local groups with which the business interacts, for instance, Chambers of Commerce

> **Now try Question 1 in the Exam Question Bank**

Chapter 2　Organisational structure

Chapter topic list

1　Purposes and objectives of organisations
2　Business functions
3　Organisation structure
4　Influences on organisation structure
5　Tall and flat organisations
6　Departmentation
7　Mechanistic and organic organisation
8　Informal organisation

The following study sessions are covered in this chapter:

		Syllabus reference
2(a)	Identify the purpose and objectives of an organisation	1(b)
2(b)	Recognise the stages needed to establish an organisation	1(b)
2(c)	Explain what influences the structure of an organisation with reference to the work of Fayol	1(b)
2(d)	Describe the business as a system with clearly defined functional areas	1(b)
2(e)	Identify organisational levels and spans of control	1(b)
2(f)	Recognise how departments within an organisation are structured	1(b)

2: Organisational structure

1 PURPOSES AND OBJECTIVES OF ORGANISATIONS

1.1 What are organisations for? What purpose do they serve? In general terms, organisations are formed because they can achieve results which individuals cannot achieve by themselves. Organisations increase the **productive capacity** of individuals by:

(a) Overcoming their physical and mental limitations through **combining their efforts**

(b) Enabling them to pool their expertise and skills. This in turn allows **specialisation**, where individuals concentrate their efforts on what they do best, allowing others to supply other skills

(c) Allowing the accumulation and sharing of **knowledge and ideas**: from different sources (through contribution by organisational members) and over time (because the organisation is continuous, building up an on-going knowledge base).

(d) Saving **time and resources**, by allowing economies of scale and task sharing

(e) Enabling **synergy**: allowing the organisation to achieve more than the same individuals would if they worked separately. In other words, 2 + 2 = 5.

1.2 In addition, organisations meet human beings' social needs for relationship, belonging and identifying with something bigger than themselves.

Organisational objectives

1.3 We will be discussing the process of business planning in detail in Chapter 3, but in broad terms, a business is likely to have a **hierarchy of objectives/goals**: one primary corporate objective and a series of subordinate objectives/goals which should combine to ensure the achievement of the overall objective.

1.4 People might disagree on the choice of the overall corporate objective. Charities and public sector organisations generally have primary objectives in relation to **service delivery** of some kind, but businesses generally have a **financial objective**: profitability, return on capital employed or earnings per share, say.

(a) Profit, in its broadest sense, measures the creation of **value**, the relationship of inputs to outputs. It thus integrates cost behaviour and revenue performance for the whole organisation.

(b) Profit also is a key indicator for **shareholders**.

(c) Profit is one of several measures that can be **compared** across organisations.

1.5 Secondary or **subordinate goals** and objectives can be listed under the following broad headings. They support the primary goal.

(a) **Market position**

Total market share of each market, growth of sales, customers or potential customers, the need to avoid relying on a single customer for a large proportion of total sales, what markets the company should be in.

(b) **Product development**

Bring in new products, develop a product range, investment in research and development, provide products of a certain quality at a certain price level.

Part A: The business and accounting environment

(c) **Technology**

Improve productivity, reduce the cost per unit of output, exploit appropriate technology.

(d) **Employees and management**

Train employees in certain skills, reduce labour turnover.

Activity 2.1

Review the list of goals and objectives above. How do you think each of them relates to the financial objectives mentioned in Paragraph 1.5? Can you see any potential conflicts between them?

1.6 Management writer Peter Drucker suggests that objectives are needed in eight key areas.

(a) **Market standing**: this includes market share, customer satisfaction, size of product range and distribution resources

(b) **Innovation** in all major aspects of the organisation

(c) **Productivity**

(d) **Physical and financial resources**

(e) **Profitability**

(f) **Manager performance and development**

(g) **Worker performance and attitude**

(h) **Public responsibility**: ethical and socially responsible business practices

2 BUSINESS FUNCTIONS

2.1 Within a typical organisation, there are many different types of activity being carried out.

- Purchasing materials and components
- Carrying out operations on purchased materials and components
- Research on and development of new products or technologies
- Communicating with customers and potential customers
- Taking and processing sales orders
- Accounting and record keeping
- Employing and managing people
- Planning and controlling all the above activities to ensure that the organisation reaches its goals.

2.2 Many of these activities can be grouped under the following broad functions.

(a) **Production or direct service provision**

This is the reason the organisation is in business. It covers the output of factories and farms and the provision of services. For manufacturing industry, purchasing of components and raw materials are important functions, and research and development expenditure is necessary in order to stay ahead technologically. Over the past few decades, manufacturing has been relocating to parts of the world where labour is cheaper and more and more food is imported into the UK, so a large proportion of the workforce is now engaged in service industries.

(b) **Sales and marketing**

The sales function covers both retail operations and the activities of sales forces who deal in large orders and contracts. This is a vital function. The outputs of a business are no value if they cannot be sold. Marketing seeks out prospective customers for the product and looks for the best way to present it to them. Marketing has become increasingly sophisticated over the past decade, with customer profiling and use of web-based technologies.

(c) **Accounting and finance**

Sales and purchases give rise to transactions (which must be recorded) and movements of funds (which must be monitored). The accounting and finance functions are there to safeguard the assets of the business, comply with statutory requirements and provide the information needed by management in order to run the business profitably.

Activity 2.2

(a) Match up each of the following activities with the person in the organisation you think would be responsible for carrying out the activity: write the appropriate number in the box next to the activity.

	Activity		Person in organisation
(i)	Delivering goods to customers	1	Purchasing manager
(ii)	Preparing cheques for suppliers	2	Accounts administrator
(iii)	Recording credit sales	3	Sales administrator
(iv)	Bank reconciliations	4	Distribution manager
(v)	Dealing with customers' enquiries	5	Factory supervisor
(vi)	Negotiating discounts with suppliers		
(vii)	Calculating wages due to production staff		

(b) For each activity, consider with which other person in the organisation (if anybody) that person might have to communicate (orally or in writing) in order to do the activity. Explain why, briefly.

(d) **Human resource planning and management**

For most businesses, personnel are the biggest cost and the most valuable asset. This becomes and more and more the case as service-based industries replace traditional manufacturing. Recruiting, keeping and training the right people is now a major function in large organisations. Planning and budgeting will also involve calculating future human resource needs.

3 ORGANISATION STRUCTURE

> **KEY TERM**
>
> **Organisation structure** is the framework for allocating tasks, delegating authority, co-ordinating activity and channelling communication between individuals and groups in the organisation.

Part A: The business and accounting environment

3.1 **Formal organisation structure** implies a framework intended to accomplish organisational objectives: think about your own organisation.

Objective of organisation structure	Reason	Your organisation
To **link individuals** in an established network of relationships	So that authority, responsibility and communications can be controlled.	There will be individuals in certain roles in your organisation who you have to deal with regularly in order to do your job. Can you identify them?
To group together the **tasks** required to fulfil the objectives of the organisation as a whole, and to allocate them to suitable individuals or groups	This must be appropriate – it may be done on the basis of **function** (sales, production, accounting and so on), **geographical area** (regional sales territories, for example), **product** or **product type**.	What departments exist in your organisation? Why?
To allocate to individuals or groups the **authority** they require to perform their functions, as well as the **responsibility to account** for their performance to their superiors	This creates a hierarchy or **chain of command**, whereby **authority** flows downwards from senior management (a chief executive, managing director or board of directors) to each level of the organisation, and your **accountability** flows back up.	Can you identify the levels of authority in your own department? Who is your immediate superior, to whom you are responsible for your work? To whom is that person accountable? Do you yourself have authority over others?
To **co-ordinate** the objectives and activities of separate units	So that overall aims are achieved without gaps or overlaps in the flow of work.	What other departments or areas of the organisation do you have to liase with regularly?
To **enable the flow** of work, information and other resources through the organisation, via clear lines of co-operation and communication	So that all the different parts of the organisation are able to meet their objectives.	Where do you get the information and resources you require to do your job? To whom do you supply information and resources in return?

Activity 2.3

Suggest a logical sequence of steps to take if you were *forming* an organisation from scratch.

Principles of organisation

3.2 Henri **Fayol** (1841 – 1925) was an early management theorist, who proposed certain universal, rational principles of organisation.

Principle	Comment
Division of work	Most rationally achieved by **specialisation**, in order to produce more and better outputs
Authority and responsibility	A person with responsibility for performing an action should be given the clear authority to do it – and a person with the authority to perform an action should be made clearly responsible for its outcome
Scalar chain	There is a chain of authority running from the top of the organisation hierarchy to the bottom. (This also forms the organisation's formal channels of communication: instructions flow down and reports flow back up.)
Unity of command	For any given action, a subordinate should receive orders from only one superior. Dual command (whether caused by imperfect boundaries of authority or by superiors ignoring the proper channels of authority) causes stress and inefficiency.
Unity of direction	For any given activity, there should be one identified 'chief' and one overall plan, so that efforts can be co-ordinated.
Subordination of individual interests	The satisfaction of one employee or group of employees should be recognised as less important than the fulfilment of the organisation's objectives.

Elements of organisation

3.3 **Henry Mintzberg** has provided a more flexible framework for discussing organisation structure, by categorising the **five basic component parts** in any organisation.

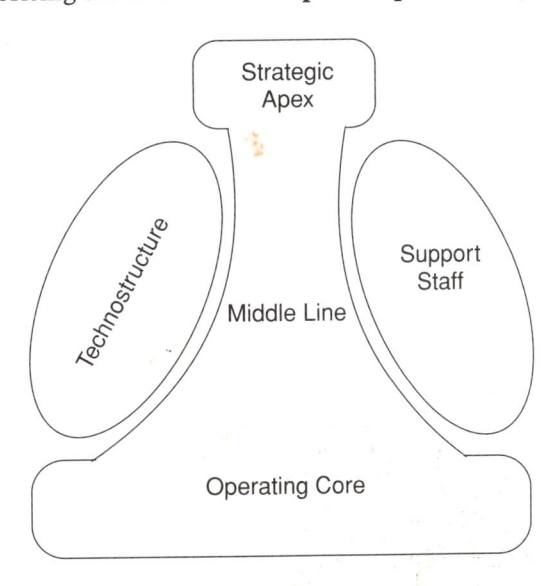

```
           ┌───────────┐
           │ Strategic │
           │   Apex    │
           └───────────┘
    ╱            │            ╲
┌─────────┐      │      ┌─────────┐
│ Techno- │      │      │ Support │
│structure│  Middle Line│  Staff  │
└─────────┘      │      └─────────┘
    ╲            │            ╱
           ┌───────────┐
           │ Operating │
           │   Core    │
           └───────────┘
```

Part A: The business and accounting environment

Element	People involved	Key tasks
Strategic apex	Senior management	Ensuring that the organisation pursues its objectives and serves the needs of its owners and stakeholders, through: • Strategic planning • Resource allocation • Boundary management (as ambassadors between the organisation and the environment).
Operating core	People directly involved in production	Securing inputs, and processing and distributing them as outputs (goods and services).
Middle line	Managers and supervisors, forming the chain of command that runs between the strategic apex and the operating core	Organising, planning and control of work. Acting as an interface between: • Senior management and operational employees • The organisation and external contacts.
Techno-structure	Specialist advisers and analysts; technical support staff	Offering technical support to the rest of the structure. Designing and maintaining systems to standardise work throughout the organisation (eg strategic planning, quality control, systems design, financial control and HR planning).
Staff support	Administrative and ancillary support staff	Offering administrative and ancillary support to the rest of the structure (eg personnel management, legal advice, research and development, maintenance, mail, security)

3.4 Each of these elements may be larger or smaller, according to the needs of the organisation, its structure and culture. For example, bureaucratic organisations (such as large banks and public-sector organisations) have traditionally had many layers of middle line, and an enlarged technostructure (to maintain all the standardised rules and procedures) and staff support. Small, simple organisations (such as a hairdressing salon or grocery store) consist mainly of the strategic apex and operating core. An accountancy firm might have little middle line or technostructure (since the operating core is made up of qualified experts) – but a substantial staff support element, providing clerical and administrative support.

Modern theories of organisation

3.5 Modern management theorists now emphasise values such as the following.

(a) **Contingency theory**. There is no 'one best way' to structure an organisation: a range of factors (such as the task, technology, members, management and environment of the organisation) will have to be taken into account in order to find the structure that best 'fits' the organisation's needs. We look at this in more detail when we consider the accounting function in Chapter 4.

(b) **Flexibility**. This is perhaps the key value in modern management theory. Arising from the competitive need to respond swiftly to rapidly-changing customer demands and

2: Organisational structure

technological changes, organisations and processes are being re-engineered. This has created a tendency towards:

  (i) **Smaller, more temporary structures**, such as project or task-force teams

  (ii) **Multi-functional units**, facilitating communication and co-ordination across departmental boundaries. This often takes the form of 'matrix' organisation (discussed later in the chapter): an employee reports both to his department superior and to a project or product manager whose job is to manage all areas of activity related to the product or project

  (iii) **Multi-skilling**, where individuals are able to switch roles according to task requirements and customer demands

  (iv) **Flexible deployment** of the labour resource: for example, through part-time and temporary working, contracting out tasks, flexitime or annual hours contracts.

(c) **Empowerment**: giving people lower down the organisation the authority and resources to take more responsibility and initiative in their area of work. This may involve removing formal controls or supervision, delegating additional authority, and including the operating core in decision-making on key issues such as quality and customer service. It is associated with the decentralisation of authority to local and customer-facing units, for greater responsiveness and flexibility.

3.6 We will discuss some of the structural implications of these principles later in the chapter.

Organisation charts

3.7 Organisation charts are a traditional way of depicting the various roles and relationships of the formal structure. They are a simplified and standardised way of showing:

(a) The units (eg departments) into which the organisation is divided and how they relate to each other

(b) Formal communication and reporting channels

(c) The structure of authority, responsibility and delegation

(d) Any problems in these areas, such as excessively long lines of communication, lack of co-ordination between units or unclear areas of authority.

3.8 The most common form of organisation chart is the vertical organisation chart, which illustrates the flow of authority downwards through the different levels of the organisation, and the pyramid shape of many organisations. (We will look at various examples in Section 6 of this chapter.) Different types of organisation may, however, be depicted in different ways.

- Mintzberg's model (shown above) is an example of a component-based chart.
- Matrix charts (shown in Paragraph 6.6 below) show both vertical and horizontal communication and authority relationships.

Activity 2.4

What are organisation charts able to show – and what can you identify as their potential limitations for managers seeking to control and develop organisational performance?

4 INFLUENCES ON ORGANISATION STRUCTURE

4.1 There are many influences on organisation structure.

(a) There are certain **internal principles of organisation**, which determine some aspects of structure. The scalar chain of authority, span of control and centralisation and decentralisation are all significant influences. According to **contingency theory**, however, there are still managerial choices to be made on the best structure for the organisation's environment and objectives.

(b) The **objectives** of the organisation, and how these are broken down to define the goals of sub-units. Diversified organisations, for example, may require more decentralised structures, with autonomous specialist units. Organisations who want to support innovation may need more flexible structures.

(c) The **task** or activity of the organisation, which will determine which line and technostructure/support functions are required, and the relative importance of each.

(d) The **technology** of the task (how it is organised, as well as the tools and techniques used). Technologies require certain forms of organisation to maximise their efficiency and the needs of the people involved.

(e) The **size** of the organisation. As structures gets larger, they tend to get more complex: formalisation, specialisation and subdivision are required in order to control and co-ordinate performance more closely. Geographical spread, on the other hand, may require more decentralised structures to take local factors into account.

(f) The **human resources** of the organisation. Their skills, abilities and expectations will influence how far authority is decentralised (giving them more responsibility) and how work is organised (facilitating team-working or utilising multi-skilled workers, for example).

(g) The **environment** of the organisation. As we saw in Chapter 1, many factors (and especially changes) in the business environment represent opportunities and threats to which organisation structure must adapt. As one example, information and communication technology (ICT or IT) has enabled organisations to adopt looser, more network-style units and to outsource areas of their activities to other organisations.

(h) The **culture** of the organisation. Managerial willingness to delegate authority will support decentralisation, and values about 'responsiveness' will lead to more flexible cultures.

5 TALL AND FLAT ORGANISATIONS

Span of control

> **KEY TERM**
>
> The **span of control** refers to the number of subordinates immediately reporting to a superior official.

5.1 Span of control or 'span of management' refers to the number of subordinates responsible to a superior. In other words, if a manager has five subordinates, the span of control is five.

2: Organisational structure

5.2 There are physical and mental limitations to a manager's ability to maintain control and relationships at the required level of detail. The span of control should therefore be restricted to between three and six.

5.3 If span of control is too wide, too much of the manager's time will be taken up with routine problems and supervision. Even so, subordinates may not get the supervision, control or communication that they require, because the manager is 'spread too thin'. On the other hand, if the span of control is too narrow, the manager may over-supervise the work of subordinates and may feel no pressure to delegate at all.

5.4 The arguments for narrow or wide spans of control therefore include the following.

Arguments for a narrow span of control	Arguments for a wide span of control
• Better control, co-ordination and communication	• More efficient use of managerial time and costs (because managers are forced to delegate more, and cannot over-supervise work)
• More efficient use of managerial time and costs (because managers spend less time on routine tasks and supervision)	• More responsibility and discretion for subordinates (which may contribute to job satisfaction and organisational flexibility)
• Reduced need for managers to delegate (eg if subordinates are not capable of accepting responsibility for complex tasks)	

5.5 Using a contingency approach, the appropriate span of control will depend on a number of factors.

(a) The manager's **capabilities** and limitations: including his ability to manage his time and to delegate effectively (wider span possible).

(b) The **nature of the manager's work load**

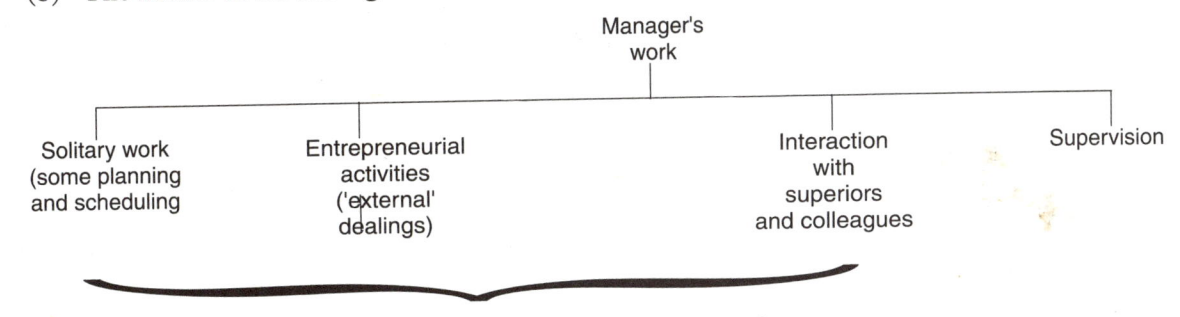

```
                        Manager's
                          work
   ┌───────────────┬──────────────┬─────────────────┬──────────────┐
Solitary work   Entrepreneurial              Interaction        Supervision
(some planning    activities                    with
and scheduling   ('external'                 superiors
                  dealings)                 and colleagues
   └──────────────────┬──────────────────────────┘
                Non-supervisory work
```

The more non-supervisory work in a manager's workload:

- The narrower the span of control
- The greater the delegation of authority to subordinates

(c) The **capabilities** of subordinates. The more competent and motivated they are, the less direct supervision they will require and the more delegated responsibility they may want – suggesting a wider span.

(d) The **nature and technology of the task**.

(i) If all subordinates do similar tasks, or tasks are highly routine, repetitive, programmed or automated, a wide span is possible. More complex, non-standard tasks, where there are high risks attached to errors, may require supervisory support, suggesting a narrow span of control.

Part A: The business and accounting environment

        (ii) Geographical dispersion of subordinates may require more attention to co-ordination, suggesting a narrower span. Effective communication systems and IT have widened spans of control, however, by enabling supervisors to programme and monitor the work of 'virtual team' members, and share information, via computer systems.

        (iii) Teamworking and interaction allows subordinates to help each other, facilitating a wider span.

5.6   Span of control has implications for the 'shape' of the organisation. An organisation with a narrow span of control will have more levels of middle line, and a longer scalar chain of command, than an organisation of the same size with a wide span of control.

KEY TERMS

A **tall organisation** is one which, in relation to its size, has a large number of levels of management hierarchy. This implies a narrow span of control, and tight supervision and control.

A **flat organisation** is one which, in relation to its size, has a small number of hierarchical levels. This implies a wide span of control and a greater degree of delegation or decentralisation of authority.

Exam alert

A whole 20-mark (compulsory) question appears on the Pilot Paper to this syllabus. The question covered a number of areas relating to this topic (defining tall and flat organisation; influences on height and width; advantages and disadvantages of flat structures). This is a good indication of the kind of detailed knowledge – and revision – required in this area of the syllabus. Make sure you get to grips with all the key concepts covered.

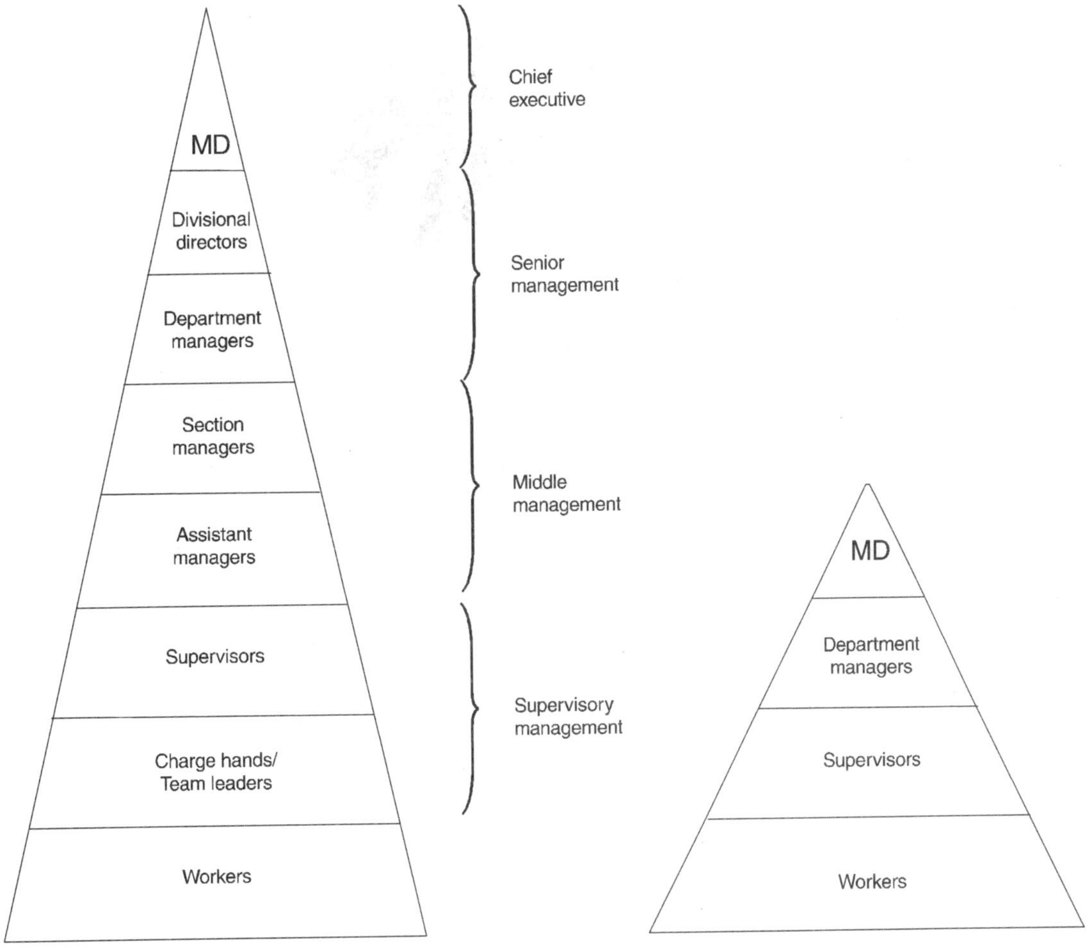
MD
Divisional directors
Department managers
Section managers
Assistant managers
Supervisors
Charge hands/ Team leaders
Workers
Chief executive
Senior management
Middle management
Supervisory management
MD
Department managers
Supervisors
Workers

Tall

Flat

5.7 The advantages and disadvantages of these organisational forms can be summarised as follows.

Tall organisation

For	Against
Advantages of narrow spans of control (discussed in Paragraph 5.4)	Inhibits delegation (possibly frustrating employees and overtaking managers)
Smaller working groups may be more satisfying to members	Rigid supervision can be imposed, blocking initiative and flexibility
More steps on the promotional ladder, supporting management development, succession and motivation	Inflexible communication and decision-making: the strategic apex is further away from the operating core and the customer
	Increases administration and overhead costs
	The same work passes through many hands, creating inefficiency and less sense of responsibility

Part A: The business and accounting environment

Flat organisation

For	Against
More delegation, supporting employee satisfaction, flexibility/responsiveness, managerial efficiency	Not all tasks can be effectively delegated
Cost-efficient in terms of managerial/supervisory costs	Sacrifices an element of control and co-ordination
Supports flexibility: empowers customer-facing units to make decisions, and keeps strategic core close to the customer	The middle line may be necessary to convert the vision of the strategic apex into terms understood by subordinates
Reduces time lags in communication and decision-making	
Supported by ICT developments: strategic apex has direct access to decision support and control information	

5.8 In highly competitive environments, the arguments are currently weighted in favour of flattening or **delayering**.

Centralisation and decentralisation

5.9 Centralisation and decentralisation refer to the extent to which authority for decision making is either retained at the top (or centre) of the organisation or delegated to lower (or outer) levels. We can look at centralisation in two ways.

(a) **Geography**. Some functions may be centralised rather than 'scattered' in different offices, departments or locations. So, for example, secretarial support, IT support and information storage may be centralised in specialist departments (whose services are shared by other functions) rather than carried out by staff/equipment duplicated in each departmental office.

(b) **Authority**. Centralisation also refers to the extent to which people have to refer decisions upwards to their superiors. Decentralisation therefore implies increased delegation, empowerment and autonomy at lower levels of the organisation.

5.10 The table on the next page summarises some of the arguments in favour of centralisation and decentralisation.

Pro centralisation	Pro decentralisation/delegation
• Decisions are made at one point and so are easier to co-ordinate.	• Avoids overburdening top managers, in terms of workload and stress.
• Senior managers in an organisation can take a wider view of problems and consequences.	• Improves motivation of more junior managers who are given responsibility- important since job challenge and entrepreneurial skills are highly valued in today's work environment.
• Senior management can keep a proper balance between different departments or functions - eg by deciding on the resources to allocate to each.	• Greater awareness of local problems by decision makers. Geographically dispersed organisations should often be decentralised on a regional/area basis.

Pro centralisation	Pro decentralisation/delegation
• Quality of decisions is (theoretically) higher due to senior managers' skills and experience.	• Greater speed of decision making, and response to changing events, since no need to refer decisions upwards. This is particularly important in rapidly changing markets.
• Possibly cheaper, by reducing number of managers needed and so lower costs of overheads.	• Helps junior managers to develop and helps the process of transition from functional to general management.
• Crisis decisions are taken more quickly at the centre, without need to refer back, get authority etc.	• Separate spheres of responsibility can be identified: controls, performance measurement and accountability are better.
• Policies, procedures and documentation can be standardised organisation-wide.	• Communication technology allows decisions to be made locally, with information and input from head office if required.

6 DEPARTMENTATION

6.1 Division of labour is one of the key principles of organisation. Once an organisation grows beyond a certain size, this typically involves the grouping together and allocation of specific aspects of the work to different **departments**. This can be done on the basis of various criteria, such as functional specialisation, geographical area or product/brand. We will look at each of these in turn.

Activity 2.5

Jason, Mark, Gary and Robbie set up in business together as repairers of musical instruments - specialising in guitars and drums. They are a bit uncertain as to how they should run the business, but when they discuss it in the pub, they decide that attention needs to be paid to three major areas: taking orders from customers, doing the repairs (of course) and checking the quality of the repairs before notifying the customers.

Suggest three ways in which they could structure their business.

Functional departmentation

6.2 **Functional organisation** involves setting up departments for people who do similar jobs. Primary functions in a manufacturing company might be production, sales, finance, and general administration. Sub-departments of marketing might be selling, distribution and warehousing.

Part A: The business and accounting environment

Functional organisation

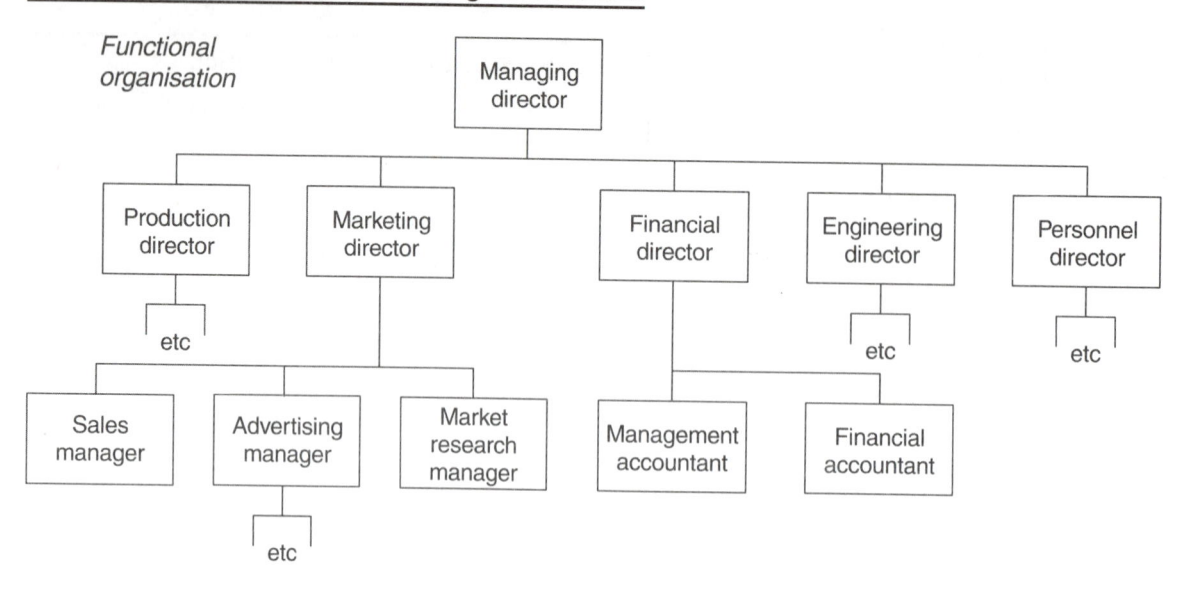

[Organisation chart: Managing director at top, with reports: Production director, Marketing director, Financial director, Engineering director, Personnel director. Marketing director reports: Sales manager, Advertising manager, Market research manager. Financial director reports: Management accountant, Financial accountant.]

Geographical departmentation

6.3 Where the organisation is structured according to geographic area, some authority is retained at Head Office but day-to-day operations are handled on a territorial basis (eg Southern region, Western region). Many sales departments are organised territorially.

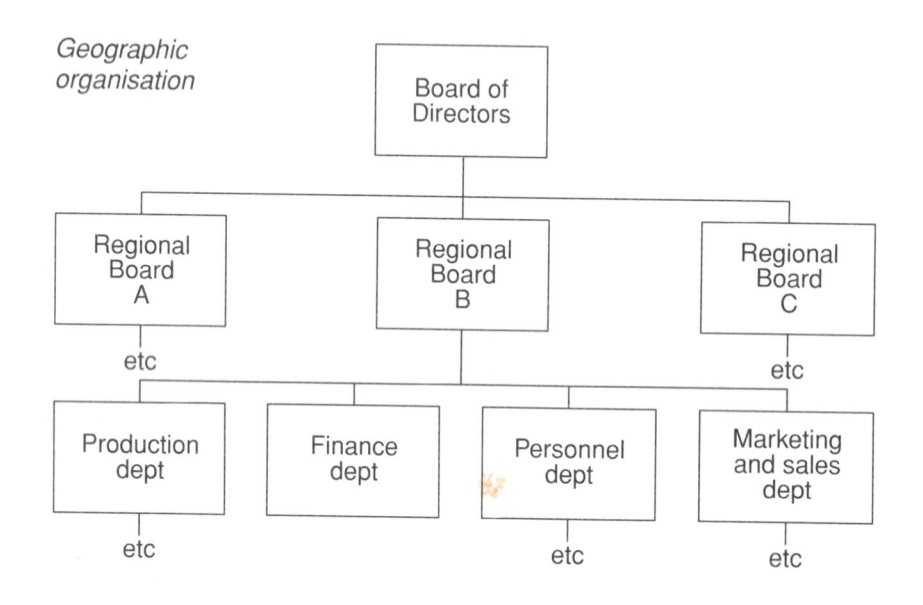

Geographic organisation

[Organisation chart: Board of Directors at top, reports: Regional Board A, Regional Board B, Regional Board C. Regional Board B reports: Production dept, Finance dept, Personnel dept, Marketing and sales dept.]

Product/brand departmentation

6.4 Some organisations group activities on the basis of **products** or product lines. Some functional departmentation remains (eg manufacturing, distribution, marketing and sales) but a divisional manager is given responsibility for the product or product line, with authority over personnel of different functions.

Product/brand organisation

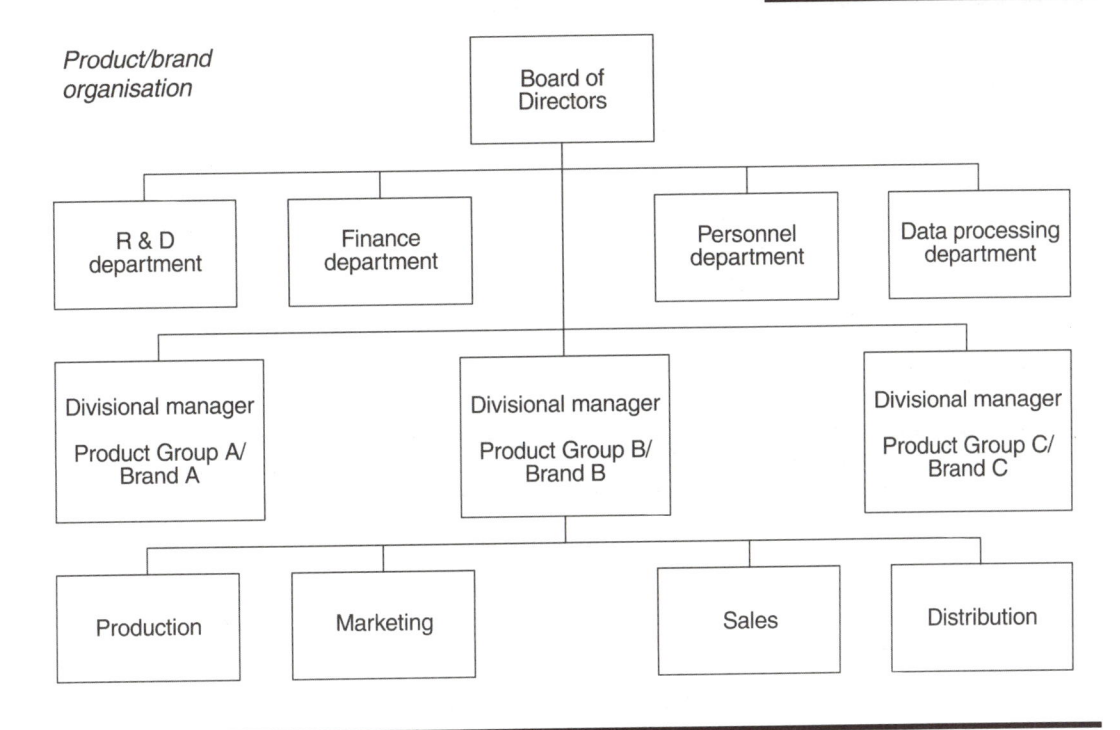

```
                        Board of Directors
        ┌───────────┬──────────┴──────────┬────────────┐
     R & D       Finance            Personnel     Data processing
   department   department          department      department
        ┌──────────────────┼──────────────────┐
   Divisional manager  Divisional manager  Divisional manager
   Product Group A/    Product Group B/    Product Group C/
       Brand A             Brand B             Brand C
                  ┌─────────┬──────┴──┬──────────┐
              Production  Marketing  Sales   Distribution
```

Activity 2.6

Looking at the 'Product/brand organisation' chart above, what types of organisation can you identify, and why are these appropriate for their purposes? What *added* type of organisation might this firm use, and in what circumstances?

Divisionalisation

> **KEY TERM**
>
> **Divisionalisation** is the division of a business into more or less autonomous regional or product-centred businesses, each with its own revenues, expenditures and capital asset purchase programmes, and therefore each with its own profit and loss responsibility.

6.5 Divisions of the organisation may be **profit or investment centres** within a company: strategic planning and other technostructure and support activities may be undertaken at a central 'head office' level or location. Divisions may also be **subsidiary companies**, owned or controlled by a holding company: often the case when businesses grow through acquisition, or require a high degree of differentiation in product or regional divisions.

Matrix structure

6.6 Matrix structure essentially 'crosses' functional and product/project organisation, so that staff in different functional or regional departments are responsible:

- To their department managers, in regard to the activities of the department and
- To a product or project manager, in regard to the given product or project.

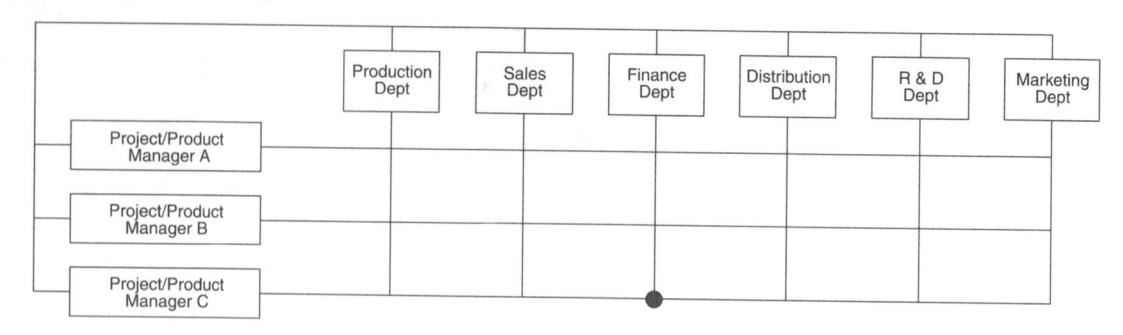

Part A: The business and accounting environment

```
                    ┌──────────┬──────────┬──────────┬──────────┬──────────┬──────────┐
                    │Production│  Sales   │ Finance  │Distribution│  R & D  │Marketing │
                    │   Dept   │   Dept   │   Dept   │   Dept   │   Dept   │   Dept   │
                    └──────────┴──────────┴──────────┴──────────┴──────────┴──────────┘
   ┌─────────────┐       │          │          │          │          │          │
   │Project/Product│─────┼──────────┼──────────┼──────────┼──────────┼──────────┤
   │  Manager A   │      │          │          │          │          │          │
   └─────────────┘       │          │          │          │          │          │
   ┌─────────────┐       │          │          │          │          │          │
   │Project/Product│─────┼──────────┼──────────┼──────────┼──────────┼──────────┤
   │  Manager B   │      │          │          │          │          │          │
   └─────────────┘       │          │          │          │          │          │
   ┌─────────────┐       │          │          │          │          │          │
   │Project/Product│─────┼──────────┼──────────┼──────────┼──────────┼──────────┤
   │  Manager C   │      │          │         •│          │          │          │
   └─────────────┘       │          │          │          │          │          │
```

6.7 The employees represented by the dot in the above diagram, for example:

- Are responsible to the Finance Manager for their work in accounting and finance

- Are responsible to the Project Manager C for their work on the project team: This may be budgeting, management reporting and payroll relevant to the project.

Activity 2.7

Q plc is a business which is divided into three product divisions. Each of these divisions has been operating from different sites and relatively old-fashioned buildings. It has become possible to acquire an eminently suitable site cheaply, to which Q plc intends to move all the divisions. It has been decided to take the opportunity to reorganise on a functional basis.

At present, the following activities take place in the divisions:

Division A	Division B	Division C
Purchasing	Purchasing	Commercial (ie sales, finance
Stamping	Machining	and administration)
Machining	Wiring	Stamping
Wiring	Drilling	Wiring
Drilling	Painting	Drilling
Commercial (ie sales, finance	Assembly	Painting
and administration)	Sales	Assembly
	Finance	

Required

(a) Draw an organisation chart showing the revised functional structure for Q plc.

(b) Suggest reasons why the decision to switch from a product organisation structure to a functional organisation structure might have been taken.

Advantages and disadvantages

6.8 The advantages and disadvantages of the various forms of organisation can be summarised as follows.

Organisation	Advantages	Disadvantages
Functional organisation	• Pools and focuses specialised skills and knowledge	• Focuses on inputs/processes rather than outputs/ customers (necessary for customer satisfaction)
	• Shares specialised technology and equipment for efficiency	
	• Facilitates the recruitment, training and management of specialist staff	• Creates vertical barriers to cross-disciplinary communication (necessary for flexibility and co-ordination)
	• Avoids duplicating functions within area/product	

2: Organisational structure

Organisation	Advantages	Disadvantages
	departments: enables economies of scale	
Geographical organisation	• Decision-making at the interface between organisation and local stakeholders (with distinctive needs) • Cost-effective (because shorter) lines of supply and communication to local markets or plants	• Duplication of functional activities • Loss of standardisation, due to local differences
Product/ brand organisation	• Clearer accountability for the profitability of different products/brands • Specialisation of production and marketing expertise • Co-ordination of different functions by product managers	• Increased managerial complexity and overhead costs • Possible fragmentation of objectives and markets
Divisionalisation	• Clear accountability for the profitability of each division • Sensitivity to region/product-specific demands and opportunities • Co-ordination and efficiencies from centralised strategic planning and control and support functions • Potential to develop managerial skills and assess promotion potential at divisional level	• Possible disintegration of objectives, including conflict between head office generalists and divisional specialists • Possible competition between divisions for resources • Units may not be large enough to support managerial overheads
Matrix organisation	• Combines the efficiency benefits of specialisation with the accountability benefits of product/project structures • Supports inter-disciplinary co-operation and multi-functional working • Develops tolerance of flexibility and ambiguity (useful for change, responsiveness, learning) • Encourages 'big picture' thinking, instead of departmental monopolies	• Possible competition and conflict between dual managers • Stress on staff 'caught' between conflicting demands • Inefficiency of ambiguous priorities and switching between tasks • Potentially slower decision-making: referring to two authorities • Costs of added management positions, meetings

Organisation	Advantages	Disadvantages
	• Encourages product/market/customer awareness	
	• Brings authority conflicts and ambiguities into the open, encouraging intentional co-operation	

Hybrid structures

6.9 'Hybrid' ('mixed') structures may involve a combination of functional departmentation, ensuring specialised attention to key functions, with elements of (for example):

(a) Product organisation, to suit the requirements of brand marketing or specific production technologies

(b) Customer organisation, particularly in marketing departments, to service key accounts

(c) Territorial organisation, particularly of sales and distribution departments, to service local requirements for marketing or distribution in dispersed regions or countries.

7 MECHANISTIC AND ORGANIC ORGANISATION

Organisational metaphors

7.1 A number of writers have come up with metaphors or analogies to discuss what organisations are 'like' and how they function. In Chapter 1, we saw one of these analogies: the organisation as an open system. Two other very influential metaphors are:

(a) The organisation as a **machine**. The idea of 'mechanistic' organisation sees organisations as a collection of many moving parts (people, processes) which act and interact in defined, routine and expected ways: altering one variable has a predictable effect on the others.

(b) The organisation as a **biological organism**. The idea of 'organic' organisation sees the organisation as a living creature, which grows, matures (over its 'life cycle'), learns and adapts to its environment, by absorbing and processing resources and influences (information, skills, technology) so that it can meet changing demands over its life span.

7.2 Burns and Stalker described 'mechanistic' and 'organic' organisational forms, and suggested that each is suited to a different type of environment.

(a) Mechanistic organisations (also known as 'bureaucracies') are stable, efficient and suitable for slow-changing operating environments.

(b) Organic organisations are flexible, adaptive and suitable for fast-changing or dynamic operating environments.

7.3 The characteristics of mechanistic and organic organisations can be summarised as follows.

Mechanistic	Organic
Centralised hierarchical authority: managers are responsible for co-ordinating tasks; control is achieved by legal contract, rules and supervision	A 'network' structure of authority, allowing decentralisation and a range of lateral relationships (crossing functional boundaries) for co-ordination and self-control on the basis of shared goals and interests
Senior managers are assumed to be the 'experts' in decision-making. Internal knowledge (of the organisation and its activities) is prized.	'Expertise' is found throughout the organisation. External knowledge (of the business environment, best practice and so on) is prized.
Vertical (rather than lateral) communication using formal channels and consisting mainly of directions and orders for the purposes of command	Lateral and diagonal communication, often using informal channels, and consisting mainly of information and advice for the purposes of consultation
Standardisation of work processes via rules, procedures and job descriptions	A 'contributive' culture of information and skill sharing, encouraging versatility (rather than specialisation) and teamworking (rather than functional departmentation)
Specialisation, demarcation and detailed definition of individual tasks and responsibilities	Job design that allows flexible definition of tasks according to the needs of the team and changing demands
Focus on process and procedures (efficiency) rather than goals or results (effectiveness)	Focus on goals and outputs (effectiveness) rather than processes

7.4 Mechanistic systems are associated with **bureaucracy**.

Bureaucracy

> **KEY TERM**
>
> A **bureaucracy** is 'a continuous organisation of official functions bound by rules' (Weber).

Part A: The business and accounting environment

7.5 The characteristics of bureaucracy can be summarised as follows.

Characteristic	Description
Hierarchy	Each lower office is under the control and supervision of a higher one.
Specialisation and training	There is a high degree of specialisation of labour.
Professional nature of employment	Officials are full-time employees; promotion is according to seniority and achievement; pay scales are prescribed according to the position or office held in the organisation structure.
Impersonal nature	Employees work within impersonal rules and regulations and act according to formal, impersonal procedures.
Rationality	The hierarchy of authority is clearly and rationally defined. Duties are established and measures of performance set.
Uniformity in the performance of tasks	Standardised procedures ensure consistent performance, regardless of who carries out a given task.
Technical competence	All officials are technically competent.
Stability	The organisation's structure, tasks and culture are consistent over time, regardless of external changes.

7.6 It is common to think of bureaucracy as an old-fashioned and dysfunctional form of organisation, but it has some advantages.

(a) Bureaucracies are ideal for **standardised, routine tasks**. For example, processing driving license applications is fairly routine, requiring systematic work.

(b) Bureaucracies can be very **efficient**. Weber considered them the most effective organisational form, in stable environments.

(c) Rigid adherence to procedures is necessary for **fairness**, adherence to the **law, safety** and **security** (eg procedures over computer use).

(d) Some people like the structured, predictable environment. Bureaucracies tend to be long-lived because they select and retain bureaucratically-minded people.

7.7 In swiftly-changing environments, however, the dysfunctions of bureaucracy become apparent.

(a) **Slow decision-making** results from the rigidity and length of authority networks.

(b) Uniformity creates **conformity**, inhibiting the personal development of staff.

(c) Bureaucracies suppress **innovation**: they can inhibit creativity and initiative.

(d) Bureaucracies find it hard to **learn** from their mistakes, because of the lack of feedback (especially upwards).

(e) Bureaucracies are **slow to change**. Environmental change therefore causes severe trauma.

(f) **Communication** is restricted to established channels, ignoring opportunities for networking, upward feedback and suggestions that contribute to customer service and innovation.

Activity 2.8

Using Mintzberg's model, what component part of the organisation is responsible for designing rules and procedures in a bureaucracy?

Flexible organisation forms

7.8 Modern trends in flexible organisation include the following.

(a) **Flat structures**. The trend is towards 'delayering': reducing the middle line of organisations. Flatter structures are more adaptive and responsive, because there is a shorter distance between the strategic apex and the operational core which serves the customer.

(b) **Horizontal structures**. This is the term given to structures which allow work and information to flow freely across the 'vertical barriers' created by functional specialisation, departmental job demarcations and formal communication channels.

(c) **Chunked** structures. So far, this has mainly meant teamworking and empowerment, creating smaller and more flexible units within the overall structure.

(d) **'Ad hoc'** structures are temporary, adaptive, creative – in contrast to bureaucracy, which tends to be permanent, rule-driven and inflexible.

(e) **Output-focused** structures, focusing on the customer and outputs/results, rather than on internal processes and functions. Project management structures, for example, are being applied to the supply of services within the organisation (to internal customers) as well as to the external market.

8 INFORMAL ORGANISATION

8.1 Within – or underneath – every formal organisation, there is a complex **informal organisation**.

8.2 Formal organisation has a well-defined, fixed structure of task-focused roles and relationships which remains stable regardless of changes of membership. Informal organisation, in contrast, is a loosely-structured, spontaneous, fluctuating network of interpersonal relationships.

8.3 The informal organisation includes:

(a) **Social networks and groups**. Examples include managers who get together to network, and office cliques and friendship groups.

(b) **Informal communication networks**. These are sometimes called the 'grapevine'. They are often much faster than formal channels – but sometimes to carry inaccurate and distorted information, in the form of rumours and gossip.

(c) **Informal ways of getting things done**: procedural short-cuts, work customs.

(d) **Informal power structures**. A charismatic team member, say, may have more influence than the designated team leader.

Part A: The business and accounting environment

8.4 These informal structures may support or undermine the formal organisation.

Positive influences	Negative influences
The grapevine can speed the spread of information, and may have greater credibility with employees than formal management statements.	Informal organisation activities may divert attention and energy from the task.
Informal networks encourage horizontal and upward communication (often lacking via formal channels), increasing co-ordination, flexibility and ideas sharing.	Informal information is often inaccurate and negative, causing stress, conflict and resistance to change.
Informal ways of working may be more efficient than formal procedures.	Informal work methods may cut corners (eg on quality or health and safety).
Informal leaders may support a manager or designated team leader in gaining the commitment of the team.	Informal leaders may undermine managerial authority.

Activity 2.9

Get hold of a copy of your organisation's chart. (Check the Office Manual, or ask the Personnel Department.) What does it tell you about the organisation, the role of the Accounts Department and your own position within it? If no chart is available, try drawing one!

Key learning points

- Organisations have general **purposes** in extending the productive capacity of individuals and satisfying social needs. They also have a hierarchy of specific **objectives**, which allow them to plan, co-ordinate and control their activities.

- Business functions include: production (or direct service delivery), sales and marketing, accounting and finance and human resource management.

- Classical organisation structure is based on the principles of **division of labour** (specialisation) and the **hierarchy of authority**, or scalar chain.

- **Mintzberg** suggested an alternative model of structure, including various common elements: strategic apex, middle line and operating core, technostructure and staff support.

- Internal influences on organisation design include **span of control** (the number of subordinates reporting to one superior) and the amount of **delegation** of authority (centralisation or decentralisation). These factors determine whether an organisation is **tall** (many management levels, narrow spans of control, centralised authority) or **flat** (fewer management levels, wider spans of control, decentralised authority).

- Organisations may be **departmentalised** or **divisionalised** in a number of different ways, including: functional (by specialism), geographical (by region or country) and product/brand organisation. These methods may be 'crossed' in a **matrix** structure of dual authority, or 'mixed' in a **hybrid** structure.

- There is an emphasis upon the need for **adaptive** organisation structures. **Mechanistic** organisation (efficient and stable in slow-change environments) can be contrasted with **organic** organisation (fluid and flexible in fast-change environments). **Bureaucracy** can be rational and efficient– but its dysfunctions in fast-changing environments have been recognised.

- Organisational approaches to **flexibility** include matrix and horizontal structures, multi-skilling, empowerment and teamworking.

- An **informal organisation** exists alongside the formal organisation, with its own communication networks, power relationships and ways of doing things.

Quick quiz

1. List six of Fayol's key principles of organisation.
2. List Mintzberg's components of the organisation.
3. List four activities of the human resources function.
4. What is span of control?
5. What is delayering?
6. What is functional organisation?
7. What is a matrix organisation?
8. List four manifestations of informal organisation.
9. 'Ad hocracy' would be an example of which type of organisation?

    A   Mechanistic
    B   Organic

10. Who is the writer most closely associated with the concept of bureaucracy?

Answers to quick quiz

1. Division of work, authority and responsibility, unit of command, unity of direction, scalar chain, subordination of individual interests

2. Strategic apex, middle line, operating core, technostructure, staff support

Part A: The business and accounting environment

3 HR planning, recruitment and selection, training and development, compliance

4 The number of subordinates directly reporting to a given official

5 The reduction in the number of management levels

6 People and tasks are grouped together around similar work or specialised skills

7 A matrix organisation is a 'grid' of dual authority whereby staff report to departmental and project/product/account managers in relation to appropriate areas of their work

8 The grapevine (informal communication), informal groups, informal work methods, informal power/leadership

9 B. ('Bureaucracy' is associated with 'mechanistic')

10 Max Weber

Answers to activities

Answer 2.1

(a) Market position. Markets are customers. Customers are source of revenue. Markets are where organisations compete with each other. Gaining market share *now* helps future profitability - but this market share may be expensive in the short term.

(b) Product development is another way of competing, to make profits to satisfy the corporate objectives. This, too, is expensive.

(c) and (d) are to do with organising the production process. This means making operations efficient and effective.

Answer 2.2

(a)
(i)	Delivering goods to suppliers	4
(ii)	Preparing cheques for suppliers	2
(iii)	Recording credit sales	2
(iv)	Bank reconciliations	2
(v)	Dealing with customers' enquiries	3
(vi)	Negotiating discounts with suppliers	1
(vii)	Calculating wages due to production staff	2

(b) (i) The sales administrator (3) would need to tell the distribution manager (4) what goods to deliver to whom.

(ii) Cheque preparation would normally go ahead without further consultation unless for some reason the purchasing manager (1) gave instructions that a certain supplier should not be paid.

(iii) The accounts administrator (2) would record sales when told by the sales administrator (3) what sales had been made. (In some systems the recording of the sale might happen automatically, however.)

(iv) Bank reconciliations would be the task of the accounts administrator (2) alone, assuming proper records had been kept.

(v) The sales administrator (3) might need to communicate with the accounts administrator (2) if the enquiry were about payment for the goods, or with the distribution manager (4) if it were about delivery.

(vi) Discount negotiation would normally be the sole preserve of the purchasing manager (1), unless the time of payment was critical (for settlement discounts) in which case the accounts administrator (2) may need to be consulted.

(vii) The factory supervisor (5) would need to provide the accounts administrator (2) with details of hours worked and so forth to enable wages to be calculated.

Answer 2.3

An organisation may be formed as follows.

(i) Formulate objectives, policies (a guiding framework for behaviour and decision-making) and plans (how to go about achieving objectives).

(ii) Identify the activities that will carry out the plans.

(iii) Classify and group those activities, for example by forming departments.

(iv) Give the groups authority to carry out their activities.

(v) Establish relationships between groups, so that there is a structure of authority and communication.

Answer 2.4

Organisation charts portray something of the structure and self-image of an organisation, and so aid managerial thinking and discussion about these aspects. However:

(a) They only offer a static 'snapshot' of the situation, whereas an organisation is dynamic, continually changing

(b) They only show the formal organisation – not the structure of informal relationships and communication that always occurs across formal channels and boundaries (discussed in Section 8 of chapter 2)

(c) They only show roles or functions – not the competence or performance of individuals – so their ability to highlight potential weaknesses is limited.

Answer 2.5

The group has identified three major functions of their business (sales, repairs and quality control) and to main product areas (guitars and drums). They might decide to structure the business in the following ways.

(a) Have one 'general manager' (whose responsibilities may include quality control) and three 'operatives' who share the sales and repair tasks.

(b) Divide tasks by function: have one person in change of sales, one quality controller and two repairers (perhaps one for drums and one for guitars).

(c) Divide tasks by product: have a two-man drums team (who share sales/repair/control tasks between them) and a similar guitar team.

Since there are only four individuals, each (we assume) capable of performing any of the functions for either of the products, they may decide to have a looser social arrangement. They may prefer to discuss who is going to do what, as and when jobs come in. A larger organisation would not have this luxury.

Answer 2.6

(a) At the head office level, there is functional organisation. This enables standardisation of policy and activity in key 'staff' or support functions shared by the various divisions.

(b) At divisional level, there is product/brand organisation. This allows the distinctive culture and attributes of each product/brand to be addressed in production processes and marketing approach.

(c) For each product/brand, there is functional organisation, enabling specialist expertise to be directed at the different activities required to produce, market and distribute a product.

This firm may further organise its marketing department by customer, if its customer base includes key (high-value, long-term) customer accounts with diverse service needs.

It may further organise its sales and distribution departments by geographical area, if the customer base is internationally or regionally dispersed: local market conditions and values, and logistical requirements of distribution, can then be taken more specifically into account.

Part A: The business and accounting environment

Answer 2.7

> *Tutorial note.* There are a variety of ways in which the organisation could be structured. This is only one suggestion. It is possible that the purchasing and stock control functions would be under much closer supervision of the accounts department. Nor do we know how the separate manufacturing operations will be organised. The three different products could still be organised in different manufacturing departments.

(a) Organisation chart

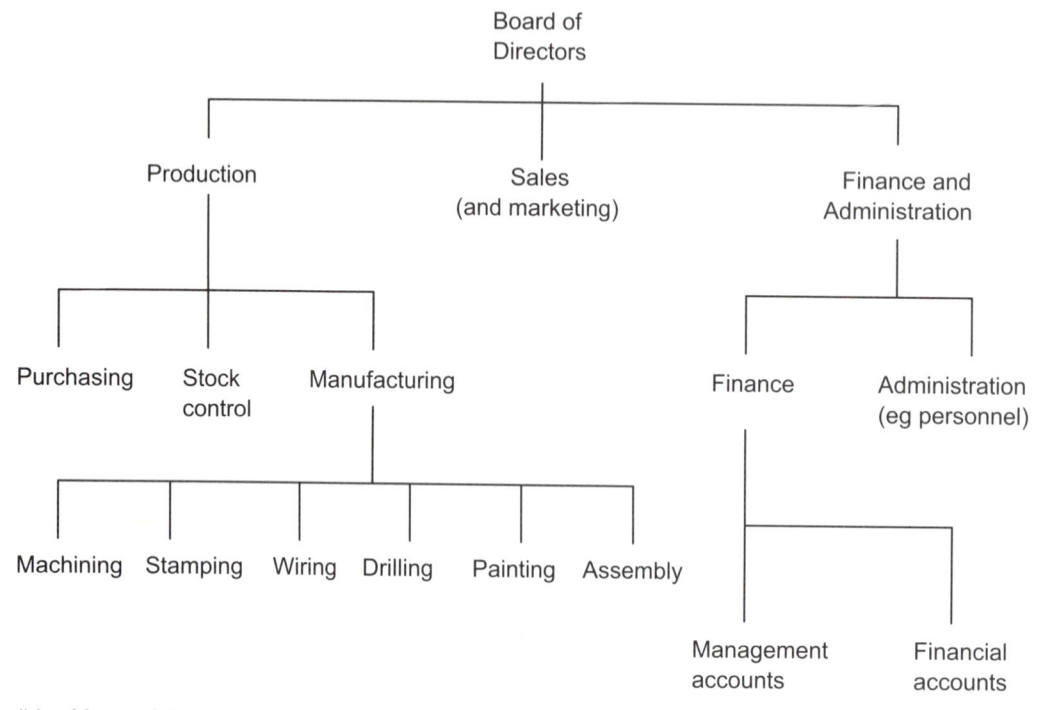

```
                            Board of
                            Directors
          ┌───────────────────┼───────────────────┐
      Production            Sales            Finance and
                       (and marketing)      Administration
   ┌──────┬──────┐                         ┌──────┴──────┐
Purchasing Stock Manufacturing           Finance    Administration
          control                                    (eg personnel)
   ┌──────┬──────┬──────┬──────┐             ┌──────┴──────┐
Machining Stamping Wiring Drilling Painting Assembly   Management   Financial
                                               accounts    accounts
```

(b) Many of the reasons for changing organisation structure are those which are disadvantages of product organisation structures in any circumstances.

Principal disadvantages of product organisation structures are as follows.

(i) Duplication of functions such as sales order administration, accounting, personnel and other administrative functions. This leads to higher costs.

(ii) Loss of other economies of scale in production and administration.

(iii) If selling and marketing are decentralised, there can be a loss of opportunities for cross-selling different products to the same market.

(iv) Conflict between different products in the market place.

In the case of Q plc, it appears that the product organisation structure was the result of the company's geographical split into three locations. Where this is the case, a product structure might make some sense, to ensure that time is not wasted on paper work going to and from a head office. However, given that Q plc is to relocate to a single site, the geographical imperative leading to a product departmentation structure no longer holds.

The advantages of moving to a functional structure for Q plc are as follows.

(i) More efficient use of resources: for example, the accounts department is likely to be in one place, and so staff time can be used more efficiently.

(ii) The pooling of administrative resources may lead to better management information systems, as there could be a more efficient division of labour.

(iii) On the production side, manufacturing planning can be enhanced, as production can be switched between different machines if production flows are uneven. There would be fewer bottlenecks.

(iv) In purchasing, it may be possible to take advantage of quantity discounts on raw materials, if this is a centralised function for each of the three products.

(v) Centralisation in one spot could make decision-making easier as all of the relevant personnel are on site, and management can react immediately to problems and opportunities.

Answer 2.8

The technostructure

Answer 2.9

The answer to this activity is specific to your own observations and examples.

> **Now try Question 2 in the Exam Question Bank**

Chapter 3   Business planning and control

Chapter topic list

1   The business plan
2   Resource planning and control
3   Co-ordination
4   Systems, policies and procedures
5   Office procedures and systems
6   Financial control procedures

The following study sessions are covered in this chapter:

		Syllabus reference
3(a)	Outline the purpose of an overall business plan	1(b)
3(b)	Describe the elements of an organisational plan	1(b)
3(b)	Describe the elements of the human resource plan	1(b)
3(c)	Explain the need for co-ordination in the planning process	1(b)
4(a)	Explain the purpose of systems, policies and procedures	1(b)
4(b)	Describe the principles of effective systems and procedures	1(b)
4(c)	Identify and explain general office procedures and systems using flowcharting techniques	1(b)
4(d)	Review the effectiveness of office procedures and identify weaknesses	1(b)
4(e)	Review the effectiveness of financial control procedures and identify potential weaknesses	1(b)

1 THE BUSINESS PLAN

1.1 If individuals and groups within an organisation are to be effective in working for the achievement of the organisation's objectives, they need to know what it is that they are expected to do. Planning allows managers to identify:

- The objectives for which they are responsible
- How far they are being successful in achieving those objectives

1.2 Planning involves decisions about:

- What to do in future
- How to do it
- When to do it
- Who should do it

1.3 Such questions are relevant at all levels of organisational activity:

(a) At a **strategic** level – deciding what business the organisation should be in, and what its overall objectives should be

(b) At a **tactical** level – deciding how it should go about achieving its overall objectives: what products it should produce, how it will organise work and so on

(c) At the **operational** level – deciding what needs to be done from day to day and task to task

1.4 **Strategic**, or **long-range,** planning looks at where the business wants to be in maybe two to three years time and works out how to get it there. This will involve consideration of environmental factors, current and potential competitors, declining and emerging markets, projected technological change, possible diversification (producing new, different products or services) and forecast movements in consumer spending. In other words, long-range planning has to deal with a lot of variables and a high level of uncertainty. The strategic plan will constantly amended in the light of new developments.

1.5 **Tactical**, or **short-range** planning takes a shorter time period, for instance a year, and decides what needs to be done within that time period to further the strategic plan. At this level, planning will look at expansion targets, market penetration, asset purchases, financing requirements, resource requirements, and any improvements which need to be made to efficiency in order to maintain and widen the gap between costs and revenues. Improvements to efficiency will then be translated into **operational planning.**

1.6 Long-term plans may sometimes conflict with short-term plans, and it is important to reconcile them. If a company has a short-term shortage of funds, for example, it might be tempted to cut costs to maintain profitability. However, if the cuts are made in research and development or marketing, the company's long-term profitability may suffer.

2 RESOURCE PLANNING AND CONTROL

2.1 The strategic and tactical plans will need resources to carry them out. Resource planning includes estimates of requirements with regard to:

- Personnel
- Equipment or machinery
- Materials and components
- Finance

Part A: The business and accounting environment

2.2 It also includes estimates of the **availability** of all these resources and what will have to be done to obtain them.

Elements of the human resource plan

2.3 The human resource plan of the organisation is prepared on the basis of the analysis of its future human resource and skills requirements. Depending on the organisation's requirements and the availability of skills within the organisation which can be developed or deployed, the human resource plan may include the following elements.

Recruitment plan	• Numbers and types of people/skills, and when required
	• Target recruitment programme (internal and external)
Training and development plan	• Skills needing to be developed within the organisation
	• Number of recruited trainees required or internal trainees to be developed
	• Programmes for transferring or retraining employees to meet skill shortages, avoid the need for redundancies or aid flexibility
Succession plan	• Programmes for identification and development of promotable individuals
	• Plans to develop replacements for key management posts
Productivity plan	• Programmes for improving productivity or reducing staffing costs
	• Productivity targets
Retention plan	• Actions to reduce avoidable staff turnover or wastage (by resignation or early retirement): review of working terms and conditions
	• Target length of employment per new recruit and per long-term employee
Redundancy plan	• Policies for selection and timing of redundancies
	• Timetable for union consultation
	• Budgets for redundancy payments
Reward plan	• Salary structure and plans for merit or performance related pay and salary rises over time
	• Budgets for salary expenditure

Each of these elements should include budgets, targets and standard. It should allocate clear responsibilities for implementation and control (reporting, monitoring achievement against plan).

2.4 The other factors of production will have to analysed in a similar fashion. If new equipment or machinery needs to be purchased, decisions will have to be made about how it will be financed.

2.5 Planning is the process of deciding what should be done. **Control** is the process of checking whether it has been done, and if not, doing something about it. Once the plan has been formulated and steps have been taken to carry it out, it is necessary to **monitor** and **measure** the actual results achieved. These results can then be compared to the planned results. This will show that either results are proceeding according to plan, or corrective action is necessary in order to ensure the plan is achieved.

2.6 Control is necessary because unexpected factors may arise and affect the system, so making actual results deviate from the expected results.

2.7 Examples of such unpredictable factors in a business system might be:
- The entry of a **powerful new competitor** into the market
- An unexpected rise in **labour costs**
- A decline in **quality standards**
- A **supplier** going out of business
- Loss of a major **customer**
- New **legislation** affecting products
- The appearance of **new technology**

2.8 A good control system will provide management with rapid **feedback** enabling it to react appropriately to changes in the business environment.

2.9 It is as well to recognise that there always **will be** unpredictable factors. Given the current pace of change in finance, technology and world markets, it would be more surprising to see a long-term, or even a short-term, plan which proceeded as envisaged without any changes being made to keep it on track. It has even been argued that long-term planning is a waste of time, as the plan is bound to be overtaken by events.

2.10 An important part of planning in this regard is the consideration of **contingencies**. Contingencies are unexpected events, which may or may not happen. **Contingency planning** looks at how the overall plan will be affected if something unexpected happens, or if some part of the business does not proceed according to plan. As part of the contingency planning process, managers will come up with alternative solutions in response to possible problems.

Activity 3.1

Rajiv is the supervisor of a small section of 10 staff, including himself. In July, which is the section's busiest time of the year, one of his staff is on honeymoon for three weeks, two are injured in a car accident and not expected back at work for the foreseeable future and one is believed to have won the lottery and has since disappeared.

Identify the problems for Rajiv's section and discuss possible ways of dealing with them.

3 CO-ORDINATION

3.1 **Co-ordination** is one of the major functions of management. Each department will have its own procedures and its own priorities. It is the job of the manager to get all of these to mesh together harmoniously and move in the direction of the common purpose.

3.2 This is nowhere more apparent than in the planning process. Each department will have its own long-term and short-term goals and purposes, and targets that it wants to achieve. There may also be bonus schemes tied into this. Each department will have its own set of priorities. Effective co-ordination will cause some of these to change, in the interests of pursuing an **overall** set of priorities.

3.3 As the business plan will cover all departments of the organisation, so all of the departmental plans and budgets must be co-ordinated, so that they are all working together to achieve the business plan. For instance, sales should be planning to sell the number of

Part A: The business and accounting environment

units which the production departments agreed to produce, otherwise there will be either unsold stock or unfilled orders.

3.4 At the production level, co-ordination will ensure that:

- Departments know what it is they need to achieve, and when
- Work 'flows' from one department to another without holdups or clashes, and without idle time or overwork for staff and machinery
- The resources required for a task are available where and when they are required
- There is no duplication of effort

4 SYSTEMS, POLICIES AND PROCEDURES

4.1 The tools by which planning and co-ordination are carried out can be categorised as follows.

Systems

4.2 A system is an agreed-upon plan or process for carrying out an activity. An **operating system** interfaces between the hardware, programs and data in a computer. It organises and schedules the tasks. A production plant will have a system which determines how production is organised, who does what, when the machines are serviced, how long the shifts run etc.

4.3 In a business, the **accounting system** will ensure that all bookkeeping and related tasks are carried out accurately and in a timely fashion. At the next level, the **management information system** will provide management with the financial information needed for planning and control.

Policies

4.4 Policies are general statements which provide guidelines for management decision making. It might be company policy, for example, to offer five year guarantees on all products, or to promote managers from within the organisation. Policy guidelines allow managers to exercise their own discretion and freedom of choice, but within certain acceptable limits.

Procedures

4.5 Procedures are chronological sequences of actions required to perform a task. They exist at all levels but are more extensive lower down the company hierarchy, where the work is more routine. They have three main advantages:

- **Efficiency**. Procedures prescribe the most efficient way of doing a job.
- **Routine**. Procedures remove the need for the exercise of discretion or ad hoc decision-making.
- **Standardisation**. This makes output more predictable and more consistent throughout the organisation.

Activity 3.2

Differentiate between systems, policies and procedures in your own organisation by giving examples of each.

5 OFFICE PROCEDURES AND SYSTEMS

5.1 Office systems and procedures are designed to allow the different administrative functions to interrelate effectively. This diagram shows, in a simplified form, the flow of funds, documentation and information in an office.

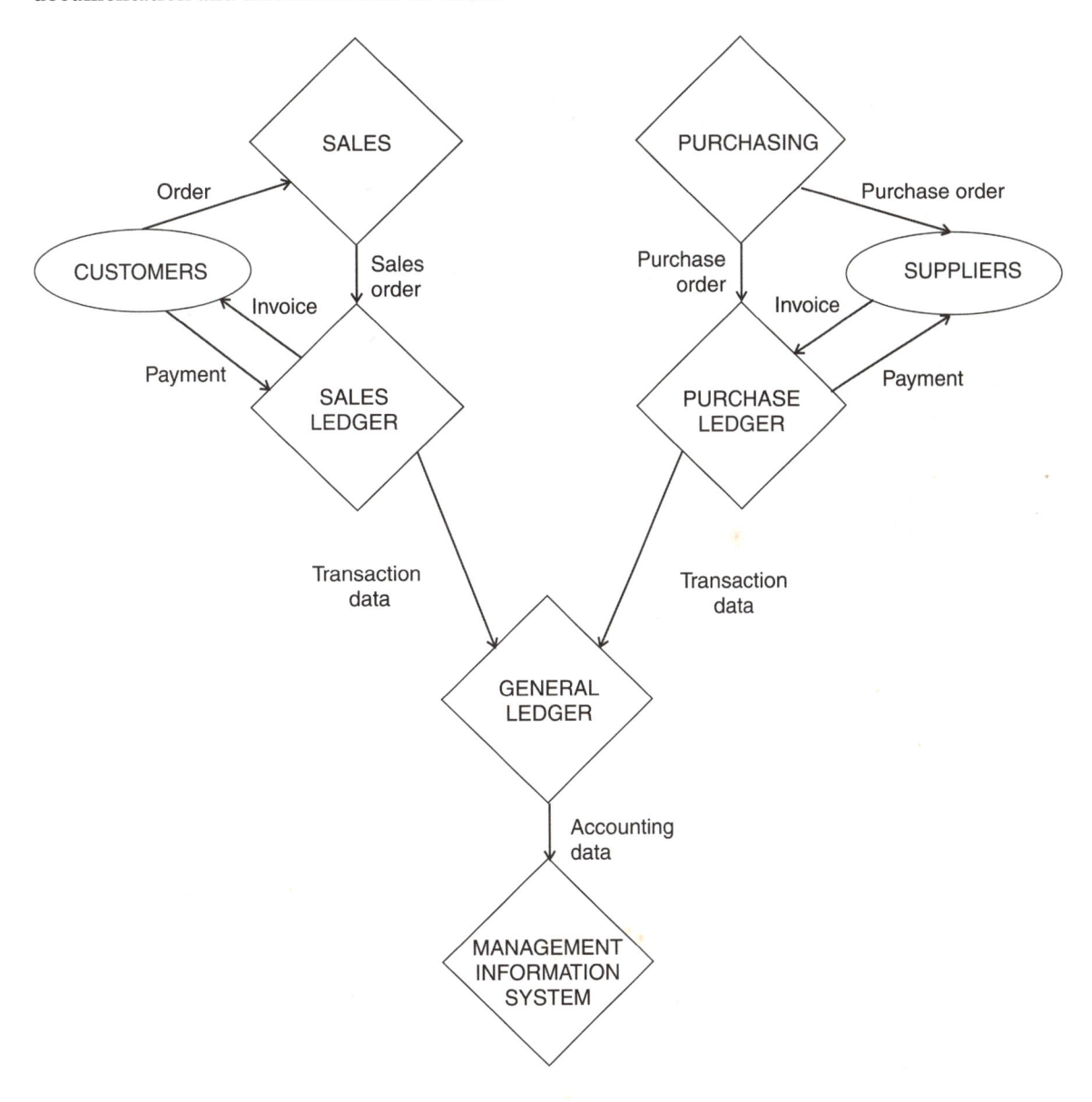

```
            SALES                              PURCHASING
    Order  ╱    ╲                           ╱            ╲  Purchase order
          ╱      ╲ Sales            Purchase              ╲
  CUSTOMERS       ╲ order           order   ╲              SUPPLIERS
          ╲ Invoice╲                         ╲ Invoice    ╱
           ╲       ╲                          ╲          ╱ Payment
    Payment ╲    SALES                      PURCHASE
             ╲  LEDGER                       LEDGER

              Transaction              Transaction
              data                     data
                    ╲                ╱
                     GENERAL
                     LEDGER
                        │
                  Accounting data
                        │
                  MANAGEMENT
                  INFORMATION
                    SYSTEM
```

5.2 Effective systems and procedures should ensure that:

- Relationships with customers are effectively managed
- Relationships with suppliers are effectively managed
- Office functions interrelate properly and are not duplicated

5.3 Within the overall system, which we can consider to be how each department relates to the other departments and to outside bodies, there will be sub-systems. For instance, the purchase ledger function will have its own system, which will be designed to ensure that only authorised payments are made, that no invoice ever gets paid twice and that expenses are coded to the correct accounts.

5.4 Weaknesses in office procedures may be signalled by:

- Arguments over job functions
- Missing paperwork

Part A: The business and accounting environment

- Disputes with customers/suppliers
- Goods not delivered

6 FINANCIAL CONTROL PROCEDURES

6.1 Financial control procedures exist specifically to ensure that:

- Financial transactions are properly carried out
- The assets of the business are safeguarded
- Accurate and timely management information is produced

6.2 These are some examples of financial control procedures:

- Cheques over a certain amount to need two signatories
- Authorisation limits for purchase orders
- Authorisation for petty cash and expenses claims
- Effective credit control procedures
- Computer security procedures and access levels

6.3 Weaknesses in financial control procedures may be signalled by:

- Cash or cheques going missing
- Excessive bad or doubtful debts
- Debtors not paying within credit terms
- Suppliers not being paid on time
- Unauthorised purchases being made
- Failure to produce accounts or other reports at the specified time

Key learning points

- Planning takes place at **strategic**, **tactical** and **operational** levels
- Plans must take account of the availability of **resources**
- A **control** system is needed to identify deviations from the plan
- Planning requires **co-ordination**
- Planning is executed through **systems, policies** and **procedures**
- Proper procedures are particularly important in the **finance** area

Quick quiz

1 What is a strategic plan?
2 Name four elements of the human resource plan.
3 Why is control a necessary part of planning?
4 What is contingency planning?
5 What does co-ordination achieve?
6 If a customer suddenly went bankrupt owing the business a large sum of money from six months ago, which system would not have been operating effectively?

Answers to quick quiz

1. A long-term plan, taking account of known environmental factors, which formulates long-range goals for the business and works out how to achieve them.

2. Any four of: recruitment, training and development, succession, productivity, retention, redundancy and reward.

3. Because only through feedback from an effective control system can managers know whether or not the plan is being carried out.

4. Planning for unforeseen developments.

5. Co-ordination gets all departments working in the same direction, by substituting overall for individual priorities.

6. This would be a serious failure of the credit control system.

Answers to activities

Answer 3.1

Rajiv's section is now seriously undermanned, and at the busiest time of the year. There is also an element of uncertainty, as he does not know whether or not the member of staff who won the lottery is going to re-appear. If he is wise, he will assume not, and plan accordingly.

These are some of his possible solutions:

- 'Borrow' staff from another section. This depends upon the willingness of other sections to help out. Of course it may also be their busiest period!

- Recruit temporary staff from an agency. This is an expensive option and these staff will need training before they become operational.

- Get his existing staff to work overtime. This is a possible solution, especially if it is made financially attractive. These are definitely the best people to have handling the work.

- Do some of the work himself. In practice, this is bound to happen!

Answer 3.2

The answer you give will depend upon your own organisation. The notes in Section 4 should help you to identify your own examples.

> **Now try Question 3 in the Exam Question Bank**

Chapter 4 The accounting function

Chapter topic list

1. The purpose and function of the accounting system
2. The structure of accounting functions
3. Accounting in the organisation
4. Manual and computerised accounting systems

The following study sessions are covered in this chapter:

Syllabus reference

5(a)	Outline the function and purpose of the accounting system	1(c)(i)
5(b)	Identify key elements of accounting systems and procedures	1(c)(i)
5(c)	Explain how accounting functions may be structured	1(c)(ii)
5(d)	Explain how accounting departments co-ordinate with other functional areas of the organisation	1(c)(iii)
5(e)	Explain the difference between manual and computerised accounting systems	1(c)(iv)

4: The accounting function

1 THE PURPOSE AND FUNCTION OF THE ACCOUNTING SYSTEM

1.1 The accounting function is part of the broader business system, and does not operate in isolation. It handles the financial operations of the organisation, but also provides information and advice to other departments. This is considered in more detail in Section 3.

1.2 Accounts are produced to aid management in planning, control and decision-making and to comply with statutory regulations. **The accounting system must be adequate to fulfil these functions**. An organisation's accounting systems are affected by the nature of its business transactions and the sort of business it is. This revisits the **contingency theory** of organisation covered in Chapter 3.

Factor	Example
Size	A **small business** like a greengrocer will have a simple, accounting system, where the main accounting record will probably be the till roll. A **large retail business,** such as a chain of supermarkets, will have elaborate accounting systems covering a large number of product ranges and sites.
Type of organisation	A **service business** might need to record the time employees take on particular jobs. Accounting on a **job or client basis** might also be a feature of service businesses. A **public sector organisation,** such as a government department, may be more concerned with the **monitoring of expenditure** against performance targets than recording revenue. A **manufacturing company** will account both for unit sales and revenue, but needs to keep **track of costs** for decision-making purposes and so forth.
Organisation structure	In a business managed by **area**, accounts will be prepared on an area basis. In a functional organisation, the accounts staff are in a separate department.

Be aware that accounting work has to comply with a wide range of regulations, including law such as the Companies Act 1985. As a result, it tends to be rather formalised and procedural in order to make sure that nothing is overlooked. Organisations often lay down their accounting rules and procedures in writing, and this may form part of an organisation manual or procedures manual.

Area organisation

1.3 Some organisations are spread over many different **countries**, and organised by area. Here is how the accounting function will be specifically affected by geography.

Difference	Comment
Currencies	**Recording information.** Customers might want to pay in local currency, but the business might have to pay for imported supplies in a different currency.
Legal and accounting requirements	In some countries, the state regulates the keeping of accounts. In the UK companies can prepare accounts as they wish, subject to the Companies Act, and financial reporting standards.
Ways of doing business	The emphasis of the accountant's job differs from country to country. In a country in which payments are made by cash, management of debtors is likely to take up far less time and effort than in a country where extended credit periods are the norm.
Economic conditions	Some countries have very high rates of inflation; this can affect accounting practice.

Part A: The business and accounting environment

Product-division structure

1.4 When an organisation has a product-based structure, accounting information must be grouped in a particular way to highlight revenue earned and costs incurred by a particular product. It is possible, then, that the product divisional basis will affect the **account coding system** of the company.

(a) **Revenue.** Recording accounting information relating to revenue is usually easy. Each product has a price, and it is relatively simple to record unit sales. Invoices may be analysed by product group.

(b) **Costs.** Some costs, such as materials, can be traced to individual products. Overheads are more difficult to deal with.

Cost information is not just a feature of a product-division structured organisation, as this information is necessary for decision making in any organisation.

1.5 In a product-division structure, administrative functions are carried out by individual product divisions. However, there will still be some areas (eg research and development) which are shared by all divisions, and it might not be easy to allocate these common costs.

External influences

1.6 Government regulations have a significant impact on the **timing** of accounting work. Quarterly VAT returns must be submitted on time to avoid heavy fines and companies have to file annual returns and accounts.

1.7 Cost and management accounting is not subject to any statutory rules. There may, however, be circumstances in which outsiders can influence the **timing** of the production of management information, and its format, or affect the procedures adopted in the accounts department.

Influence	Effect
Investors	People who have invested in the business need to know how well it is doing.
Banks	Banks often make it a condition of their loan that they be supplied with regular monthly management accounts or cash flow projections.
Suppliers	They insist on having their bills paid early.
Customers	Can also sometimes have an impact on the operation of an accounting system.
Bench-marking	Some industries have standard formats for management reports so that companies can be compared anonymously via inter-firm comparison or benchmarking.
Privatised utilities	Former public sector bodies like British Gas have their costs and revenues closely scrutinised by their regulators.

Activity 4.1

Review the accounting information produced by your department. Identify all the different users, internal and external. How have they influenced the information presented?

2 THE STRUCTURE OF ACCOUNTING FUNCTIONS

2.1 In UK companies, the head of the accounting management structure is usually the **finance director**. The finance director has a seat on the **board of directors** and is responsible for routine accounting matters and also for broad financial policy.

2.2 In many larger companies the finance director has one or more deputies below him.

(a) Some responsibilities of the **Financial Controller**

- Routine accounting
- Providing accounting reports for other departments
- Cashiers' duties and cash control

(b) Management accounting is such an important function that a **Management Accountant** is often appointed with status equal to the financial controller and separate responsibilities.

- Cost accounting
- Budgets and budgetary control
- Financial management of projects

(c) A very large organisation might have a **Treasurer** in charge of treasury work.

- Raising funds by borrowing
- Investing surplus funds on the money market or other investment markets
- Cash flow control

2.3 Sections in the accounts department

(a) The **financial accounts** section is divided up into sections, with a supervisor responsible for each section (eg for credit control, payroll, purchase ledger, sales ledger etc).

(b) Similarly, **management accounting** work is divided up, with a number of cost accountants as supervisors of sections responsible for keeping cost records of different items (eg materials, labour, overheads; or production, research and development, marketing).

(c) Some companies that spend large amounts on **capital projects** might have a section assigned exclusively to capital project appraisal (payback appraisal, DCF appraisal, sensitivity analysis, the capital budget).

2.4 An accounts function is depicted in the diagram on the next page. People are grouped together by the type of work they do. In an area structure, accounts staff might be dispersed throughout the different regions of an organisation. Management accounting work is often decentralised to departments because it provides vital information for management control purposes.

Part A: The business and accounting environment

```
                        FINANCE
                        DIRECTOR
           ┌───────────────┼───────────────┐
        TREASURER      FINANCIAL       MANAGEMENT
                       CONTROLLER      ACCOUNTANT
                           │               │
                       FINANCIAL         COST
                       ACCOUNTANTS     ACCOUNTANTS
           │
        CASHIER
```

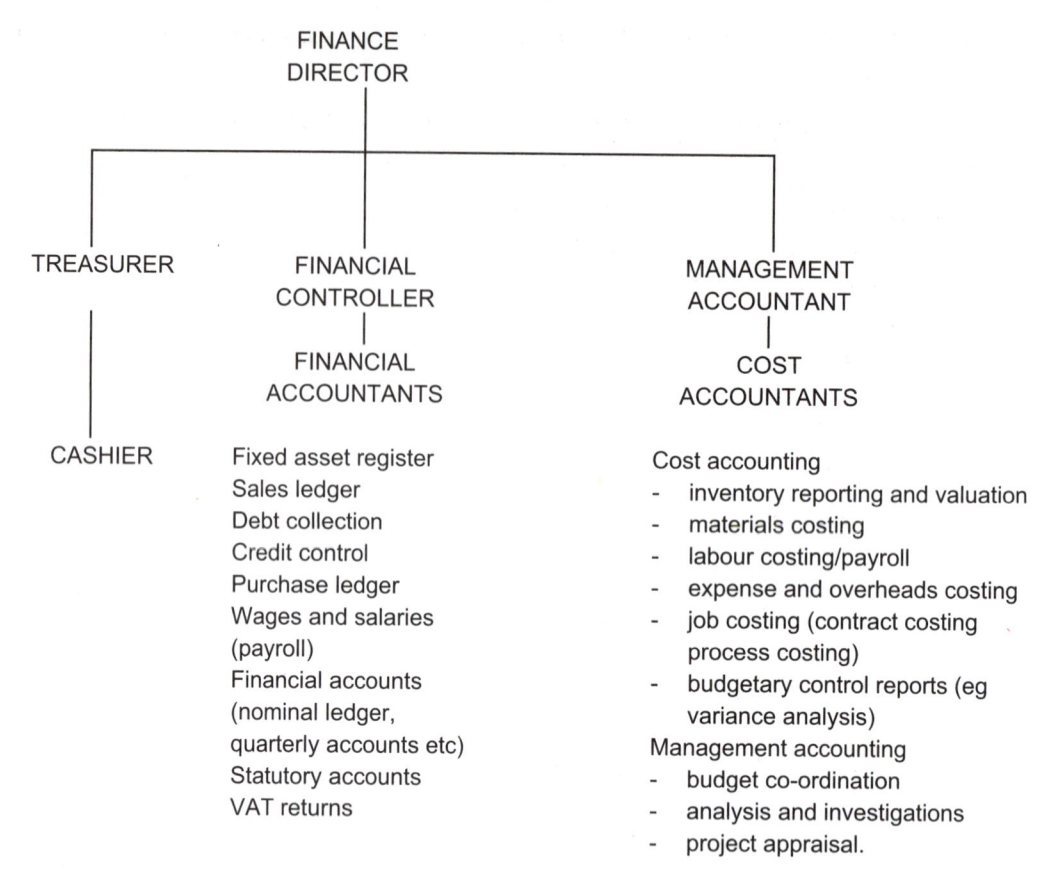

Fixed asset register	Cost accounting
Sales ledger	- inventory reporting and valuation
Debt collection	- materials costing
Credit control	- labour costing/payroll
Purchase ledger	- expense and overheads costing
Wages and salaries (payroll)	- job costing (contract costing process costing)
Financial accounts (nominal ledger, quarterly accounts etc)	- budgetary control reports (eg variance analysis)
Statutory accounts	Management accounting
VAT returns	- budget co-ordination
	- analysis and investigations
	- project appraisal.

2.5 Many organisations have an **internal audit department**. This functions as an internal financial control. One of its responsibilities is to control the risks of fraud and error. For this reason it should be separate from the finance department and the chief internal auditor should report to the audit committee of the board of directors, bypassing the Financial Director.

3 ACCOUNTING IN THE ORGANISATION

3.1 In very broad terms, accounting work can be seen as a mixture of two types of work.

(a) **Handling the financial operations** of an organisation.

- Handling receipts and payments - ie managing the **cash flows** of the business
- Acting as a collection and reporting agency for the **government** (payroll, VAT)
- Receiving and checking invoices from **suppliers**
- Sending out invoices to **credit customers** and chasing up late payers; keeping a record of debts owed to the organisation
- **Borrowing** money and repaying loans
- Keeping the financial position of the organisation - cash flows, gearing and debt - in good order
- Through **internal controls**, preventing errors or fraudulent practices, and ensuring that the assets of the business are safeguarded.

(b) **Providing information** (and advice if required) to the managers of other departments to help them do their work better. The accounts department has to liase with other departments all the time. **Performance reports** enable managers and others to judge how well the organisation is doing.

(i) **Planning information**: for instance information for budgets is often provided by accountants.

(ii) **Control information** helps other managers to identify problem areas and take control decisions. Budgetary control variance reports are an example of this.

(iii) **Information to make one-off decisions.** Sometimes, a decision has to be taken by management, and some knowledge about the financial consequences of each choice needs to be available. Accountants can provide such information (eg information about the costs and likely cash benefits of capital expenditure proposals).

3.2 In each case, **input information** from **other departments** is necessary to carry out the accounting activity. The **procedures** for communication with other departments may be set out in manuals or schedules of duties. For example, before an invoice for raw material supplies is paid, the accounting department will need to check the details of the invoice against the **purchase order form** (co-ordination with the purchasing department) and the **goods received note** (co-ordination with the stores department).

Other departments and sections

3.3 Accounting management provides a good example of the **need for close co-ordination** between managers and sections, and this need is particularly acute in financial accounts work because of the **internal controls dividing up responsibilities**.

Department	Accounts section	Relationship
Purchases dept (PD)	Purchase ledger (PL)	PD advises PL of purchase orders
		PD indicates valid invoices
	Cashier (C)	C informs PD and PL of payment
Personnel dept	Payroll	Personnel gives details of wage rates, starters and leavers, to payroll
Sales dept (SD)	Sales ledger (SL)	SD advises SL of sales order
Credit control (CC)		SL might give CC information about overdue debts
		SL might give details about debtors ageing and other reports
Operations, stock controllers	Cost accounting staff	Operations might give details of movements of stock, so that the accounts staff can value stock and provide costing reports
Senior management	Financial accounting and cost accounting staff	The accounts department as a whole produces management information for decision making and control

Importance of the relationship

3.4 The accounts department is crucial to the organisation.

- If it provides the wrong information, managers will make bad decisions

Part A: The business and accounting environment

- It if confuses the data, important transactions might slip through the net, and fraud may result.
- There is a legal duty to ensure that accounting records are in good order.

4 MANUAL AND COMPUTERISED ACCOUNTING SYSTEMS

4.1 Most accounting systems are computerised and anyone training to be an accountant should be able to work with them. The most important point to remember is that the **principles** of computerised accounting are the same as those of **manual accounting**. You should by now have a good grasp of these principles.

4.2 Most reference to computerised accounting talks about accounting **packages**. This is a rather general term, but most of us can probably name the accounting package that we use at work. An accounting package consists of several accounting **modules**, eg sales ledger, nominal ledger.

4.3 We are going to look specifically at 'applications software', that is packages of computer programs that carry out specific tasks.

   (a) Some applications are devoted specifically to an accounting task, for example a payroll package, a fixed asset register or a stock control package.

   (b) Other applications have many uses in business, including their use for accounting purposes. Examples of this are databases and spreadsheets.

Accounting packages

> **IMPORTANT!**
>
> One of the most important facts to remember about computerised accounting is that in principle, it is exactly the same as manual accounting.

4.4 Accounting functions retain the same names in computerised systems as in more traditional written records. Computerised accounting still uses the familiar ideas of day books, ledger accounts, double entry, trial balance and financial statements. The principles of working with computerised sales, purchase and nominal ledgers are exactly what would be expected in the manual methods they replace.

4.5 The only difference is that these various books of account have become invisible. Ledgers are now computer files which are held in a computer-sensible form, ready to be called upon.

Advantages

4.6 The advantages of accounting packages compared with a manual system are as follows:

   (a) The packages can be used by **non-specialists**.
   (b) A large amount of **data can be processed very quickly**.
   (c) Computerised systems are **more accurate** than manual systems.
   (d) A computer is capable of handling and processing **large volumes** of data.

4: The accounting function

(e) Once the data has been input, computerised systems can **analyse data** rapidly to present useful control information for managers such as a trial balance or a debtors schedule.

Disadvantages

4.7 The advantages of computerised accounting system far outweigh the disadvantages, particularly for large businesses. However, the following may be identified as possible disadvantages.

(a) The initial **time and costs** involved in installing the system, training personnel and so on.

(b) The need for **security checks** to make sure that unauthorised personnel do not gain access to data files.

(c) The necessity to develop a **system of coding** (see below) and checking.

(d) **Lack of 'audit trail'**. It is not always easy to see where a mistake has been made.

Coding

4.8 Computers require vital information to be expressed in the form of codes. For example, nominal ledger accounts might be coded individually by means of a two-digit code:

- 00 Ordinary share capital
- 01 Share premium
- 05 Profit and loss account
- 15 Purchases
- 22 Debtors ledger control account
- 41 Creditors ledger control account
- 42 Interest
- 43 Dividends

In the same way, individual accounts must be given a unique code number in the sales ledger and purchase ledger.

4.9 EXAMPLE: CODING

When an invoice is received from a supplier (example code 1234) for £3,000 for the purchase of raw materials, the transaction might be coded for input to the computer as:

Supplier Code	Nominal ledger Debit	Nominal ledger Credit	Value	Stock Code	Quantity
1234	15	41	£3,000	56742	150

Code 15 in our example represents purchases, and code 41 the creditors control account from the list in Paragraph 4.8. This single input could be used to update the purchase ledger, the nominal ledger, and the stock ledger. The stock code may enable further analysis to be carried out, perhaps allocating the cost to a particular department or product. Thus the needs of both financial accounting and cost accounting can be fulfilled at once.

Part A: The business and accounting environment

Modules

> **KEY TERM**
>
> A **module** is a program which deals with one particular part of a business accounting system.

4.10 An accounting package will consist of several modules. A simple accounting package might consist of only one module (in which case it is called a stand-alone module), but more often it will consist of several modules. The name given to a set of several modules is a **suite**. An accounting package, therefore, might have separate modules for:

- Invoicing
- Stock
- Sales ledger
- Purchase ledger
- Nominal ledger
- Payroll
- Cash book
- Job costing
- Fixed asset register
- Report generator

Integrated software

4.11 Each module may be integrated with the others, so that data entered in one module will be passed automatically or by simple operator request through into any other module where the data is of some relevance. For example, if there is an input into the invoicing module authorising the despatch of an invoice to a customer, there might be **automatic links**:

(a) To the sales ledger, to update the file by posting the invoice to the customer's account

(b) To the stock module, to update the stock file by:

- Reducing the quantity and value of stock in hand
- Recording the stock movement

(c) To the nominal ledger, to update the file by posting the sale to the sales account

(d) To the job costing module, to record the sales value of the job on the job cost file

(e) To the report generator, to update the sales analysis and sales totals which are on file and awaiting inclusion in management reports.

Advantages

4.12 (a) It becomes possible to make just one entry in one of the ledgers which automatically updates the others.

(b) Users can specify reports, and the software will automatically extract the required data from all the relevant files.

(c) Both of the above simplify the workload of the user, and the irritating need to constantly load and unload disks is eliminated.

4: The accounting function

Disadvantages

4.13 (a) Usually, it requires more computer memory than separate (stand-alone) systems - which means there is less space in which to store actual data.

(b) Because one program is expected to do everything, the user may find that an integrated package has fewer facilities than a set of specialised modules.

Activity 4.2

What outputs would you expect to see from a computerised purchase ledger?

> **Key learning points**
>
> - The nature of an organisation's business determines the **size and complexity** of the accounting system.
> - **Deadlines** for producing reports and information may be influenced by **external bodies**, such as tax authorities and banks.
> - The accounts department needs to **liaise closely** with other departments, especially sales and purchasing.
> - **Financial accounting** and **management accounting** will be separate sections in any large accounting department.
> - **Computerised accounting** is the same in principle as **manual accounting**.

Quick quiz

1. What additional records may need to be kept by a service business?
2. How will costs be allocated in a product-based structure?
3. Accounting is made up of two types of work. What are they?
4. What functions are carried out by a Treasurer?
5. What is the function of the internal audit department?
6. What is an accounting module?
7. What do we mean by integrated software?

Answers to quick quiz

1. Records of hours spent by staff, to be recharged to clients.
2. Direct costs will be allocated to products and overheads will be apportioned by some agreed method.
3. Handling the financial operations of the business, and providing financial information to management.
4. Raising funds
   Investing surplus funds
   Controlling cash flow
5. Monitoring internal financial controls in order to prevent fraud and error.
6. A program which deals with one particular part of an accounting system, for instance, sales ledger.
7. Software in which a number of modules can be simultaneously updated.

Part A: The business and accounting environment

Answers to activities

Answer 4.1

Produce a table for your company like that in Paragraph 1.7.

Answer 4.2

A computerised purchase ledger will produce the following outputs:

- A list of suppliers with whom the business has accounts
- A list of purchase invoices input that day
- A report of postings from the purchase ledger to the nominal ledger
- A listing of invoices due for payment
- A cash requirements report, showing the cost of paying a specified list of invoices
- An aged creditors report
- If it's configured to do so, a pile of computer-generated cheques!

Part B
Effective management of business and accounting systems

Chapter 5 Monitoring business and accounting systems

Chapter topic list

1 Internal control
2 Internal audit and internal control
3 The external auditor

The following study sessions are covered in this chapter:

Syllabus reference

6(a) Explain the importance of internal controls in an organisation 2(d)

6(b) Describe the responsibilities of management with respect to internal control 2(a)

6(c) Describe the different roles of the internal and external auditors 2(a)

6(d) Recognise the weaknesses of controls and the features of effective control procedures 2(b)

Part B: Effective management of business and accounting systems

1 INTERNAL CONTROL

1.1 **Control** is defined as 'ensuring that the desired results are obtained'. It is a key management function. Most organisations need to measure their performance and compare what should have happened with what has actually happened. **Control systems** make sure that the organisation drives its plans forward, and achieves its objectives. An **effective** control system will also promote corrective actions when necessary.

Internal control systems and internal controls

> **KEY TERM**
>
> An **internal control system** is 'the whole system of controls, financial and otherwise, established by the management in order to carry on the business of the enterprise in an orderly and efficient manner, ensure adherence to management policies, safeguard the assets and secure as far as possible the completeness and accuracy of the records. The individual components of an internal control system are known as controls or internal controls'. (Auditing guideline: *Internal controls*).

1.2 This definition of **internal control** should draw your attention to several matters which you should keep clear in your mind.

(a) **Internal control** refers to **control by management** - that is, controls applied from within the organisation itself.

(b) A system of internal control **extends beyond matters that relate to accounting** and the work of the finance and accounting department of an organisation. It embraces all types of controls implemented by management - such as controls over late attendance by employees and control over operator efficiency levels.

Types of internal control

1.3 **Types of internal controls**

(a) **Administrative controls**. These consist of all methods and procedures that are concerned with operational efficiency and adherence to management policies. These controls will emphasise statistical analysis performance reports, quality control, employee training programmes and so on.

(b) **Accounting controls**. These consist of all **methods** and **procedures** that are concerned with the safeguarding of assets and the reliability of financial records. Such controls will include systems of authorisation and approval, separation of duties concerned with asset custody, physical controls over assets and internal auditing.

5: Monitoring business and accounting systems

> **KEY TERM**
>
> There are eight types of control listed. One way of remembering them is to use the mnemonic **SPAM SOAP**.
>
> **S**egregation of duties
>
> **P**hysical
>
> **A**uthorisation and approval
>
> **M**anagement
>
> **S**upervision
>
> **O**rganisation
>
> **A**rithmetical and accounting
>
> **P**ersonnel

Segregation of duties

1.4 Clear **job descriptions** should segregate **execution** from **control** tasks. One of the prime means of control is the separation of those responsibilities or duties which would, if combined, **enable one individual to record and process a complete transaction**.

Segregation of duties reduces the risk of intentional manipulation or error and increases the element of checking. Some functions should be separated whenever possible.

- Authorisation
- Execution
- Custody
- Recording
- Systems development and daily operations

1.5 EXAMPLE

A classic example of segregation of duties, which both internal and external auditors look for, concerns the **receipt, recording and banking of cash**. It is not a good idea for the person who **opens the post** to be the person responsible for **recording that the cash has arrived**. It is even poorer practice for that person to be responsible for **taking the cash to the bank**. If these duties are not segregated, there is always the chance that the person will simply pocket the cash, and nobody would be any the wiser. More about this when we cover fraud in the next chapter.

Physical controls

1.6 **Procedures and security measures** are needed to ensure that access to **assets** is limited to authorised personnel. Such controls include locks, safes and entry codes.

Authorisation and approval

1.7 All transactions should be authorised or approved by an appropriate responsible person. The limits for these authorisations should be specified.

Part B: Effective management of business and accounting systems

1.8 EXAMPLE

A company might make a regulation that the head of a particular department may authorise revenue expenditure up to £500, but that for anything more expensive he must seek the approval of a director. Such authorisation limits will vary from company to company: £500 could be quite a large amount for a small company, but seem insignificant to a big one.

Management controls

1.9 Management controls are exercised by management outside the day-to-day routine of the system.

- Overall supervisory controls
- Review of management accounts and comparison with budgets
- Internal audit function
- Special review procedures

Supervisory controls

1.10 Any system of internal control should include the **supervision** by responsible officials of day-to-day transactions and recording thereof.

Organisation as a control

1.11 Enterprises should have a plan of their organisation, defining and allocating responsibilities and identifying **lines of reporting** for all aspects of the enterprise's operations, including the controls. The **delegation of authority and responsibility** should be clearly specified.

1.12 EXAMPLE

An employee in a company may work for two managers, say a brand manager (who is responsible for the marketing and profitability of one particular product) and a production manager who supervises the production of all products. As you know, a company which is organised in this overlapping fashion is said to have a matrix organisation. The point here is that all the employee's actions must be supervised by one or other of the two managers.

Arithmetical and accounting controls

1.13 These controls within the recording function **which** check that the transactions to be recorded and processed have **been authorised**, that they are all **included** and that they are **correctly recorded** and **accurately processed**.

- Checking the arithmetical accuracy of the records
- The maintenance and checking of totals
- Reconciliations
- Control accounts
- Trial balances
- Accounting for documents

Personnel controls

1.14 **Personnel controls** are procedures to ensure that personnel have capabilities appropriate to their responsibilities, since the proper functioning of any system depends on the competence and integrity of those operating it. The qualifications, selection and training of

5: Monitoring business and accounting systems

the personnel involved are important features to be considered in setting up any control system.

1.15 EXAMPLE

A company accountant should be suitably qualified. Nowadays, qualified tends to mean someone who possesses a professional qualification of some sort, but it is important to remember that others are still able to do a job because of work experience - they are qualified through that experience.

The internal control system

1.16 A company will select internal controls from the SPAM SOAP list in Paragraph 1.3 and incorporate them into its organisation. Which controls it selects depends on the particular circumstances of the company, but the range of internal controls it ends up with is called the company's **internal control system**.

1.17 An organisation may not possess all of the SPAM SOAP internal controls - or indeed may not be able to implement all of them. For example, a very small organisation may have insufficient staff to be able to organise a desirable level of segregation of duties.

1.18 **If controls are absent, managers should be aware of the risk**. It is then the responsibility of management to decide whether the risk is acceptable, or whether the missing control should be instituted.

Internal checks

1.19 Internal controls should not be confused with **internal checks**, which have a more restricted definition.

> **KEY TERM**
>
> **Internal checks** are defined as the checks on the day-to-day transactions whereby **the work of one person is proved independently or is complementary to the work of another**, the object being the prevention or early detection of errors and fraud. It includes matters such as the delegation and allocation of authority and the division of work, the method of recording transactions and the use of independently ascertained totals, against which a large number of individual items can be proved.

1.20 Internal checks are an important feature of the day-to-day control of financial transactions and the accounting system. **Arithmetical** internal checks include pre-lists, post-lists and control totals.

Part B: Effective management of business and accounting systems

> **KEY TERMS**
>
> A **pre-list** is a list that is drawn up before any processing takes place.
> A **post-list** is a list that is drawn up during or after processing.
>
> A **control total** is a total of any sort used for control purposes by comparing it with another total that ought to be the same.

1.21 A pre-list total is a control total, so that for example, when cash is received by post and a pre-list prepared and the receipts are recorded individually in the cash book, and a total of amounts entered in the cash book is obtained by adding up the individual entries, the control total obtained from the cash book can be compared with, and should agree with, the pre-list control total. Control totals, as you should already be aware, are frequently used within computer processing.

1.22 **Aims of internal checks**

(a) **Segregate tasks**, so that the responsibility for particular actions, or for defaults or omissions, can be traced to an individual person.

(b) **Create and preserve** the records that act as confirmation of physical facts and accounting entries.

(c) **Break down routine procedures** into separate steps or stages, so as to facilitate an even flow of work and avoid bottlenecks.

(d) **Reduce the possibility of fraud and error**. The aim should be to **prevent** fraud and error rather than to be able to **detect** it after it has happened. Efficient internal checks make extensive fraud virtually impossible, except by means of collusion between two or more people.

1.23 **Internal checks**, importantly, imply a **division of work**, so that the work of one person is either **proved independently** or else is complementary to the work of another person

Activity 5.1

The Geton Company specialises in providing cleaning services. It is currently undertaking an expansion programme, much of which is achieved by supplying services previously carried out by employees of client organisations. In many cases these same employees are then recruited by Geton to work on the contracts using the improved procedures developed through its specialisation in this type of work.

For each large contract, or a number of small contracts in the same location, a supervisor is appointed to oversee the activities of the employees and to provide basic control data for hours worked, materials issued, use of equipment and so on. Invoices are prepared centrally as are wages. These are paid weekly in arrears via BACS. Each supervisor has a van in which the materials are kept and replenished from a central store. Equipment is normally kept at the purchasing organisation.

As a senior accounts assistant with Geton you have been asked to oversee the clerical activities associated with the work of the supervisors.

(a) Outline and explain the basic data you would expect to be completed by the supervisor.

(b) Explain what checks you would apply to confirm the correctness of the data provided.

Characteristics of a good internal control system

1.24 (a) **A clearly defined organisation structure**

  (i) **Different operations must be separated** into appropriate divisions and sub-divisions.

  (ii) Officers must **be appointed to assume responsibility** for each division.

  (iii) **Clear lines of responsibility** must exist between each division and sub-division and the board.

  (iv) There must be overall **co-ordination of the company's activities** (through corporate planning).

(b) **Adequate internal checks**

  (i) **Separation of duties** for **authorising** a transaction, **custody** of the assets obtained by means of the transaction and **recording** the transaction.

  (ii) '**Proof measures**' such as control totals, pre-lists and bank reconciliations should be used.

(c) **Acknowledgement** of work done: persons who carry out a particular job should acknowledge their work by means of signatures, initials, rubber stamps and so on.

(d) Protective devices for **physical security**.

(e) **Formal documents should acknowledge the transfer of responsibility for goods**. When goods are received, a goods received note should be used to acknowledge receipt by the storekeeper.

(f) **Pre-review:** the authorisation of a transaction (for example a cash payment, or the purchase of an asset) should not be given by the person responsible without first checking that all the proper procedures have been carried out.

(g) A clearly defined **system for authorising transactions** within specified spending limits.

(h) **Post-review:** completed transactions should be reviewed after they have happened; for example, monthly statements of account from suppliers should be checked against the purchase ledger accounts of those suppliers.

(i) There should be **authorisation, custody** and **re-ordering** procedures.

  (i) Funds and property of the company should be kept under **proper custody**. Access to assets (either direct or by documentation) should be **limited to authorised personnel**.

  (ii) Expenditure should only be incurred after authorisation and all expenditures are properly accounted for.

  (iii) All revenue must be properly accounted for and received in due course.

(j) **Personnel** should have the capabilities and qualifications necessary to carry out their responsibilities properly.

(k) An **internal audit** department should be able to verify that the control system is working and to review the system to ensure that it is still appropriate for current circumstances.

Part B: Effective management of business and accounting systems

Limitations on the effectiveness of internal controls

1.25 Not only must a control system include sufficient controls, but also these **controls must be applied properly and honestly**.

(a) Internal controls depending on **segregation of duties can be avoided by the collusion** of two or more people responsible for those duties.

(b) **Authorisation controls can be abused** by the person empowered to authorise the activities.

(c) **Management can often override the controls they have set up themselves.**

2 INTERNAL AUDIT AND INTERNAL CONTROL

2.1 Internal audit

> **KEY TERM**
>
> **Internal audit** has been defined as:
>
> An independent appraisal activity established within an organisation as a service to it. It is a control which functions by examining and evaluating the adequacy and effectiveness of other controls. The investigative techniques developed are applied to the analysis of the effectiveness of all parts of an entity's operations and management.

2.2 The work of internal audit is distinct from the external audit which is carried out for the benefit of shareholders only and examines published accounts. **Internal audit is part of the internal control system**.

The features of internal audit

2.3 From these definitions the two main features of internal audit emerge.

(a) **Independence:** although an internal audit department is part of an organisation, it should be independent of the line management whose sphere of authority it may audit.

(b) **Appraisal:** internal audit is concerned with the appraisal of work done by other people in the organisation, and internal auditors should not carry out any of that work themselves. The appraisal of operations provides a service to management.

Types of audit

2.4 Internal audit is a management control, as it is a tool used to ensure that other internal controls are working satisfactorily. An internal audit department may be asked by management to look into any aspect of the organisation.

2.5 Five different types of audit can be distinguished. (The first three types are considered further in the following paragraphs.)

- Operational audit
- Systems audit
- Transactions audit
- Social audit
- Management investigations

2.6 **Operational audits** can be concerned with **any sphere** of a company's activities. Their prime objective is the monitoring of management's performance at every level, to ensure optimal functioning according to pre-determined criteria. They concentrate on the outputs of the system, and the efficiency of the organisation. They are also known as '**management**', '**efficiency**' or '**value for money**' audits.

2.7 A **systems audit** is based on a testing and evaluation of the **internal controls** within an organisation so that those controls may be relied on to ensure that resources are being managed effectively and information provided accurately. Two types of tests are used.

(a) **Compliance tests** seek evidence that the internal controls are being applied as prescribed.

(b) **Substantive tests** substantiate the entries in the figures in accounts. They are used to discover **errors and omissions**.

2.8 The auditor will be interested in a variety of processing errors when performing compliance tests.

- At the wrong time
- Incompleteness
- Omission
- Error
- Fraud

2.9 The key importance of the two types of test is that **if the compliance tests reveal that internal controls are working satisfactorily, then the amount of substantive testing can be reduced**, and the internal auditor can concentrate the audit effort on those areas where controls do not exist or are not working satisfactorily.

2.10 **EXAMPLE**

Suppose a department within a company processes travel claims which are eventually paid and recorded on the general ledger.

(a) When conducting **compliance tests**, the internal auditor is **looking at the controls** in the travel claim section to see if they are working properly. This is not the same as looking at the travel claims themselves. For example, one of the internal controls might be that a clerk checks the addition on the travel claim and initials a box to say that he has done so. If he fails to perform this arithmetic check, then there has been a control failure - regardless of whether the travel claim had, in fact, been added up correctly or incorrectly.

(b) When conducting **substantive tests**, the internal auditor is examining figures which he has extracted directly from the company's financial records. For this sort of test, the auditor is concerned only with establishing whether or not the figure in the ledger is correct. He or she is not concerned as to how it got there.

2.11 **A transactions or probity audit** aims to detect fraud and uses only substantive tests.

Accountability

2.12 Ideally, the internal auditor should be directly responsible to the highest executive level in the organisation, preferably to the audit committee of the Board of Directors. There are three main reasons for this requirement.

Part B: Effective management of business and accounting systems

- The auditor needs access to all parts of the organisation.
- The auditor should be free to comment on the performance of management.
- The auditor's report may need to be actioned at the highest level to ensure its effective implementation.

In practice, however, the internal auditor is often responsible to the head of the finance function.

Independence

2.13 Given an acceptable line of responsibility and clear terms of authority, it is vital that the internal auditor **is and is seen to be independent**. Independence for the internal auditor is established by three things.

- The responsibility structure
- The auditor's mandatory authority
- The auditor's own approach

2.14 Internal audit requires a highly professional approach which is objective, detached and honest. Independence is a fundamental concept of auditing and this applies just as much to the internal auditor as to the external auditor. The internal auditor should not install new procedures or systems, neither should he engage in any activity which he would normally appraise, as this might compromise his independence.

Activity 5.2

The Midas Mail Order Company operates a central warehouse from which all merchandise is distributed by post or carrier to the company's 10,000 customers. An outline description of the sales and cash collection system is set out below.

Sales and cash collection system

Stage	Department/staff responsible	Documentation
(1) Customer orders merchandise (Orders by phone or through the postal system)	Sales dept Sales assistants	Multiple copy order form (with date, quantities, price marked on them) Copies 1-3 sent to warehouse. Copy 4 sent to accounts dept. Copy 5 retained in sales dept
(2) Merchandise requested from stock rooms by despatch clerks	Storekeepers	Copies 1-3 handed to storekeepers. Forms marked as merchandise taken from stock. (Note. If merchandise is out of stock the storekeepers retain copies 1-3 until stockroom is re-stocked). Copies 1-2 handed to despatch clerks. Copy 3 retained by store-keepers.
(3) Merchandise despatched	Despatch bay Despatch clerks	Copy 2 marked when goods despatched and sent to accounts department
(4) Customers invoiced	Accounts dept: sales ledger clerks	2-copy invoice prepared from invoiced details on copy 2 of order form received from despatch bay Copy 1 of invoice sent to customer. Copy 2 retained by accounts dept and posted to sales ledger
(5) Cash received (as cheques, bank giro credit, or cash)	Accounts dept: cashier	2-copy cash receipt list Copy 1 of cash receipt list retained by cashier Copy 2 passed to sales ledger clerk

5: Monitoring business and accounting systems

(a) State four objectives of an internal control system.

(b) For the Midas Mail Order Company list four major controls which you would expect to find in the operation of the accounting system described above, and explain the objective of each of these controls.

(c) For each of the four controls identified above, describe briefly two tests which you would expect an internal auditor to carry out to determine whether the control was operating satisfactorily.

3 THE EXTERNAL AUDITOR

> **KEY TERM**
>
> An **external audit** is an independent examination of, and expression of opinion on the financial statements of an enterprise.

3.1 If the 'enterprise' is a limited company, 'external audit' means statutory audit, that is, under the Companies Act 1985.

3.2 External auditors are generally firms of chartered or certified accountants. They summarise their conclusions on the company's financial statements by issuing an audit report, addressed to the shareholders. The report must state whether, in the auditors opinion:

(a) The **balance sheet** gives a **true and fair view** of the state of affairs of the company at the end of the financial year.

(b) The **profit and loss account** gives a true and fair view of the profit or loss of the company for the financial year.

(c) The financial statements have been **properly prepared** in accordance with the Companies Act 1985.

> **KEY TERM**
>
> '**True and fair**' is not defined in company law or accounting standards. The words are used together rather than separately and the term is generally taken to mean 'reasonably accurate and free from bias or distortion'.

3.3 The Companies Act 1985 states that the directors may depart from any provisions of company law or accounting standards if these are inconsistent with the requirement to give a true and fair view. This 'true and fair override' has been treated as an important loophole in the law and has been the cause of much argument and dissatisfaction within the accounting profession.

Differences between internal and external audit

3.4 There are three main differences between internal and external audit.

(a) **Appointment**. External auditors are appointed by the shareholders (although they are usually only ratifying the directors' choice) and must be independent of the company, whereas internal auditors are employees of the organisation.

Part B: Effective management of business and accounting systems

(b) **Responsibility**. External auditors are responsible to the owners (ie shareholders, the public or Parliament), whereas internal auditors are responsible to senior management.

(c) **Objectives**. The objectives for external auditors are defined by statute, whereas those for internal auditors are set by management. In other words, management - perhaps the internal auditors themselves - decide what parts of the organisation or what systems they are going to look at, and what type of audit should be carried out.

3.5 Contrary to popular belief, it is not the responsibility of external auditors to detect fraud; they are merely obliged to plan their audit tests so that they have a reasonable expectation of detecting fraud. It is the responsibility of the **directors** to set up an adequate system of internal control to deter and expose fraud.

Key learning points

- There are various types of control in an organisation.
- The main **internal controls** that an organisation may adopt are those covered by the SPAM SOAP mnemonic.
- **Internal checks** are part of the internal controls in an accounting system: they are designed to check that everything that should be recorded is recorded, that any errors come to light and that assets and liabilities genuinely exist and are recorded at the correct amount.
- Internal audit is itself an internal control whose function is to assess the adequacy of other internal controls. The main types of audit are systems audits, transactions audits and value for money audits.

Quick quiz

1. What is an internal control system?
2. Distinguish between administrative controls and accounting controls.
3. What is the well-known mnemonic for the eight types of internal control, and what does it stand for?
4. The person who authorises a transaction should ideally be separate from the person who executes it. Give an example of this and state what other functions should be kept separate.
5. What is the purpose of arithmetical and accounting controls? Give some examples.
6. What is an internal check?
7. Briefly describe five characteristics of a good internal control system.
8. Are internal controls foolproof? If not, why not?
9. What is internal audit?
10. Distinguish between internal audit, internal control and internal check.

Answers to quick quiz

1. An internal control system is 'the whole system of controls, financial and otherwise, established by the management in order to carry on the business of the enterprise in an orderly and efficient manner, ensure adherence to management policies, safeguard the assets and secure as far as possible the completeness and accuracy of the records. The individual components of an internal control system are known as controls or internal controls'. The overall system of internal control consists of a number of individual controls known as internal controls.

2. Administrative controls consist of the plan of organisation and methods and procedures that are concerned with operational efficiency and adherence to management policies. Examples are time and motion study, performance reports, quality control, and employee training programmes. Accounting controls consist of methods and procedures that are concerned with, and relate directly to,

5: Monitoring business and accounting systems

safeguarding of assets and the reliability of financial records. Examples are systems of authorisation and approval, separation of duties concerned with asset custody, physical controls over assets and internal auditing.

3   The eight types of control can be remembered using the mnemonic SPAM SOAP.

- **S**egregation of duties
- **P**hysical controls
- **A**uthorisation and approval controls
- **M**anagement controls, such as internal audit or review of management accounts
- **S**upervision
- **O**rganisation (that is, the formal structure of authority and responsibility)
- **A**rithmetical and accounting controls
- **P**ersonnel controls

4   An example would be the authorisation for the payment of a supplier's invoice and the drawing up and signing of the cheque. Other functions that should be kept separate are the custody of assets (for example cheque books), and the recording of transactions (writing up the payment in the cash book and purchase ledger). The Auditing Guideline also gives the example, in the case of a computer-based accounting system, of systems development and daily operations.

5   Accounting and arithmetical controls check that the transactions to be recorded and processed have been authorised, that they are all included and that they are correctly recorded and accurately processed. Here are some examples.

- Checking the arithmetical accuracy of the records
- The maintenance and checking of totals
- Reconciliations
- Control accounts
- Trial balances
- Accounting for documents

6   Internal checks are: the checks on the day-to-day transactions whereby the work of one person is proved independently or is complementary to the work of another, the object being the prevention or early detection of errors and fraud. Control totals and pre-lists are examples of them.

7   **Characteristics of good internal control**

   (i)   A clearly defined organisation structure

   (ii)   Adequate internal checks

   (iii) Acknowledgement of work done

   (iv)   Protective devices for physical security

   (v)   The use of formal documents to acknowledge the transfer of responsibility for goods

   (vi)   Pre-review of transactions

   (vii) A clearly defined system for authorising transactions within specified spending limits

   (viii) Post-review: completed transactions should be reviewed after they have happened.

   (ix)   Authorisation, custody and re-ordering procedures over the funds, property and expenditure of the organisation

   (x)   Personnel should be adequately trained, and there should be appropriate remuneration, welfare, promotion and appointment schemes (adequate 'hygiene' and 'motivation', in Herzberg's terms). There should also be adequate supervision by responsible officials and management

   (xi)   An internal audit department should be able to verify that the control system is working and to review the system to ensure that it is still appropriate for (changing) current circumstances.

Part B: Effective management of business and accounting systems

8   Internal controls have to be applied properly and honestly in order to work.

9   Internal audit is a form of control which has been defined as 'An independent appraisal activity established within an organisation ... which functions by examining and evaluating the adequacy and effectiveness of other controls'. It can be applied to the analysis of the effectiveness of all parts of an organisation's operations and management.

10 Internal controls embrace all controls (both financial and non-financial) established by management to ensure efficiency and adherence to management policies, properly safeguarded assets and complete and accurate records. Internal checks are specific types of internal controls in an accounting system, and are procedures designed to ensure complete and correct recording of transactions and other accounting information, and the discovery of errors or irregularities in processing accounting information. Internal audit is a part of the internal control system acting as a 'watchdog' over the other internal controls.

Answers to activities

Answer 5.1

(a) *Basic data to be completed by the supervisor*

   (1) **Materials usage**. This will be determined by records of the use of van materials by job, materials drawn from central store to replenish the van and so forth. To assess usage the quantity and type of materials in stock at the beginning and the end of the week may need to be recorded, unless a running total is kept. Although the supervisor keeps the van topped up, it is not certain whether there is a minimum level kept in the van.

   (2) **Van expenses**. It is a relatively simple matter to record the miles run on company business. Supervisors will need to keep receipts for amounts paid for petrol and oil, to enable reimbursement. Alternatively, a company charge card might be used.

   (3) **Hours worked**. For each employee, the employee's name, grade if appropriate, hours at basic rate, and hours at overtime rates, type or category of work (if the company analyses its time in this way) should be recorded.

(b) *Checks to ensure data accuracy*

   Geton can take a variety of approaches. They could require a great deal of documentation to ensure that errors do not arise. They could have a roaming inspection department to check on compliance with recording procedures. Other controls include the following.

   (i) **Materials usage**

   - Comparison between different jobs for reasonableness
   - Van stock counts
   - Reconciliation of van stock counts with recorded usage
   - Materials usage could be part of the budget

   (ii) **Van expenses**

   (1) The company will not pay for private mileage so the mileage recorded must be reasonable. Van mileages can be checked. Supervisors might be required to log journeys and to produce all garage receipts, including those for cleaning the van.

   (2) A mileage budget could be established to check for the reasonableness of any claims. Again, mileage on a job can be compared with other similar jobs.

   (iii) **Work done**

   (1) A budget can be set for each job. Actual hours worked can be compared to it: the difference may be perfectly reasonable but the supervisor will have to explain any significant variance. On occasions, a member of the inspection team can carry out further checks.

   (2) The job to be done should be specified and the job specification might arise out of the contract itself. One of the supervisor's jobs will be to ensure that the work is done as required. In addition, an inspection team may visit the site now and then to ensure that standards are adhered to. Clients can also be sent questionnaires asking them about their satisfaction with the service.

Answer 5.2

(a) **Four objectives of an internal control system**

  (i) To enable management to carry on the business of the enterprise in an orderly and efficient manner

  (ii) To satisfy management that their policies are being adhered to

  (iii) To ensure that the assets of the company are safeguarded

  (iv) To ensure, as far as possible, that the enterprise maintains complete and accurate records

(b) **Four major controls**

  (i) **Control over customers' creditworthiness.** Before any order is accepted for further processing, established procedures should be followed in order to check the creditworthiness of that customer. For new customers procedures should exist for obtaining appropriate references before any credit is extended. For all existing customers there should be established credit limits and before an order is processed the sales assistants should check to see that the value of the current order will not cause the debtor's balance to rise above their agreed credit limit.

  The objective of such procedures is to try to avoid the company supplying goods to debtors who are unlikely to be able to pay for them. In this way the losses suffered by the company as a result of bad debts should be minimal.

  (ii) **Control over the recording of sales and debtors.** The most significant document in the system is the multiple order form. These forms should be sequentially pre-numbered and controls should exist over the supplies of unused forms and also to ensure that all order forms completed can be traced through the various stages of processing and agreed to the other documents raised and the various entries made in the accounting records.

  The main objective here will be to check the completeness of the company's recording procedures in relation to the income which it has earned and the assets which it holds in the form of debtors.

  (iii) **Control over the issue of stocks and the despatch of goods.** Control procedures here should be such that goods are not issued from stores until a valid order form has been received and the fact of that issue is recorded both on the order form (copies 1-3) and in the stock records maintained by the store-keepers.

  The objectives here are to see that no goods are released from stock without appropriate authority and that a record of stock movements is maintained.

  (iv) **Control over the invoicing of customers.** The main control requirement here will be to use sequentially pre-numbered invoices with checks being carried out to control the completeness of the sequence. Checks should also be conducted to ensure that all invoices are matched with the appropriate order form (Copy 2) to confirm that invoices have been raised in respect of all completed orders.

  The major concern here will be to ensure that no goods are despatched to customers without an invoice subsequently being raised.

  (v) (*Tutorial note.* The question merely required four controls to be considered, but for the sake of completeness, each of the five main stages in processing as indicated by the question are considered here.)

  Control over monies received. There should be controls to ensure that there is an adequate segregation of duties between those members of staff responsible for the updating of the sales records in respect of monies received and those dealing with the receipt, recording and banking of monies. There should also be a regular independent review of aged debtor balances together with an overall reconciliation of the debtors' ledger control account with the total of outstanding debts on individual customer accounts.

  The objectives here are to ensure that proper controls exist with regard to the complete and accurate recording of monies received, safe custody of the asset cash and the effectiveness of credit control procedures.

Part B: Effective management of business and accounting systems

(c) Appropriate tests in relation to each of the controls identified in (b) above would be as follows.

    (i) **Controls over customers' creditworthiness**

        (1) For a sample of new accounts opened during the period check to see that suitable references were obtained before the company supplied any goods on credit terms and that the credit limit set was properly authorised and of a reasonable amount.

        (2) For a sample of customers' orders check to see that at the time they were accepted, their invoice value would not have been such as to cause the balance on that customers' account to go above their agreed credit limit.

    (ii) **Controls over the recording of sales and debtors**

        (1) On a sample basis check the completeness of the sequence of order forms and also that unused stocks of order forms are securely stored.

        (2) For a sample of order forms raised during the period ensure that they can be traced through the system such that there is either evidence that the order was cancelled or that a valid invoice was subsequently raised.

    (iii) **Control over the issue of stocks and the despatch of goods**

        (1) For a sample of entries in the stock records check to ensure that a valid order form exists for all issues recorded as having been made.

        (2) Attend the stockrooms to observe the procedures and check that goods are not issued unless a valid order form has been received and that the appropriate entries are made in the stock records and on the order form at the time of issue.

    (iv) **Control over the invoicing of customers**

        (1) On a sample basis check the completeness of the sequence of invoices raised and also that the unused stocks of invoice forms are securely stored.

        (2) For a sample of invoices raised during the period ensure that they have been properly matched with the appropriate order form (copy 2).

Now try Question 4 in the Exam Question Bank

Chapter 6 Identifying and preventing fraud

Chapter topic list
1 What is fraud?
2 Implications of fraud for the organisation
3 Potential for fraud
4 Systems for detecting and preventing fraud
5 Responsibility for detecting and preventing fraud

The following study sessions are covered in this chapter:

Syllabus reference

7(a) Describe the prerequisites for fraud	2(c)
7(b) Identify the common types of fraud	2(c)
7(c) Explain the implications of fraud for the organisation	2(c)
7(d) Identify the scope for fraud using manual and computer systems	2(c)
7(e) Describe systems and procedures to discover and prevent fraud	2(c)
7(f) Understand the role of auditors in dealing with fraud	2(c)
7(g) Identify the duties and responsibilities of management in the detection and prevention of fraud	2(c)

Part B: Effective management of business and accounting systems

1 WHAT IS FRAUD?

> **KEY TERM**
>
> No precise legal definition of fraud exists. However, **fraud** may be generally defined as 'deprivation by deceit'.

1.1 In a corporate context, fraud can fall into one of two main categories.

Category	Comment
Removal of funds or assets from a business	The most obvious example of this is outright **theft**, either of cash or of other assets. However, this form of fraud also encompasses more subtle measures, such as overstatement of claims.
Intentional misrepresentation of the financial position of the business	This includes the **omission or misrecording of the company's accounting records.**

1.2 Let us consider some practical examples within each category.

> **EXAM ALERT**
>
> This is not an exhaustive list of examples. Every business is unique in its own way and offers different opportunities for fraud to be committed. You need to be able to think about a situation and identify for yourself areas and ways in which frauds could be occurring.

Removal of funds or assets from a business

1.3 **Theft of cash.** Employees with access to cash may be tempted to steal it. A prime example is theft from petty cash. Small amounts taken at intervals may easily go unnoticed.

1.4 **Theft of stock.** Similarly, employees may pilfer items of stock. The most trivial example of this is employees taking office stationery, although larger items may be taken also. These examples are of unsophisticated types of fraud, which generally go undetected because of their immateriality. On the whole, such fraud will tend to be too insignificant to have any serious impact on results or long-term performance.

1.5 **Payroll fraud.** Employees within or outside the payroll department can perpetrate payroll fraud.

(a) Employees external to the department can falsify their timesheets, for example by claiming overtime for hours which they did not really work.

(b) Members of the payroll department may have the opportunity deliberately to miscalculate selected payslips, either by applying an inflated rate of pay or by altering the hours to which the rate is applied.

(c) Alternatively, a fictitious member of staff can be added to the payroll list. The fraudster sets up a bank account in the bogus name and collects the extra cash himself. This is most feasible in a large organisation with high numbers of personnel, where management is not personally acquainted with every employee.

1.6 **Teeming and lading.** This is one of the best known methods of fraud in the sales ledger area. Basically, **teeming and lading** is the theft of cash or cheque receipts. Setting subsequent receipts, not necessarily from the same debtor, against the outstanding debt conceals the theft.

1.7 **Fictitious customers.** This is a more elaborate method of stealing stock. Bogus orders are set up, and goods are despatched on credit. The 'customer' then fails to pay for the goods and the cost is eventually written off as a bad debt. For this type of fraud to work, the employee must have responsibility for taking goods orders as well as the authority to approve a new customer for credit.

1.8 **Collusion with customers.** Employees may collude with customers to defraud the business by manipulating prices or the quality or quantity of goods despatched.

   (a) For example, a sales manager or director could **reduce the price** charged to a customer in return for a cut of the saving. Alternatively, the employee could write off a debt or issue a credit note in return for a financial reward.

   (b) Another act of collusion might be for the employee to **suppress invoices** or under-record quantities of despatched goods on delivery notes. Again, the customer would probably provide the employee with a financial incentive for doing this.

1.9 **Bogus supply of goods or services.** This typically involves senior staff who falsely invoice the firm for goods or services that were never supplied. One example would be the supply of consultancy services. To enhance authenticity, in many cases the individual involved will set up a personal company that invoices the business for its services. This type of fraud can be quite difficult to prove.

1.10 **Paying for goods not received.** Staff may collude with suppliers, who issue invoices for larger quantities of goods than were actually delivered. The additional payments made by the company are split between the two parties.

1.11 **Meeting budgets/target performance measures.** Management teams will readily agree that setting budgets and goals is an essential part of planning and an important ingredient for success. However, such targets can disguise frauds. In some cases, knowing that results are unlikely to be questioned once targets have been met, employees and/or management siphon off and pocket any profits in excess of the target.

1.12 **Manipulation of bank reconciliations and cash books.** Often the simplest techniques can hide the biggest frauds. We saw earlier how simple a technique teeming and lading is for concealing a theft. Similarly, other simple measures such as incorrect descriptions of items and use of compensating debits and credits to make a reconciliation work frequently ensure that fraudulent activities go undetected.

1.13 **Misuse of pension funds or other assets.** This type of fraud has received a high profile in the past. Ailing companies may raid the pension fund and steal assets to use as collateral in obtaining loan finance. Alternatively, company assets may be transferred to the fund at significant over-valuations.

1.14 **Disposal of assets to employees.** It may be possible for an employee to arrange to buy a company asset (eg a car) for personal use. In this situation, there may be scope to manipulate the book value of the asset so that the employee pays below market value for it. This could be achieved by over-depreciating the relevant asset.

Part B: Effective management of business and accounting systems

Intentional misrepresentation of the financial position of the business

1.15 Here we consider examples in which the intention is to overstate profits. Note, however, that by reversing the logic we can also use them as examples of methods by which staff may deliberately understate profits. You should perform this exercise yourself.

1.16 **Over-valuation of stock.** Stock is a particularly attractive area for management wishing to inflate net assets artificially. There is a whole range of ways in which stock may be incorrectly valued for accounts purposes.

 (a) Stock records may be manipulated, particularly by deliberate miscounting at stock counts.

 (b) Deliveries to customers may be omitted from the books.

 (c) Returns to suppliers may not be recorded.

 (d) Obsolete stock may not be written off but rather held at cost on the balance sheet.

1.17 **Bad debt policy may not be enforced.** Aged debtors who are obviously not going to pay should be written off. However, by not enforcing this policy management can avoid the negative effects it would have on profits and net assets.

1.18 **Fictitious sales.** These can be channelled through the accounts in a number of ways.

Activity 6.1

An exercise in spotting how the system could be abused! See if you can come up with three ways of generating fictitious sales transactions or sales values.

1.19 **Manipulation of year end events.** Cut off dates provide management with opportunities for window dressing the financial statements. Sales made just before year end can be deliberately over-invoiced and credit notes issued with an apology at the start of the new year. This will enhance turnover and profit during the year just ended. Delaying the recording of pre-year-end purchases of goods not yet delivered can achieve the same objective.

1.20 **Understating expenses.** Clearly, failure to record all expenses accurately will inflate the reported profit figure.

1.21 **Manipulation of depreciation figures.** As an expense that does not have any cash flow effect, depreciation figures may be easily tampered with. Applying incorrect rates or inconsistent policies in order to understate depreciation will result in a higher profit and a higher net book value, giving a more favourable impression of financial health.

2 IMPLICATIONS OF FRAUD FOR THE ORGANISATION

2.1 Whilst it is clear that fraud is bad for business, the precise ways in which the firm is affected depends on the type of fraud being carried on.

 (a) **Removal of funds or assets from a business**

 (i) **Immediate financial implications**

6: Identifying and preventing fraud

Profits are lower than they should be. The business has less cash or fewer assets, and therefore the net asset position is weakened. Returns to shareholders are likely to fall as a result.

(ii) **Long term effects on company performance**

The reduction in working capital makes it more difficult for the company to operate effectively. In the most serious cases, fraud can ultimately result in the collapse of an otherwise successful business, such as Barings.

(b) **Intentional misrepresentation of the financial position of the business**

(i) Financial statements do not give a true and fair view of the financial situation of the business. Results may be either artificially enhanced or, less frequently, under-reported.

(ii) It is also possible that managers in charge of a particular **division** can artificially enhance their division's results, thereby deceiving senior management.

Activity 6.2

Try to think of reasons why someone might want to:

(a) Artificially enhance the results
(b) Under-report the results

2.2 **If results are overstated**:

(a) A company may **distribute too much** of its profits to shareholders.

(b) **Retained profits will be lower than believed**, leading to potential shortfalls in working capital. This makes the day-to-day activities more difficult to perform effectively.

(c) **Incorrect decisions will be made**, based on inaccurate knowledge of available resources.

(d) The effects of fraudulent activities can also affect **stakeholders** if the financial statements upon which they rely are misrepresentations of the truth.

(i) **Investors** making decisions based on inaccurate information will find actual returns deviating from expectations.

(ii) **Suppliers** will extend credit without knowing the financial position of the company.

2.3 If results are **understated**:

(a) Returns to investors may be reduced unnecessarily.

(b) If the company is quoted on the stock exchange, the share price might fall and market strength may be eroded.

(c) Access to loan finance may be restricted if assets are understated.

(d) The **negative publicity** can damage the business by affecting the public's perceptions.

2.4 **Legal consequences**. Finally, fraudsters open themselves up to the possibility of arrest. Depending on the scale and seriousness of the offence some may even find themselves facing a prison sentence.

Part B: Effective management of business and accounting systems

3 POTENTIAL FOR FRAUD

3.1 The UK has witnessed a number of high profile frauds, most notably the BCCI, Maxwell and Barings Bank cases. The real incidence of fraud is difficult to gauge, particularly because companies are often loath to publicise such experiences. However, all business – without exception – face the **risk of fraud**: the directors' responsibility is to manage that risk.

Prerequisites for fraud

3.2 There are three broad pre-requisites or 'pre-conditions' that must exist in order to make fraud a possibility: dishonesty, motivation and opportunity. These are useful to know, because if one or more of them can be eliminated, the risk of fraud is reduced!

3.3 **Dishonesty.** Honesty is a subjective quality, which is interpreted variously according to different ethical, cultural and legal norms. However, we may define dishonesty as an individual's pre-disposition or tendency to act in ways which contravene accepted ethical, social, organisational and legal norms for fair and honest dealing. This tendency may arise from:

(a) Personality factors: a high need for achievement, status or security; a competitive desire to gain advantage over others; low respect for authority;

(b) Cultural factors: national or familial values, which may be more 'flexible' or anti-authority than the law and practice prevailing in the organisation. (Cultural values about the ethics of business 'bribes' – or 'gifts' – for example, vary widely. 'Lying' is also a very fluid concept: some cultures value 'saving face' or agreeing over giving strictly truthful responses.)

Activity 6.3

List some examples of behaviours that would be considered dishonest in your work context. (Don't confine yourself only to financial fraud.) Include an example of dishonest behaviour that the person doing it might not even be aware was dishonest.

3.4 **Motivation.** In addition to a general predisposition or willingness to act dishonestly, should the opportunity arise, the individual needs a specific motivation to do so. We will be discussing the concept of motivation in Chapter 12, but broadly, it involves a **calculation** of whether a given action is worthwhile. Individuals weigh up:

(a) The **potential rewards** of an action: the satisfaction of some need, or the fulfilment of some goal; **in relation to**

(b) The **potential sanctions** or negative consequences of an action, or the deprivations required to carry it through.

3.5 The individual's goal or motive for fraudulent behaviour may be:

(a) Financial needs or wants, or envy of others (in the case of theft or fraud for monetary gain)

(b) A desire to exercise negative power over those in authority

(c) A desire to avoid punishment (in the case of cover ups, say)

6: Identifying and preventing fraud

3.6 **Opportunity.** Even if a person is willing to act dishonestly, and has a motive for doing so, (s)he must still find an opportunity or opening to do so: a 'loophole' in the law or control system that:

- Allows fraudulent activity to go undetected, or
- Makes the risk of detection acceptable, given the rewards available.

3.7 An individual will have a high incentive to commit fraud if (s)he is predisposed to **dishonesty** and the **rewards** for the particular fraud are high and there is an **opportunity** to commit fraudulent action with **little chance of detection** or with insignificant sanctions if caught.

Activity 6.4

Just considering the three prerequisites of fraud, what immediate control strategies can you suggest for preventing fraud?

Assessing the risk of fraud

3.8 The starting point for any management team wanting to set up internal controls to prevent and detect fraud must be an assessment of the extent to which the firm is exposed to the risk of fraud. The best approach is to consider separately the extent to which **external** and **internal** factors may present a risk of fraud.

3.9 **External factors**

Step 1. First, consider the market place as a whole. The general environment in which the business operates may exhibit factors that increase the risk of fraud. For instance, the trend to de-layer may reduce the degree of supervision exercised in many organisations, perhaps without putting anything in its place.

Step 2. Next, narrow the focus a little and consider whether the industry in which the firm operates is particularly exposed to certain types of fraud. For example, the building industry may be particularly prone to the risk of theft of raw materials, the travel industry may face risks due to the extensive use of agents and intermediaries and the retail industry must be vigilant to the abuse of credit cards.

Activity 6.5

Think of some examples of such general external factors that might influence the degree of risk that a company is exposed to.

3.10 **Internal factors**

Having considered the big picture, the next step is to apply the same logic at a company level. Focus on the general and specific risks in the firm itself.

Be alert to circumstances that might increase the risk profile of a company.

- Changed operating environment
- New personnel
- New or upgraded management information systems
- New overseas operations
- Rapid growth
- New technology
- New products
- Corporate restructuring

Part B: Effective management of business and accounting systems

3.11 A number of factors tend to crop up time and time again as issues that might indicate potential fraud. Attention should be drawn to them if any of these factors come to light when assessing external and internal risks.

3.12 **Business risks**

An alert management team will always be aware of the industry or business environment in which the organisation operates.

(a) **Profit levels/margins deviating significantly from the industry norm**

As a rule of thumb, if things seem too good to be true, then they generally are. If any of the following happen, alarm bells should start ringing.

(i) The company suddenly starts to exhibit profits far above those achieved by other firms in the same industry.

(ii) Turnover rises rapidly but costs do not rise in line.

(iii) Demand for a particular product increases significantly.

(iv) Investors seem to find the firm unusually attractive.

Such patterns can indicate problems such as the manipulation of accounting records, collusion with existing customers or the creation of fictitious customers.

Similarly, results showing that the organisation is under-performing relative to competitors may be an indication of theft, collusion with suppliers or deliberate errors in the accounting records.

(b) **Market opinion**

If the market has a low opinion of the firm, this might indicate something about the company's products, its people or its way of doing business.

(c) **Complex structures**

(i) Organisations with complex group structures, including numerous domestic and overseas subsidiaries and branches, may be more susceptible to fraud.

(ii) The sheer size of the group can offer plenty of opportunities to 'lose' transactions or to hide things in intercompany accounts.

(iii) Furthermore, vast staff numbers contribute to a certain degree of employee anonymity, making it easier to conceal fraudulent activities.

3.13 **Personnel risks**

Fraud is not usually an easy thing to hide. A person's behaviour often gives clues to the fact that they are engaging in fraud.

(a) **Secretive behaviour**

A High Court judge once described secrecy as 'the badge of fraud'. If an individual starts behaving in a more secretive way than is generally considered normal, then there may be cause for concern.

(b) **Expensive lifestyles**

A well-known indicator of fraud is a life-style beyond an individual's earnings. A recent case involved an Inspector of Taxes who started driving expensive sport cars, taking lavish holidays and so forth. It was later discovered that he was being paid by a wealthy businessman in return for assisting him to evade tax.

(c) **Long hours or untaken holidays**

Workaholics and staff who do not take their full holiday entitlement may be trying to prevent a temporary replacement from uncovering a fraud.

(d) **Autocratic management style**

In some organisations a sole manager or director has exclusive control over a significant part of the business. This can provide ample scope for fraud, particularly when the situation is compounded by little, if any, independent review of those activities by anyone else at a senior level.

(e) **Lack of segregation of duties**

Employees occasionally have more than one area of responsibility, particularly in small businesses where staff numbers are low. This can make it easy for the employee to conduct and conceal fraudulent actions. For example, if the employee who prepares the payslips were also the person who authorises the payments, payroll fraud would be relatively simple to put into practice.

(f) **Low staff morale**

One motive for fraud is resentment towards the firm. Staff may start defrauding the firm because they feel that they are not rewarded sufficiently for their work or because they were passed over for a promotion that they believed they deserved. Alternatively, low staff morale may lead to the breakdown of internal controls, yielding opportunities for fraud.

Potential for computer fraud

3.14 Organisations are becoming increasingly dependent on computers for operational systems as well as accounting and management information. With this dependency comes an increased **exposure** to fraud. The computer is frequently the vehicle through which fraudulent activities are carried out.

3.15 Problems particularly associated with computers.

(a) **Computer hackers**. The possibility of unknown persons trying to hack into the systems increases the potential for fraud against which the firm must protect itself.

(b) **Lack of training within the management team**. Many people have an inherent lack of understanding of how computer systems work. Senior management can often be the least computer literate. They may also be the most reluctant to receive training, preferring to delegate tasks to assistants. Without management realising it, junior staff can secure access to vast amounts of financial information and find ways to alter it.

(c) **Identifying the risks**. Most firms do not have the resources to keep up to date with the pace of development of computer technology. This makes it ever more difficult to check that all major loopholes in controls are closed, even if management are computer literate.

(d) **Need for ease of access and flexible systems**. In most cases, a firm uses computers in order to simplify and speed up operations. To meet these objectives, there is frequently a need for ease of access and flexible systems. However, implementing strict controls can sometimes suppress these features.

3.16 We will be discussing data security, including computer security, in Chapter 18 of this Text.

Part B: Effective management of business and accounting systems

Activity 6.6

Report: exposure to fraud

Smiths Ltd is a small, family-run manufacturing firm that makes office furniture. The directors, Stuart and his sister Michelle, share responsibility for running the business, although Stuart concentrates on trying to bring in new business while Michelle takes a more active role in day-to-day management.

John runs the purchasing department. Martha, who has just recently been recruited to the firm, looks after the cash book and is responsible for performing monthly bank reconciliations.

John keeps records of all purchases and related expenses as well as looking after creditor accounts. When an invoice comes in, he checks the details against the purchase ledger details. If he is satisfied that the invoice is correct, he draws up a cheque for Michelle to sign. He also supervises Martha's work.

All accounting systems are computerised. The firm employs one staff member, Craig, in an IT capacity. Craig has full control of the computer network, with access to all programs and reporting systems.

You are required to produce a report to the directors in which you advise them on ways in which the firm is exposed to the risk of fraud.

4 SYSTEMS FOR DETECTING AND PREVENTING FRAUD

Detection and prevention

4.1 A primary aim of any system of internal controls should be to **prevent fraud**. However, the very nature of fraud means that people will find ways to get around existing systems. It is equally important, therefore, to have controls in place to **detect fraud** if and when it happens.

Internal controls

4.2 Controls must be developed in a structured manner, taking account of the whole spectrum of risk and focusing on the key risks identified in each area of the business.

4.3 We looked at internal controls generally in Chapter 5. Let us think about appropriate controls that could be introduced to combat fraud.

4.4 **Physical controls**

Basic as it seems, physical security is an important tool in preventing fraud. Keeping tangible assets under lock and key makes it difficult for staff to access them and can go a long way towards discouraging theft.

4.5 **Segregation of duties**

(a) Staff who have responsibility for a range of tasks have more scope for committing and concealing fraud. Therefore the obvious way to control the risk is to segregate duties.

(b) If an employee's duties do not extend beyond one domain, it will be more difficult for an employee to conceal a fraud. It is more likely that it will be picked up at the next stage in the process.

(c) So, for example, the employee responsible for recording sales orders should not be the same person responsible for maintaining stock records. This will make it more difficult to falsify sales or stock records, as a discrepancy between sales figures and stock balances would show up.

6: Identifying and preventing fraud

(d) Segregating responsibility for packaging goods for delivery from either of the recording tasks would also help to minimise the risk of theft and increase the likelihood of detection.

4.6 Authorisation policies

Requiring written authorisation by a senior member of staff is a good preventative tool. It increases accountability and also makes it harder to conceal a fraudulent transaction.

4.7 Customer signatures

Requiring customers to inspect and sign for receipt of goods or services ensures that they cannot claim that the delivery did not match their order.

It also provides confirmation that the delivery staff actually did their job and that what was delivered corresponded to what was recorded.

4.8 Using words rather than numbers

Insist that all quantities be written out in full. It is much more difficult to change text than to alter a figure.

4.9 Documentation

Separate documents should be used to record sales order, despatch, delivery and invoice details. A simple matching exercise will then pick up any discrepancies between them and lead to detection of any alterations.

4.10 Sequential numbering

Numbering order forms, delivery dockets or invoices makes it extremely simple to spot if something is missing.

4.11 Dates

Writing the date on forms and invoices assists in cut-off testing. For example, if a delivery docket is dated pre-year end but the sale is recorded post-year end it is possible that results are being manipulated.

4.12 Standard procedures

Standard procedures should be defined clearly for normal business operations and should be known to all staff. For example:

- Independent checks should be made on the existence of new customers.
- Credit should not be given to a new customer until his/her credit history has been investigated.
- All payments should be authorised by a senior member of staff.
- Wages/payslips must be collected in person.

Any deviations from these norms should become quite visible.

4.13 Holidays

As we have said, fraud is difficult to conceal. Enforcing holiday policy by insisting that all staff take their full holiday entitlement is therefore a crucial internal control. A two-week absence is frequently sufficient time for a fraud to come to light.

Part B: Effective management of business and accounting systems

4.14 Recruitment policies

Personnel policies play a vital part in developing the corporate culture and deterring fraud. Something as obvious as checking the information and references provided by applicants may reduce the risk of appointing dishonest staff.

4.15 Computer security

This will be discussed in detail in chapter 18. However, many of the above controls (access controls, segregation of duties, authorisations and so on) will apply.

5 RESPONSIBILITY FOR DETECTING AND PREVENTING FRAUD

The responsibility of directors

5.1 In a **limited company**, or plc, it is the responsibility of the directors to prevent and detect fraud. They should:

(a) Ensure that the **activities** of the entity are conducted honestly and that its **assets** are safeguarded

(b) Establish arrangements to **deter** fraudulent or other dishonest conduct and to **detect** any that occurs

(c) Ensure that, to the best of their knowledge and belief, **financial information**, whether used internally or for financial reporting, is reliable.

The role of the auditor

5.2 The responsibility of the external auditor is only to express an opinion upon whether the financial statements give a true and fair view of the company's financial situation and results.

5.3 The auditor should design audit procedures so as to have a **reasonable expectation** of detecting misstatements arising from fraud or error. It should be emphasised that, in the case of a sophisticated fraud, which has been designed to escape detection by the auditors, a **reasonable expectation** is all that they can have.

5.4 If the auditors become aware, during the audit, that fraud or error may exist, they should document their findings and report them to management.

5.5 In the case of fraud, the auditors should then consider whether the matter should be reported to an appropriate authority in the public interest. If they decide that this is the case, they request that **the directors** make the report. If the directors do not do so, or if the fraud casts doubt upon the integrity of the directors, the auditors should make the report themselves.

5.6 If the auditor takes the view that the financial statements are affected by fraud or error, he should qualify his report accordingly.

5.7 It is the responsibility of the **directors** to take reasonable steps to detect and prevent fraud and error.

6: Identifying and preventing fraud

Key learning points

- **Fraud** may be generally defined as 'deprivation by deceit'.
- In a corporate context, fraud can fall into one of two main categories:
  - **Removal of funds** or assets from a business; and/or
  - **Intentional misrepresentation** of the financial position of the business
- The three broad **prerequisites for fraud** are: dishonesty, motivation and opportunity.
- The key to devising successful internal controls is to **identify the risks** clearly: once they are known, they can be managed effectively.
- A number of factors tend to crop up frequently as **indicators** of potential fraud situations: these can be categorised under business and personnel risks.
- **Internal controls** must be developed in a structured manner, taking account of the whole spectrum of risk and focusing on the key risks identified in each area of the business.
- It is the responsibility of the directors to take such steps as are reasonably open to them to **prevent and detect** fraud.

Quick quiz

1. What is fraud?
2. What are the two main types of fraud from a corporate perspective?
3. Give two consequences of each type.
4. Give three examples of each type.
5. Why do computers increase the risk of fraud?
6. What is the key to devising successful internal controls?
7. What is the first step in assessing the risks faced by an organisation?
8. List five common indicators of fraud
9. In what manner should controls be developed?
10. List five examples of internal controls (not computer-related).

Answers to quick quiz

1. Fraud may generally be defined as 'deprivation by deceit'.
2. The two types of corporate fraud are removal of funds or assets from a business and intentional misrepresentation of the financial position of the business.
3. Consequences of the former include lower profits and a reduction in working capital. Consequences of the latter include incorrect decision-making by management or by investors and fluctuations in share price.
4. Examples of the former include theft of cash or other assets, payroll fraud and teeming and lading. Examples of the latter include overvaluation of stock, failure to adhere to bad debt or depreciation policy and manipulation of year-end events.
5. Computers tend to increase exposure to fraud because they are frequently the vehicles through which fraudulent activities are carries out.
6. The key to devising successful internal controls is to identify the risks clearly first.
7. The first step is to consider separately the extent to which external and internal factors may present a risk.

Part B: Effective management of business and accounting systems

8   Common indicators of fraud include trends that start to deviate from the industry norms, complex changes to business structures, secretive behaviour, evidence of an expensive lifestyle not commensurate with earnings and an autocratic management style.

9   Controls must be developed in a structured manner, taking account of the whole spectrum of risk and focusing on the key risks identified in each area of business.

10 Examples include physical controls, segregation of duties, authorisation policies, using words rather than numbers and enforcing holiday policy.

Answers to activities

Answer 6.1

The following are just three obvious suggestions:

(a) Generation of false invoices
(b) Overcharging customers for goods or services
(c) Selling goods to friends (with a promise of buying them back at a later date)

Answer 6.2

(a) Reasons for overstating profits and/or net assets

- To ensure achievement on paper, may have to meet targets in order to secure a promotion, bonuses or remuneration may be linked to performance
- Trying to conceal another form of fraud, such as theft
- Need a healthy balance sheet to convince bank to give loan finance
- Ailing company may be trying to entice equity investors

(b) Reasons for understating profits and/or net assets

- To facilitate a private purchase of an asset from the business at less than market value
- To defraud the Inland Revenue by reducing taxable profits or gains
- Trying to force the share price down so that shares can be bought below market value by friends or relatives

Answer 6.3

Examples of dishonesty in a typical UK context would include:

(a) Various financial malpractices and manipulations discussed in Section 1 of the chapter
(b) Being absent from work pretending to be sick when you aren't
(c) Blaming a colleague for mistakes you have made
(d) Tampering with data and information on the computer system
(e) Sending personal e-mails on work time and computers (where this is not permitted)
(f) Falsifying time sheets or expenses lists (for reimbursement)
(g) Covering up for others who do any of the above.

A person might not know they are being dishonest if, for example, they use office stationery for personal correspondence.

Answer 6.4

(a) Don't employ people with pre-dispositions to **dishonesty**, if possible: carry out legitimate and appropriate background and CV checks when carrying out recruitment and selection. (The more opportunity for fraud there is in the job, the more carefully dishonesty should be screened.)

(b) Reduce **motivations** for fraud. This is highly subjective, but the organisation should give attention to matters such as: ensuring equity in pay and rewards; monitoring employees for signs of financial difficulty and its possible causes (eg gambling addiction) and offering counselling and support where

6: Identifying and preventing fraud

required; providing generally good and equitable working terms and conditions; establishing clear rules and strong sanctions for fraudulent behaviour; and so on.

(c) Reduce **opportunities** for fraud. This is the function of a range of internal checks and controls, discussed in Section 4 of the chapter: separating duties so no one person has sole control over a system; requiring authorisations for expense/time sheets, cheques and so on; using data security measures such as passwords; security checks; identification on office equipment to deter theft; and so on.

Answer 6.5

You might have thought of some of the following.

- Technological developments
- New legislation or regulations
- Economic or political changes
- Increased competition
- Changing customer needs

Answer 6.6

Report: exposure to fraud

Date: 30 June 200X
To: Stuart and Michelle Smith, Directors, Smiths Ltd
From: Accounting Technician
Subject: Risk of fraud

You have asked me to advise on ways in which Smiths Ltd is exposed to the risk of fraud. My report has been based on discussions with you both about the established work practices and on a review of the company's books.

Findings

Due to the small number of staff employed by the firm, there is little segregation of duties. This automatically enhances exposure to risk of fraud.

(a) Martha is responsible for both the cash book and bank reconciliations. This makes it easy for her to conceal theft or to manipulate accounting records. Simple measures such as the use of compensating debits and credits to make the reconciliation work or incorrect narratives facilitate such frauds.

(b) John keeps the records of all purchases and expenses but yet he is also responsible for confirming that invoice details agree to purchase ledger details and for maintaining creditor accounts. He therefore has ample opportunity to manipulate accounting records, such as turnover figures. He is also responsible for drawing up the cheques for Michelle to sign. This means he could easily steal from the firm by drawing up cheques for fictitious creditors.

(c) Craig has sole control of all computer systems. He has unlimited access to files and is in a unique position to carry numerous types of fraud. The firm essentially relies on nothing more than trust to ensure that he does not engage in any fraudulent activities.

(d) As Stuart focuses almost entirely on bringing in new business, he has little time to spend on the supervision of day-to-day activities. The bulk of this work falls on Michelle. The sheer weight of her responsibilities means that in many cases there is little independent review or supervision of her work.

Overall, the firm suffers from a high level of exposure to risk. In order to manage that risk effectively, a system of internal controls should be introduced to prevent and detect incidences of fraud.

Now try Question 5 in the Exam Question Bank

Chapter 7 Improving control procedures

Chapter topic list

1 Controlling the payroll system
2 Controlling the purchases cycle
3 Controlling the sales cycle
4 Controlling cash
5 Control and integrated systems

The following study sessions are covered in this chapter:

		Syllabus reference
8(a)	Describe the payroll system and appropriate controls	2(d)(ii)
8(b)	Describe the purchase cycle and appropriate controls	2(d)(ii)
8(c)	Describe the sales cycle and appropriate controls	2(d)(ii)
8(d)	Describe the cash system and appropriate controls	2(d)(ii)
8(e)	Explain how controls are more effective if systems are integrated	2(d)(ii)

1 CONTROLLING THE PAYROLL SYSTEM

1.1 The purpose of a payroll system is to compute the gross wages and salaries of employees and produce payslips, cheques and/or listings sent to banks instructing them to make payments. A computerised payroll system will be expected to carry out these tasks in accordance with how much employees should receive, how they should receive it and when it should be paid. The system should also be able to calculate tax deductions, national insurance deductions, savings, loan repayments etc, as well as printing various other outputs connected with employees' pay.

Data held on a payroll file

1.2 Payroll files will consist of an individual record for each employee.

   (a) **Standing** data on each employee will include:
   - Personal details (eg name, employee number, job grade, address etc)
   - Rate of pay
   - Details of deductions (including tax code)
   - Holidays

   (b) **Variable** (transaction) data will include:
   - Gross pay to date
   - Tax to date
   - Pension contributions etc

Inputs to a payroll system

1.3 The main inputs into a **wages system** (ie into a weekly-paid payroll) are as follows.

   (a) Clock cards or time sheets (sometimes both are used). Details of overtime worked will normally be shown on these documents. Sometimes payroll might be directly linked to an electronic time recording system.

   (b) Amount of bonus, or appropriate details if the bonus is calculated by the computer.

1.4 **Salary systems** (ie a monthly-paid payroll) are similar to those for wages but it is usual for the monthly salary to be generated by the computer from details held on the master file and therefore (with the exception of overtime, bonuses etc) there is no need for any transaction input. So the inputs for a salary system are just overtime, bonuses etc (because the basic salary is already on the master file).

Processing in a payroll system

1.5 The primary action involved in processing a payroll is calculating an employee's gross pay, calculating and implementing the various deductions in order to find net pay, and then making payment by the appropriate method.

1.6 In the case of wages, this means taking the input data on hours worked and pay details, and calculating the weekly wage due to the employee. The same calculation is carried out every week.

1.7 In the case of salaries, payroll processing might just mean picking an option to pay all the monthly-paid employees the same amount as they received the previous month. This could

Part B: Effective management of business and accounting systems

happen in theory, but in practice there are usually some amendments to make to the monthly pay details, and these are implemented during payroll processing.

Outputs from a payroll system

1.8 Typical outputs in a payroll system are:

(a) Payslips

(b) Payroll (this is often a copy of the payslips)

(c) Payroll analysis, including analysis of deductions (tax, national insurance etc) and details for costing purposes

(d) Various forms required for PAYE (Pay As You Earn) tax purposes

(e) Coin analysis, cheques, credit transfer forms

(f) In some cases, a floppy disk with payment details for despatch to the bank and payment through the BACS system

1.9 In the previous chapter we looked at types of fraud, including payroll fraud. Now we will look at the controls which are designed to prevent this. You will notice that segregation of duties within the payroll department is particularly important. Well-planned fraud, such as the payment of 'ghost' employees, then requires collusion involving two or more people, and is consequently less likely to take place.

1.10 The most important aims of the control system relating to wages and salaries are:

Feature	Aims
Setting of wages and salaries	• **Employees** are **only paid** for **work** that they have **done** • **Gross pay** has been **calculated correctly** and **authorised**
Recording of wages and salaries	• **Gross** and **net pay** and **deductions** are **accurately recorded** on the payroll • **Wages** and **salaries paid** are **recorded correctly** in the **bank** and **cash records** • Wages and salaries are **correctly recorded** in the **general ledger**
Payment of wages and salaries	• The **correct employees** are **paid**
Deductions	• Statutory and non-statutory **deductions** have been **calculated correctly** and are **authorised** • The **correct amounts** are **paid** to the **taxation authorities**

Controls

1.11 While in practice separate arrangements are generally made for dealing with wages and salaries, the considerations involved are broadly similar and for convenience the two aspects are here treated together.

General arrangements

1.12 Responsibility for the preparation of pay sheets should be delegated to a suitable person, and adequate staff appointed to assist him. The extent to which the staff responsible for preparing wages and salaries may perform other duties should be clearly defined. In this connection full advantage should be taken where possible of the **division of duties,** and checks available where automatic wage-accounting systems are in use.

1.13 Setting of wages and salaries

- **Staffing** and **segregation of duties**
- **Maintenance of personnel records** and regular checking of wages and salaries to details in personnel records
- **Authorisation** required for:
    - Engagement and discharge of employees
    - Changes in pay rates
    - Overtime
    - Non-statutory deductions (for example pension contributions)
    - Advances of pay
- **Recording** of **changes** in **personnel** and **pay rates**
- **Recording** of hours worked by **timesheets, clocking in and out** arrangements
- **Review of hours worked**
- **Recording** of **advances** of **pay**
- **Holiday pay** arrangements
- **Answering queries**
- **Review** of **wages against budget**

1.14 Recording of wages and salaries

- **Bases** for **compilation** of payroll
- **Preparation, checking** and **approval** of payroll
- Dealing with **non-routine matters**

1.15 Payment of cash wages

- **Segregation of duties**
    - Cash sheet preparation
    - Filling of pay packets
    - Distribution of wages
- **Authorisation** of **wage cheque**
- **Custody** of cash
    - Encashment of cheque
    - Security of pay packets
    - Security of transit arrangements
    - Security and prompt banking of unclaimed wages
- **Verification of identity**
- **Recording** of distribution

1.16 Payment of salaries

- **Preparation** and **signing** of cheques and bank transfer lists

- Comparison of cheques and bank transfer list with payroll
- Maintenance and reconciliation of wages and salaries bank account

1.17 Deductions from pay

- **Maintenance** of **separate employees' records**, with which pay lists may be compared as necessary
- **Reconciliation** of **total pay** and **deductions** between one pay day and the next
- **Surprise cash counts**
- **Comparison** of actual pay totals with **budget estimates** or standard costs and the investigation of variances
- **Agreement** of **gross earnings** and **total tax deducted** with PAYE returns to the Inland Revenue

1.18 Appropriate arrangements should be made for dealing with statutory and other authorised deductions from pay, such as national insurance, PAYE, pension fund contributions, and savings held in trust. A primary consideration is the establishment of adequate controls over the **records,** and **authorisation** of deductions.

Activity 7.1

What are the possible financial implications of the following shortcomings in payroll procedures?

(a) No written notices regarding termination of employment
(b) No verification of overtime hours
(c) No timekeeping records for hourly paid staff
(d) Cheques and bank transfer lists not compared with payroll

2 CONTROLLING THE PURCHASES CYCLE

2.1 Purchasing is an important area to control, especially where items of high value are concerned. There are likely to be specific authorisation procedures for the purchase of fixed assets.

Inputs to a purchase ledger system

2.2 Bearing in mind what we expect to see held on a purchase ledger, typical data input into a purchase ledger system is:

- Details of purchases recorded on invoices
- Details of returns to suppliers for which credit notes are received
- Details of payments to suppliers
- Adjustments

Processing in a purchase ledger system

2.3 The primary action involved in updating the purchase ledger is adjusting the amounts outstanding on the supplier accounts. These amounts will represent money owed to the suppliers. This processing is identical to updating the accounts in the sales ledger, except that the sales ledger balances are debits (debtors) and the purchase ledger balances are credits (creditors).

7: Improving control procedures

Outputs from a purchase ledger system

2.4 Typical outputs in a computerised purchase ledger are as follows.

(a) Lists of transactions posted - produced every time the system is run.

(b) An analysis of expenditure for nominal ledger purposes. This may be produced every time the system is run or at the end of each month.

(c) List of creditors balances together with a reconciliation between the total balance brought forward, the transactions for the month and the total balance carried forward.

(d) Copies of creditors' accounts. This may show merely the balance b/f, current transactions and the balance c/f. If complete details of all unsettled items are given, the ledger is known as an **open-ended ledger**.

(e) Any purchase ledger system can be used to produce details of payments to be made. For example:

- Remittance advices (usually a copy of the ledger account)
- Cheques
- Credit transfer listings

(f) Other special reports may be produced for:

- Costing purposes
- Updating records about fixed assets
- Comparisons with budget
- Aged creditors list

2.5 Businesses have to ensure that only **properly authorised purchases** which are necessary for the business are made. All stages of the purchase process – ordering, receiving goods and being charged for them – should be documented and matched. In this way it can be ensured that the business gets what it ordered and only pays for what it orders and receives. The purchase ledger makes it possible for the business to keep track of what it owes each supplier.

2.6 The most important aims of the control system relating to creditors and purchases are:

Feature	Aims
Ordering	• All **orders for**, and expenditure on, **goods and services** are properly **authorised**, and are for **goods and services** that are actually **received** and are **for the company**
	• **Orders** are only **made** to **authorised suppliers**
	• **Orders** are **made** at **competitive prices**
Receipt and invoices	• **Goods and services** received are **used** for the **organisation's purposes** and not private purposes
	• **Goods and services** are **only accepted** if they have been **ordered**, and the **order** has been authorised
	• All **goods and services received** are accurately **recorded**
	• **Liabilities** are **recognised** for all **goods and services** that have been **received**
	• All **credits** to which business is due are **claimed**
	• **Receipt** of goods and services is **necessary** to **establish** a **liability**

Part B: Effective management of business and accounting systems

Feature	Aims
Accounting	• All **expenditure** is **authorised** and is for goods that are **actually received**
	• All **expenditure** that is made is **recorded** correctly in the general and purchase ledger
	• All **credit notes** that are received are **recorded** in the general and purchase ledger
	• All **entries** in the **purchase ledger** are **made** to the **correct purchase ledger accounts**
	• **Cut-off** is **applied correctly** to the purchase ledger

Activity 7.2

What can go wrong at the following stages of the purchase cycle?
(a) Ordering
(b) Receipt of goods
(c) Accounting

Controls

2.7 The following controls should be in place over **ordering**.

- **Central policy** for choice of suppliers
- Evidence needed of **requirements** for purchase before purchase authorised (re-order quantities and re-order levels)
- **Order forms** prepared only when a purchase requisition has been received
- **Authorisation** of order forms
- **Prenumbered order forms**
- **Safeguarding** of blank order forms
- **Review** of orders not received
- **Monitoring** of **supplier terms** and taking advantage of favourable conditions (bulk order, discount)

2.8 The client should carry out the following checks on **goods received** and **invoices** from **suppliers**.

(a) **Examination** of goods inwards
- Quality
- Quantity
- Condition

(b) **Recording arrival** and **acceptance** of goods (prenumbered goods received notes)

(c) **Comparison** of **goods received notes** with **purchase orders**

(d) **Referencing** of supplier invoices; numerical sequence and supplier reference

(e) **Checking** of **suppliers' invoices**
- Prices, quantities, accuracy of calculation
- Comparison with order and goods received note

7: Improving control procedures

  (f) **Recording return of goods** (prenumbered good returned notes)

  (g) Procedures for **obtaining credit notes** from suppliers

2.9 The following controls should be in place over **accounting procedures**.

  (a) **Segregation** of **duties:** accounting and checking functions

  (b) Prompt **recording** of **purchases** and **purchase returns** in day books and ledgers

  (c) **Regular maintenance** of **purchase ledger**

  (d) **Comparison** of **supplier statements** with **purchase ledger balances**

  (e) **Authorisation** of **payments**

   (i) Authority limits

   (ii) Confirmation that goods have been received, accord with purchase order, and are properly priced and invoiced

  (f) **Review** of **allocation** of expenditure

  (g) **Reconciliation** of **purchase ledger** control account to total of purchase ledger balances

  (h) **Cut-off** accrual of unmatched goods received notes at year-end

3 CONTROLLING THE SALES CYCLE

3.1 For sales, businesses want to give credit only to customers who will pay their debts. The processes of handling sales, matched orders, despatching goods and invoicing all need to be **documented** and **matched**, so that customers receive what they ordered and are correctly billed. The **sales ledger** makes it possible to keep track of what is owed by each customer.

Input to a sales ledger system

3.2 Bearing in mind what we expect to find in a sales ledger, we can say that typical data input into sales ledger system is as follows.

  (a) **Amendments**

   - Amendments to customer details, eg change of address or credit limit
   - Insertion of new customers
   - Deletion of old 'non-active' customers

  (b) **Transaction data relating to**:

   - Sales transactions, for invoicing
   - Customer payments
   - Credit notes
   - Adjustments (debit or credit items)

3.3 Some computerised sales ledgers produce invoices, so that basic sales data is input into the system. But other businesses might have a specialised invoicing module, so that the sales ledger package is not expected to produce invoices. The invoice details are already available (as output from the specialised module) and are input into the sales ledger system rather than basic sales data.

Part B: Effective management of business and accounting systems

Processing in a sales ledger system

3.4 The primary action involved in updating the sales ledger is modifying the amount outstanding on the customer's account. How the amount is modified depends on what data is being input (ie whether it is an invoice, credit note, remittance etc).

3.5 When processing starts, the balance on an account is called the **brought-forward** balance. When processing has finished, the balance on the account is called the **carried-forward** balance. These terms are often abbreviated to b/f and c/f.

3.6 What a computer does is to add or subtract whatever you tell it to from the b/f balance, and end up with a c/f balance.

	£	£
Brought forward account balance		X
Add:		
Invoice value	X	
Adjustments (+)	X	
		X
		X
Deduct:		
Credit note value	X	
Adjustments (-)	X	
Remittances	X	
		X
Carried forward account balance		X

This method of updating customer accounts is called the **balance forward method**.

3.7 Most systems also offer users the **open item method** of processing the data, which is much neater. Under this method, the user identifies specific invoices, and credits individual payments against specific invoices. Late payments of individual invoices can be identified and chased up. The customer's outstanding balance is the sum of the unpaid open items. The open item method follows best accounting practice, but it is more time consuming than the balance forward method.

Outputs from a sales ledger system

3.8 Typical outputs in a computerised sales ledger are as follows.

(a) **Day book listing**. A list of all transactions posted each day. This provides an audit trail - information which the auditors of the business can use when carrying out their work. Batch and control totals will be included in the listing.

(b) **Invoices** (if the package is one which is expected to produce invoices.)

(c) **Statements**. End of month statements for customers.

(d) **Aged debtors list**. Probably produced monthly.

(e) **Sales analysis reports**. These will analyse sales according to the sales analysis codes on the sales ledger file.

(f) **Debtors reminder letters**. Letters can be produced automatically to chase late payers when the due date for payment goes by without payment having been received.

(g) **Customer lists** (or perhaps a selective list). The list might be printed on to adhesive labels, for sending out customer letters or marketing material.

(h) **Responses to enquiries,** perhaps output on to a VDU screen rather than as printed copy, for fast response to customer enquiries.

(i) **Output onto disk file for other modules,** eg to the stock control module and the nominal ledger module, if these are also used by the organisation, and the package is not an integrated one.

3.9 There are a number of controls which need to be in place over sales and debtors. Bear in mind that, quite apart from safeguarding actual transactions, there must be no possibility of turnover figures being falsified. A number of people may have bonuses and commissions based on them!

3.10 The most important aims of the control system relating to debtors and sales are these:

Feature	Aims
Ordering and granting of credit	• **Goods** and **services** are **only supplied** to **customers** with **good credit ratings** • **Customers** are encouraged to **pay promptly** • **Orders** are **recorded correctly** • **Orders** are **fulfilled**
Despatch and invoicing	• All **despatches** of goods are **recorded** • All **goods and services** sold are **correctly invoiced** • All **invoices** raised **relate to goods and services** that have been **supplied** by the business • **Credit notes** are only given for **valid reasons**
Recording, accounting and credit control	• All sales that have been **invoiced** are **recorded** in the general and sales ledgers • All **credit notes** that have been **issued** are **recorded** in the general and sales ledgers • All **entries** in the sales ledger are **made** to the **correct** sales ledger accounts • **Cut-off** is applied correctly to the sales ledger • Potentially **doubtful debts** are **identified**

Activity 7.3

What can go wrong at the following stages of the sales cycle?
(a) Ordering by customers
(b) Despatch of goods
(c) Accounting

Controls

3.11 The following controls relate to the **ordering** and **credit control** process; note the importance of controls over credit terms, ensuring that goods are only sent to customers who are likely to pay promptly.

(a) **Segregation** of duties; credit control, invoicing and stock despatch

Part B: Effective management of business and accounting systems

(b) **Authorisation** of **credit terms** to customers
- References/credit checks obtained
- Authorisation by senior staff
- Regular review

(c) **Authorisation** for changes in **other customer data**
- Change of address supported by letterhead
- Requests for deletion supported by evidence balances cleared/customer in liquidation

(d) **Orders** only **accepted** from **customers** who have no credit problems

(e) **Sequential numbering** of blank **order documents**

(f) **Matching** of **customer orders** with production orders and despatch notes

3.12 The following checks relate to **despatches** and **invoice preparation**.

(a) **Authorisation** of **despatch** of **goods**
- Despatch only on sales order
- Despatch only to authorised customers
- Special authorisation of despatches of goods free of charge or on special terms

(b) **Examination** of **goods outwards** as to quantity, quality and condition

(c) **Recording** of **goods outwards**

(d) **Agreement** of **goods outwards records** to **customer orders**, **despatch notes** and **invoices**

(e) **Prenumbering** of despatch notes and delivery notes and regular checks on sequence

(f) **Condition** of **returns checked**

(g) Recording of goods returned on **goods returned notes**

(h) **Signature** of **delivery notes** by customers

(i) Preparation of invoices and credit notes
- **Authorisation** of **selling prices**/use of **price lists**
- **Authorisation** of **credit notes**
- **Checks on prices, quantities, extensions** and totals on invoices and credit notes
- **Sequential numbering of** blank invoices and credit notes, and regular tests on sequence

(j) **Stock records updated**

(k) **Matching** of **sales invoices** with despatch and delivering notes and sales orders

(l) Regular **review** for **orders** which have not yet been delivered

3.13 The following controls relate to **accounting** and **recording**.

(a) **Segregation of duties:** recording sales, maintaining customer accounts and preparing statements

(b) **Recording** of **sales invoices** sequence and **control** over **spoilt invoices**

(c) **Matching** of **cash receipts** with **invoices**

(d) **Retention** of **customer remittance advices**

(e) **Separate recording** of **sales returns, price adjustments** etc

(f) **Cut-off procedures** to ensure goods despatched and not invoiced (or vice versa) are properly dealt within the correct period

(g) Regular **preparation** of **debtor statements**

(h) **Checking** of **debtors' statements**

(i) **Safeguarding** of **debtor statements** so that they cannot be altered before despatch

(j) **Review** and **follow-up** of **overdue accounts**

(k) **Authorisation** of **writing off** of **bad debts**

(l) **Reconciliation** of **sales ledger control account**

(m) **Analytical review** of **sales ledger** and **profit margins**

4 CONTROLLING CASH

4.1 Although we still talk in terms of cash, very few business transactions involve its use. Even at the retail level, many purchases are now being made by debit and credit card.

4.2 When we consider sales and purchases made on credit between businesses, transfer of funds will probably be by:

- Company cheque
- Bank transfer
- Internet transfer, or in some cases
- Standing order/direct debit

4.3 The only use of cash in non-retail businesses will probably be for petty cash. So what controls need to be in place?

Control over receipts

4.4 In any business controls over cash **receipts** are fundamental if the company is to keep a healthy cash position. **Control over cash receipts** will concentrate on three main areas.

- Receipts must be **banked promptly**.
- The **record of receipts must be complete.**
- The loss of receipts through **theft or accident** must be prevented.

The difference between these three controls can be demonstrated with an example.

4.5 **EXAMPLE: CONTROL OVER CASH RECEIPTS**

Suppose that your company sells goods for £10,000 during the month of April to XYZ & Co. You receive a payment of £10,000 by cheque along with a remittance advice which shows exactly which invoices the cheque covers.

(a) You examine the cheque to ensure it is valid and completed correctly and you pay it in to the company account within 24 hours as company policy dictates (**banked promptly**).

(b) A colleague records the cheque details and compares the amount of the cheque to the remittance advice (**checking for completeness**). Usually the payment would also be checked against the total amount owed by the customer as part of the completeness check.

Part B: Effective management of business and accounting systems

(c) The **segregation of duties** between the person who banks the money and the person who records it is considered to be a very good control to prevent **theft and accidental loss**. This prevents the fraud known as 'teeming and lading' where receipts for customers are misappropriated and this is then covered up by misposting future receipts.

(d) Now that cheques can only be paid into the account in whose name they are made out, the opportunities for misappropriation of cheque receipts are much less.

Controls over payments

4.6 Controls over payments by a business must be **strict**. This should apply to all payments, from the smallest to the largest. The need for controls should be fairly obvious: if any business allowed some of its employees to pay out its money without needing to obtain permission, the scope for cheating and dishonesty would be very wide.

4.7 There are three main steps in applying controls over payments.

Step 1. Obtaining **documentary evidence** of the reason why the payment is being made and the amount of the payment. In the case of payments to suppliers, the documentary evidence will be a supplier's invoice (or statement).

Step 2. **Authorisation** of the payment, which means giving formal 'official' approval to make the payment.

Step 3. **Restricting the authority to actually make the payment** to certain specified individuals.

The difference between Steps 1, 2 and 3 can be illustrated with an example.

4.8 EXAMPLE: CONTROLLING A PAYMENT

Suppose that a company buys goods costing £5,000.

Step 1. It will receive an invoice from the supplier. This is the **documentary evidence** of the reason for and amount of the payment.

Step 2. The invoice will be approved by the purchasing director. This approval is the **authorisation of the payment**.

Step 3. At some time later, the payment will be made to the supplier, probably by cheque. For a payment of £5,000, perhaps only the finance director or managing director will be permitted to sign the cheque, and so the **authority to make the payment** would be limited to these two people.

Authorisation

4.9 Every payment must be approved by an **authorised person**. This person will often be a manager or supervisor in the department that initiated the expense, but every organisation has its own system. The following control limits must be set.

- **Which individuals** can authorise particular expenses
- The **maximum amount** of expenditure that an individual can authorise

4.10 The controls described above are designed to **prevent** fraud and error in the cash cycle. The most important controls designed to **detect** fraud and error which may already have taken place are **reconciliations**.

4.11 **Petty cash** should be reconciled whenever there is a need to replenish the float. The vouchers plus the remaining cash should equal the original float. If this balances, the only other check needed is to make sure that the vouchers are all valid and authorised.

4.12 A **bank reconciliation** should be done at least once a month. Many businesses, even those with sophisticated computer systems, still keep a manual cash book. If not, a printout of the bank record from the computer can be used. This is reconciled to the bank statement. There will always be differences, but they should come into the following categories.

- Timing differences due to unpresented cheques
- Timing differences due to uncredited lodgements
- Standing orders and direct debits not entered in the cash book
- Bank charges not entered in the cash book
- Funds received by transfer and not recorded in the cash book

5 CONTROL AND INTEGRATED SYSTEMS

5.1 An **integrated system** ties together the different modules of an accounting package, such as sales, purchases and stock, through automatic links. In this way, data entered into one module can automatically update files in another module.

5.2 For example, a sales invoice generated by the system could then update

- The sales ledger
- The stock module, recording the movement out of the goods
- The sales account in the nominal ledger

5.3 There are a number of implications to this.

(a) Fewer people need to be involved in input. This is not very good for segregation of duties, but it makes it possible to have more restricted access to the computer system, which enhances control.

(b) Errors in one module are unlikely to go unnoticed, because they will impinge upon other areas.

(c) Frauds involving just one accounting area are difficult to maintain because queries will arise in other areas

5.4 For these reasons, a higher level of control can be maintained in an integrated system.

Part B: Effective management of business and accounting systems

Key learning points

- The sales and purchases systems will be the most important components of most company accounting systems.

- The tests of controls of the **sales system** will be based around:
    - **Selling** (authorisation)
    - **Goods outwards** (custody)
    - **Accounting** (recording)

- Similarly, the **purchases systems** tests will be based around:
    - **Buying** (authorisation)
    - **Goods inwards** (custody)
    - **Accounting** (recording)

- Obviously, most manufacturing companies will have a large payroll. **Wages and salaries** are usually dealt with in very different ways, but they are often grouped together for audit testing purposes.

- Key controls over **wages** cover:
    - **Documentation** and **authorisation** of staff changes
    - **Calculation** of wages and salaries
    - **Payment** of wages and salaries
    - **Authorisation** of **deductions**

- Cash and petty cash must be regularly **reconciled**

- Control is enhanced by an **integrated accounting system**

Quick quiz

1. What are the key elements in authorisation of credit terms to customers?
2. What should auditors check when reviewing sales invoices?
3. How can a company ensure that quantities of goods ordered do not exceed those that are required?
4. What are the important checks that should be made on invoices received from suppliers?
5. What are the most important authorisation controls over amounts to be paid to employees?
6. What are the three main steps in controlling payments?

Answers to quick quiz

1. References and credit checks should be obtained before customers are given credit. Credit limits should be authorised by senior staff and should be regularly reviewed.

2. When checking sales invoices, auditors should check:

    (a) Quantities
    (b) Prices charged with price lists
    (c) Correct calculation of discounts
    (d) Calculations and additions
    (e) Invoices have been correctly entered and analysed in the sales day book
    (f) VAT has been properly dealt with
    (g) Invoices have been posted to the sales ledger

3. A company can ensure goods ordered do not exceed requirements by setting re-order quantities and re-order limits.

4. Invoices from suppliers should be checked for correctness of prices and quantities and accuracy of calculation. They should be compared with purchase orders and goods received notes.

5　The most important authorisation controls over wages and salaries are controls over:

　　(a)　Engagement and discharge of employees
　　(b)　Changes in pay rates
　　(c)　Overtime
　　(d)　Non-statutory deductions
　　(e)　Advances of pay

6　(a)　Obtaining documentary evidence of the reason for the payment
　　(b)　The payment being authorised
　　(c)　Control over cheque signing

Answers to activities

Answer 7.1

(a)　This allows the possibility of wages continuing to be paid to an employee who has left
(b)　This means that employees can be paid for hours not worked – or not paid for hours that were worked
(c)　As above
(d)　In a large payroll, the absence of this check means that payments can be made to fictitious employees

Answer 7.2

(a)　(i)　All purchases may not be recorded.
　　(ii)　Goods and services may be purchased which are not required.
　　(iii)　The company may fail to buy at the best prices.

(b)　(i)　Goods may be accepted which have not been ordered.
　　(ii)　Goods may be damaged or the quantity may be wrong.

(c)　(i)　Invoices may be received for goods that have not been ordered.
　　(ii)　Invoices may be incorrect.
　　(iii)　Accounts may not be correctly updated.

Answer 7.3

(a)　(i)　Orders may never be recorded.
　　(ii)　The goods may never be sent.
　　(iii)　Goods may be sold to a customer who is unable to pay.

(b)　(i)　Goods may never be despatched.
　　(ii)　Damaged or incorrect goods may be despatched.
　　(iii)　The customer may never receive the goods.

(c)　(i)　Goods may never be invoiced.
　　(ii)　Invoicing errors may occur.
　　(iii)　Accounts may remain overdue.
　　(iv)　Accounts may not be correctly updated.

Now try Question 6 in the Exam Question Bank

Chapter 8 Management information and reporting systems

Chapter topic list

1 Management information
2 Collecting management information
3 The management information system (MIS)
4 Management reports

The following study sessions are covered in this chapter:

		Syllabus reference
9(a)	Describe the main features of an MIS	2(e)
9(b)	Describe the information flows within the accounting system	2(e)
9(c)	Draft examples of relevant management reports	2(e)
9(d)	Understand how data and transactions are processed and stored within the accounting system	2(e)

8: Management information and reporting systems

1 MANAGEMENT INFORMATION

1.1 What sort of knowledge or data might the people in charge of running a business wish to be told?

- How much it costs to make a product in their factory
- How many products the company sold last month
- How much was spent on wages last year
- How many staff the company currently employs

1.2 These are just some of the questions that management might wish to have answers for. Management information can be as follows.

- Financial information (measured in terms of money)
- Non-financial information (not measured in terms of money)

1.3 Good management information has the following qualities.

(a) **Reliable**. It is important that management have an accurate picture of what is really happening.

(b) **Timely**. Information should be available in time for decisions to be made.

(c) **Relevant**. Management information should be relevant to the needs of the organisation and the individual.

1.4 So now you know what management information is, let's go on to look at the second question: **why is management information needed**?

1.5 In order to manage their resources, managers in any organisation need to know on a regular basis how their particular department or section is performing. They will also wish to know whether activities are going as planned and whether any problems have arisen. Accounting systems must therefore provide them with **reliable, up-to-date information** which is **relevant** to the **decisions** they have to take.

1.6 Management information assists in the following areas of management activity.

- **Planning**
- **Control**
- **Decision making**

1.7 **Planning**. Management needs to decide what the objectives of the company are and how they can be achieved. Management information is used to help management **plan** the resources that a business will require and how they will be used.

1.8 **Control**. Once management puts a plan of action into operation, there needs to be some **control** over the business's activities to make sure that they are carrying out the original plans.

1.9 **Decision making**. Management at all levels within an organisation take decisions. Decision making always involves a **choice between alternatives**. It is the role of the management accountant to provide information so that management can reach an informed decision.

1.10 The information required by a manager will vary according to the nature of the organisation and individual responsibilities. Look at the following examples.

Part B: Effective management of business and accounting systems

(a) Senior management will usually be interested in the financial statements (balance sheet and profit and loss account), on a monthly basis.

(b) A supervisor in a large factory may want a daily output report for every production shift.

(c) A sales manager may want a weekly report of orders achieved by the sales team.

1.11 Management information is used for a wide variety of purposes. We have already mentioned **planning**, **control** and **decision making**. Management information is also needed for the following.

- Pricing
- Valuing stock
- Assessing profitability
- Deciding on the purchase of capital assets

1.12 In the present business environment where the rate of change is increasing, good management information systems are seen by many as the key to success. Although such systems give a basis for improved management decisions they do not guarantee good management. Poor information, however, is likely to reduce a manager's chances of success.

2 COLLECTING MANAGEMENT INFORMATION

2.1 Basic (prime) sources of management information include sales invoices and purchase invoices. These will also provide information for the financial accounts of a company.

2.2 In most organisations, this accounting information will be keyed into a **computer system** and the **coding structure** (also called the **chart of accounts**) for this system should be set up to provide information in the categories required.

2.3 For example, if the organisation is divided into different business units, costs and income must be coded to the correct unit. In a factory which makes different products, raw materials must be coded to the product which uses them. Errors in coding will lead to inaccurate information.

2.4 Other **sources of information** may include reports from various departments of the organisation.

- Timesheets, employee and wage information from the personnel department
- Goods received notes and material requisition notes from the warehouse
- Price lists (in-house and suppliers)
- The organisation's policy manual (to ensure that consistent procedures are followed)

2.5 Information will be sorted and amalgamated through the **coding structure** so that the reports required by management can be produced. Ways in which information can be collected include the following.

(a) **Cost centres** (physical locations which use resources, for example a department, a machine).

(b) **Profit centres** (sections of the business which use resources and generate income to match against them).

(c) **Projects,** for example, research projects, activities (for example invoice processing) or other outputs (for example a job for a specific customer).

8: Management information and reporting systems

> **KEY TERMS**
>
> - A **cost centre** is a physical location in the organisation which uses resources (usually a department or section of a department).
> - A **cost code** is a 'shorthand' description of a cost using numbers, letters, or a combination of both.

2.6 EXAMPLE: A TYPICAL COMPUTER COST CODE STRUCTURE

An example of the outline for an 8 digit code is shown as follows.

01	172	301
Originating department	Type of cost or revenue	End product/service
Cost centre or location		Eg project, contract, job, service, product

Therefore the code 01172301 will tell us where the cost came from, what type of cost (or income) it was and which end product or service it should be charged to. For example, it could be from factory department 1, wages, chargeable to product 301.

Activity 8.1

What is the purpose of a computer coding structure?

3 THE MANAGEMENT INFORMATION SYSTEM (MIS)

> **KEY TERM**
>
> A **management information system (MIS)** is a system to **convert data** from internal and external sources into **information** and to communicate that information, in an appropriate form, to **managers** at all levels. This information can then be used to make timely and effective decisions for planning, directing and controlling the activities for which they are responsible.

3.1 If we get the idea of the accounting system as a whole, starting at the bottom with source documents, then moving through the books of prime entry, through the ledgers and then up to the financial statements, we could position the **management information system** at the top.

3.2 As we move up through the system, the financial information available becomes more useful and more meaningful. A bunch of invoices do not tell a manager very much, a total of sales invoiced that month tells him a bit more, a year to date profit and loss account gives him more useful information. But when we arrive at the management information system, the manager can obtain information he can really do something with. For instance, he can have a year to date profit and loss account compared to budget and compared to the same time last year.

Part B: Effective management of business and accounting systems

3.3 A sophisticated MIS can also use **external** information sources, such as the published accounts of competitors, forecast changes in interest rates etc. to assist with financial planning.

3.4 An **integrated accounting system,** such as that represented in the diagram below, supports an MIS. In a system like this, users can specify reports and the software will automatically extract the required data from all the relevant files. The MIS will also use a spreadsheet application to manipulate figures and produce the required reports.

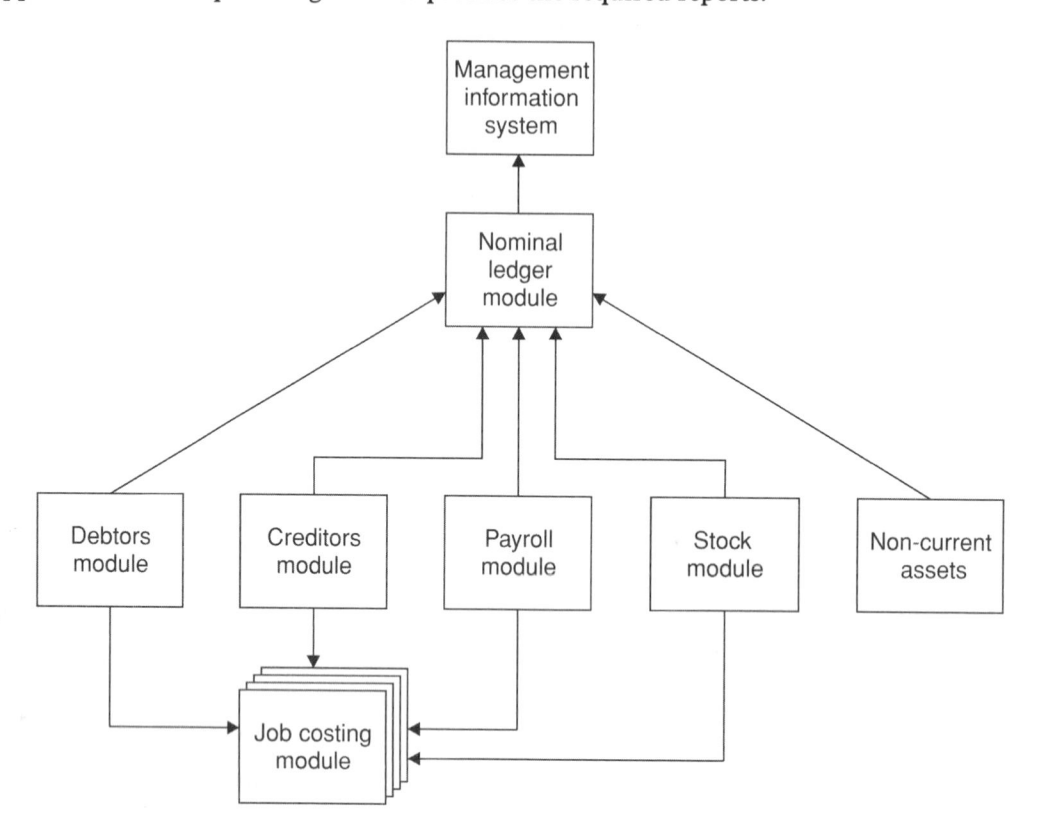

```
                    ┌──────────────┐
                    │  Management  │
                    │  information │
                    │    system    │
                    └──────▲───────┘
                           │
                    ┌──────┴───────┐
                    │   Nominal    │
                    │    ledger    │
                    │    module    │
                    └──────────────┘
          ▲      ▲      ▲      ▲      ▲
          │      │      │      │      │
     ┌────┴──┐┌──┴───┐┌─┴────┐┌┴─────┐┌┴────────┐
     │Debtors││Credi-││Payroll││Stock ││Non-current│
     │module ││tors  ││module ││module││  assets   │
     │       ││module││       ││      ││           │
     └───┬───┘└──┬───┘└───────┘└──┬───┘└───────────┘
         │      │                 │
         │      ▼                 │
         │  ┌────────┐            │
         └─▶│  Job   │◀───────────┘
            │costing │
            │ module │
            └────────┘
```

3.5 Data is amalgamated and stored in the ledgers. It can then be extracted and manipulated to produce the required information.

3.6 A system like this will allow a sales manager to obtain reports such as:

- Gross profit margins of particular products
- Slow-moving stock
- Success in particular markets

4 MANAGEMENT REPORTS

4.1 Most management reports are made meaningful by the use of **comparison**.

Comparisons with previous periods

4.2 The most common comparison of a previous period is when **one year's final figures** are **compared** with the **previous year's**. A business's statutory financial accounts contain comparative figures for the previous year as well as the figures for the actual year. As financial accounts are sent to shareholders, this comparison is obviously of great interest to them.

8: Management information and reporting systems

4.3 Some companies' financial accounts contain figures for the last five years. Comparing the figures for five years may be more valuable than comparing the figures for two years. **Long-term trends** become more apparent over five years. If the comparison is only over two years, one or other year might be unusual for various reasons. This will distort the comparison.

4.4 For management accounting purposes year-on-year comparisons are insufficient by themselves. Management will wish to pick up problems a lot sooner than the end of the financial year. Hence comparisons are often made for management accounting purposes **month-by-month** or **quarter-by-quarter**.

Comparisons with corresponding periods

4.5 Making comparisons month-by-month or quarter-by-quarter is most useful when you expect figures to be reasonably even over time. However demand for many products fluctuates **season-by-season**. In this case you would compare with the same season last year. This is the **corresponding period**.

Comparisons with forecasts

4.6 Businesses make forecasts for a number of purposes. A very common type of forecast is a **cash flow forecast.**

4.7 EXAMPLE: CASH FLOW FORECAST

	Jan £	Feb £	Mar £
Estimated cash receipts			
From credit customers	14,000	16,500	17,000
From cash sales	3,000	4,000	4,500
Proceeds on disposal of fixed assets	-	2,200	-
Total cash receipts	17,000	22,700	21,500
Estimated cash payments			
To suppliers of goods	8,000	7,800	10,500
To employees (wages)	3,000	3,500	3,500
Purchase of fixed assets	-	12,500	-
Rent and rates	-	-	1,000
Other overheads	1,200	1,200	1,200
Repayment of loan	2,500	-	-
	14,700	25,000	16,200
Net surplus/(deficit) for month	2,300	(2,300)	5,300
Opening cash balance	1,200	3,500	1,200
Closing cash balance	3,500	1,200	6,500

4.8 The purpose of making this forecast is for the business to be able to see how likely it is to have problems **maintaining** a **positive cash balance**. If the cash balance becomes negative, the business will have to obtain a loan or overdraft which will involve interest costs.

4.9 At the end of the period management will **compare** the **actual figures** with the **forecast figures,** and try to assess why they differ. Differences are likely to be a sign that some of the **assumptions** made when drawing up the original forecast were **incorrect**. Hence management, when making forecasts for future periods, may wish to change the assumptions that are made.

Part B: Effective management of business and accounting systems

Comparison with budgets

> **KEY TERM**
>
> A **budget** is an organisation's plan for a forthcoming period, expressed in monetary terms.

4.10 You can use budgets to check that the plan is working by **comparing** the **planned results** for the day, week, month or year to date **with** the **actual results**.

4.11 Budgets, like forecasts, represent a view of the future. However the two are not identical. Forecasts represent a prediction of what is **likely to happen**, the most likely scenario. Budgets may be a **target** rather than a prediction.

Comparisons within organisations

4.12 Organisations may wish to compare the performance of different departments and sales regions.

4.13 EXAMPLE: ANALYSIS OF RESULTS BY SALES AREA

	Area 1 £'000	Area 2 £'000	Area 3 £'000	Total £'000
Sales (A)	600	500	150	1,250
Direct costs by areas:				
Cost of goods sold	320	250	60	630
Transport & outside warehousing	60	35	15	110
Regional office expenses	40	45	28	113
Salespeople's expenses	30	25	11	66
Other regional expenses	20	15	8	43
Total direct cost by areas (B)	470	370	122	962
Gross profit (A – B)	130	130	28	288

4.14 Alternatively comparisons may be on a product by product basis.

4.15 EXAMPLE: ANALYSIS OF RESULTS BY PRODUCT

	Product A £'000	Product B £'000	Product C £'000	Total £'000
Sales	200	350	250	800
Variable costs of goods sold	95	175	90	360
Gross contribution	105	175	160	440
Variable marketing costs:				
Transport and warehousing	5	26	37	68
Office expenses	8	20	7	35
Sales salaries	15	44	25	84
Other expenses	2	7	6	15
Total variable marketing costs	30	97	75	202
Contribution	75	78	85	238

4.16 **Contribution** is an important term. It refers to how much each product contributes to fixed costs and profit.

Comparisons with other organisations

4.17 An obvious way of assessing how a business is performing in its chosen market is to **compare** its **results** and **financial position with** its **main competitors**. The main information that will generally be available will be the competitor's annual statutory financial accounts. Thus the comparisons are generally made on an annual basis.

4.18 For management purposes comparisons with competitors' positions as shown in the accounts will often give only a broad indication of performance. The information available in statutory accounts is limited. For example the accounts will not give a product by product breakdown of sales.

4.19 EXAMPLE: A HOSPITAL CASUALTY DEPARTMENT

A hospital casualty department will aim to deal with incoming patients quickly, efficiently and effectively but numbers and types of patients are hard to predict. Comparing waiting times or cases dealt with per day will be misleading if one day includes the victims of a serious train crash and another covers only minor injuries. Long term comparisons might give a clearer picture and help to identify usage patterns (for example busy Saturday nights). Comparisons with other casualty departments might be even more revealing.

Activity 8.2

Do you think the comparisons given to the following individuals are the right ones to help them to assess the performance of their work teams?

(a) Daily output in units compared with the same day, for the previous week, for a shift supervisor in a car factory

(b) December sales value compared with the previous month for the sales manager of a firm trading in Christmas decorations

(c) This year's examination results compared with last year for a secondary school headteacher

Note. Think about the relevance and completeness of the information.

Identifying differences

4.20 Differences are only meaningful if they **compare like with like**.

4.21 For example if the heating bill for the summer quarter is less than that for the winter quarter, the difference does not tell you anything about organisational performance, only about the weather.

4.22 If production quantities change from the amount planned or the amount produced in previous periods, then obviously costs will change, but by how much? The detailed techniques for dealing with this problem are beyond the scope of this Text. In essence what you do is **adjust** the figures that you are comparing actual data with to take account of the changed quantities.

4.23 If production is 10% more than it was in the previous period, then we can expect the costs of direct materials to rise by about 10%. The effect on labour costs will depend on whether workers are paid a flat rate or by what they produce. Most factory overheads should not vary with the change in quantities produced.

Part B: Effective management of business and accounting systems

4.24 Identifying differences only in financial terms may not be very helpful in finding out why they have actually occurred. For example if raw material expenditure is greater than forecast, this could be due to having spent a greater amount or used a greater quantity than planned. In this situation **reporting quantities as well as prices** will be helpful.

Activity 8.3

Here is part of a sales budget for an ice cream manufacturer.

MONTH	Jan	Feb	Mar	Apr	May	June	Jul	Aug
000 5 litres	1.0	1.0	1.1	1.1	1.2	1.4	1.4	1.5
Sales price £ per 5l	8.00	8.00	8.00	8.00	8.00	8.50	8.50	8.50

(a) The sales department complains that they only get information on quantities sold and would like to know what revenue they have earned. They ask you to compare budgeted sales revenue with actual for the last three months (April, May and June). Where would you find the actual sales figures?

(b) You find the figures which are April £9,000, May £10,200 and June £11,800. The sales department telephones you to say that the price rise planned for 1 June was actually brought forward to 1 May.

Produce the report the sales department has asked for and compose a note to go with it, commenting on the effect of the price rise.

4.25 Here is a report on the conveyancing department of a firm of solicitors for the year 20X1.

	Planned	Actual	Last year
Number of conveyances	300	290	295
Number of staff	3	3	2.5
£'000 Fees generated	155	156	145
£'000 Staff costs	62	65	56
£'000 Share of overheads	38	38	35
£'000 Departmental profit	55	53	54

4.26 This shows us that fees earned are well up on last year and better than planned, despite the fact that the number of conveyances are less than planned. Overheads are on target but staff costs are greater than expected.

4.27 Sometimes reports will include information in the form of **ratios or percentages** such as output per employee, profit as a percentage of revenue etc. In the example above, the number of conveyances per employee last year was 118, but this year it is only 96.7. Unless staff are doing more complex work, this needs investigation.

4.28 A further point that should be made about management reports is that they need to be easy to interpret and they need to make it possible for managers to quickly find the information that they need without wading through a mass of figures. In a very detailed report, it is easy for the reader to miss the important data. For this reason, reports are often produced which list only **exceptions** (favourable or unfavourable) from some agreed-upon standard.

4.29 This is known as **exception reporting**. It reports only the exceptions to the rule. This type of reporting gives managers exactly the information that they require and takes up very little of their time. For instance, managers could require reports listing:

- Account customers who have exceeded their credit limits
- Products making more that 40% gross profit

8: Management information and reporting systems

- Expense categories for which spending is currently over budget

Activity 8.4

Fill in the missing words:

Management information helps managers to plan,............ and make .... It should be relevant, ... and .... In most organisations it is sorted through a computer by using a .... to produce relevant reports. These reports should not be too detailed as this wastes .... and tends to obscure vital ....

Key learning points

- Good management information is:
  - **Reliable**
  - **Timely**
  - **Relevant**
- Management information is used for:
  - **Planning**
  - **Control**
  - **Decision making**
- The computer **coding structure** allows information to be sorted and amalgamated in order to produce useful information
- An **integrated accounting system** supports an MIS
- An MIS can also utilise **external** information
- Managers can assess the **significance** of financial information by the use of **comparison**

Quick quiz

1. Information is sorted and amalgamated through the _____ structure.
2. Why is an integrated accounting system an advantage in terms of providing management information?
3. For which type of product do comparisons have to be made using corresponding periods?
4. The purpose of a cash flow forecast is:
   - A To show how the cash has been spent
   - B To predict profit for the next quarter
   - C To predict whether a positive cash balance can be maintained
   - D To see whether the business is making any money
5. Is a budget the same as a forecast?
6. What measure is used to compare the financial viability of different products?
7. What is exception reporting?

Answers to quick quiz

1. The coding structure
2. Because it enables the MIS to automatically extract data from all relevant files
3. Seasonal products
4. C

Part B: Effective management of business and accounting systems

5   No. A budget is a target to be achieved. A forecast is a prediction of what is expected to happen

6   Contribution

7   Exception reporting reports only exceptional items, for instance figures which are above or below average by a certain amount.

Answers to activities

Answer 8.1

The purpose of a computer coding structure is to allow information to be sorted and grouped for management information and financial accounting purposes.

Answer 8.2

Note. In (a) the information is not precise enough, in (b) you are not comparing like with like and in (c) other comparisons are needed.

(a) Daily figures will not help the supervisor to judge the performance of his particular shift (there are other shifts during the day).

(b) You would expect December sales to be the highest for the year so comparison with December last year and the year-to-date with last year might be more meaningful.

(c) Exam results only measure one aspect of a school's objectives and will be affected by the quality of pupils as well as teachers.

Answer 8.3

Note. In (b) you need to quantify why the differences arose.

(a) Actual sales revenue could be found in the ledger accounts for sales.

(b)

Sales Revenue Report April to June

	April		May		June		Total	
	Actual	Budgeted	Actual	Budgeted	Actual	Budgeted	Actual	Budgeted
	£'000	£'000	£'000	£'000	£'000	£'000	£'000	£'000
	9.0	8.8	10.2	9.6	11.8	11.9	31.0	30.3

Note

Sales revenue for the three months is £700 more than budgeted.

In April, the quantity sold was greater than budget resulting in £200 revenue over budget. In May, a price rise of 50p per 5l (not in the budget until June) resulted in an increase in revenue of £600 over budget although the amount sold was as planned. In June, the quantity sold was under budget resulting in a £100 revenue shortfall.

Answer 8.4

Management information helps managers to plan, control and make decisions. It should be relevant, reliable and timely. In most organisations it is sorted through a computer by using a coding system to produce relevant reports. These reports should not be too detailed as this wastes time and tends to obscure vital information.

> **Now try Question 7 in the Exam Question Bank**

Part C
Management theory, principles and techniques

Chapter 9 Leadership, management and supervision

Chapter topic list

1   Authority and responsibility
2   Delegation
3   The role of management
4   The role of the supervisor
5   The role of the leader
6   Leadership skills and styles

The following study sessions are covered in this chapter:

Syllabus reference

10(a)	Describe the process of determining authority and responsibility	3(a)
10(b)	Describe the skills, traits and characteristics of a leader	3(a)
10(c)	Explain the role of management	3(a)
10(d)	Explain the role of the supervisor in achieving tasks, building the team and developing individuals	3(a)
10(e)	Describe the principles of effective delegation	3(a)
10(f)	Compare and contrast the terms 'leadership', 'management', 'supervision' and 'delegation'.	3(a)

Part C: Management theory, principles and techniques

1 AUTHORITY AND RESPONSIBILITY

1.1 We have already discussed some of the principles of management and organisation, and how positions of authority are determined, in Chapter 2 on organisation structure.

1.2 In this chapter, we look at some of the 'human' aspects of the organisation: what people in authority actually do. In following chapters, we focus in more detail on specific managerial skills and techniques in team management and motivation.

Power

1.3 A manager or supervisor without power, of whatever kind, cannot do his/her job properly. Power is not something a person has in isolation: it is exercised over other individuals or groups.

1.4 Power has been classified into six types or sources.

Type of power	Description
Coercive power	This is the power of physical force or punishment. Physical power is rare in business organisations, but organisations can sometimes use hidden forms of coercion to get what they want.
Reward (or resource) power	Access to or control over valued resources is a source of power. For example, managers have a resource of information or other contacts. The amount of resource power a person has depends on the scarcity of the resource, how much the resource is valued by others, and how far the resource is under the manager's control.
Legitimate (or position) power	This is power associated with a particular job or position in the hierarchy. For example, your boss has the power to authorise certain expenses, or organise work.
Expert power	A person may have power if his/her experience, qualifications or expertise are recognised. Accountants have a type of expert power because of their knowledge of the tax system, for example.
Referent (or personal) power	A person may be powerful simply by force of personality, which can influence other people, inspire them etc.
Negative power	This is the power to disrupt operations, such as strike, refusal to communicate information.

KEY TERM

Authority is the right to get things done: to ask someone else to do something and expect it to be done. Authority is thus another word for position or legitimate power.

Responsibility and accountability

> **KEY TERMS**
>
> **Responsibility** is the obligation a person has to fulfil a task, which (s)he has been given.
>
> **Accountability** is a person's liability to be called to account for the fulfilment of tasks they have been given.

1.5 The definitions given above have been created because **responsibility** is used in two ways.

   (a) A person is said to be responsible **for** a piece of work when he or she is required to ensure that the work is done.

   (b) The same person is said to be responsible **to** a superior when he or she is given work by that superior.

1.6 The word **accountable** has come to be used instead of **responsible** in the meaning given in 1.5(b) above. A person is thus **accountable to** a superior and **responsible for** work.

1.7 The principle of **delegation** (which we discuss later) is that a manager may make subordinates **responsible for** work, but remains **accountable to** his or her own superior for ensuring that the work is done. Appropriate decision-making **authority** must be delegated alongside the delegated responsibility.

Responsibility without authority

1.8 In practice, matters are rarely clear-cut. Authority without responsibility is a recipe for arbitrary and irresponsible behaviour. Responsibility without authority places a subordinate in an impossible and stressful position. These situations may arise when the organisation is doing something new or in a different way, its existing rules and procedures may be out of date or unable to cope with the new development. Various people may try to 'empire build'.

Activity 9.1

You have just joined a small accounts department. The financial controller keeps a very close eye on expenditure and, being prudent, believes that nothing should be spent that is not strictly necessary. She has recently gone on a three week holiday to Venezuela. You have been told that you need to prepare management accounts, and for this you have to obtain information from the payroll department in two weeks' time. This is standard procedure. However, there are two problems. One of the other people in your department has gone sick, and a temporary replacement will be needed very shortly. The personnel department say: 'We need a staff requisition from the financial controller before we can get in a temp. Sorry, you'll just have to cancel your weekend'. The payroll department is happy to give you the information you need - except directors' salaries, essential for the accounts to be truly accurate.

What is the underlying cause of the problem and what, in future, should you ask the financial controller to do to put it right?

Part C: Management theory, principles and techniques

2 DELEGATION

> **KEY TERM**
>
> **Delegation** of authority is the process whereby a superior gives to a subordinate part of his or her own authority to make decisions.

2.1 Note that delegation can only occur if the superior initially possesses the authority to delegate. A subordinate cannot be given organisational authority to make decisions unless it would otherwise be the superior's right to make those decisions personally.

2.2 Managers and supervisors must delegate some authority for three reasons.

(a) There are **physical and mental limitations** to the work load of any individual or group in authority.

(b) Managers and supervisors are free to **concentrate on the aspects of the work** (such as planning), which only they are competent (and paid) to do.

(c) The **increasing size and complexity** of some organisations calls for specialisation, both managerial and technical.

2.3 However, by delegating authority to assistants, the supervisor takes on two extra tasks:

- **Monitoring** their performance
- **Co-ordinating** the efforts of different assistants.

How to delegate

2.4 The process of delegation can be outlined as follows.

Step 1. **Specify performance:** the goals and standards expected of the subordinate, keeping in mind his or her level of expertise

Step 2. **Formally assign tasks** to the subordinate, who should formally agree to do them

Step 3. **Allocate resources and authority** to the subordinate to enable him or her to carry out the delegated tasks at the expected level of performance

Step 4. **Back off** and allow the subordinate to perform the delegated tasks

Step 5. **Maintain contact,** to review progress made, make constructive criticism and be available to give help and advice if requested

2.5 The decision of **when to delegate** is equally important.

(a) Is the **acceptance** of staff affected required for morale, relationships or ease of implementation of the decision?

(b) Is the **quality** of the decision most important? Many technical financial decisions may be of this type, and should be retained by the supervisor if he or she alone has the knowledge and experience to make them.

(c) Is the **expertise or experience** of assistants relevant or **necessary** to the task, and will it enhance the quality of the decision?

(d) Can **trust** be placed in the competence and reliability of the assistants?

(e) Does the **decision** require tact and confidentiality, or, on the other hand, maximum exposure and assimilation by employees?

> **Exam alert**
>
> A major pitfall in this area is being able to distinguish accurately between the three terms: authority, responsibility and delegation.
>
> Make sure you can define each of them. You should also be able to outline important practical considerations, such as how to delegate effectively, and what might happen if there is a mismatch between authority, power and responsibility.

Problems of delegation

2.6 Many managers and supervisors are **reluctant to delegate** and attempt to do many routine matters themselves in addition to their more important duties. This may happen for the following reasons.

(a) **Low confidence and trust** in the abilities of their staff: the suspicion that 'if you want it done well, you have to do it yourself'.

(b) The burden of **accountability for the mistakes of subordinates**, aggravated by (a) above.

(c) A **desire to 'stay in touch'** with the department or team – both in terms of workload and staff – particularly if the manager does not feel 'at home' in a management role.

(d) **Feeling threatened.** An unwillingness to admit that assistants have developed to the extent that they could perform some of the supervisor's duties.

(e) **Poor control and communication systems** in the organisation, so that the manager feels he has to do everything himself if he is to retain real control and responsibility for a task.

(f) An **organisational culture** that has failed to reward or recognise effective delegation, so that the manager may not feel that delegation is positively regarded.

(g) **Lack of understanding** of what delegation involves – ie not giving assistants total control, or making the manager himself redundant.

(h) **Lack of training** and development of managers in delegation skills and related areas (such as assertiveness and time management).

2.7 There is a **trust-control dilemma** in a superior-subordinate relationship. The sum of trust and control is a constant amount:

$T + C = Y$

where $T =$ the trust the superior has in the subordinate, and the trust which the subordinate feels the superior has in him
 $C =$ the degree of control exercised by the superior over the subordinate
 $Y =$ a constant, unchanging value

If there is any increase in C (if the superior retains more 'control' or authority), the subordinate will immediately recognise that (s)he is being trusted less. If the superior wishes to show more trust in the subordinate, he can only do so by reducing C: by delegating more authority.

Part C: Management theory, principles and techniques

Overcoming the reluctance of managers to delegate

2.8 Encouraging managers to delegate therefore involves increasing trust.

(a) **Train the subordinates** so that they are capable of handling delegated authority in a responsible way. If subordinates are of the right 'quality', supervisors will be prepared to trust them more.

(b) Have a system of **open communications**, in which the supervisor and subordinates freely interchange ideas and information. If the subordinate is given all the information needed to do the job, and if the supervisor is aware of what (s)he is doing:

- The subordinate will make better-informed decisions.
- The supervisor will not panic because he does not know what is going on.

(c) **Ensure that a system of control is established**. If responsibility and accountability are monitored at all levels of the management hierarchy, the risks of relinquishing authority and control to subordinates are significantly lessened.

Activity 9.2

You are the manager of an accounts section of your organisation and have stopped to talk to one of the clerks in the office to see what progress he is making. He complains bitterly that he is not learning anything. He gets only routine work to do and it is the same routine. He has not even been given the chance to swap jobs with someone else. You have picked up the same message from others in the office. You discuss the situation with Jean Howe the recently appointed supervisor. She appears to be very busy and harassed. When confronted with your observations she says that she is fed up with the job. She is worked off her feet, comes early, goes late, takes work home and gets criticised behind her back by incompetent clerks.

What has gone wrong?

3 THE ROLE OF MANAGEMENT

> **KEY TERM**
>
> **Management:** 'Getting things done through other people'.

Functions of management

3.1 Fayol classified five **functions of management** which apply to any organisation.

Function	Comment
Planning	This involves selecting **objectives**, and the strategies, policies, programmes and procedures for achieving the objectives either for the organisation as a whole or for a part of it.
Organising	Establishing a structure of tasks which need to be performed to achieve the goals of the organisation; grouping these tasks into jobs for an individual; creating groups of jobs within sections and departments, **delegating** authority to carry out the jobs; and providing **systems of information** and communication, for the co-ordination of activities.
Commanding	Giving **instructions** to subordinates to carry out tasks over which the manager has authority for decisions and responsibility for performance

Function	Comment
Co-ordinating	**Harmonising** the activities of individuals and groups within the organisation, which will inevitably have different ideas about what their own goals should be. Management must reconcile differences in approach, effort, interest and timing of these separate individuals and groups.
Controlling	**Measuring** and **correcting** the activities of individuals and groups, to ensure that their performance is in accordance with plans. Deviations from plans are identified and corrected.

3.2 You may be struck by two key 'omissions' from Fayol's classification.

(a) '**Motivating**' is not mentioned. It is assumed that subordinates will carry out tasks when 'commanded' or instructed to do so, regardless of whether or how far they may 'want' to.

(b) '**Communicating**' is not mentioned, although it is implied by the process of commanding (giving instructions), co-ordinating (sharing information) and controlling (giving feedback).

This reflects the classical view of the function of management as a matter of controlling resources and processes rather than people. An awareness of management as a primarily **interpersonal** process, involving communication and influence, only developed later with the **human relations school** of management theory.

Mayo: reaction to scientific management

3.3 It is clear to us today that treating work people as though they are machines is not a recipe for either harmony in the workplace or for high quality work. In the 1920s research began to show that managers needed to consider the complexity of **human behaviour.**

3.4 In the 1930s, there developed a renewed understanding that organisations are made up of **people** – not just functions. By robbing the worker of any sense of **contribution** to the total product or task, the organisation was losing out on an important source of energy and creativity. A new approach set out to redress the balance.

Human relations

3.5 The '**human relations**' **approach** emphasised the importance of human attitudes, values and relationships for the efficient and effective functioning of work organisations. Its pioneer, **Elton Mayo** (1880-1949) wrote: 'We have thought that first-class technical training was sufficient in a modern and mechanical age. As a consequence we are **technically competent** as no other age in history has been, and we combine this with **utter social incompetence.**'

3.6 Early work focused on the idea that people need companionship and belonging, and seek satisfaction in the **social relationships** they form at work. This emphasis resulted from a famous set of experiments (the **Hawthorne Studies**) carried out by Mayo and his colleagues for the Western Electric Company in the USA. The company was using a group of girls as 'guinea pigs' to assess the affect of lighting on productivity: they were astonished to find that productivity shot up, whatever they did with the lighting. Their conclusion was that: 'Management, by **consultation** with the girl workers, by clear **explanation** of the proposed experiments and the reasons for them, by accepting the workers' verdict in several

Part C: Management theory, principles and techniques

instances, unwittingly scored a success in two most important human matters – the girls became a self-governing team, and a team that **co-operated** wholeheartedly with management.'

3.7 Mayo's ideas were followed by various social psychologists (like **Maslow** and **Herzberg** whom we will meet later in this text), who shifted attention towards human beings' 'higher' **psychological needs** for growth, challenge, responsibility and self-fulfilment. Herzberg suggested that only these things could positively encourage or motivate employees to improved work performance. This has had a profound effect on the way management is perceived – as we will see when we look at fashionable concepts such as empowerment.

3.8 As we have seen, early theorists saw the organisation primarily as a structure of **tasks and authority** which could be drawn in an organisation chart. But that is like a snapshot of an organisation, showing what it looks like frozen at a particular moment in time. In fact, organisations are neither self-contained nor static: they are **open systems**.

> **Exam alert**
>
> The Pilot Paper for this syllabus set a compulsory question on the duties of a supervisor and the role of a manager in a typical accounting system, with examples. As you read the material in this chapter, compare the theory of duties, functions and roles to your own experience.

The management process

3.9 **Peter Drucker** worked in the 1940s and 1950s as a business adviser to a number of US corporations. He was also a prolific writer on management.

3.10 Drucker argued that the manager of a business has a basic function - **economic performance**. In this respect, the business manager is different from the manager of any other type of organisation. Management can only justify its existence and its authority by the economic results it produces, even though as a consequence of its actions, significant non-economic results occur as well.

3.11 Drucker grouped the work of the manager into five categories.

(a) **Setting objectives for the organisation**. Managers decide what the objectives of the organisation should be and quantify the targets of achievement for each objective. They must then communicate these targets to other people in the organisation.

(b) **Organising the work**. The work to be done in the organisation must be divided into manageable activities and manageable jobs. The jobs must be integrated into a formal organisation structure, and people must be selected to do the jobs.

(c) **Motivating** employees and communicating information to them to enable them to do their work.

(d) **The job of measurement**. Management must:

(i) Establish **objectives** or yardsticks of performance for every person in the organisation

(ii) Analyse **actual performance**, appraise it against the objectives or yardsticks which have been set, and analyse the comparison

(iii) Communicate the findings and explain their significance both to subordinate employees and also to superiors

9: Leadership, management and supervision

(e) **Developing people**. The manager 'brings out what is in them or he stifles them. He strengthens their integrity or he corrupts them'.

3.12 Every manager performs all five functions listed above, no matter how good or bad a manager he is. Drucker emphasised the importance of **communication** in the functions of management, which should be evident in items (a), (c) and (d) above.

Managers as innovators

3.13 In *When Giants Learn to Dance*, Rosabeth Moss Kanter described some of the impossible or incompatible demands made on managers when seeking improved performance and excellence through innovation.

DEMANDS MADE ON MANAGERS

Be entrepreneurial and risk taking	but	Don't lose money
Invest in the future	but	Keep profitable now
Do everything you're doing now but even better	but	Spend more time communicating, on teams and new projects
Lead and direct	but	Participate, listen, co-operate
Know everything about your business	but	Delegate more
Work all hours	but	Keep fit
Be single-minded in your commitment to ideas	but	Be flexible and responsive

DEMANDS MADE ON ORGANISATIONS

Be 'lean and mean'	but	Be a good employer
Be creative and innovative	but	'Stick to the knitting'
Decentralise to small, simple autonomous units	but	Centralise to be efficient and integrative
Have a sense of urgency	but	Deliberately plan for the future

The manager's roles

3.14 Henry **Mintzberg** did a study of a relatively small sample of US corporations to see how senior managers actually spend their time. He suggests that in their daily working lives, managers fulfil three types of **managerial role**.

Role category	Role	Comment
Interpersonal, from formal authority and position	**Figurehead** (or ceremonial)	Representing the company at dinners, conferences etc
	Leader	Hiring, firing and training staff, motivating employees, and reconciling individual needs with the requirements of the organisation
	Liaison	Making contacts with people in other departments

Part C: Management theory, principles and techniques

Role category	Role	Comment
Informational Managers have: • Access to all their staff • Many external contracts	**Monitor**	The manager monitors the environment, and receives information from subordinates, superiors and peers in other departments. It might be gossip or speculation.
	Spokesperson	The manager provides information to interested parties either within or outside the organisation
	Disseminator	The manager disseminates this information to subordinates
Decisional The manager's formal authority and access to information mean that no one else is in a position to take decisions relating to the work of the department as a whole.	**Entrepreneur**	A manager initiates projects, a number of which may be on the go at any one time.
	Disturbance handler	A manager has to respond to pressures over which the department has no control, taking decisions in unusual or unexpected situations.
	Resource allocator	A manager takes decisions relating to the allocation of scarce resources. The manager determines the department's direction and authorises decisions taken by subordinates.
	Negotiator	Both inside and outside the organisation takes up a great deal of management time.

3.15 Mintzberg's researches challenged the classical view of the manager as separate to, or above, routine demands of day-to-day work.

(a) Managers are not reflective, systematic planners.

(b) Managerial work is disjointed and discontinuous.

(c) Managers do have routine duties to perform, especially of a ceremonial nature (receiving important guests) or related to authority (signing cheques as a signatory) contrary to the myth that all routine work is done by juniors.

(d) Managers prefer verbal and informal information to the formal output of management information systems. Verbal information is 'hotter' and probably easier to grasp.

(e) Management cannot be a science or a profession. According to Mintzberg we do not know what procedures managers use, so they cannot be analysed scientifically or codified into an examinable body of theory.

3.16 Mintzberg states that general management is, in practice, a matter of **judgement and intuition**, gained from **experience** in **particular situations** rather than from abstract principles. 'Fragmentation and verbal communication' characterise the manager's work.

4 THE ROLE OF THE SUPERVISOR

4.1 There are different levels of management in most organisations. A **finance department** in an organisation might be headed by the **finance director** (A) supported by a chief **financial accountant** (B) and chief **management accountant** (C). Lower down in the hierarchy assistant accountants might report to (B) and (C).

4.2 The **supervisor** is the lowest level of management, at the **interface** between managerial and non-managerial staff.

> **KEY TERM**
>
> 'A **supervisor** is a person selected by middle management to take charge of a group of people, or special task, to ensure that work is carried out satisfactorily ... the job is largely reactive dealing with situations as they arise, allocating and reporting back to higher management.' (Savedra and Hawthorn).

4.3 The key features of supervision are as follows.

(a) A supervisor is usually a **front-line manager**, dealing with the levels of the organisation where the bread-and-butter work is done. (S)he will deal with matters such as staffing and health and safety at the day-to-day operational level, where a manager might deal with them at a policy-making level.

(b) A supervisor does not spend all his or her time on the managerial aspects of his job. Much of the time will be spent doing **technical/operational work**.

(c) A supervisor is a **gatekeeper** or filter for communication between managerial and non-managerial staff, both **upward** (conveying reports and suggestions) and **downward** (conveying policies, instructions and feedback).

(d) The supervisor monitors and controls work by means of **day-to-day, frequent and detailed information:** higher levels of management plan and control using longer-term, less frequent and less detailed information, which must be 'edited' or selected and reported by the supervisor.

4.4 It may be argued that supervisors carry out **Fayol's five functions of management at a lower level**.

What do supervisors do?

4.5 The following may give a more practical flavour of the actual responsibilities undertaken by managerial staff at different levels.

4.6 **Planning**
- Planning work so as to meet work targets or schedules set by more senior management
- Planning the work for each employee; making estimates of overtime required
- Planning the total resources required by the section to meet the total work-load
- Planning work methods and procedures
- Attending departmental planning meetings
- Preparing budgets for the section
- Planning staff training and staff development
- Planning the induction of new staff
- Planning improvements in the work

4.7 **Organising and overseeing the work of others**
- Ordering materials and equipment from internal stores or external suppliers
- Authorising spending by others on materials, sundry supplies or equipment
- Interviewing and selecting staff

Part C: Management theory, principles and techniques

- Authorising overtime
- Allocating work to staff
- Allocating equipment to staff
- Reorganising work (for example when urgent jobs come in)
- Establishing performance standards for staff
- Organising transport
- Deciding job priorities
- General 'housekeeping' duties
- Maintaining liaison with more senior management

Activity 9.3

Bert Close has decided to delegate the task of identifying the reasons for machine 'down' time (when machines are not working) over the past three months to Brenda Cartwright. This will involve her in talking to operators, foremen and supervisors and also liaising with other departments to establish the effects of this down time. What will Bert need to do to delegate this task effectively? List at least four items he will need to cover with Brenda.

4.8 **Controlling:** making sure the work is done properly

- Keeping records of total time worked on the section
- Deciding when sub-standard work must be re-done
- Attending progress control meetings
- Dealing with trade union representatives
- Dealing with personal problems of staff
- Disciplining staff (for late arrival at work and so on)
- Counselling staff
- Ensuring that work procedures are followed
- Ensuring that the quality of work is sustained to the required levels
- Ensuring that safety standards are maintained
- Checking the progress of new staff/staff training, on-the-job training
- Co-ordinating the work of the section with the work of other sections
- Ensuring that work targets are achieved, and explaining the cause to senior management of any failure to achieve these targets

4.9 **Motivating employees, and dealing with others**

- Dealing with staff problems
- Dealing with people in other sections
- Reporting to a senior manager
- Dealing with customers
- Motivating staff to improve work performance
- Applying disciplinary measures to subordinates who act unreasonably or work badly
- Helping staff to understand the organisation's goals and targets
- Training staff, and identifying the need for more training

4.10 **Communicating**

- Telling employees about plans, targets and work schedules
- Telling managers about the work that has been done
- Filling in reports (for example absentee reports for the personnel department)
- Writing memos, notes and reports
- Passing information between employees and managers, and between sections

9: Leadership, management and supervision

- Collecting information and distributing it to the other persons interested in it.
- Keeping up-to-date with developments

Activity 9.4

Look at the job of the supervisor (or similar position) in your office (your own job, if you are in such a position).

(a) Identify the (i) managerial and (ii) technical aspects of the job, and list as many as you can. Think of the duties they entail.

(b) Get hold of a copy of the job description of a supervisory job (or have a look at one in the organisation manual). Does it bear any relation to the list you compiled yourself? Is it a realistic description of the actual work of the supervisor? Is the 'supervisory' part of the job well-defined (as compared with the technical part)? Are there targets or standards, and training requirements?

(c) Consider your own experience of promotion to a supervisory post (or ask your supervisor). What preparation, training, coaching, and/or advice was given by the manager for this first step into managerial work - was it 'sink or swim'?

---

5 THE ROLE OF THE LEADER

What is leadership?

> **KEY TERM**
>
> **Leadership** has been defined as:
>
> 'The activity of influencing people to strive willingly for group objectives' (Terry)
>
> 'Interpersonal influence exercised in a situation and directed, through the communication process, toward the attainment of a specialised goal or goals' (Tannenbaum et al)

Management and leadership

5.1 The terms 'management' and 'leadership' are often used interchangeably. In some cases, management skills and theories have simply been relabelled to reflect the more fashionable term. However, there have been many attempts to distinguish meaningfully between them.

(a) **Kotter** (2001) argues that leadership and management involve two distinct sets of action. Management is about coping with **complexity**: its functions are to do with logical, structure, analysis and control, and are aimed at producing order, consistency and predictability. Leadership, by contrast, is about coping with **change**: its activities include creating a sense of direction, communicating strategy, and energising, inspiring and motivating others to translate the vision into action.

(b) **Yukl** (1998) suggests that while management is defined by a prescribed role and position in the structure of the organisation, leaders are given their roles by the perception of others, through election, choice or influence. Leadership is an interpersonal process. In other words, managers have **subordinates**, but leaders have **followers**.

(c) **Zaleznik** (1992) suggests that managers are mainly concerned with order and **maintaining the status quo**, exercising their skills in diplomacy and focusing on decision-making processes within the organisation. Leaders, in contrast, direct their energies towards introducing **new approaches and ideas**. They create excitement and vision in order to arouse motivation, and focus with empathy on the meanings of events and actions for people. Leaders search out opportunities for change.

(d) **Katz and Kahn** (1974) point out that while management aims to secure compliance with stated organisational objectives, leadership aims to secure willingness, enthusiasm and commitment. Leadership is the **influential increment** over and above mechanical compliance with the routine directives of the organisation.

5.2 Management can be exercised over resources, activities, projects and other essential non-personal things. Leadership can only be exercised over **people**.

5.3 Whetten and Cameron argue that the distinction between managers and leaders is no longer very useful.

> 'Managers cannot be successful without being good leaders, and leaders cannot be successful without being good managers... Effective management and leadership are inseparable ... No organisation in a post-industrial, hyperturbulent, twenty-first century environment will survive without executives capable of providing both management and leadership.'

Why should managers be 'leaders'?

> **Exam alert**
>
> Eight marks were available in the Pilot Paper for this syllabus for suggesting why senior managers might require leadership qualities to support their managerial capabilities. This is an important point.

5.4 Whether or not we make the distinction between management and leadership, attempts to define what makes leadership 'special' (such as those outlined above) have suggested some key points about the benefits effective leadership can bring and why it is valuable.

(a) Leaders energise and support **change**, which is essential for survival in highly competitive and fast-changing business environments. By setting visionary goals, and encouraging contribution from teams, leaders create environments that:

- Seek out new information and ideas
- Allow challenges to existing procedures and ways of thinking
- Invite innovation and creativity in finding better ways to achieve goals
- Support and empower people to cope with the turbulence.

(b) Leaders secure **commitment**, mobilising the ideas, experience and motivation of employees – which contributes to innovation and improved quality and customer service. This is all the more essential in a competitive, customer-focused, knowledge-based business environment.

(c) Leaders set **direction**, helping teams and organisations to understand their purpose, goals and value to the organisation. This facilitates team-working and empowerment (allowing discretion and creativity about how to achieve the desired outcomes) without loss of co-ordination or direction.

(d) Leaders support, challenge and develop **people**, maximising their contribution to the organisation. Leaders use an influence-based facilitate-empower style rather than a command-control style, and this is better suited to the expectations of empowered teams and the need for information-sharing in modern business environments.

Activity 9.5

Reflect on your own experience of working under the direction of others. Identify the 'best' leader you have ever 'followed'. (You may need to think about non-work leaders such as a sports coach or school teacher.) Think about how this person behaved and interacted with you and others.

What qualities make you identify this person as a 'great leader', from your point of view as a follower?

Theories of leadership

5.5 There are three basic 'schools' of leadership theory.

School	Comment
Trait theories	Based on analysing the **personality characteristics** or preferences of successful leaders.
Style theories	Based on the view that leadership is an **interpersonal process** whereby different **leader behaviours** influence people in different ways. More or less effective patterns of behaviour (or 'styles') can therefore be adopted.
Contingency theories	Based on the belief that there is no 'one best way' of leading, but that effective leaders adapt their behaviour to the specific and changing variables in the leadership context: the nature of the task, the personalities of team members, the organisation culture and so on.

We will look at each of these in the next section.

6 LEADERSHIP SKILLS AND STYLES

Traits of leadership

6.1 Early theories suggested that there are certain personality characteristics common to 'great men' or successful leaders. In other words, 'leaders are born, not made'. Various studies have attempted to determine exactly which traits are essential in a leader. One American study (cited by Rosemary Stewart) cites the following fifteen traits.

Judgement	Initiative	Integrity	Foresight	Energy
Drive	Human relations skill	Decisiveness	Dependability	Emotional stability
Fairness	Ambition	Dedication	Objectivity	Co-operation

6.2 Trait theory has been more or less discredited.

(a) The premise that certain traits are absolutely necessary for effective leadership has never been substantiated.

(b) The lists of traits proposed for leaders have been vast, varied and contradictory.

(c) 'A person does not become a leader by virtue of the possession of some combination of traits, but the pattern of personal characteristics must bear some relevant relationship to the characteristics, activities and goals of the followers' (Stodgill).

Styles of leadership

6.3 There are various classifications of leadership style. Although the labels and definitions of styles vary, style models are often talking about the same thing: a continuum of behaviours from:

Part C: Management theory, principles and techniques

(a) Wholly **task-focused, directive leadership behaviours** (representing **high leader control**) at one extreme, and

(b) Wholly **people-focused, supportive/relational leadership behaviours** (representing **high subordinate discretion**) at the other

A continuum of leadership styles

6.4 Tannenbaum and Schmidt proposed a continuum of behaviours (and associated styles) which reflected the balance of control exercised in a situation by the leader and the team.

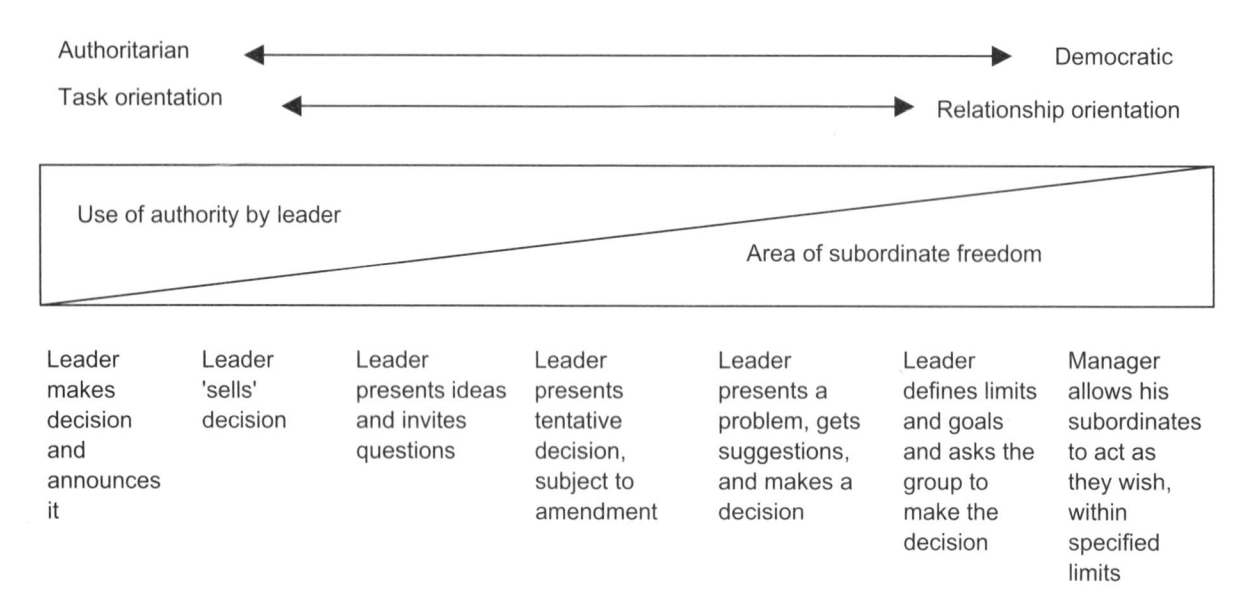

Authoritarian ←————————————→ Democratic

Task orientation ←————————————→ Relationship orientation

Use of authority by leader

Area of subordinate freedom

| Leader makes decision and announces it | Leader 'sells' decision | Leader presents ideas and invites questions | Leader presents tentative decision, subject to amendment | Leader presents a problem, gets suggestions, and makes a decision | Leader defines limits and goals and asks the group to make the decision | Manager allows his subordinates to act as they wish, within specified limits |

The Ashridge Management College model

6.5 The Research Unit at Ashridge Management College distinguished four different management styles. (These are outlined, with their strengths and weaknesses, in the following full-page table.)

6.6 The Ashridge studies came to the following conclusions.

(a) In an ideal world, subordinates preferred the 'consults' style of leadership.

(b) People led by a 'consults' manager had the most favourable attitude to their work.

(c) Most subordinates feel they are being led by a 'tells' or 'sells' manager.

(d) In practice, **consistency** was far more important to subordinates than any particular style. The least favourable attitudes were found amongst subordinates who were unable to perceive any consistent style of leadership in their superiors.

Activity 9.6

Suggest an appropriate style of management for each of the following situations. Think about your reasons for choosing each style in terms of the results you are trying to achieve, the need to secure commitment from others, and potential difficulties with both.

(a) Due to outside factors, the personnel budget has been reduced for your department and one-quarter of your staff must be made redundant. Records of each employee's performance are available.

(b) There is a recurring administrative problem which is minor, but irritating to every one in your department. Several solutions have been tried in the past, but without success. You think you

9: Leadership, management and supervision

have a remedy which will work, but unknown problems may arise, depending on the decisions made.

Style	Characteristics	Strengths	Weaknesses
Tells (autocratic)	The manager makes all the decisions, and issues instructions which must be obeyed without question.	(1) Quick decisions can be made when speed is required. (2) It is the most efficient type of leadership for highly-programmed routine work.	(1) It does not encourage the sub-ordinates to give their opinions when these might be useful. (2) Communications between the manager and subordinate will be one-way and the manager will not know until afterwards whether the orders have been properly understood. (3) It does not encourage initiative and commitment from subordinates.
Sells (persuasive)	The manager still makes all the decisions, but believes that subordinates have to be motivated to accept them in order to carry them out properly.	(1) Employees are made aware of the reasons for decisions. (2) Selling decisions to staff might make them more committed. (3) Staff will have a better idea of what to do when unforeseen events arise in their work because the manager will have explained his intentions.	(1) Communications are still largely one-way. Sub-ordinates might not accept the decisions. (2) It does not encourage initiative and commitment from subordinates.
Consults	The manager confers with subordinates and takes their views into account, but has the final say.	(1) Employees are involved in decisions before they are made. This encourages motivation through greater interest and involvement. (2) An agreed consensus of opinion can be reached and for some decisions consensus can be an advantage rather than a weak compromise. (3) Employees can contribute their knowledge and experience to help in solving more complex problems.	(1) It might take much longer to reach decisions. (2) Subordinates might be too inexperienced to formulate mature opinions and give practical advice. (3) Consultation can too easily turn into a façade concealing, basically, a sells style.
Joins (democratic)	Leader and followers make the decision on the basis of consensus.	(1) It can provide high motivation and commitment from employees. (2) It shares the other advantages of the consultative style (especially where subordinates have expert power).	(1) The authority of the manager might be undermined. (2) Decision-making might become a very long process, and clear decisions might be difficult to reach. (3) Subordinates might lack enough experience.

Part C: Management theory, principles and techniques

Rensis Likert

6.7 Likert (*New patterns of Management*) also described a range of four management styles or 'systems':

(a) System 1: **Exploitative authoritative**. The leader has no confidence or trust in his subordinates, imposes decisions, never delegates, motivates by threat, has little communication with subordinates and does not encourage teamwork.

(b) System 2: **Benevolent authoritative**. The leader has only superficial trust in subordinates, imposes decisions, never delegates, motivates by reward and, though sometimes involving others in problem-solving, is basically paternalistic.

(c) System 3: **Participative**. The leader has some confidence in subordinates, listens to them but controls decision making, motivates by reward and a level of involvement, and will use the ideas and suggestions of subordinates constructively.

(d) System 4: **Democratic**. The leader has complete confidence in subordinates who are allowed to make decisions for themselves. Motivation is by reward for achieving goals set by participation, and there is a substantial amount of sharing of ideas, opinions and co-operation.

6.8 Likert's research suggested that effective managers naturally use a System 3 or System 4 style. Both are seen as viable approaches, balancing the needs of the organisation and the individual.

Blake and Mouton's Managerial Grid

6.9 **Robert Blake** and **Jane Mouton** carried out research (The Ohio State Leadership Studies) into managerial behaviour and observed two basic dimensions of leadership: **concern for production** (or task performance) and **concern for people.**

6.10 Along each of these two dimensions, managers could be located at any point on a **continuum** from very low to very high concern. Blake and Mouton observed that the two concerns did not seem to correlate, positively or negatively: a high concern in one dimension, for example, did not seem to imply a high or low concern in the other dimension. Individual managers could therefore reflect various permutations of task/people concern.

The managerial grid

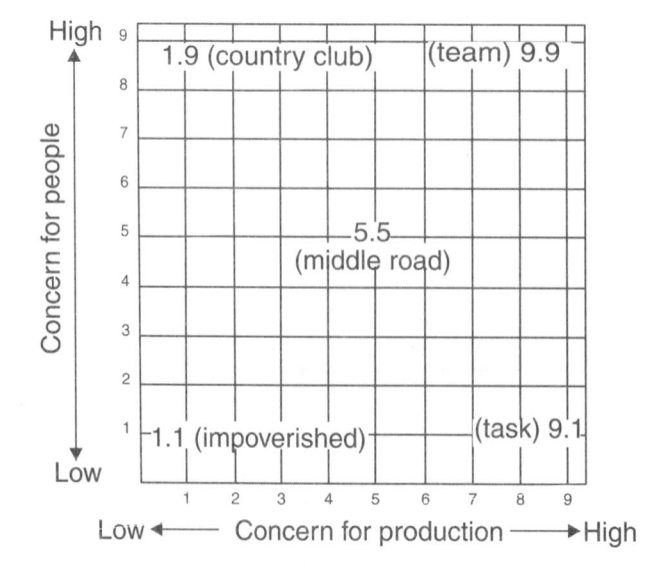

9: Leadership, management and supervision

6.11 The extreme cases shown on the grid are these.

(a) 1.1 **impoverished:** the manager is lazy, showing little interest in either staff or work.

(b) 1.9 **country club:** the manager is attentive to staff needs and has developed satisfying relationships. However, there is little attention paid to achieving results.

(c) 9.1 **task management:** almost total concentration on achieving results. People's needs are virtually ignored.

(d) 5.5 **middle of the road** or the **dampened pendulum:** adequate performance through balancing the necessity to get out work while maintaining morale of people at a satisfactory level.

(e) 9.9 **team:** high performance manager who achieves high work accomplishment through 'leading' committed people who identify themselves with the organisational aims.

6.12 The managerial grid was intended as an **appraisal and management development tool.** It recognises that a balance is required between concern for task and concern for people, and that a high degree of both is possible (and highly effective) at the same time.

6.13 However, the grid is a **simplified** model, and as such has **practical limitations.**

(a) It assumes that 9.9 is the desirable model for effective leadership. In some managerial contexts, this may not be so. Concern for people, for example, would not be necessary in a context of comprehensive automation: compliance is all that would be required.

(b) It is open to oversimplification. Scores can appear polarised, with judgements attached about individual managers' suitability or performance. The Grid is intended as a simplified 'snapshot' of a manager's preferred style, not a comprehensive description of his or her performance.

(c) Organisational context and culture, technology and other 'givens' influence the manager's style of leadership, not just the two dimensions described by the Grid.

(d) Any managerial theory is only useful in so far as it is useable in practice by managers: if the grid is used only to inform managers that they 'must acquire greater concern for people', it may result in stress, uncertainty and inconsistent behaviour.

Activity 9.7

Here are some statements about a manager's approach to meetings. Which position on Blake's Grid do you think each might represent?

(a) I attend because it is expected. I either go along with the majority position or avoid expressing my views.

(b) I try to come up with good ideas and push for a decision as soon as I can get a majority behind me. I don't mind stepping on people if it helps a sound decision.

(c) I like to be able to support what my boss wants and to recognise the merits of individual effort. When conflict rises, I do a good job of restoring harmony.

Part C: Management theory, principles and techniques

Limitations of style approaches

6.14 Perhaps the most important criticism of the style approach is that it does not consider all the variables that contribute to the operation of effective leadership.

(a) The manager's personality may simply not be flexible enough to utilise different styles effectively.

(b) The demands of the task, technology, organisation culture and other managers constrain the leader in the range of styles effectively open to him. (If his own boss practices an authoritarian style, and the team are incompetent and require close supervision, no amount of theorising on the desirability of participative management will make it possible.)

(c) Consistency is important to subordinates. If a manager adapts his style to changing situations, they may simply perceive him to be fickle, or may suffer insecurity and stress.

6.15 Huczynski and Buchanan note that 'There is therefore no simple recipe which the individual manager can use to decide which style to adopt to be most effective.'

6.16 It is the consideration of this wide set of variables that has led to the development of the contingency approach to leadership.

Contingency approaches

6.17 In essence, contingency theory sees effective leadership as being dependent on a number of variable or contingent factors. There is no one right way to lead that will fit all situations. Gillen *(Leadership Skills)* suggests that: 'Using only one leadership style is a bit like a stopped clock: it will be right twice a day but, the rest of the time, it will be inaccurate to varying degrees. Leaders need to interact with their team in different ways in different situations. This is what we mean by "leadership style".'

Charles Handy

6.18 Handy argued that the ability of a manager to lead and to influence the work group will vary according to three factors.

(a) The **leader**: his personality and preferred style of operating

(b) The **subordinates**: their individual and collective personalities, and their preference for a particular style of leadership

(c) The **task**: its structure, complexity and variety

6.19 In addition, there is the wider leadership 'context', including:

(a) The position of **power** held by the leader within the organisation and the group. A leader with power is better able to manage the other variables.

(b) The norms, structure and technology of the **organisation** as a whole. No manager can act contrary to organisational constraints.

6.20 Each of the key variables can be plotted on a spectrum from 'tight' to 'flexible'. Handy suggests that the most effective managerial approach in any situation is one that brings all three variables as close as possible to a '**best fit**', where they all align on the same level in the spectrum. While there may be long-term benefits to be achieved from re-defining the task (eg job enlargement) or from development the subordinates, in the short term the most easily changed variable is often the leader's style.

9: Leadership, management and supervision

	The leader	The subordinates	The task
Tight ↑ The Spectrum	Preference for autocratic style, high estimation of his own capabilities and a low estimation of his subordinates. Dislikes uncertainty.	Low opinion of own abilities, do not like uncertainty in their work and like to be ordered. They regard their work as trivial; past experience in work leads to acceptance of orders, cultural factors lean them towards autocratic/dictatorial leaders.	Job requires no initiative, is routine and repetitive or has a certain outcome; short time scale for completion. Trivial tasks.
↓ Flexible	Preference for democratic style, confidence in his subordinates, dislikes stress, accepts reasonable risk and uncertainty.	High opinion of own abilities; likes challenging important work; prepared to accept uncertainty and longer time scales for results; cultural factors favour independence.	Important tasks with a longer timescale; problem-solving or decision-making involved, complex work.

Hersey and Blanchard

6.21 In their influential **Situational Leadership** model, Hersey and Blanchard (1988) focus on the **readiness of the team members** to perform a given task, in terms of their **task ability** (experience, knowledge and skills) and willingness (whether they have the confidence, commitment and motivation) to complete the task successfully.

- High-readiness (R4) teams are able and willing. They do not need directive or supportive leadership: the most appropriate leadership style may be a joins or 'delegating' (S4) style.

- High-moderate readiness (R3) teams are able, but unwilling or insecure. They are competent, but require supportive behaviour to build morale: the most appropriate leadership style may be a consults or 'participating' (S3) style.

- Low-moderate readiness (R2) teams are willing and confident, but lacking ability. They require both directive and supportive behaviour to improve their task performance without damaging morale: the most appropriate leadership style may be a 'selling' (S2) style.

- Low-readiness (R1) teams are lacking ability and motivation/confidence. They require more directive behaviours in order to secure an adequate level of task performance: the most appropriate leadership style may be a 'telling' (S1) style.

6.22 This can be summed up as follows.

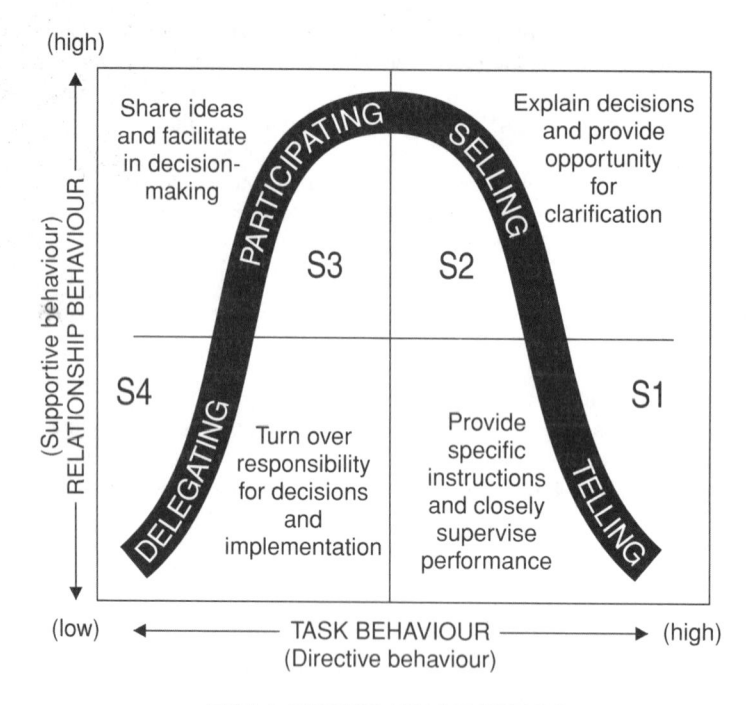

```
                           (high)
                             ▲
                             │
                    ┌────────┼────────┐
   (Supportive      │ Share  │ Explain│
    behaviour)      │ ideas  │decisions│
         ▲          │ and    │ and    │
         │          │facilitate│provide│
   RELATIONSHIP     │   PARTICIPATING/SELLING
   BEHAVIOUR        │   S3   │   S2   │
         │          │────────┼────────│
         │          │   S4   │   S1   │
         ▼          │DELEGATING/TELLING
                    │ Turn   │Provide │
                    │ over   │specific│
                    │respons.│instruc.│
                    └────────┼────────┘
                             │
   (low) ◄──── TASK BEHAVIOUR ────► (high)
              (Directive behaviour)

              FOLLOWER READINESS
   │ high  │    moderate    │  low  │
   │  R4   │   R3   │   R2  │  R1   │
   │Able & │Able but│Unable │Unable │
   │willing│unwilling│but    │and    │
   │or     │or      │willing│unwilling│
   │confid.│insecure│or conf.│or insecure│
```

(Diagram: Hersey & Blanchard Situational Leadership model — S1 Telling, S2 Selling, S3 Participating, S4 Delegating; Follower readiness R1–R4.)

An appraisal of contingency theory

6.23 Contingency theory usefully makes people aware of the factors affecting the choice of leadership style. However, Schein has pointed out that:

(a) Key variables such as task structure, power and relationships are difficult to measure in practice

(b) Contingency theories do not always take into account the need for the leader to have technical competence relevant to the task

6.24 Perhaps the major difficulty for any leader seeking to apply contingency theory, however, is actually to modify his or her behaviour as the situation changes.

Key learning points

- **Power** is the ability to get things done. There are many types of power in organisations: position or **legitimate power**, expert power, personal power, resource power and negative power are examples.

- **Authority** is related to legitimate or position power. It is the right to take certain decisions within certain boundaries.

- **Delegation** is necessary to get work distributed throughout the organisation. Successful delegation requires the resolution of the Trust-Control dilemma. Some managers and supervisors are reluctant to delegate.

- Organisations typically employ managers to direct them. The classic functions of managers were: **planning**, **organising**, **commanding**, **co-ordinating** and **controlling** (Fayol). In businesses, we can add the need to achieve **economic results.**

- A manager's job is not clear-cut and systematic in practice. More recent descriptions of the manager's role (Mintzberg) describe **interpersonal** roles (figurehead, leader, liaison), **informational** roles (monitor, disseminator, spokesperson) and **decisional** roles (entrepreneur, disturbance-handler, resource allocator, negotiator).

- The **supervisor** is at the first level of management, being closest to operational work. A supervisor is a person normally selected to take charge of a group of people or special task to ensure that work is carried out satisfactorily, as well as fulfilling his or her own tasks.

- There are many different definitions of **leadership**. Key themes (which are also used to distinguish leadership from management) include: interpersonal influence; securing willing commitment to shared goals; creating direction and energy; and an orientation to change.

- Leadership offers key **benefits** in a competitive, turbulent environment: activating commitment, setting direction, developing people and energising and supporting change.

- There are three basic schools of leadership theory: trait theories, style theories and contingency theories.

- **Leadership styles** are clusters of leadership behaviour that are used in different ways in different situations. While there are many different classifications of style, they mainly relate to the extent to which the leader is focused primarily on task/performance (directive behaviour) or relationships/people (supportive behaviour). Key style models include:

    - The Ashridge Model: tells, sells, consults, joins
    - Likert: exploitative authoritative, benevolent authoritative, consultative, participative
    - Blake and Mouton's Managerial Grid: concern for task, concern for people

- Leaders need to adapt their style to the needs of the team and situation. This is the basis of **contingency approaches** such as:

    - Hersey and Blanchard's 'situational leadership' model
    - Handy's 'best fit' model

Quick quiz

1. Power arising from an individual's formal position in the organisation is called:

    A Referent power
    B Legitimate power
    C Expert power
    D Resource power

2. Why can't accountability be delegated?

3. List the stages in the process of delegation.

4. List some problems in delegation.

5. List Fayol's management functions.

Part C: Management theory, principles and techniques

6   List three categories of managerial roles.

7   'A supervisor's job is like any other manager's.' Do you agree?

8   What is the difference between a manager and a leader?

9   If a manager confers with subordinates, takes their views and feelings into account, but retains the right to make a final decision, this is a:

    A   Tells style
    B   Sells style
    C   Consults style
    D   Joins style

10   What is the most effective style suggested by Blake and Mouton's Managerial Grid? Why is it so effective in theory, and why might it not be effective in practice?

Answers to quick quiz

1   B (or 'position' power).

2   Because the delegator has been given the task by his/her own boss.

3   Specify performance levels; formally assign task; allocate resources and authority; back off; give feedback.

4   Low trust, low competence, fear, worry about accountability.

5   The functions of management are: planning, organising, co-ordinating, controlling and commanding.

6   Interpersonal, informational, decisional

7   No - a supervisor is in charge of non-managerial employees, whereas a manager might be in charge of other managers in the levels below; a supervisor's job often contains a technical aspect.

8   See Paragraphs 5.1 and 5.2 for a full range of points.

9   C. Make sure you can define the other styles as well.

10   9.9. It is effective if there is sufficient time and resources to attend fully to people's needs, if the manager is good at dealing with people and if the people respond. It is ineffective when a task has to be completed in a certain way or by a certain deadline, whether or not people like it.

Answers to activities

Answer 9.1

The immediate problem is that the financial controller should have considered these issues before she went to Venezuela. The underlying cause, as far as you are concerned, is that you have responsibility to do a task but without the authority - to obtain all the information you need and to hire a temp - to do the job. In future the financial controller should, when delegating the task, delegate the authority to do it.

Answer 9.2

The problem appears to be that the new supervisor is taking too much of the department's work on to herself. While she is overworked, her subordinates are apparently not being stretched and as a result motivation and morale amongst them are poor. The supervisor herself is unhappy with the position and there is a danger that declining job satisfaction will lead to inefficiencies and eventually staff resignations.

There could be a number of causes contributing to the problem.

(a)   Jean Howe may have been badly selected, ie she may not have the ability required for a supervisory job.

(b)   Alternatively she may just be unaware of what is involved in a supervisor's role. She may not have realised that much of the task consists of managing subordinates; she is not required to shoulder all the detailed technical work herself.

9: Leadership, management and supervision

(c) There may be personality problems involved. Jean Howe regards her clerks as incompetent and this attitude may arise simply form an inability to get on with them socially. (Another possibility is that her staff actually are incompetent.)

(d) The supervisor does much of the department's work herself. This may be because she does not understand the kind of tasks which can be delegated and the way in which delegation of authority can improve the motivation and job satisfaction of subordinates.

As manager you have already gone some way towards identifying the actual causes of the problem You have spoken to some of the subordinates concerned and also to the supervisor. You could supplement this by a review of personnel records relating to Jean Howe to discover how her career has progressed so far and what training she had received (if any) in the duties of a supervisor. You may then be in a position to determine which of the possible causes of the problems are operating in this case.

Answer 9.3

- Identify task objectives
- Explain limits within which Brenda will work
- Deadlines
- Formats of reporting results
- Progress monitoring

Answer 9.4

Answer according to your own observations and experience.

Answer 9.5

Own observation. Bear in mind that, according to Yukl, the essence of leadership is inspiring 'followership': to an extent anyone you identify as a good leader (and would be prepared to follow) is a leader – whatever their position in the organisation.

Answer 9.6

Styles of management suggested in the situations described, using the tells-sells-consults-joins model.

(a) You may have to 'tell' here: nobody is gong to like the idea and, since each person will have his or her own interests at heart, you are unlikely to reach consensus. You could attempt to 'sell', if you can see a positive side to the change in particular cases: opportunities for retraining, say.

(b) You could 'consult' here: explain your remedy to staff and see whether they can suggest potential problems. They may be in a position to offer solutions - and since the problem effects them too, the should be committed to solving it.

Answer 9.7

Blake's Grid positioning of the given managerial approaches are:

(a) 1.1: low task, low people
(b) 9.1: High task, low people
(c) 1.9: high people, low task

> **Now try Question 8 in the Exam Question Bank**

Chapter 10 Individual and group behaviour

Chapter topic list

1. Individuals at work
2. Groups at work
3. Individual and team contribution
4. Organisation culture

The following study sessions are covered in this chapter:

		Syllabus reference
11(a)	Explain the concept of organisational culture and discuss its limitations	3(b)
11(b)	Discuss the differences between individual and group behaviour	3(b)
11(c)	Outline the contribution of individuals and teams to organisational success	3(b)
11(d)	Identify work that benefits from either an individual or team approach	3(b)
11(e)	Recognise behaviour facilitating and inhibiting organisational success	3(b)

1 INDIVIDUALS AT WORK

1.1 Individual behaviour and interpersonal behaviour (between two or more individuals) is a vast area of study. We will merely highlight some useful concepts. (Interpersonal behaviour is covered further in Chapter 14.)

Personality

1.2 In order to identify, describe and explain the differences between people, psychologists use the concept of **personality**.

> **KEY TERM**
>
> **Personality** is the total pattern of characteristic ways of thinking, feeling and behaving that constitute the individual's distinctive method of relating to the environment.

1.3 Personality develops from dynamic processes whereby the individual interacts with the environment and other people, through experience.

   (a) **Self-image.** If people regularly praise your hard work, for example, you may have an image of yourself as a successful worker. People tend to behave, and expect to be treated, in accordance with their self-image.

   (b) **Personality development.** People tend, as they mature, to become more actively independent, to take on more equal or superior relationships (moving from child-adult, to adult-adult and adult-child relationships) and to develop self control and self awareness.

1.4 Attempts to describe the 'components' of personality, or the ways people differ, focus on two broad concepts: traits and types.

   (a) Personality **traits** are relatively stable, enduring qualities of an individual's personality which cause a tendency to behave in particular ways. If we say that someone is 'impulsive', for example, we are identifying one of his personality traits. This trait will make him tend to respond to situations in habitual ways: for example, by making rapid decisions and taking immediate liking to people.

   (b) Personality **types** are distinct clusters of personality characteristics, which reflect the psychological preferences of the individual. If we say that someone is an 'extravert', for example, we may be suggesting that they are sociable, expressive, impulsive, practical and active. An 'introvert', by contrast, is unsociable, inhibited, controlled, reflective and inactive.

1.5 The well-known **Myers Briggs Type Inventory** is based on detailed analysis of personality types. The aim of the inventory (and the value of personality theories to managers) is:

   (a) To provide a shared language with which people can discuss and explore individual uniqueness (their own natural style) and ways of developing to their full potential

   (b) To help people to understand areas of difference which might otherwise be the source of misunderstanding and mis-communication, and

   (c) To encourage people to appreciate diversity by highlighting the value and complementary contributions of all personality types

Part C: Management theory, principles and techniques

Activity 10.1

How is your personality 'cut out' to be an accountant? This is not a technical question: it merely invites you to think about your personality traits – and stereotypes about the 'type of person' who chooses to be an accountant or makes a good accountant.

1.6 An individual's personality should be compatible with his or her work requirements in three ways.

Compatibility	Comments
With the **task**	Different personality types suit different types of work. A person who appears unsociable and inhibited will find sales work, involving a lot of social interactions, intensely stressful - and will probably not be very good at it.
With the **systems** and **management culture** of the organisation	Some people hate to be controlled, for example, but others want to be controlled and dependent in a work situation, because they find responsibility threatening.
With other **personalities** in the team	Personality clashes are a prime source of conflict at work. An achievement-oriented personality, for example, tends to be a perfectionist, is impatient and unable to relax, and will be unsociable if people seem to be getting in the way of performance: such a person will clearly be frustrated and annoyed by laid-back sociable types working (or not working) around him.

1.7 Where incompatibilities occur, the manager or supervisor has three options.

(a) **Restore compatibility**: this may be achieved by reassigning an individual to tasks more suited to his personality type, for example, or changing management style to suit the personalities of the team.

(b) **Achieve a compromise**: individuals should be encouraged to:

  (i) **Understand the nature** of their differences. Others have the right to be themselves (within the demands of the team); personal differences should not be taken personally, as if they were adopted deliberately to annoy.

  (ii) **Modify their behaviour** if necessary.

(c) **Remove the incompatible personality**. In the last resort, obstinately difficult or disruptive people may simply have to be weeded out of the team.

Perception

KEY TERM

Perception is the psychological process by which stimuli or in-coming sensory data are selected and organised into patterns which are meaningful to the individual.

1.8 Perception may be determined by any or all of the following.

(a) **The context**. People see what they want to see: whatever is necessary or relevant in the situation in which they find themselves. You might notice articles on management in the newspapers while studying this module which normally you would not notice.

(b) **The nature of the stimuli**. Our attention tends to be drawn to large, bright, loud, unfamiliar, moving and repeated stimuli. Advertisers know it.

(c) **Internal factors**. Our attention is drawn to stimuli that match our personality, needs, interests, expectations and so on. If you are hungry, for example, you will pick the smell of food out of a mix of aromas. Similarly, people are able to avoid seeing things that they don't want to see: things that are threatening to their security of self-image, or things that are too painful for them.

1.9 People do not respond to the world as it really is, but as they **perceive it to be**. If people act in ways that seem illogical or contrary to you, it is probably because they simply do not see things in the same way you do.

(a) Consider whether **you** might be misinterpreting the situation

(b) Consider whether **others** might be misinterpreting the situation or interpreting it differently from you

(c) When tackling a task or a problem get the people involved to **define the situation** as they see it

(d) Be aware of the most common clashes of perception at work

    (i) **Managers and staff.** The experience of work can be very different for managerial and non-managerial personnel. Efforts to bridge the gap may be viewed with suspicion.

    (ii) **Work cultures.** Different functions in organisations may have very different time-scales and cultures of work, and will therefore perceive the work, and each other, in different ways.

    (iii) **Race and sex.** A joke, comment or gesture that one person may see as amusing may be offensive - and construed as harassment under the law - to another.

Activity 10.2

Identify the perceptual problem(s) in the following cases.

(a) An autocratic manager tries to adopt a more participative style of management, in order to improve the morale of his staff. He tells them they will be given more responsibility, and will be 'judged and rewarded accordingly'. For some reason, morale seems to worsen, and several people ask to transfer to other departments.

(b) A woman has just be promoted to the management team. At the first management meeting, the chairman introduces her to her new colleagues - all male - and says: 'At least we'll get some decent tea in these meetings from now on, eh?' Almost everyone laughs. For some reason, the woman does not contribute much in the meeting, and the chairman later tells one of his colleagues: 'I hope we haven't made a mistake. She doesn't seem to be a team player at all.'

(c) A new employee wanders into the office canteen, and is offered a cup of coffee by a youngster in jeans and a T-shirt, who has been chatting to the canteen supervisor. The youngster joins the man at his table (to his surprise) and asks how he likes working there so far. After a while, glancing uneasily at the man behind the serving counter, the new employee asks: 'Is it OK for you to be sitting here talking to me? I mean, won't the boss mind?' The youngster replies: 'I am the boss. Actually, I'm the boss of the whole company. Biscuit?'

Part C: Management theory, principles and techniques

2 GROUPS AT WORK

2.1 As an employee your relationship with the organisation is as an individual: after all, the employment contract is with you as an individual, and you are recruited as an individual. In your working life, though, you will generally find yourself working as part of a **group** or **team**. Teamworking and team management are discussed in Chapter 11. Here, we will merely highlight some of the distinctive features of group behaviour (as opposed to individual behaviour) at work.

Groups

> **KEY TERM**
>
> A **group** is 'any number of people who (1) interact with one another; (2) are psychologically aware of one another; and (3) perceive themselves to be a group.'
>
> *(Schein)*

2.2 Groups have certain attributes that a random 'crowd' does not possess.

(a) **A sense of identity**. There are acknowledged **boundaries** to the group which define who is 'in' and who is 'out', who is 'us' and who is 'them'.

(b) **A sense of inclusion and belonging. Loyalty to the group,** and acceptance within the group. This expresses as **cohesion**, or solidarity, and as **conformity**, or the acceptance of shared norms of behaviour and attitudes within the group.

(c) **Interdependence and interaction.** Group processes (such as communication and decision-making) are aimed at **collaborative activity** in pursuit of **shared purposes**.

2.3 People in organisations will be drawn together into groups by a variety of forces.

- A **preference for small networks,** where closer relationships can develop
- The **need to belong** and to make a contribution that will be noticed and appreciated
- **Familiarity:** a shared office or canteen
- **Common** rank, specialisms, objectives and interests
- The attractiveness of a particular group **activity** (joining an interesting club, say)
- **Resources** offered to groups (for example sports facilities)
- **Power** greater than the individuals could muster alone (trade union, pressure group)
- **Formal** directives

2.4 **Informal** groups will invariably be present in any organisation. Informal groups include workplace cliques, and networks of people who regularly get together to exchange information or groups of 'mates' who socialise outside work. They have a constantly fluctuating membership and structure.

2.5 **Formal** groups will be consciously organised by the organisation, for a task which they are held responsible - they are task oriented, and become **teams**. Although many people enjoy working in teams, their popularity in the work place arises because of their effectiveness in fulfilling the organisation's work.

Activity 10.3

What groups are you a member of in your study or work environment(s)? How big are these groups? How does the size of your class, study group, work-team – or whatever – affect your ability to come up with questions or ideas and give you the help and support to do something you couldn't do alone?

What is group behaviour?

2.6 Being in a group affects how individuals behave. (You may have seen this in its extreme form in very large groups, such as crowds at sporting events.) Again, we will just look at a few concepts which might be helpful to a manager or team member wanting to understand what is 'going on' in a team.

Social influence

2.7 **Social influence** is the way in which the presence (and even the implied or imagined presence of other people) influences the attitudes, beliefs, decisions and actions of an individual.

(a) Individuals often perform tasks better in the presence of others who are observing or working on the same task. This effect is known as **social facilitation**. The presence of others appears to facilitate (make easier) the performance of a task: the individual wants to make a good impression. This helps to explain the positive synergistic effect of group working: people working in groups can often accomplish more than the same individuals working alone.

(b) On the other hand, individuals in a group tend to exert less effort when they feel they are pooling their efforts toward attaining a common goal than when they feel they are individually accountable: they feel less accountable, or as if their contribution is less needed (or not fairly rewarded) or they feel they could work more efficiently on their own. As the size of the group increases, individual effort decreases: this effect is known as **social loafing**.

Activity 10.4

What might you do to address the problem of negative social facilitation if you identified it in your work team?

What might you do to address the problem of social loafing if you identified it in your work team?

Group influence

2.8 **Group influence** is the way in which interactions and dynamics within the group affect how individuals behave.

(a) **Group conformity**

Groups formally or informally establish **group norms**: ways of thinking and behaving to which all members of the group are expected to conform. This helps the group to function, by letting everyone know the kinds of behaviour that are acceptable in a given context: it avoids embarrassment and preserves the cohesion of the group. Conformity to group norms may be:

(i) **Positively reinforced** (eg by allowing the individual to feel that he belongs and is accepted by the group and has access to its rewards) or

(ii) **Negatively reinforced** (eg by threatening the individual with ridicule, rejection or expulsion from the group if he fails to conform).

(b) **Group cohesion**

Cohesion is the sum of all the forces that attract members to the group and motivate them to remain part of it: it is associated with group solidarity, loyalty and identity. (Cohesion is discussed in more detail below.)

(c) **Group polarisation**

If a group is like-minded, discussion will tend to amplify or strengthen its prevailing tendencies and attitudes. This can distort group discussion and decision-making, resulting in the tendency of groups to take greater risks (known as **risky-shift**) or fewer risks (**cautious-shift**) than the individual members would do on their own.

2.9 **Group cohesion** is considered a key positive factor in group performance and member satisfaction. It strengthens the shared commitment to collaborative activity that is the key to teamworking. However, there are drawbacks to group cohesion.

(a) It increases group influence and conformity – which may be positive or negative, depending on the norms of the group. (Groups can work together to undermine a manager's authority, or to reduce work output to manipulate incentive schemes, say.)

(b) It demands attention to group maintenance and priorities, diverting energy and attention away from the task and organisational goals.

2.10 A very cohesive group can become blinkered to outside information and feedback, to the point where its decision-making processes are dangerously distorted. Irving Janis described this phenomenon as **group think**: 'the psychological drive for consensus at any cost, that suppresses dissent and appraisal of alternatives in cohesive decision-making groups'. Symptoms of group think include:

(a) Resistance to criticism, contradiction and new information (from inside or outside the group)

(b) Strong group pressure for all members to 'toe the line'

(c) A sense of invulnerability, blinding the group to problems and risks

(d) A tendency to stereotype all outsiders as competitors and enemies

(e) Poor – because persistently uncriticised – decision-making

Group process

2.11 **Group process** refers to what is happening to and between group members while the group is working. Observing group process (how people contribute, how they communicate, how they go about negotiating decisions and so on) highlights issues such as group morale, atmosphere, influence, participation, leadership, conflict, competition and co-operation. These observations can be used to diagnose potential blockages and barriers to successful team working.

2.12 Some key components of group process include the following.

Stages of group development	Groups develop over time: different issues and dynamics confront the group at different stages of its life. (Group development models are discussed in Chapter 11.)
Role differentiation	In an effectively functioning group, members find and adopt a role or set of roles that works for them and for the group, according to task and group maintenance requirements. (Group roles are discussed in Chapter 11.)
Communication/ interaction	Effectively functioning groups tend to move from a leader-centred, leader-initiated pattern of communication to one where interaction is multi-directional, including all members.
Task and maintenance	Effectively functioning groups achieve a balance between meeting individual needs (satisfaction and contribution), group needs (achieving and maintaining cohesion) and task needs (meeting objectives).
Decision-making	In an effectively functioning group, decision-making will become less leader-centred: processes for constructive problem-solving will be carried out with appropriate member involvement and information sharing (without degenerating into group think).

3 INDIVIDUAL AND TEAM CONTRIBUTION

3.1 Individuals and teams are the building blocks of organisations.

3.2 Teams are particularly well adapted to fulfilling the following purposes.

Type of role	Comments
Work organisation	Teams combine the skills of different individuals.
	Teams are a co-ordinating mechanism: they avoid complex communication between different business functions.
Control	Fear of letting down the team can be a powerful motivator: group norms and expectations can be used to control the performance and behaviour of individuals.
Ideas generation	Teams can generate ideas, eg through brainstorming and information sharing.
Decision-making	Decisions are evaluated from more than one viewpoint, with pooled information. Teams make fewer, but better-evaluated, decisions than individuals.

3.3 Teams and teamworking are very much in fashion, but there are potential drawbacks.

(a) Teamworking is not suitable for all jobs.

(b) Teamwork should be introduced because it leads to better performance, not because people feel better or more secure.

(c) Team processes (especially seeking consensus) can delay good decision-making. The team might produce the compromise decision, not the right decision.

(d) Social relationships might be maintained at the expense of other aspects of performance.

Part C: Management theory, principles and techniques

(e) Group norms may restrict individual personality and flair.

(f) Group think: team consensus and cohesion may prevent consideration of alternatives or constructive criticism.

(g) Personality clashes and political behaviour within a team can get in the way of effective performance.

Activity 10.5

Identify some differences between your contribution as an individual to your organisation and your contribution as a team member.

4 ORGANISATION CULTURE

What is 'culture'?

> **KEY TERM**
>
> **Culture**: the collective programming of the mind which distinguishes the members of one category of people from another'.
>
> *(Hofstede)*

4.1 Culture may be identified as ways of behaving, and ways of understanding, that are shared by a group of people. Schein referred to it as: 'The way we do things round here.'

4.2 Culture can be discussed on many different levels. The 'category' or 'group' of people whose shared behaviours and meanings may constitute a culture include:

- A nation, region or ethnic group
- Women versus men ('gender culture')
- A social class (eg 'working class culture')
- A profession or occupation
- A type of business (eg 'advertising culture')
- An organisation ('**organisational culture**')

If you are a male (or female) accountant in an organisation operating in a given business sector in a particular region of your country of residence (which may not be your country of origin), you may be influenced by all these different spheres of culture!

4.3 Trompenaars suggested that in fact there are different levels at which culture can be understood.

(a) The **observable**, expressed or 'explicit' elements of culture include:

(i) **Behaviour**: norms of personal and interpersonal behaviour; customs and rules about behaviours that are 'acceptable' or unacceptable.

(ii) **Artefacts**: concrete expressions such as art and literature, architecture and interior design (eg of office premises), dress codes, symbols and 'heroes' or role models.

(iii) **Rituals**: patterns of collective behaviour which have traditional or symbolic value, such as greeting styles, business formalities, social courtesies and ceremonies.

(b) Beneath these observable phenomena lie **values and beliefs** which give the behaviours, artefacts and rituals their special meaning and significance. For example, the design of office space (artefact) may imply status and honour, or reflect the importance of privacy, or reflect spiritual beliefs (as in feng shui) within a culture: it 'means' more than the observable features. Values and beliefs may be overtly expressed in sayings, mottos and slogans.

(c) Beneath values and beliefs lie **assumptions**: foundational ideas that are no longer consciously recognised or questioned by the culture, but which 'programme' its ways of thinking and behaving. Examples include the importance of the individual in many Western cultures: this is taken for granted in designing HR (human resources) policies, for example.

4.4 Cultural assumptions, values and beliefs influence the behaviour of individuals, groups and organisations. They create a shared 'style' of operating within a given culture – but also the potential for misunderstanding and conflict between different cultural groups.

Organisation culture

> **KEY TERM**
>
> **Organisation culture** may be defined as the complex body of shared beliefs, attitudes and values that shape behavioural norms in an organisation.

4.5 Layers of culture, following Trompenaars' elements, include the following.

Item	Example
Beliefs and values, which are often unquestioned	'The customer is always right'
Behaviour	In the City of London, standard business dress is still generally taken for granted and even 'dress down Fridays' have their rules.
Artefacts	**Microsoft** encourages communication between employees by setting aside informal spaces for the purpose.
Rituals	In some firms, sales people compete with each other, and there is a reward, given at a ceremony, for the salesperson who does best in any period.
Symbols	Corporate logos are an example of symbols, but they are directed outwards. Within the organisation, symbols can represent power: dress, make and model of car, office size and equipment and access to facilities can all be important symbols.

4.6 **Manifestations of culture** in an organisation may thus include:

- **Communication:** formality, open-ness
- Office **layout** and decor
- The type of **people** employed
- **Symbols, legends,** corporate **myths**

Part C: Management theory, principles and techniques

- **Management** style
- **Freedom** for subordinates to show initiative
- Attitudes to **quality**
- Attitudes to **risk**
- Attitudes to the **customer**
- Attitudes to **technology**

Activity 10.6

What do you think would differentiate the culture of:

- A regiment in the Army
- An advertising agency?

What shapes organisation culture?

4.7 **Influences on organisational culture**:

(a) The organisation's **founder**. A strong set of values and assumptions is set up by the organisation's founder, and even after he or she has retired, these values have their own momentum. Or, to put it another way, an organisation might find it hard to shake off its original culture.

(b) The organisation's **history**.

   (i) Culture reflects the **era when the organisation was founded**.

   (ii) The effect of history can be determined by **stories, rituals and symbolic behaviour**. They legitimise behaviour and promote priorities.

(c) **Leadership and management style**. An organisation with a strong culture recruits managers who naturally conform to it, who perpetuate the culture.

(d) The **organisation's environment**. As we have seen, nations, regions, occupations and business types have their own distinctive cultures, and these will affect the organisation's style.

Culture and structure

4.8 Writing in 1972, Roger Harrison suggested that organisations could be classified into four types. His work was later popularised by Charles **Handy** in his book 'Gods of Management'. The four types are differentiated by their structures, processes and management methods. The differences are so significant as to create **distinctive cultures**, to each of which Handy gives the name of a Greek God.

4.9 **Zeus** is the god representing the **power culture** or **club culture**. Zeus is a dynamic entrepreneur who rules with snap decisions. Power and influence stem from a central source, perhaps the owner-directors or the founder of the business. The degree of formalisation is limited, and there are few rules and procedures. Such a firm is likely to be organised on a **functional** basis.

(a) The organisation is capable of adapting quickly to meet change.

(b) Personal influence decreases as the size of an organisation gets bigger. The power culture is therefore best suited to smaller entrepreneurial organisations, where the leaders have direct communication with all employees.

(c) Personnel have to get on well with each other for this culture to work. These organisations are clubs of 'like-minded people introduced by the like-minded people, working on empathetic initiative with personal contact rather than formal liaison.'

4.10 **Apollo** is the god of the **role culture** or bureaucracy. There is a presumption of logic and rationality.

(a) These organisations have a formal structure, and operate by well-established rules and procedures. Individuals are required to perform their job to the full, but not to overstep the boundaries of their authority. Individuals who work for such organisations tend to learn an expertise without experiencing risk; many do their job adequately, but are not over-ambitious.

(b) The bureaucratic style can be very efficient in a stable environment, when the organisation is large and when the work is predictable.

4.11 **Athena** is the goddess of the **task culture.** Management is seen as completing a succession of projects or solving problems.

(a) The task culture is reflected in project teams and task forces. In such organisations, there is no dominant or clear leader. The principal concern in a task culture is to get the job done. Therefore the individuals who are important are the experts with the ability to accomplish a particular aspect of the task.

(b) Performance is judged by **results**.

(c) Task cultures are expensive, as experts demand a market price.

(d) Task cultures also depend on variety, and to tap creativity requires a tolerance of perhaps costly mistakes.

4.12 **Dionysus** is the god of the **existential** or **person culture**. In the three other cultures, the individual is subordinate to the organisation or task. An existential culture is found in an organisation whose purpose is to serve the interests of the individuals within it. These organisations are rare, although an example might be a partnership of a few individuals who do all the work of the organisation themselves (with perhaps a little secretarial or clerical assistance).

(a) Barristers (in the UK) work through chambers. The clerk co-ordinates their work and hands out briefs, but does not control them.

(b) Management in these organisations are often lower in status than the professionals and are labelled secretaries, administrators, bursars, registrars and chief clerk.

(c) The organisation depends on the **talent of the individuals**; management is derived from the consent of the managed, rather than the delegated authority of the owners.

Part C: Management theory, principles and techniques

Activity 10.7

Review the following statements. Ascribe each of them to one of Handy's four corporate cultures.

People are controlled and influenced by:

(a) The personal exercise of rewards, punishments or charisma

(b) Impersonal exercise of economic and political power to enforce procedures and standards of performance

(c) Communication and discussion of task requirements leading to appropriate action motivated by personal commitment to goal achievement

(d) Intrinsic interest and enjoyment in the activities to be done, and/or concern and caring for the needs of the other people involved

The importance of culture

4.13 In 1982, Tom Peters and Robert Waterman published *In Search of Excellence*. Using an anecdotal approach, they set about describing and analysing what it was that made successful companies successful.

Excellent companies, according to Peters and Waterman, are good at two things:

- Producing commercially viable **new products**
- Responding to **changes in their environment**

4.14 A feature of excellent companies was their use of **cultural values** to guide business processes and motivate employees.

(a) Cultural norms can replace rules and guidelines, focusing on output values such as quality and customer service, and freeing employees to make more flexible decisions in pursuit of those values.

(b) Valued cultural symbols can be used as rewards and incentives, to help employees feel 'heroic' in pursuing organisational aims.

(c) Cultural values can be used to drive organisational change, on the basis that if values change, behaviour will follow.

Changing the organisation culture

4.15 A rigid culture can make an organisation inflexible, unable to learn or adapt, and a victim of entrenched negative cultural values (such as information hoarding, sticking to rules for their own sake, industrial conflict and so on).

4.16 Kilmann suggests the following steps for closing 'culture gaps'.

Step 1. Find out about what norms and values are currently present. In other words, find out about attitudes toward performance/excellence, teamwork, communication, leadership, profitability, staff relations, customer relations, honesty and security, training and innovation. This can be done through attitude surveys, interviews and managerial listening!

Step 2. Decide the ways in which norms need to be changed

Step 3. Establish new norms. This needs:

- Top management commitment
- Leadership by example

- Support for positive behaviour and confrontation of negative behaviour
- Consistency between the reward system and positive behaviour
- Clear communication of desired norms
- Recruitment and selection of people who fit the new norms
- Induction programmes for new employees on the desired norms
- Training and skills development in line with the new norms

Key learning points

- **Personality** is the total pattern of an individual's thoughts, feelings and behaviours.
- **Perception** is the process by which the brain selects and organises information in order to make sense of it. People behave according to what they perceive – not according to the world as it 'really is'.
- A **group** is a collection of individuals who (1) interact with one another, (2) are psychologically aware of one another and (3) perceive themselves to be a group.
- Individuals behave differently in groups than they do working separately, due to factors such as:
    - **Social influence**: the effect of the presence of others on individual behaviour (such as social facilitation and social loafing)
    - **Group influence**: the effect of group dynamics on individual behaviour (such as conformity, cohesion and polarisation)
    - **Group process**: group formation, role differentiation, communication/interaction, task and maintenance functions and group decision-making.
- Individuals and groups **contribute** differently to the organisation. While teamworking is highly fashionable, it can be less effective than individual contribution, due to effects such as **group think**, risky shift, the need for consensus in decision-making and so on.
- **Culture** is 'the collective programming of the mind which distinguishes the members of one category of people from another' (including organisations).
- **Elements of culture** include observable behaviour, artefacts, rituals and symbols; underlying values and beliefs; hidden assumptions.
- **Types of culture**, and related structures, were identified by Harrison and Handy as follows.
    - Power culture (Zeus)
    - Role culture (Apollo)
    - Task culture (Athena)
    - Existential or person culture (Dionysus)
- **Cultural values** can be used:
    - to guide organisational processes without the need for tight controls
    - to motivates employees, by emphasising the heroic dimension of the task
    - to drive change (although they can also be a powerful force for preserving the status quo).

Quick quiz

1. List three factors for a manager to consider in managing 'personality' at work.
2. Give three examples of areas where people's perceptions commonly conflict.
3. What is 'social loafing'?
4. List the arguments for and against group cohesion.
5. What three types of needs should be balanced in an effectively functioning group?
6. What types of work are groups particularly good at?

Part C: Management theory, principles and techniques

7   What are the elements of culture, according to Trompenaars?

8   'Bureaucracy' might be another name for a:

    A   Power culture
    B   Role culture
    C   Task culture
    D   Existential culture

9   A project team is most likely to be a role culture. True or false?

Answers to quick quiz

1   The compatibility of the individual's personality with the task, with the systems and culture of the organisation and with other members of the team.

2   Managers and staff, work culture, race, gender

3   Social loafing is the tendency of individuals to exert less effort when they feel they are pooling their efforts toward attaining a common goal.

4   For cohesion: positive factor in group performance and member satisfaction; strengthens the shared commitment to collaborative activity (teamworking); strengthens group conformity to positive values

    Against cohesion: strengthens group conformity to negative values; diverts energy from the task; risk of group think and poor decision-making

5   Individual, group maintenance, task achievement

6   Work organisation, control, ideas generation, decision-making

7   Observable phenomena (behaviour, artefacts, rituals), values and beliefs, assumptions

8   B

9   False: it is most likely to be a task culture

Answers to activities

Answer 10.1

Your own thoughts.

Answer 10.2

The perceptual problems in the situations given are as follows.

(a) The manager perceives himself as 'enlightened', and his style as an opportunity and gift to his staff. he clearly thinks that assessment and reward on the basis of more responsibility is a positive thing, probably offering greater rewards to staff. He does not perceive his use of the work 'judged' as potentially threatening: he uses it as another word for 'assessed'. His staff obviously see things differently. 'More responsibility' means their competence - maybe their jobs - are on the line. Feeling this way, and with the expectations they have of their boss (based on past experience of his autocratic style), they are bound to perceive the work 'judged' as threatening.

(b) The chairman thinks he is being funny. Maybe he is only joking about the woman making the tea - but he may really perceive her role that way. He lacks the perception that his new colleague may find his remark offensive. From the woman's point of view, she is bound to be sensitive and insecure in her first meeting and with all male colleague: small wonder that, joke or not, she perceives the chairman's comment as a slap in the face. The chairman later fails to perceive the effect his joke has had on her, assuming that her silence is a sign of poor co-operation or inability to communicate.

(c) This is a case of closure leading to misinterpretation. The new employee sees the informal dress, the position behind the counter, and the offer of coffee: his brain fills in the gaps, and offers the perception that the youngster must be the tea-boy. Perceptual selectivity also plays a part filtering out awkward information that does not fit his expectations (like the fact that the 'tea-boy' comes to chat with him).

Answer 10.3

The primary groups are probably your tutor group or class. If at work, it would be the section in which you work. If the groups are large, you may feel reluctant to put forward ideas or ask questions, but even within a large group you should feel there is support and that help is at hand if you need it.

Answer 10.4

Once you are aware of negative social facilitation, you may decide to 'back off' when someone is performing a complex task which they have not yet mastered, and to encourage others to do so: clear up any impression the person may have that (s)he is being 'watched'.

Once you are aware of social loafing, you might attempt to: bring loafing into the open and challenge the perception that 'everyone's doing it'; make it clear that each member of the group is accountable for pulling his or her weight; highlight members' individual contributions, so they do not think they can loaf unnoticed; positive reinforce (praise, reward) contribution.

Answer 10.5

Individuals contribute:	Groups contribute:
• A set of skills	• A mix of skills
• Objectives set by manager	• Some teams can set their own objectives under the corporate framework
• A point of view	• A number of different points of view, enabling a swift overview of different ways of looking at a problem
• Creative ideas related to the individual's expertise	• Creative ideas arising from new combinations of expertise
• 'I can't be in two places at once'	• Flexibility as team members can be deployed in different ways
• Limited opportunity for self-criticism	• Opportunity for exercising control

Answer 10.6

Here are some hints. The Army is very disciplined. Decisions are made by officers; behaviour between ranks is sometimes very formal. The organisation values loyalty, courage and discipline and team work. Symbols and artefacts include uniforms, medals, regimental badges and so on. Rituals include imitations, parades and ceremonies.

An advertising agency, with a different mission, is more fluid. Individual flair and creativity, within the commercial needs of the firm, is expected. Artefacts may include the style of creative offices, awards or prizes, and the agency logo. Rituals may include various award ceremonies, team meetings and social gatherings.

Answer 10.7

(a) Zeus
(b) Apollo
(c) Athena
(d) Dionysus

Now try Question 9 in the Exam Question Bank

Chapter 11   Team management

Chapter topic list

1. Teams
2. Team formation and roles
3. Development of the team
4. Team building
5. Team evaluation and rewards

The following study sessions are covered in this chapter:

		Syllabus reference
12(a)	Define the purpose of a team	3(c)
12(b)	Outline the composition of successful teams	3(c)
12(c)	Explain the stages in team development	3(c)
12(d)	Identify and explain team building techniques and blockages	3(c)
12(e)	Describe the main ways of rewarding a team	3(c)
12(f)	Identify appropriate methods to evaluate team performance	3(c)

1 TEAMS

> **KEY TERM**
>
> A **team** is a 'small number of people with *complementary skills* who are committed to a *common* purpose, performance goals and approach, for which they hold themselves *mutually accountable*.' (Katzenbach & Smith)

1.1 The basic **work units** of organisations have traditionally been specialised functional departments. In more recent times, as discussed in Chapter 2, organisations have adopted smaller, more flexible units. **Teamworking** allows work to be shared among a number of individuals, so that it gets done faster and with a greater range of skills and information than by individuals working alone.

1.2 A team may be called together temporarily, to achieve specific task objectives (**project team**), or may be more or less permanent, with responsibilities for a particular product, product group or stage of the production process (a **product** or **process team**).

1.3 There are two basic approaches to the organisation of team work: multi-disciplinary teams and multi-skilled teams.

Multi-disciplinary teams

1.4 Multi-disciplinary teams bring together individuals with different skills and specialisms so that their skills, experience and knowledge can be pooled or exchanged. Such teams are typically project-, customer- or product-focused and represent **matrix** structures (discussed in Chapter 2).

1.5 Multi-disciplinary teams:

(a) Increase workers' awareness of their overall objectives and targets

(b) Aid co-ordination and communication across functional boundaries

(c) Help to generate new ideas and solutions to problems, since the team has access to more perspectives and 'pieces of the jigsaw'.

Multi-skilled teams

1.6 A multi-skilled team brings together a number of individuals who can perform any of the group's tasks. These tasks can then be shared out in a more flexible way between group members, according to who is available and best placed to do a given job at the time it is required.

1.7 Multiskilling is the cornerstone of team empowerment, since it cuts across the barriers of job descriptions and demarcations to enable teams to respond flexibly to changing demands.

Self-managed teams

1.8 Self-managed teams are the most highly-developed form of team working. They are permanent structures in which team members **collaboratively decide** all the major issues affecting their work: work processes and schedules, task allocation, the selection and development of team members, the distribution of rewards and the management of group processes (problem-solving, conflict management, internal discipline and so on). The **team leader** is a member of the team, acting in the role of coach and facilitator: leadership roles may be shared or rotated as appropriate.

1.9 **Self-managed teamworking** is said to have advantages in:

(a) Saving managerial costs

(b) Gains in quality and productivity, by harnessing the commitment of those who perform the work

(c) Encouraging individual initiative and responsibility, enhancing organisational responsiveness (particularly in front-line customer-facing units)

(d) Gains in efficiency, through multi-skilling, the involvement of fewer functions in decision-making and co-ordinating work, and (often) the streamlining of working methods by groups.

Virtual teams

1.10 The development of Information and Communications Technology (ICT) has enabled communication and collaboration among people in remote locations, via teleconferencing and video-conferencing, locally networked PCs and the World Wide Web. This has created the concept of the 'virtual team': an interconnected group of people who may never be present in the same office – and may even be on different sides of the world – but who share information and tasks, make joint decisions and fulfil the collaborative functions of a 'physical' team.

1.11 Localised virtual teams have been used for some time in the form of 'teleworking': the process of working from home, or from a satellite office, with the aid of computers, fax machine, modems, mobile phones and other forms of telecommunication equipment.

1.12 Members of virtual teams have to consider the following concerns.

(a) Team members need to develop trust that people will perform when they're away from direct supervision.

(b) Team members need to be self-motivated, able to work without detailed instruction or structure, and strong communications.

(c) Team leaders need to set up regular 'virtual meetings' to share expectations, objectives and debriefings, and to provide ongoing monitoring and honest feedback about how the team is doing.

Applications of team working

1.13 The collaborative nature of teams makes them particularly effective for **increasing communication**, generating new ideas and evaluating ideas from different viewpoints. Common applications of teamworking therefore include the following.

(a) **Problem-solving or brainstorming groups**: generating creative ideas for problem-solving and innovation. Small groups of people are invited to contribute ideas, without any initial evaluation or censorship: this freedom encourages people to 'bounce' ideas off each other and build on each other's ideas, creating more innovative ideas than would otherwise be possible.

(b) **Quality and service circles**: drawing people together from different disciplines to share ideas about quality and service issues. This has been a popular technique in involving employees at different levels of the organisation in quality assurance, as part of a Total Quality Management (TQM) orientation. Such discussions are said to result not only in specific suggestions for quality improvements, but to a greater awareness and discussion of performance issues in the organisation, and to higher morale in employees. Similar options include **health and safety circles** and other groups that meet regular to discuss matters of concern.

(c) **Project teams**: set up to handle particular tasks or projects. This enables a range of cross-functional expertise to collaborate on a project, creating a 'horizontal' organisation. In the case of **account teams**, dedicated to particular customers or clients (eg advertising agency accounts), this offers the customer a more satisfying 'horizontal' experience of the organisation than having to be constantly transferred between departments.

(d) **Representative groups**: set up to discuss and put forward the views of interest groups in the organisation. An employee representative team (a works council, the local branch of a trade union or staff association, say) might consult and negotiate with management, for example, representing the views and interests of employees. This is often an important channel of upward communication, so that management can benefit from 'grass roots' knowledge of issues at the front line of the organisation.

(e) **Briefing groups**: allowing information and instructions to be presented to a number of people together.

Activity 11.1

What functions do teams perform in your own organisation? List a number of different teams of which you are aware (or perhaps a member). What is their function – and why is this function most effectively performed by a team (as opposed to individuals working on their own)?

2 TEAM FORMATION AND ROLES

Putting the team together

2.1 R Meredith Belbin, one of the most influential modern writers on teams, identifies a number of basic steps in the early stages of team building.

(a) **Articulating the purpose** and terms of reference of the team: setting clear and meaningful goals

(b) **Selecting team membership** and 'casting' team members in appropriate roles

(c) **Deciding the 'style'** in which the team will operate: whether through meetings, independent working, working in pairs – or whatever suits the members.

2.2 Team members may be pre-selected as representatives of specific functions/departments or interest groups. Members may be **selected** on the basis of:

(a) The skills, knowledge and expertise required by the task

(b) Power or influence in the wider organisation, required to champion the team's interests or to mobilise resources

(c) The skills required for task processes: skills in stimulating discussion, skills in checking and attending to detail, skills in implementation and follow-through

Part C: Management theory, principles and techniques

(d) The skills required for teamworking: skills in discussion, conflict resolution and so on.

2.3 Belbin suggested that process roles – the ways people contribute to discussion, decision-making and teamworking – are at least as important as functional roles: whether a person is an accounting, marketing or technical expert.

Belbin: Team roles

2.4 Belbin researched business game teams at the Henley Management College and drew up a widely-used framework for understanding roles within work groups. He identifies nine team roles.

Role and description	Team-role contribution	Allowable weaknesses
Plant Creative, imaginative, unorthodox	Solves difficult problems	Ignores details, too preoccupied to communicate effectively
Resource investigator Extrovert, enthusiastic, communicative	Explores opportunities, develops contacts	Over-optimistic, loses interest once initial enthusiasm has passed
Co-ordinator Mature, confident, a good chairperson	Clarifies goals, promotes decision-making, delegates well	Can be seen as manipulative, delegates personal work
Shaper Challenging, dynamic, thrives on pressure	Has the drive and courage to overcome obstacles	Can provoke others, hurts people's feelings
Monitor evaluator Sober, strategic and discerning	Sees all options, judges accurately	Lacks drive and ability to inspire others, overly critical
Teamworker Co-operative, mild, perceptive and diplomatic	Listens, builds, averts friction, calms the waters	Indecisive in crunch situations, can be easily influenced
Implementer Disciplined, reliable, conservative and efficient	Turns ideas into practical actions	Somewhat inflexible, slow to respond to new possibilities
Completer Painstaking, conscientious, anxious	Searches out errors and omissions, delivers on time	Inclined to worry unduly, reluctant to delegate, can be a nitpicker
Specialist Single-minded, self-starting, dedicated	Provides knowledge and skills in rare supply	Contributes only on a narrow front, dwells on technicalities, overlooks the 'big picture'

11: Team management

2.5 These team roles are not fixed within any given individual. Team members can occupy more than one role, or switch to 'backup' roles if required: hence, there is no requirement for every team to have nine members. However, since role preferences are based on personality, it should be recognised that:

- Individuals will be naturally inclined towards some roles more than others
- Individuals will tend to adopt one or two team roles more or less consistently
- Individuals are likely to be more successful in some roles than in others

2.6 The nine roles are complementary, and Belbin suggested that an 'ideal' team should represent a **mix or balance** of all of them. If managers know employees' team role preferences, they can strategically select, 'cast' and develop team members to fulfil the required roles.

2.7 Belbin insists that a sharp distinction needs to be made between:

(a) **Team role** ('a tendency to behave, contribute and interrelate with others at work in certain distinctive ways'), and

(b) **Functional role** ('the job demands that a person has been engaged to meet by supplying the requisite technical skills and operational knowledge')

Activity 11.2

The following phrases and slogans project certain team roles: identify which. (Examples drawn from Belbin, 1993.)

(a) The small print is always worth reading.
(b) Let's get down to the task in hand.
(c) In this job you never stop learning.
(d) Without continuous innovation, there is no survival.
(e) Surely we can exploit that?
(f) When the going gets tough, the tough get going.
(g) I was very interested in your point of view.
(h) Has anyone else got anything to add to this?
(i) Decisions should not be based purely on enthusiasm.

How do people contribute?

2.8 In order to evaluate and manage team dynamics, it may be helpful for the team leader to:

(a) Assess who (if anybody) is performing each of Belbin's **team roles**. Who is the team's plant? co-ordinator? monitor-evaluator? and so on. There should be a mix of people performing task and team maintenance roles.

(b) Analyse the frequency and type of **individual members' contributions** to group discussions and interactions.

  (i) Identify which members of the team habitually make the most contributions, and which the least. (You could do this by taking a count of contributions from each member, during a sample 10-15 minutes of group discussion.)

  (ii) If the same people tend to dominate discussion whatever is discussed (ie regardless of relevant expertise), the team has a problem in its communication process.

2.9 **Neil Rackham and Terry Morgan** have developed a helpful categorisation of the types of contribution people can make to team discussion and decision-making.

Part C: Management theory, principles and techniques

Category	Behaviour	Example
Proposing	Putting forward suggestions, new concepts or courses of action	'Why don't we look at a flexi-time system?'
Building	Extending or developing someone else's proposal.	'Yes. We could have a daily or weekly hours allowance, apart from a core period in the middle of the day.'
Supporting	Supporting another person or his/her proposal.	'Yes, I agree, flexi-time would be worth looking at.'
Seeking information	Asking for more facts, opinions or clarification.	'What exactly do you mean by "flexi-time"?'
Giving information	Offering facts, opinions or clarification.	'There's a helpful outline of flexi-time in this article.'
Disagreeing	Offering criticism or alternative factors or opinions which contradict a person's proposals or opinions.	'I don't think we can take the risk of not having any staff here at certain periods of the day.'
Attacking	Attempting to undermine another person or their position: more emotive than disagreeing.	'In fact, I don't think you've thought this through at all.'
Defending	Arguing for one's own point of view.	'Actually, I've given this a lot of thought, and I think it makes sense.'
Blocking/ difficulty stating	Putting obstacles in the way of a proposal, without offering any alternatives.	'What if the other teams get jealous? It would only cause conflict.'
Open behaviour	Risking ridicule and loss of status by being honest about feelings and opinions.	'I thing some of us are afraid that flexi-time will show up how little work they really do in a day.'
Shutting-out behaviour	Interrupting or overriding others; taking over.	'Nonsense. Let's move onto something else - we've had enough of this discussion.
Bringing-in behaviour	Involving another member; encouraging contribution.	'Actually, I'd like to hear what Fred has to say. Go on, Fred.'
Testing understanding	Checking whether points have been understood.	'So flexi-time could work over a day or a week; have I got that right?'
Summarising	Drawing together or summing up previous discussion.	'We've now heard two sides to the flexi-time issue: on the one hand, flexibility; on the other side possible risk. Now … '

2.10 Each type of behaviour may be appropriate in the right situation at the right time. A team may be low on some types of contribution - and it may be up to the team leader to encourage, or deliberately adopt, desirable behaviours (such as bringing-in, supporting or seeking information) in order to provide balance.

3 DEVELOPMENT OF THE TEAM

3.1 You probably have had experience of being put into a group of people you do not know. Many teams are set up this way and it takes some time for the team to become effective.

3.2 Four stages in this development were identified by **Tuckman** (1965).

Step 1. **Forming**

The team is just coming together. Each member wishes to impress his or her personality on the group. The individuals will be trying to find out about each other, and about the aims and norms of the team. There will at this stage probably be a wariness about introducing new ideas. The objectives being pursued may as yet be unclear and a leader may not yet have emerged. This period is essential, but may be time wasting: the team as a unit will not be used to being autonomous, and will probably not be an efficient agent in the planning of its activities or the activities of others.

Step 2. **Storming**

This frequently involves more or less open conflict between team members. There may be changes agreed in the original objectives, procedures and norms established for the group. If the team is developing successfully this may be a fruitful phase as more realistic targets are set and trust between the group members increases.

Step 3. **Norming**

A period of settling down: there will be agreements about work sharing, individual requirements and expectations of output. Norms and procedures may evolve which enable methodical working to be introduced and maintained.

Step 4. **Performing**

The team sets to work to execute its task. The difficulties of growth and development no longer hinder the group's objectives.

3.3 Later writers added two stages to Tuckman's model.

(a) **Dorming**. Once a group has been performing well for some time, it may get complacent, and fall back into self-maintenance functions, at the expense of the task.

(b) **Mourning/adjourning**. The group sees itself as having fulfilled its purpose – or, if it is a temporary group, is due to physically disband. This is a stage of confusion, sadness and anxiety as the group breaks up. There is evaluation of its achievements, and gradual withdrawal of group members. If the group is to continue, going on to a new task, there will be a re-negotiation of aims and roles: a return to the forming stage.

3.4 An alternative model was developed by Woodcock, who classified teams into four categories.

Category	Comment
Undeveloped	The team-leader takes most decisions. People are not quite sure what the objectives should be. Personal interaction is based on hiding feelings.
Experimenting	The group turns in on itself, with people raising and facing key issues.
Consolidating	The task and its objectives become clear, people begin to get along with each other on a personal level, and people begin to agree on procedures.
Mature	Working methods are methodical, people are open with their feelings 'leadership style is contributory and the group recognises its responsibilities to the rest of the organisation'.

Team leadership

3.5 You should note that, in all of the above stages, the role of the **team leader** is very important. Team leaders need to manage the process of team development, as colleagues get to know each other, conflicts emerge which need to be resolved, and the team eventually settles together to become committed to achieving tasks.

3.6 Leadership of the team may need to vary in some circumstances, if **specialists** are needed to assume control of some part of the task. In general, however, team leaders must address the following areas.

(a) Focus on the team's **task** and **objectives**.

(b) Assess the **size** of the team, and the **skills** needed.

(c) Evaluate individual **strengths and weaknesses** and allocate tasks.

(d) Assess **training** needs.

(e) Find ways to create harmony, and **motivate** the team.

(f) Establish clear lines and methods of **communication** to keep team members informed of progress.

The leader therefore must give appropriate attention to the needs of the **task**, the needs of the **team** and the needs of the **individuals** within it.

Activity 11.3

Read the following descriptions of team behaviour and decide to which category they belong (forming, storming, norming, performing, dorming).

(a) Two of the group arguing as to whose idea is best
(b) Progress becomes static
(c) Desired outputs being achieved
(d) Shy member of group not participating
(e) Activities being allocated

4 TEAM BUILDING

4.1 In Section 3, we suggested that teams have a natural evolutionary life cycle, and that various stages can be identified. Not all teams develop into mature teams and might be stuck in one of the sub-performing stages. In addition, the process towards 'performing' may need to be accelerated, for example in the case of a temporary project team.

11: Team management

4.2 **Team-building** may be described as a systematic attempt to develop the processes of collaborative functioning within a team (such as communication, problem-solving, decision-making and conflict resolution) in such a way as to help the team to overcome any barriers to effective pursuit of its shared goals.

4.3 So, it often falls to the supervisor or manager to build the team. There are three main issues involved in team building.

(a) **Team identity:** get people to see themselves as part of the group

(b) **Team solidarity:** encourage loyalty so that members put in extra effort for the sake of the team

(c) **Shared objectives**: encourage the team to commit itself to shared work objectives and to co-operate willingly and effectively in achieving them.

4.4 **Woodcock** identifies a number of **blockages** and **building blocks** in the team building process. Adapted, these are as follows.

Issue	Blockage	Building block
Leadership	Inappropriate	Adopting a leadership style that fits the task, team and situation (as discussed in Chapter 9)
Membership	Insufficient or unbalanced mix of skills and role preferences	Ensuring a suitable mix of competencies and member roles
Climate	Unconstructive	Striving to create a co-operative atmosphere and style based on trust
Objectives	Not clear	Clarifying and articulating specific, meaningful and achievable goals which can be shared by the whole team
Achievement	Poor	Creating opportunities to learn: celebrating learning and improvement
Work methods	Ineffective	Developing workable procedures for task and group functioning
Communications	Not open; people are afraid to challenge or confront key issues	Facilitating openness and honesty, information sharing, ideas generation and constructive feedback
Individuals	Development needs not attended to	Giving team members opportunities to grow and develop within and through the team (eg by multi-skilling)
Creativity	Low	Facilitating generation of new ideas (eg through brainstorming); respecting and reinforcing new ideas and risk-taking
Interpersonal relations	Poor and unconstructive	Helping members to get to know one another; controlling conflict; facilitating trust and co-operation
Review and control	Non-existent	Regularly evaluating and giving feedback on team performance and improvement needs

Part C: Management theory, principles and techniques

> **Exam alert**
>
> Be aware that Tuckman's team development model, Belbin's team roles and Woodcock's teambuilding factors are specifically mentioned in the Study Guide for this paper. Make sure you have mastered the basic terminology (and authorship!) of each model.

4.5 We can now discuss some of the techniques for building team identity, team solidarity and the commitment to shared objectives. But first try the question below.

Activity 11.4

Why might the following be effective as team-building exercises?

(a) Sending a project team (involved in the design of electronic systems for racing cars) on a recreational day out karting.

(b) Sending two sales teams on a day out playing 'War Games, each being an opposing combat team trying to capture the other's flag, armed with paint guns

(c) Sending a project team on a conference at a venue away from work, with a brief to review the past year and come up with a vision for the next year

These are actually commonly-used techniques. If you are interested, you might locate an activity centre or company near you which offers outdoor pursuits, war games or corporate entertainment and ask them about team-building exercises and the effect they have on people.

4.6 A manager might seek to reinforce the **sense of identity** of the group. Arguably this is in part the creation of boundaries, identifying who is in the team and who is not.

(a) **Name**. Staff at McDonald's restaurants are known as the Crew. In other cases, the name would be more official describing what the team actually does (eg Systems Implementation Task Force)

(b) **Badge or uniform**. This often applies to service industries, but it is unlikely that it would be applied within an organisation

(c) Expressing the team's **self-image:** teams often develop their own jargon, especially for new projects

(d) Building a team **mythology** - in other words, stories from the past ('classic mistakes' as well as successes.)

(e) **A separate space**: it might help if team members work together in the same or adjacent offices, but this is not always possible

4.7 **Team solidarity** implies cohesion and loyalty inside the team. A team leader might be interested in:

(a) Expressing solidarity

(b) Encouraging **interpersonal relationships** - although the purpose of these is to ensure that work does get done

(c) **Dealing with conflict** by getting it out into the open; disagreements should be expressed and then resolved

(d) **Controlling competition**. The team leader needs to treat each member of the team fairly and to be seen to do so; favouritism undermines solidarity.

11: Team management

(e) **Encouraging some competition** with other groups if appropriate. For example, sales teams might be offered a prize for the highest monthly orders; London Underground runs best-kept station competitions.

4.8 Getting **commitment to the team's shared objectives** may involve a range of leader activity.

(a) Clearly setting out the objectives of the team (particularly in the case of 'virtual' teams)

(b) Allowing the team to participate in setting objectives, targets and standards, and agreeing methods of organising work and team processes

(c) Giving regular feedback on progress and results, with constructive criticism where required, and getting the team involved in providing performance feedback

(d) Exploiting formal and informal communication channels to ensure that team members continually share information and ideas, and generally maintain contact (particularly in dispersed, virtual or independent-working teams)

(e) Offering positive reinforcement (praise etc) for co-operative working and task achievement

(f) Championing the success of the team within the organisation

Controlling group cohesion

4.9 Remember that, as we saw in Chapter 10, it is possible for teams to become too cohesive, and to run the risk of **groupthink**, resulting in irresponsible decision-making and conflict with other groups.

4.10 In order to avoid groupthink, the team leader must encourage the group:

- Actively to seek outside ideas and feedback
- To welcome self-criticism and constructive disagreement within the group
- Consciously to evaluate evidence and opinions that may conflict with the group's ideas

---

Activity 11.5

Brainstorm some methods by which geographically dispersed, independently working or 'virtual' team members could be 'brought together' as a team in your own work context, using:

(a) Informal and
(b) Formal communication mechanisms

---

5 TEAM EVALUATION AND REWARDS

Evaluating teams

5.1 The task of the team leader is to build a 'successful' or 'effective' team. The criteria for team effectiveness include:

(a) **Task performance**: fulfilment of task and organisational goals

(b) **Team functioning**: constructive maintenance of team working, managing the demands of team dynamics, roles and processes

(c) **Team member satisfaction**: fulfilment of individual development and relationship needs

Part C: Management theory, principles and techniques

5.2 There are a number of factors, both quantitative and qualitative, that may be assessed to decide whether or how far a team is operating effectively. Some factors cannot be taken as evidence on their own, but may suggest underlying problems: accident rates may be due to poor safety systems, for example – but may also suggest poor morale and lack of focus due to team problems.

5.3 Some of the characteristics of effective and ineffective teams may be summarised as follows.

Factor	Effective team	Ineffective team
Quantitative		
Labour turnover	Low	High
Accident rate	Low	High
Absenteeism	Low	High
Output and productivity	High	Low
Quality of output	High	Low
Individual targets	Achieved	Not achieved
Stoppages and interruptions to the work flow	Low	High (eg because of misunderstandings, disagreements)
Qualitative		
Commitment to targets and organisational goals	High	Low
Understanding of team's work and why it exists	High	Low
Understanding of individual roles	High	Low
Communication between team members	Free and open	Mistrust
Ideas	Shared for the team's benefit	'Owned' (and hidden) by individuals for their own benefit
Feedback	Constructive criticism	Point scoring, undermining
Problem-solving	Addresses causes	Only looks at symptoms
Interest in work decisions	Active	Passive acceptance
Opinions	Consensus	Imposed solutions
Job satisfaction	High	Low
Motivation in leader's absence	High	'When the cat's away...'

Activity 11.6

Try to interview somebody who manages a work team, who would be willing to talk to you for just 10 or 15 minutes. Run through the checklist of factors given above, asking your interviewee to give a 'Yes' or 'No' to each of the statements. Put a question mark (?) where is was difficult for the respondent to answer, because the factor was not easy to define or measure. You might want to reconsider some of our factors, or the way they are phrased in the light of the answers you get. What conclusions can you draw from your survey?

Rewarding effective teams

5.4 Organisations may try to encourage effective team performance by designing reward systems that recognise team, rather than **individual** success. Indeed, individual performance rewards may act against **team** co-operation performance.

(a) They emphasise individual rather than team performance.

(b) They encourage team leaders to think of team members only as individuals rather than relating to them as a team.

5.5 For **team rewards** to be effective, the team must have certain characteristics.

- Distinct roles, targets and performance measures
- Significant autonomy and thus influence over performance
- Maturity and stability
- Co-operation
- Interdependence of team members

5.6 **Reward schemes** which focus on team (or organisation) performance include:

(a) **Profit sharing** schemes, based on a pool of cash related to profit

(b) **Gainsharing** schemes, using a formula related to a suitable performance indicator, such as added value. Improvements in the performance indicator must be perceived to be within the employees' control, otherwise there will be no incentive to perform.

(c) **Employee share option** schemes, giving staff the right to acquire shares in the employing company at an attractive price

Part C: Management theory, principles and techniques

Key learning points

- A **team** is more than a group. It has joint **objectives** and **accountability** and may be set up by the organisation under the supervision or coaching of a team leader, although **self-managed teams** are growing in popularity.

- Teamworking may be used for: **organising** work; **controlling** activities; **generating** ideas; **decision-making**; pooling **knowledge**.

- **Multidisciplinary** teams contain people from different departments, pooling the skills of specialists.

- **Multi-skilled** teams contain people who themselves have more than one skill.

- Ideally team members should perform a balanced mix of **roles**. **Belbin** suggests: co-ordinator, shaper, plant, monitor-evaluator, resource-investigator, implementer, team-worker, finisher and specialist.

- Team members make different types of **contribution** (eg proposing, defending, blocking)

- A team develops in **stages**: forming, storming, norming, performing (Tuckman) and dorming or mourning/adjourning.

- Team development can be facilitated by active **team building** measures to support team identity, solidarity and commitment to shared objectives.

- A team can be evaluated on the basis of quantifiable and qualitative factors, covering its **operations** and its **output**, and team member **satisfaction**.

Quick quiz

1. What is a team?
2. List Belbin's nine roles for a well-rounded team?
3. Who described the stages of group development?

    A Woodcock
    B Belbin
    C Tuckman
    D Rackman and Morgan

4. List the teambuilding issues identified by Woodcock.
5. Suggest five ways in which a manager can get a team 'behind' task objectives.
6. List six of Rackham and Morgan's categories of contribution to group discussion.
7. High labour turnover is a characteristic of effective teams. True or false?

Answers to quick quiz

1. A small number of people with complementary skills who are committed to a common purpose, performance goals and approach for which they hold themselves basically accountable.

2. Co-ordinator, shaper, plant, monitor-evaluator, resource-investigator, implementer, teams worker, finisher, specialist.

3. C: Tuckman. You should be able to identify the team-relevant theories of Woodcock and Belbin as well.

4. Leaders, Members. Climate. Objectives. Achievement. Work methods. Communications. Individuals, Creativity. Interpersonal communications. Review and control.

5. Set clear objectives, get the team to set targets/standard, provide information and resources, give feedback, praise and reward, and champion the team in the organisation.

6. Proposing, building, supporting, seeking information, giving information, disagreeing.

7. False.

Answers to activities

Answer 11.1

Your own observation: remember, these will be useful examples to use, if asked in an exam.

Answer 11.2

(a) Completer/finisher
(b) Implementer
(c) Specialist
(d) Plant
(e) Resource investigator
(f) Shaper
(g) Teamworker
(h) Co-ordinator
(i) Monitor evaluator

Answer 11.3

Categorising the behaviour of group members in the situations described results in the following: (a) storming, (b) dorming, (c) performing, (d) forming, (e) norming.

Answer 11.4

(a) Recreation helps the team to build informal relationships: in this case, the chosen activity also reminds them of their tasks, and may make them feel special, as part of the motor racing industry, by giving them a taste of what the end user of their product does.

(b) A team challenge purses the group to consider its strengths and weaknesses, to find it's natural leader. This exercise creates and 'us' and 'them' challenge: perceiving the rival team as the enemy heightens the solidarity of the group.

(c) This exercise encourages the group the raise problems and conflicts freely, away from the normal environment of work and also encourages brainstorming and the expression of team members' dreams for what the team can achieve in the future.

Answer 11.5

Examples of informal methods include:

(a) A team notice board (or the electronic equivalent on the corporate Intranet) where team members can leave messages, suggestions or progress updates

(b) Encouraging regular telephone, e-mail or instant messaging conversations

(c) Working through a Co-ordinator or team networkers who passes information on

(d) Arranging to meet members whenever possible ('touching base')

(e) Rotating team meetings around different sites (where relevant)

Examples of formal methods are most likely to include:

(a) Scheduled team meetings at regular intervals

(b) Distributing written confirmations of deadlines, action plans and responsibilities after meetings

(c) Requesting short, regular progress reports from each team member

(d) Publishing a regular team bulletin of progress made, successes, issues arising

Answer 11.6

Your own research.

> Now try Question 10 in the Exam Question Bank

Chapter 12　Motivation

Chapter topic list

1. Motivation and performance
2. Content theories of motivation
3. Process theories of motivation
4. The job as a motivator
5. Pay as a motivator
6. Discipline

The following study sessions are covered in this chapter:

		Syllabus reference
13(a)	Outline the key theories of motivation	3(d)
13(b)	Outline the difference between content and process theories	3(d)
13(c)	Describe how management can motivate staff	3(d)
13(d)	Explain the importance of the reward system in the process of motivation	3(d)
13(e)	Explain the importance of feedback	3(d)

Part C: Management theory, principles and techniques

1 MOTIVATION AND PERFORMANCE

1.1 A well trained, experienced individual who is poorly motivated is unlikely to be very productive. A young and enthusiastic trainee may learn very fast and produce a return on the organisation's investment very quickly. **Motivation** is therefore a very important element in the management of individuals. It can be a very useful tool for improving productivity, which might be cheaper than, say, new equipment.

1.2 It is in the manager's best interests to have good motivation throughout a company, from the sales office to the production line. **Well-motivated** staff are probably more **productive**, make fewer mistakes, and convey a more **positive** and enthusiastic air to customers.

1.3 So, managers should not ignore motivation as a **tool to get work done**. The key areas, which involve little or no additional resources, are:

- Giving employees **freedom** to achieve an objective
- **Recognition** and genuine appreciation for good work done
- Good **interpersonal relations**

1.4 These ideas reflect the preoccupations of the **human relations school** of management theory, which we discussed in Chapter 9.

What is motivation?

> **KEY TERMS**
>
> **Motivation** is 'a decision-making process through which the individual chooses the desired outcomes and sets in motion the behaviour appropriate to acquiring them'. (Huczynski and Buchanan).
>
> **Motives:** 'learned influences on human behaviour that lead us to pursue particular goals because they are socially valued'. (Huczynski and Buchanan).

1.5 In practice the words **motives** and **motivation** are commonly used in different contexts to mean the following.

(a) **Goals or outcomes** that have become desirable for a particular individual. We say that money, power or friendship are motives for doing something.

(b) The **mental process of choosing desired outcomes**, deciding how to go about them (and whether the likelihood of success warrants the amount of effort that will be necessary) and setting in motion the required behaviours.

(c) The **social process** by which other people motivate us to behave in the ways they wish. Motivation in this sense usually applies to the attempts of organisations to get workers to put in more effort.

1.6 From a manager's point of view, motivation is the controlling of the work environment, rewards and sanctions in such a way as to encourage desired behaviours and performance from employees.

What does motivation achieve?

1.7 You may be wondering whether motivation is really so important. It could be argued that if a person is employed to do a job, he will do it: no question of motivation arises. If the person doesn't want to do the work, he can resign. So why try to motivate people?

1.8 The argument is that if individuals can be 'motivated', they will perform better and more willingly – **above mere compliance** with rules and procedures. If their personal needs and goals are integrated with those of the team and organisation, individuals will work more efficiently (so that productivity will rise) or produce a better quality of work, or might contribute more of their creativity and initiative to the job.

1.9 There is on-going debate about exactly what motivation strategies can aim to achieve in the way of productivity, quality and other business benefits, but it has become widely accepted that **committed** employees add value to the organisation. This is particularly true in environments where initiative and flexibility are required of employees in order to satisfy customer demands and keep pace with environmental changes.

1.10 **Job satisfaction** is an even more ambiguous concept, although (as we will see) it is associated with motivation.

(a) It is difficult to prove that 'happy bees make more honey'.

(b) Job satisfaction is difficult to define: it means different things to different people, and over time – according to the individual's changing needs, goals and expectations.

1.11 On the other hand, low morale, dissatisfaction or de-motivation can cause direct and indirect **performance problems**, through effects such as:

(a) Higher than usual (or higher than acceptable) **labour turnover**

(b) Higher levels of **absenteeism**, and deterioration in time-keeping and discipline

(c) **Reduction in upward communication**, employee involvement (such as participation in suggestion schemes or quality circles)

(d) Higher incidence of **employee disputes** and grievances

(e) **Restricted output** quantity and/or quality (through lack of commitment or deliberate sabotage)

Activity 12.1

What factors in yourself or your job or organisation motivate you to:

- Turn up to work at all?
- Do an average day's work?
- 'Bust a gut' to do your best on a task, or for a boss or customer?

Rewards and incentives

> **KEY TERMS**
>
> A **reward** is a token (monetary or otherwise) given to an individual or team in recognition of some contribution or success.
>
> An **incentive** is the offer or promise of a reward for contribution or success, designed to motivate the individual or team to behave in such a way as to earn it.

1.12 Not all the incentives that an organisation can offer its employees are directly related to **monetary** rewards. The satisfaction of **any** of the employee's wants or needs may be seen as a reward for past, or incentive for future, performance.

1.13 Different individuals have different goals, and get different things out of their working life: in other words they have different **orientations** to work. There are any number of reasons why a person works, or is motivated to work well.

(a) The **human relations** school of management theorists regarded **work relationships** as the main source of satisfaction and reward offered to the worker.

(b) Later writers suggested a range of 'higher-order' motivations, notably:

- **Job satisfaction**, interest and challenge in the job itself - rewarding work
- **Participation** in decision-making - responsibility and involvement

(c) **Pay** has always occupied a rather ambiguous position, but since people need money to live, it will certainly be part of the reward package.

1.14 Rewards offered to the individual at work may be of two basic types.

(a) **Extrinsic rewards** are separate from (or external to) the job itself, and dependent on the decisions of others (that is, also external to the control of the workers themselves). Pay, benefits, cash and non-cash incentives and working conditions are examples of extrinsic rewards.

(b) **Intrinsic rewards** are those which arise from the performance of the work itself. They are therefore psychological rather than material and relate to the concept of job satisfaction. Intrinsic rewards include the satisfaction that comes from completing a piece of work, the status that certain jobs convey, and the feeling of achievement that comes from doing a difficult job well.

1.15 **Child** has outlined **management criteria for a reward system**. Such a system should do six things.

(a) Encourage people to **fill job vacancies** and not leave.

(b) Increase the **predictability of employees' behaviour**, so that employees can be depended on to carry out their duties consistently and to a reasonable standard.

(c) Increase **willingness to accept change** and flexibility. (Changes in work practices are often 'bought' from trade unions with higher pay.)

(d) Foster and **encourage innovative behaviour**.

(e) **Reflect the nature of jobs** in the organisation and the skills or experience required. The reward system should therefore be consistent with seniority of position in the organisation structure, and should be thought fair by all employees.

12: Motivation

(f) **Motivate**, that is, increase commitment and effort.

Negative and positive motivation

1.16 Note that motivation can be a negative process (appealing to an individual's need to avoid unpleasantness, pain etc) as well as a positive one (appealing to the individual's need to attain certain goals or satisfy certain wants). Negative motivation may involve threatening sanctions such as disciplinary action for poor performance. We discuss **discipline** as an aspect of motivation in Section 6 of this chapter.

Theories of motivation

1.17 Many theories try to explain motivation and why and how people can be motivated. One classification is between content and process theories.

(a) **Content theories** ask the question: '**What** are the things that motivate people?'

They assume that human beings have a set of needs or desired outcomes. Maslow's hierarchy theory and Herzberg's two-factor theory, both discussed below, are two of the most important approaches of this type.

(b) **Process theories** ask the question: '**How** can people be motivated?'

They explore the process through which outcomes **become** desirable and are pursued by individuals. This approach assumes that people are able to select their goals and choose the paths towards them, by a conscious or unconscious process of calculation. Expectancy theory and Handy's 'motivation calculus', discussed later, are theories of this type.

> **Exam alert**
>
> The distinction between process and content theories is a basic point – and a common pitfall for students. Make sure you can define each type of theory clearly and cite relevant examples. Note, as you read on, that despite the popularity of Maslow and Herzberg, they have their limitations – and they are not the only theories of motivation.

1.18 We will now look at some of the main content and process models of motivation.

2 CONTENT THEORIES OF MOTIVATION

2.1 According to content theories, people behave in particular ways in order to reduce the tension they experience as a result of an unsatisfied need. The task of management is therefore to offer the individual the means of satisfying his needs.

Maslow's hierarchy of needs

2.2 Abraham Maslow described five needs and put forward certain propositions about the motivating power of each need.

Part C: Management theory, principles and techniques

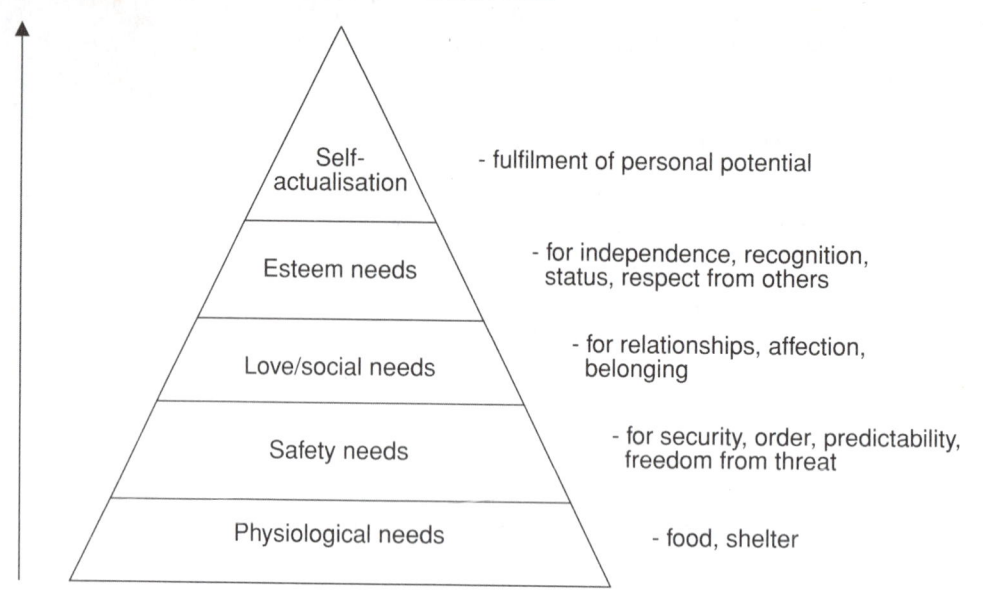

```
          /\
         /  \
        /Self-\      - fulfilment of personal potential
       /actual-\
      /isation  \
     /------------\
    / Esteem needs \   - for independence, recognition,
   /                \    status, respect from others
  /------------------\
 /  Love/social needs \  - for relationships, affection,
/                      \   belonging
/------------------------\
/     Safety needs        \  - for security, order, predictability,
/                          \    freedom from threat
/----------------------------\
/    Physiological needs      \  - food, shelter
/------------------------------\
```

(a) Any individual's needs can be arranged in a '**hierarchy** of relative pre-potency' (as shown).

(b) Each level of need is **dominant until satisfied**; only then does the next level of need become a motivating factor.

(c) A need which has been satisfied no longer motivates an individual's behaviour. The need for self-actualisation can rarely be satisfied.

Activity 12.2

Decide which of Maslow's categories the following fit into.

(a) Receiving praise from your manager
(b) A family party
(c) An artist forgetting to eat
(d) A man washed up on a desert island
(e) A pay increase
(f) Joining a local drama group
(g) Being awarded the OBE
(h) Buying a house

2.3 Maslow's hierarchy is simple and intuitively attractive: you are unlikely to worry about respect if you are starving! However, it is only a theory and has been shown to have several major limitations.

(a) An individual's behaviour may be in response to **several needs**. Work, after all, can either satisfy or thwart the satisfaction of a number of needs.

(b) The same need may cause **different behaviour** in different individuals.

(c) The hierarchy ignores the concept of **deferred gratification** by which people are prepared to ignore current suffering for the promise of future benefits.

(d) **Empirical verification** of the hierarchy is hard to come by. The role of pay is ambiguous (since money can be the means of satisfying a wide range of needs) and self-actualisation is highly subjective.

(e) Research has revealed that the hierarchy reflects UK and US cultural values, which may not transfer to other contexts.

McClelland's need theory

2.4 David McClelland identified three types of motivating need.

(a) **The need for power**. People with a high need for power usually seek positions in which they can influence and control others.

(b) **The need for affiliation**. People who need a sense of belonging and membership of a social group tend to be concerned with maintaining good personal relationships.

(c) **The need for achievement**. People who need to achieve have a strong desire for success and a strong fear of failure.

Herzberg's two-factor theory

2.5 In the 1950s, Frederick Herzberg interviewed engineers and accountants in Pittsburgh to find out what 'critical incidents' had made them feel good or bad about their work. Analysis revealed two distinct sets of factors: those which created satisfaction (which Herzberg called **motivator factors**) and those which created dissatisfaction (**hygiene** or **maintenance factors**).

2.6 Herzberg highlighted two basic needs of individuals.

(a) The **need to avoid unpleasantness**. Hygiene factors satisfy this need, temporarily – in the same way that hygiene or sanitation minimises threats to health. Hygiene factors can be manipulated to prevent dissatisfaction in the short term, but cannot offer lasting satisfaction or motivation.

(b) The **need for personal growth and fulfilment**. Motivator factors satisfy this need, and actively create job satisfaction, motivating the individual to superior performance and effort.

Hygiene factors	Motivator factors
Company policy and administration	Recognition
Salary	Responsibility
Style of supervision/management	Challenging work
Interpersonal relations within the team	Achievement
Working conditions	Growth and development in the job
Job security	

2.7 Herzberg suggested that 'when people are dissatisfied with their work it is usually because of discontent with environmental factors... Satisfaction can only arise from the job.' He recommended various approaches to job design which would build motivator factors into the work. We discuss them in Section 4 below.

2.8 Like Maslow's hierarchy, Herzberg's model is simple and accessible, and embraces a wide range of possible rewards and working conditions, but it has been criticised on a number of grounds.

(a) **Empirical verification** and measurement of the claim that motivator factors increase productivity have been hard to find.

(b) The research findings are **context-specific**: they describe specific groups of workers in a single cultural context, whose values cannot necessarily be generalised to other contexts.

(c) The original study was based on an inadequately **small sample size** to draw conclusions.

The model's main contribution is highlighting the potential **intrinsic rewards** of work, contributing to job design and the 'quality of working life' movement.

3 PROCESS THEORIES OF MOTIVATION

Vroom's expectancy theory

3.1 Expectancy theory basically states that the strength of an individual's motivation to do something will depend on the extent to which he expects the results of his efforts to contribute to his personal needs or goals.

3.2 Victor Vroom stated a formula by which human motivation could be assessed and measured. He suggested that the strength of an individual's motivation is the product of two factors.

  (a) **The strength of his preference for a certain outcome**. Vroom called this **valence**: it can be represented as a positive or negative number, or zero – since outcomes may be desired, avoided or regarded with indifference.

  (b) **His expectation that the outcome will in fact result** from a certain behaviour. Vroom called this 'subjective probability' or **expectancy**. As a probability, it may be represented by any number between 0 (no chance) and 1 (certainty).

3.3 In its simplest form, the expectancy equation may be stated as:

$$F = V \times E$$

Where

F = the force or strength of the individual's motivation to behave in a particular way
V = valence: the strength of the individual preference for a given outcome or reward and
E = expectancy: the individual's perception that the behaviour will result in the outcome/reward.

3.4 In this equation, the lower the values of either valence or expectancy, the less the motivation. An employee may have a high expectation that increased productivity will result in promotion (because of managerial promises, say), but if he is indifferent or negative towards the idea of promotion (because he dislikes responsibility), he will not be motivated to increase his productivity. Likewise, if promotion was very important to him – but he did not believe higher productivity would get him promoted (because he has been passed over before, perhaps), his motivation would also be low.

Activity 12.3

How might a manager use this theory to improve the motivation of team members?

3.5 Equity theory (usually associated with the work of JS Adams) is a **process theory** of motivation which focuses on people's sense of whether they have been fairly treated in comparison with the way others have been treated.

3.6 It is based on exchange theory, which suggests that people expect certain **outcomes** or rewards in exchange for their **inputs** or contributions. If they perceive that the ratio of their outcomes to inputs is unequal to that of other people, they experience a sense of **inequity** – whether positive (they feel they have been treated 'unfairly' well) or negative (they feel they have been treated 'unfairly' badly). If someone feels they are not getting paid enough for their work, compared to others, for example, he will have a sense of negative inequity.

3.7 A sense of inequity causes unpleasant tension, or dissonance, which motivates people to attempt to remove or reduce the perceived inequity by:

- Changing the inputs (eg reducing their hours or quality of work)
- Changing the outcomes (eg demanding better pay)
- Cognitive distortion (eg believing they aren't really working as hard as they are)
- Withdrawal (eg absenteeism or resignation)
- Influencing others to do any of the above (eg getting co-workers to put in extra hours)
- Changing the comparison (eg comparing themselves with a different set of people)

Handy's motivation calculus

3.8 Charles Handy's motivation calculus is another expectancy approach. Individuals decide how much effort to invest towards a given goals by doing a calculation, weighing up:

- The strength or 'salience' of a need
- The expectancy that effort will lead to a particular result, and
- The likely effectiveness of that result in satisfying the need

3.9 The most appealing aspect of Handy's model is his identification of 'E' factors: a range of factors which an individual invests in action when motivated to do so. We have so far used the term 'effort', but this is only one 'E' factor: others include energy, excitement, expenditure, endeavour and excellence.

Managerial implications of process theories

3.10 Expectancy theory suggests that:

(a) **Intended results should be made clear**, so that the individual can complete the calculation by knowing what is expected, the reward, and how much effort it will take.

(b) Individuals are likely to be more committed to **specific goals** which they **have helped to set themselves**, taking their needs and expectations into account.

(c) Immediate and on-going **feedback** should be given. Without knowledge of actual results, there is no check that 'E' expenditure was justified (or will be justified in future).

(d) If an individual is **rewarded** according to performance tied to standards (management by objectives), however, he or she may well set lower standards: the expectancy part of the calculation (likelihood of success and reward) is greater if the standard is lower, so less expense of 'E' is indicated.

4 THE JOB AS A MOTIVATOR

4.1 The job itself can be used as a motivator, or it can be a cause of dissatisfaction.

4.2 Frederick Herzberg suggest three ways of improving job design, to make jobs more interesting to the employee, and hopefully to improve performance: job enrichment, job enlargement and job rotation.

Job enrichment

> **KEY TERM**
>
> **Job enrichment** is planned, deliberate action to build greater responsibility, breadth and challenge of work into a job. Job enrichment is similar to **empowerment**.

4.3 Job enrichment represents a 'vertical' extension of the job into greater levels of responsibility, challenge and autonomy. A job may be enriched by:

- Giving the job holder **decision-making tasks** of a higher order
- Giving the employee greater **freedom** to decide how the job should be done
- Encouraging employees **to participate** in the planning decisions of their superiors
- Giving the employee regular **feedback**

Job enlargement

> **KEY TERM**
>
> **Job enlargement** is the attempt to widen jobs by increasing the number of operations in which a job holder is involved.

4.4 Job enlargement is a 'horizontal' extension of the job by increasing task variety and reducing task repetition.

(a) Tasks which span a larger part of the total production work should reduce boredom and add to task meaning, significance and variety.

(b) Enlarged jobs might be regarded as having higher status within the department, perhaps as stepping stones towards promotion.

4.5 Job enlargement is, however, limited in its intrinsic rewards, as asking a worker to complete three separate tedious, unchallenging tasks is unlikely to be more motivating than asking him to perform just one tedious, unchallenging task.

Job rotation

> **KEY TERM**
>
> **Job rotation** is the planned transfer of staff from one job to another to increase task variety.

4.6 Job rotation is a 'sequential' extension of the job. Job rotation is also sometimes seen as a form of training, where individuals gain wider experience by rotating as trainees in different positions.

4.7 It is generally admitted that the developmental value of job rotation is limited – but it can reduce the monotony of repetitive work.

Job design for job satisfaction

4.8 There are five 'core job dimensions' which are thought to contribute to job satisfaction.

(a) **Skill variety**: the opportunity to exercise different skills and perform different operations

(b) **Task identity**: the integration of operations into a 'whole' tasks (or meaningful segment of the task)

(c) **Task significance**: the task is perceived to have a role, purpose, meaning and value

(d) **Autonomy**: the opportunity to exercise discretion or self-management (eg in areas such as target-setting and work methods)

(e) **Feedback**: the availability of performance feedback enabling the individual to assess his progress and the opportunity to give feedback, be heard and influence results

Management style as a motivator

4.9 Although Herzberg identified management style as a hygiene factor, you should recognise that management style can contribute significantly to the core job dimensions listed above.

Activity 12.4

Suggest how a manager could build core dimensions into the job without job redesign: just through management style.

4.10 Two influential models illustrate how managers' **assumptions about worker motivation** can affect morale and performance.

- Douglas McGregor's Theory X and Theory Y
- William Ouchi's Theory Z

Theory X and Theory Y

4.11 **Douglas MacGregor** suggested that managers in the USA tended to behave as though they subscribed to one of two opposing philosophies about people's attitudes to work: **Theory X** and **Theory Y**.

(a) **Theory X** suggests that most people dislike work and responsibility and will avoid both if possible. Because of this, most people must be coerced, controlled, directed and/or threatened with punishment to get them to make an adequate effort. Managers who operate according to these assumptions will tend to supervise closely, apply detailed rules and controls, and use 'carrot and stick' motivations.

(b) **Theory Y** suggests that physical and mental effort in work is as natural as play or rest. The ordinary person does not inherently dislike work: according to the conditions it may be a source of satisfaction or punishment. At present the potentialities of the average person are not being fully used. A manager with this sort of attitude to his staff is likely to be a democratic, consultative type.

4.12 Both are intended to be extreme sets of assumptions – not actual types of people. However, they also tend to be self-fulfilling prophecies. Employees treated as if 'Theory X' were true will begin to behave accordingly. Employees treated as if 'Theory Y' were true – being challenged to take on more responsibility Y – will rise to the challenge and behave accordingly.

Part C: Management theory, principles and techniques

4.13 Theory X and Theory Y can be used to heighten managers' awareness of the assumptions underlying their management style.

Theory Z

4.14 When the Japanese economy was performing well, a generation ago, it became fashionable to study Japanese management methods and promote them as a solution to the West's then seemingly intractable industrial problems. Profiling American management culture as 'Theory A' and typical Japanese management as 'Theory J', William Ouchi sought to synthesize the two, to propose a form of Japanese-style management that could be successfully applied in Western contexts. Ouchi called these methods 'Theory Z'.

4.15 The characteristics of a Theory Z organisation offer some interesting contrasts with the Western way of doing things, notably in key Japanese values such as consensus decision-making and mutual loyalty in the employment relationship.

Ouchi described the Theory Z organisation as being characterised by:

(a) Long-term employment, with slow-progressing managerial career paths (as in the Japanese system, but with a more Western specialisation of skills)

(b) Broad concern for employee welfare, both inside and outside the work context (not just work performance, as in the Western system): commitment to the 'organisation family'

(c) Implicit informal controls (such as guiding values) alongside explicit, formal measures

(d) Collective consensus decision-making processes (Japanese), but with individual retention of ultimate responsibility for defined areas of accountability (Western)

(e) Industrial relations characterised by trust, co-operation and mutual adjustment, rather than unionisation, demarcation and artificial status barriers

4.16 Theory Z was welcomed as a more human and therefore more effective way of managing employee relations: Marks and Spencer in the UK has been cited as an organisation operating on principles akin to Theory Z. Elements of the approach have been incorporated into the 'Human Resource Management' (HRM) orientation to management, which regards people as the key resource of a business. However, it is less easy to transfer cultural values to foreign contexts than it is to apply methods and techniques: employee development programmes and quality circles have been adopted without necessarily being underpinned by Theory Z values.

Culture as a motivator

4.17 Peters and Waterman (*In Search of Excellence*) suggested that employees can be 'switched on' to extraordinary loyalty and effort through organisation culture, if:

(a) **'The cause is perceived to be in some sense great'**. Managers need to 'reaffirm the heroic dimension of work': emphasising that quality and customer satisfaction are worthwhile goals, celebrating successes and so on.

(b) **People are treated as winners**. 'Label a man a loser and he'll start acting like one'. Tight controls and negative reinforcements (by threats, punishments and reprimands) break down people's confidence: positive reinforcement (by rewards, praise, recognition and attention) creates positive energy.

(c) People are enabled to satisfy their dual needs to be a **confirming, secure part** of something bigger than themselves and to be a **'star' in their own right**.

Activity 12.5

How (if at all) does your own organisation go about creating the three cultural motivators suggested by Peters and Waterman? How do you personally respond to 'feel good factor' attempts to motivate you at work: motivational posters, celebrations and so on?

5 PAY AS A MOTIVATOR

5.1 Pay is important because:

- It is an important cost for the organisation
- People feel strongly about it: it 'stands in' for a number of human needs and goals
- It is a legal issue (minimum wage, equal pay legislation)

How is pay determined?

5.2 There are a number of ways by which organisations determine pay.

(a) **Job evaluation** is a systematic process for establishing the relative worth of jobs within an organisation, in order to:

   (i) Provide a rational basis for the design and maintenance of an equitable and defensible pay structure

   (ii) Help manage differentials in the pay of different jobs within the organisation

   (iii) Enable equal pay to be offered for work of equal value, as required by Equal Pay legislation

   The salary structure is based on **job content**, and not on the personal merit of the job-holder. (The individual job-holder can be paid extra personal bonuses in reward for performance.)

(b) **Fairness.** Pay must be **perceived** and felt to match the level of work, and the capacity of the individual to do it.

(c) **Negotiated pay scales.** Pay scales, differentials and minimum rates may have been negotiated at plant, local or national level, according factors such as legislation, government policy, the economy, trade unions, the labour market.

(d) **Market rates.** Market rates of pay will have most influence on pay structures where there is a standard pattern of supply and demand in the open labour market. If an organisation's rates fall below the benchmark rates in the local or national labour market from which it recruits, it will have trouble attracting and holding employees.

(e) **Individual performance in the job**, resulting in merit pay awards, or performance-related bonuses.

What do people want from pay?

5.3 Pay has a central – but ambiguous – role in motivation theory. It is not mentioned explicitly in any need list, but it offers the satisfaction of many of the various needs. Individuals may also have needs unrelated to money, however, which money cannot satisfy, or which the pay system of the organisation actively denies. So to what extent is pay an inducement to better performance: a motivator or incentive?

5.4 Although the size of their income will affect their standard of living, most people tend not to be concerned to **maximise** their earnings. They may like to earn more but are probably more concerned to:

(a) Earn **enough**

(b) Know that their pay is **fair** in comparison with the pay of others both inside and outside the organisation

5.5 Pay is more of a 'hygiene' factor than a motivator factor. It gets taken for granted, and so is more usually a source of dissatisfaction than satisfaction. However, pay is the most important of the hygiene factors, according to Herzberg. It is valuable not only in its power to be converted into a wide range of other satisfactions but also as a consistent measure of worth or value, allowing employees to compare themselves and be compared with other individuals or occupational groups inside and outside the organisation.

5.6 Research has illustrated an **instrumental orientation** to work: the attitude that work is not an end in itself but a means to other ends.

5.7 Pay is only one of several intrinsic and extrinsic rewards offered by work. If pay is used to motivate, it can only do so in a wider context of the job and the other rewards. Thanks, praise and recognition are alternative forms of positive reinforcement.

Activity 12.6

Herzberg says that money is a **hygiene** factor in the motivation process. If this is true, it means that lack of money can demotivate, but the presence of money will not in itself be a motivator.

How far do you agree with this proposition? Can individuals be motivated by a pay rise? What are the arguments against trying to motivate people purely by means of monetary incentives?

6 DISCIPLINE

> **KEY TERM**
>
> **Discipline** can be considered as: 'a condition in an enterprise in which there is orderliness, in which the members of the enterprise behave sensibly and conduct themselves according to the standards of acceptable behaviour as related to the goals of the organisation'.

6.1 Another definition makes the distinction between methods of maintaining sensible conduct and orderliness which are technically co-operative, and those based on warnings, threats and punishments.

(a) **Positive (or constructive) discipline** relates to procedures, systems and equipment in the work place which have been designed specifically so that the employee has **no option** but to act in the desired manner to complete a task safely and successfully. A machine may, for example, shut off automatically if its safety guard is not in place.

(b) **Negative discipline** is then the promise of **sanctions** designed to make people choose to behave in a desirable way. Disciplinary action may be punitive (punishing an offence), deterrent (warning people not to behave in that way) or reformative (calling attention to the nature of the offence, so that it will not happen again).

12: Motivation

6.2 The best discipline is **self discipline**. Even before they start to work, most mature people accept the idea that following instructions and fair rules of conduct are normal responsibilities that are part of any job. Most team members can therefore be counted on to exercise self discipline.

Types of disciplinary situation

6.3 There are many types of disciplinary situations which may require attention by the manager. Here is a handy mnemonic.

STRICT DISCIPLINE

Sleeping while on duty
Threatening co-workers
Refusing to perform assigned duties
Intoxication
Conviction of criminal offence
Tarnishing of company image

Disobedience
Infraction of company policies
Safety procedures ignored
Carrying out illegal/immoral activities in company premises
Irregular attendance
Poor performance
Lying
Improper behaviour
Negative attitude
Embezzlement

Disciplinary action

6.4 The purpose of discipline is not punishment or retribution. Disciplinary action must have as its goal the improvement of the future behaviour of the employee and other members of the organisation. The purpose obviously is the avoidance of similar occurrences in the future.

6.5 The suggested progress of disciplinary action follows guidelines set out by the Advisory Conciliation and Arbitration Service (ACAS) in the UK.

Step 1. **The informal talk**

If the infraction is of a relatively minor nature and if the employee's record has no previous marks of disciplinary action, an informal, friendly talk will clear up the situation in many cases. Here the manager discusses with the employee his or her behaviour in relation to standards which prevail within the enterprise.

Step 2. **Oral warning or reprimand**

In this type of interview between employee and manager, the latter emphasises the undesirability of the subordinate's repeated violation, and that ultimately it could lead to serious disciplinary action.

Step 3. **Written or official warning**

These form part of the ACAS Code of Practice. A written warning is of a formal nature insofar as it becomes a permanent part of the employee's record.

Step 4. **Disciplinary layoffs, or suspension**

This course of action would be next in order if the employee has committed repeated offences and previous steps were of no avail. Disciplinary lay-offs usually extend over several days or weeks.

Step 5. **Dismissal**

Dismissal is a drastic form of disciplinary action, and should be reserved for the most serious offences. For the organisation, it involves waste of a labour resource, the expense of training a new employee, and disruption caused by changing the make-up of the work team. There also may be damage to the morale of the group.

Activity 12.7

How (a) accessible and (b) clear are the rules and policies of your organisation/office: do people really know what they are and are not supposed to do? Have a look at the rule book or procedures manual in your office. How easy is it to see - or did you get referred elsewhere? is the rule book well-indexed and cross-referenced, and in language that all employees will understand?

How (a) accessible and (b) clear are the disciplinary procedures in your office? Are the employees' rights of investigation and appeal clearly set out, with ACAS guidelines? Who is responsible for discipline?

Relationship management in disciplinary situations

6.6 Even if the manager uses sensitivity and judgement, imposing disciplinary action tends to generate **resentment** because it is an unpleasant experience. The challenge is to apply the necessary disciplinary action so that it will be least resented.

(a) **Immediacy**

Immediacy means that after noticing the offence, the manager proceeds to take disciplinary action as speedily as possible, subject to investigations while at the same time avoiding haste and on-the-spot emotions which might lead to unwarranted actions.

(b) **Advance warning**

Employees should know in advance (eg in a Staff Handbook) what is expected of them and what the rules and regulations are.

(c) **Consistency**

Consistency of discipline means that each time an infraction occurs appropriate disciplinary action is taken. Inconsistency in application of discipline lowers the morale of employees and diminishes their respect for the manager.

(d) **Impersonality**

Penalties should be connected with the act and not based upon the personality involved, and once disciplinary action has been taken, no grudges should be borne.

(e) **Privacy**

As a general rule (unless the manager's authority is challenged directly and in public) disciplinary action should be taken in private, to avoid the spread of conflict and the humiliation or martyrdom of the employee concerned.

(f) **Fairness**

Disciplinary proceedings should be based on investigated facts, not hearsay. The employee should be given every opportunity to explain and defend (if necessary) his actions.

6.7 **Disciplinary interviews** should be carefully prepared and conducted, to minimise any real or perceived unfairness.

Step 1. The manager will explain the purpose of the interview.

Step 2. The charges against the employee will be delivered, clearly, unambiguously and without personal emotion.

Step 3. The manager will explain the organisation's position with regard to the issues involved: disappointment, concern, need for improvement, impact on others. This can be done frankly - but tactfully, with as positive an emphasis as possible on the employee's capacity and responsibility to improve.

Step 4. The organisation's expectations with regard to future behaviour/performance should be made clear.

Step 5. The employee should be given the opportunity to comment, explain, justify or deny. If he is to approach the following stage of the interview in a positive way, he must not be made to feel 'hounded' or hard done by.

Step 6. The organisation's expectations should be reiterated, or new standards of behaviour set for the employee.

(i) They should be specific and quantifiable, performance related and realistic.

(ii) They should be related to a practical but reasonably short time period. A date should be set to review his progress.

(iii) The manager agrees on measures to help the employee should that be necessary. It would demonstrate a positive approach if, for example, a mentor were appointed from his work group to help him check his work. If his poor performance is genuinely the result of some difficulty or distress outside work, other help (temporary leave, counselling or financial aid) may be appropriate.

Step 7. The manager should explain the reasons behind any penalties imposed on the employee, including the entry in his personnel record of the formal warning. He should also explain how the warning can be removed from the record, and what standards must be achieved within a specified timescale. There should be a clear warning of the consequences of failure to meet improvement targets.

Step 8. The manager should explain the organisation's appeals procedures: if the employee feels he has been unfairly treated, there should be a right of appeal to a higher manager.

Step 9. Once it has been established that the employee understands all the above, the manager should summarise the proceedings briefly.

Records of the interview will be kept for the employee's personnel file, and for the formal follow-up review and any further action necessary.

Part C: Management theory, principles and techniques

Key learning points

- People have certain innate needs (Maslow: physiological, security, love/social, esteem, self-actualisation). People also have goals, through which they expect their needs to be satisfied.

- **Content theories** of motivation suggest that the best way to motivate an employee is to find out what his/her needs are and offer him/her rewards that will satisfy those needs.

    ○ **Maslow** identified a hierarchy of needs which an individual will be motivated to satisfy, progressing towards higher order satisfactions, such as self-actualisation.

    ○ **Herzberg** identified two basic need systems: the need to avoid unpleasantness and the need for personal growth. He suggested factors which could be offered by organisations to satisfy both types of need: hygiene and motivator factors respectively.

- **Process theories** of motivation help managers to understand the dynamics of employees' decisions about what rewards are worth going for (eg the expectancy model: F = V × E).

- There is little evidence that a satisfied worker actually works harder.

- **Pay** is the most important of the hygiene factors, but it is ambiguous in its effect on motivation.

- Ways in which managers can improve employees' motivation include **job design** (including job enrichment, job enlargement and job rotation), a supportive and challenging **management style** and a **positive culture**.

- Managerial approaches to motivation depend to an extent on the manager's assumptions about workers. Douglas McGregor illustrated extreme sets of assumptions as **Theory X** and **Theory Y**. William Ouchi highlighted cultural values in his synthesis of American and Japanese motivational approaches: **Theory Z**.

- **Discipline** has the same end as **motivation** - ie to secure a range of desired behaviour from members of the organisation.

    ○ Motivation may even be called a kind of **self discipline** - because motivated individuals exercise choice to behave in the way that the organisation wishes.

    ○ Discipline however, is more often related to **negative motivation**, an appeal to the individual's need to avoid punishment, sanctions or unpleasantness.

Quick quiz

1. What is (a) 'positive reinforcement' and (b) self actualisation?
2. List the five categories in Maslow's Hierarchy of Needs.
3. List three ways in which an organisation can offer motivational satisfaction.
4. What is the difference between a reward and an incentive?
5. According to Herzberg, leadership style is a motivator factor. True or false?
6. Explain the formula 'F = V × E'.
7. 'People will work harder and harder to earn more and more pay.' Do you agree? Why (or why not)?
8. A 'horizontal' extension of the job to increase task variety is called:

    A   Job evaluation
    B   Job enrichment
    C   Job enlargement
    D   Job rotation

9. The assumption that people inherently dislike work and responsibility, and must be coerced and controlled in order to pursue organisational goals is called 'Theory _____'.
10. What factors should a manager bear in mind in trying to control a disciplinary situation?

Answers to quick quiz

1. (a) Encouraging a certain type of behaviour by rewarding it
   (b) Personal growth and fulfilment of potential

2. Physiological, safety, love/social, esteem, self-actualisation.

3. Relationships, belonging, challenge, achievement, progress, security, money.

4. A reward is given for some contribution or success. An incentive is an offer of reward.

5. False: it is a hygiene factor.

6. Force of motivation - Valence × Expectation

7. See Paragraphs 4.3 to 4.7.

8. C. Make sure you can define all the other terms as well.

9. X.

10. Immediacy, advance warning, consistency, impersonality, privacy, fairness.

Answers to activities

Answer 12.1

Your own reflections. Do attempt this exercise: it will cast an interesting light on the theoretical models covered in the rest of the chapter.

Answer 12.2

Maslow's categories for the listed circumstances are as follows.

(a) Esteem needs
(b) Social needs
(c) Self-actualisation needs
(d) He will have physiological needs
(e) Safety needs initially; esteem needs above in a certain income level
(f) social needs or self-actualisation needs
(g) Esteem needs
(h) Safety needs or esteem needs

Answer 12.3

Expectancy theory has various practical applications.

(a) Motivation can be measured and responses to incentives (to an extent) predicted, using attitude surveys or interviews in which team members are invited to state valence and expectancy.

(b) Managers need to fulfil their promises of rewards – otherwise expectancy will be lowered next time.

(c) Managers need to give some thought to the value of incentives and rewards to individual employees – otherwise valence will be low. (Some organisations offer a 'cafeteria' system of rewards and benefits, allowing employees to select those that they value.)

(d) Managers need to give employees clear information on expected results, offered rewards and progress – via on-going feedback – in order for them to make motivational calculations.

Answer 12.4

(a) Skill variety: the manager could coach and mentor team members to take advantage of learning opportunities in the work.

(b) Task identity: the manager could explain team members' roles and contributions in terms of the whole task and organisational goals.

Part C: Management theory, principles and techniques

(c) Task significance: the manager could explain the significance of the task to the organisation, in terms of meaningful values such as added value, quality or customer service

(d) Autonomy: the manager could remove some controls, or consult with team members on goal setting and work methods where possible

(e) Feedback: the manager can make an immediate impact simply by providing on-going constructive performance feedback, and by listening to team members in return.

Answer 12.5

Your own observations. Bear in mind that the cultural messages given by organisations reflect their values, and that people 'buy in or get out', to an extent: from the outside, strong upbeat cultural messages may seem false or embarrassing... Don't worry if you don't particularly like the idea of motivational posters, badges, reward ceremonies and so on: find your own suggestions for being positive, supportive and challenging towards team members – which is what Peters and Waterman's ideas amount to.

Answer 12.6

Your own observations. Be aware that there are arguments against offering purely financial incentives.

(a) Not everyone has an instrumental orientation to work: monetary rewards may be ineffective if other factors weigh against them.

(b) Monetary incentives can foster an instrumental orientation to work: workers may 'cut corners' on safety or quality in order to earn more.

(c) Monetary incentives work only where there is immediacy between effort/achievement and reward: they tend to create a focus on short-term performance indicators, and may lead to neglect of longer-term values such as innovation or quality.

(c) Monetary incentives tend to be a source of dissatisfaction, as it is difficult to make them fair (or felt to be fair), especially in regard to team working, where one or more people may not be felt to be 'pulling their weight'. Performance-related rewards are difficult to apply fairly, in jobs where success is determined by factors outside the individual's control.

Answer 12.7

Your own research.

Now try Question 11 in the Exam Question Bank

Part D
Individual effectiveness at work

Chapter 13 Planning and organising personal work

Chapter topic list

1. Work roles and responsibilities
2. Personal time management
3. Priorities
4. Personal work planning
5. Planning aids
6. Managing resources

The following study sessions are covered in this chapter:

		Syllabus reference
14(a)	Explain the benefits of planning and organising personal work	4(a)
14(a)	Understand roles and responsibilities	4(a)(i)
14(a)	Identify effective work methods, practices and reporting procedures	4(a)(i)
14(a)	Use work planning and planning aids	4(a)(ii)
14(a)	Prioritise work and practise personal time management	4(a)(iii)

Part D: Individual effectiveness at work

1 WORK ROLES AND RESPONSIBILITIES

1.1 We will be discussing roles, authority and working with others in the context of **interpersonal relationships** in Chapter 14 of this Text. In this chapter, we simply want to call your attention to those aspects which **influence your ability to organise and manage your own workload**.

Defining your work role: job description

1.2 Certain tasks need to be done in order for the department and organisation to meet their objectives. Those tasks must be allocated to particular positions or individuals, who will be responsible for seeing that they are complete according to plan.

1.3 A **job description** is a concise statement of the tasks, responsibilities and relationships involved in a given job.

 (a) **Job title** may include: department and job code number, where relevant; grading of the job (for salary purposes).

 (b) **Job summary** – brief account of the purpose, main tasks and special conditions (if any) of the job).

 (c) **Job content** – list of the main duties that constitute the job.

 (d) **Reporting structure** – the extent (and limits) of the jobholder's **authority and responsibility. Relation of job to other closely associated jobs,** including superior and subordinate positions and liaison required with other departments.

 (e) **Job requirements and conditions** – working hours, basis of pay and benefits, and conditions including location, special pressures, or health hazards (if any).

 (f) **Opportunities** for training, transfer and promotion.

 (g) Possibly, also, **objectives and expected results**, which will be compared against actual performance during employee appraisal.

Activity 13.1

(a) If a job description exists for your position, obtain a copy: ask your manager, or the personnel department, if you do not have ready access to one. Read it through carefully, and consider whether it is an up-to-date, accurate and full description of what you actually do in your job. Draft your own version of your job description, in the light of this appraisal.

(b) If a job description does not exist for your position, draft one!

Work systems and procedures

1.4 Individuals in an organisation cannot simply do their own thing in their own way in their own time: **standard**, **predictable** and **dependable** methods help everyone to work together to a common purpose and timetable.

 (a) A **system** is a pre-determined logical plan or process for doing something.

 (b) An **administrative system** structures the relationship between tasks, procedures, data and resources to ensure a consistent, efficient and effective flow of information in and around an organisation. Examples include communication systems, management information systems, filing systems – and, of course, accounting systems.

(c) A **procedure** is a standard sequence of steps or operations necessary to perform an activity.

(d) **Administrative procedures are** basically programmed activities relating to the flow of business information. Here is an example of such a procedure.

- All cash receipts are entered in the cash book
- At the end of the day, the totals are added up
- The addition is checked
- The totals in the cash book are posted into the main accounting records

Work methods and practices

1.5 The work methods, practices and procedures of your department and organisation arise from a number of factors.

(a) The nature and logic of the **task**: what needs to be done, in what order and in what manner, in order for the purpose of the task to be fulfilled

(b) The requirements of the **law, regulations** and **Codes of Practice** established to ensure that tasks are completed safely, fairly and in accordance with the rights of individuals and society

(c) The requirements of **organisational policy**, formulated to reflect the organisation's values and intentions

(d) **Formal instructions** from people in positions of authority. Where there is no set policy, procedure or legal constraints, a manager can to an extent dictate how things are done

(e) **Informal ground rules** or **customs**, developed over time by the work group or the organisational culture.

Activity 13.2

Give some examples of procedures affecting your work that arise from each of the influences listed in Paragraph 1.5 above.

1.6 Many organisations have a **procedures manual** which is a useful source of information – and a point of reference in case of dispute. This should contain information on:

- The organisation's structure, products and services, with relevant guidelines
- Accounting and reporting systems
- Health and safety procedures
- Disciplinary and grievance procedures

1.7 Make sure that you are aware of any such formal guidelines provided by your organisation, as well as:

- **Instructions** given by your manager, colleagues and trainers
- Posted **notices**
- **Manuals and handbooks** accompanying equipment and machinery
- **Employee bulletins**, which often highlight changes

Know how each of your tasks should be performed in accordance with organisational procedures and legal requirements.

Part D: Individual effectiveness at work

Working with others

1.8 Your work role and responsibilities cannot be considered in isolation from organisational objectives and structures. Nor can they be considered in isolation from **other people**.

   (a) Where you are working in a department, section or team, you will have **joint objectives and goals**, which require you to pool your resources, information and efforts.

   (b) Your individual role will almost certainly involve **co-ordinating** your objectives and goals with those of other individuals and departments.

1.9 **Co-ordination** means integrating your work with other people's.

   (a) The organisation is a collection of individuals and groups, each with their own interests and goals. These must be given a common direction if the organisation is to achieve its objectives.

   (b) The organisation's activities involve a variety of people, tasks, resources and technologies which will have to be co-ordinated if smooth operations are to be maintained.

   (c) Some activities of the organisation will be dependent on the successful and timely completion of other activities. Individuals need to ensure that they are aware of the requirements, plans and deadlines of others.

2 PERSONAL TIME MANAGEMENT

What is time management?

2.1 **Time is a resource, like money, information and materials.** You have a fixed and limited amount of it, and various demands in your work (and non-work) life compete for a share of it. If you work in an organisation, your 'time is money': you will be paid for it, or for what you accomplish with it.

2.2 Time, like any other resource, needs to be managed, if it is to be used efficiently (without waste) and effectively (productively). The **key principles of time management** can be depicted as follows.

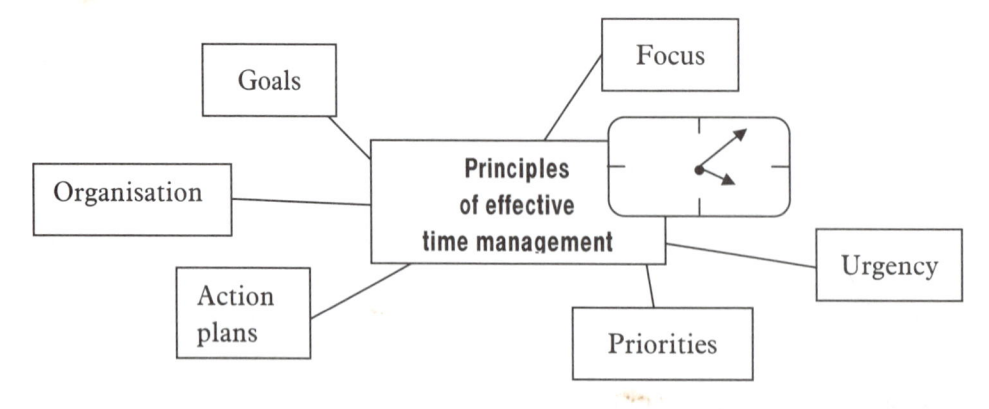

```
                    Goals            Focus

        Organisation    ┌─────────────┐
                        │  Principles │
                        │ of effective│
                        │   time      │
                        │ management  │
                        └─────────────┘     Urgency
        Action
        plans                   Priorities
```

Goals

2.3 If you have no idea what it is you are supposed to accomplish all the time in the world will not be long enough to get it done. Nor is there any way of telling whether you have done it or not. To be useful, goals need to be SMART:

Specific

Measureable

Attainable

Realistic and

Time-bounded

2.4 In work terms you could probably set **specific goals** by reference to your job description: 'prepare and despatch invoices for all goods sold'; 'issue monthly statements'; 'monitor slow paying customers'.

2.5 However, **measurable** and **time-bounded goals** are very important for **effective time management**. If you say 'My goal is to see that invoices are issued and despatched for all goods sold on the day of sale' you have a very clear and specific idea of what it is that you have to achieve and whether you are achieving it or not.

Action plans

2.6 Now you must make **written action plans that set out how you intend to achieve your goals**: the timescale, the deadlines, the tasks involved, the people to see or write to, the resources required, how one plan fits in with (or conflicts with) another. These need not be lengthy or formal plans: start with **notes, lists** or **flowcharts** that will help you to capture and clarify your ideas and intentions.

Work planning will be considered in Section 4 below.

Priorities

2.7 Now you can set priorities from your plan. You do this by deciding which tasks are the most important: what is the most valuable use of your time at that very moment?

2.8 Which task would you do if you only had time to do one task? That is your first priority. Then imagine that it will turn out that you have enough time to do one more thing before you have to leave. What would you do next? That is your second priority. Continue in this vein until you have identified three or four top priorities. Then get on with them, in order.

We discuss prioritising in more detail in Section 3 below.

Focus: one thing at a time

2.9 Work on **one thing at a time** until it is finished, where possible.

(a) If a task cannot be completely finished in one 'session', complete everything that it is in your power to complete at that time and use a **follow-up system** to make sure that it is not forgotten in the future. Correspondence, in particular, will involve varying periods of delay between question and answer, action and response.

(b) **Make sure that everything that you need is available before you start work.** If it isn't, you may not be able to do the task yet, but one of the things on your 'to do' list will be to order supplies of the necessary forms or stationery, or to obtain the required information or do whatever it is that is holding you up.

Part D: Individual effectiveness at work

(c) **Before you start a task clear away everything from your desk that you do not need for that particular task.** Put them where you will be able to retrieve them when you come to deal with the tasks that you need them for. It is quite hard to discipline yourself to do this because it might take some time and you might feel that that time could be spent doing other things. However, once tidy working becomes a habit, it will take no time at all, because your desk will always be either clear or have on it only the things you are using at that precise moment. One of the best ways of helping yourself to concentrate and handle things one at a time is to remove distractions.

Urgency: do it now!

2.10 **Do not put off large, difficult or unpleasant tasks simply because they are large, difficult or unpleasant.** If you put it off, today's routine will be tomorrow's emergency: worse, today's emergency will be even more of an emergency tomorrow. Do it now!

2.11 **Think for a moment about how you behave when you know something is very urgent.** If you oversleep, you leap out of bed the moment you wake up. If you suddenly find out that a report has to go out last post today rather than tomorrow afternoon, then you get on with it at once. We are saying that you should **develop the ability to treat everything that you have to do in this way**.

Organisation

2.12 Apart from working to plans, checklists and schedules (discussed in Section 4), your work organisation might be improved by the following.

(a) **An ABCD method of in-tray management.** When a task or piece of paper comes into your in-tray or 'to do' list, you should never merely look at it and put it back for later. This would mean you would handle it more than once – usually over and over again, if it is a trivial or unpleasant item! Resolve to take one of the following approaches

Act on the item immediately

Bin it, if you are sure it is worthless, irrelevant and unnecessary

Create a definite plan for coming back to the item: get it on your schedule, timetable or 'to do list'

Delegate it to someone else to handle

(b) **Organise your work in batches** of jobs requiring the same activities, files, equipment and so on. Group your filing tasks or word processing tasks, for example, and do them in a session, rather than having to travel to and fro or compete for equipment time for each separate task.

(c) **Take advantage of your natural work patterns.** Self-discipline is aided by developing regular hours or days for certain tasks, like dealing with correspondence first thing, or filing at the end of the day. If you are able to plan your own schedules, you might also take into account your personal patterns of energy, concentration, alertness etc. Large or complex tasks might be undertaken in the mornings before you get tired.

Activity 13.3

Which of the following apply in your case and which do not? Add explanatory notes where applicable.

	True	False	Explanatory notes
I work with a tidy desk.			
All my drawers, shelves and cabinets are tidy.			
Items that I use frequently are always ready to hand.			
Whenever I have finished with a file or a book I put it back where it belongs immediately.			
I write everything down and never forget anything.			
I work on one task at a time until it is finished.			
I do daily tasks daily except in very exceptional circumstances, in which case I catch up the next day.			
Every routine task that I do is done at a regular time each day.			
I never pick up a piece of paper without taking action on it (writing a reply, filing it, binning it, whatever).			
I organise my work into batches and do all of one type of work at the same time.			
I never run out of stationery that takes a while to obtain: I keep an eye on this and order in advance.			
My routine work could easily be taken over by someone else if I were unavoidably absent because I keep proper notes of what I am doing.			
I try to anticipate likely work and I ask my boss what is expected of me over the next week or so, so that I can plan out my work.			
I am able to estimate how long any task will take fairly accurately.			
I never miss deadlines.			
I do not panic under pressure.			

3 PRIORITIES

What is 'prioritising'?

3.1 **Prioritising** basically involves arranging all the tasks which may face an individual at the same time (this week, or today) in order of '**preference**'. Because of the individual's responsibility to the organisation, this will not just be what he would 'like' to get done (or do first), but what will be most valuable to the attainment of his immediate or long-term goals.

What makes a piece of work 'high priority'?

3.2 A piece of work will be **high priority** in the following circumstances.

(a) **If it has to be completed by a deadline.** The closer the deadline, the more urgent the work will be. A report which is to be typed for a board meeting the following day will take precedence in planning the day's work over the preparation of an agenda to be circulated in a week's time: **routine work comes lowest on the list,** as it can usually be 'caught up with' later if necessary.

(b) **If other tasks depend on it**: if the preparation of a sales invoice, or notes for a meeting, depends on a particular file, the first task may be to send a request for it to the file registry. Work can't start unless the file is there. Begin at the beginning!

(c) **If other people depend on it**. An item being given low priority by one individual or department – for example, retrieval or reproduction of a particular document – may hold up the activities of others.

(d) **If it is important**. There may be a clash of priorities between two urgent tasks, in which case relative **consequences** should be considered: if an important decision or action rests on a task (for example, a report for senior management, or correction of an error in a large customer order) then that task should take precedence over, say, the preparation of notes for a meeting, or processing a smaller order.

Routine and unexpected priorities

3.3 Routine priorities, or regular peak times include:

- Preparation of the weekly payroll
- Monthly issue of account statements
- Year end accounts preparation

They can be planned ahead of time, and other tasks postponed or redistributed around them.

3.4 **Non-routine priorities** occur when **unexpected demands** are made: events crop up, perhaps at short notice, or errors are discovered and require corrective action. If these are **important** (as well as sudden) they should be regarded as high priority.

Priority and urgency

3.5 Just because a task is **urgent** (that is, its deadline is close), it does not necessarily mean it is **high priority**. A task may be urgent but **unimportant**, compared to a task which has a more distant deadline.

On the other hand, as we noted earlier, you should **treat all important tasks as if they were urgent**.

3.6 In other words, **you need to be aware of changing priorities**. You need to:

(a) **Monitor** incoming work for unexpected or non-routine demands.

(b) Immediately **prioritise** each new task in relation to your existing list of tasks: it may not belong at the bottom of your 'to do' list but at the top!

(c) Adapt your schedule accordingly. This may simply involve changing the order of your 'to do' list in order to tackle new priorities before lesser ones. If your schedule is 'tight', however, there may be less room to manoeuvre. You may find that if you tackle the new high-priority task first, you will have difficulties completing a lesser-priority (but potentially still important) task by your target or deadline. In this case you may need to:

(i) Ask your manager to confirm that your priorities are correct.

(ii) Notify your manager, and any other people affected, of potential difficulties in meeting previously-arranged commitments.

13: Planning and organising personal work

    (iii) Request assistance with meeting the new or previous demands.

(d) Adapt any relevant resource allocations accordingly.

Again, this may simply involve re-allocating your own time (or that of others under your authority), machine hours or services (eg secretarial support) to the new priority. Again, however, this may have to be authorised and/or negotiated with your supervisor and others affected by the change.

What is a deadline?

3.7 A deadline is the **latest date or time** by which a task **must be completed** in order for its objectives to be fulfilled.

3.8 The important points about deadlines are:

- They have been set for a reason
- They get closer!

Activity 13.4

List four reasons to avoid missing deadlines.

4 PERSONAL WORK PLANNING

Work planning

4.1 Work planning, as the term implies, means planning how, when and by whom work should be done, in order that objectives can be efficiently met. At an individual level, this may involve the following.

Planning activity	Example
Scheduling **routine tasks** so that they will be completed at pre-determined times	You plan to complete bank reconciliations every month.
Handling **high-priority tasks and deadlines**: working into the routine any urgent tasks which interrupt the usual level of working	You adjust your plans so that you can prepare an urgent costing requested by the sales manager.
Adapting to **changes and unexpected demands**	A colleague may go off sick: there should be a contingency plan to enable to you to provide cover for him or her.
Setting **standards** against which performance will be measured	You set a target to complete a certain number of costings to a certain level of accuracy.
Co-ordinating your own plans and efforts with those of others	You plan to get your costings to the sales meeting in time for sales staff to prepare a quote for a client.

Part D: Individual effectiveness at work

4.2 Work planning consists of a number of basic steps.

(a) **Allocating work** to people and machines (sometimes called **loading**)

(b) Determining the **order** in which activities are performed (prioritising: sometimes called **activity scheduling** or **task sequencing**)

(c) Determining exactly **when** each activity will be performed (timetabling: sometimes called **time scheduling**)

(d) Establishing **checks and controls** to ensure that deadlines are being met and that routine tasks are still achieving their objectives

Loading

4.3 The allocation of tasks to other people, or machines, will depend upon a number of factors.

- The skills and expertise required to do the task
- The other work already allocated to people with the appropriate skills
- The demand for commonly used facilities (such as computers and printers)

Sequencing

4.4 We have already discussed prioritising on the basis of commitments, urgency and importance. If these issues are not involved, here are some other possible criteria for sequencing tasks.

(a) **Arrival time**. This is the first come, first served basis that you encounter all the time, in the bank, or whenever you ring somebody, for example. The order in which things are done are determined by the things themselves.

(b) **Most nearly finished**. This is not very scientific, but it recognises that great frustration can be caused by interrupting a job just before it is completed.

(c) **Shortest queue at next operation**. For example, seeing that the typist is about to run out of work, you might draft some letters before making the lengthy series of phone calls that you are due to make.

(d) **Least changeover cost**. For example if you have too much to do and are about to go on holiday, you should finish off all the things that it will be difficult for someone else to take over while you are away.

(e) **Shortest task first, then next shortest, and so on**. This is not very scientific, but it gets lots of things out of the way quickly.

(f) **Longest job first, then next longest, and so on**. Again this is not very scientific, but it gets the most daunting task out of the way rather than letting it hang about becoming ever more daunting.

Scheduling

4.5 **Activity scheduling** provides a list of activities, in the order in which they must be completed: we have called this task sequencing. **Time scheduling** adds to this the timescale or start and end times/dates for each activity.

4.6 Determining the time that it will take to do a task – for the purpose of setting targets – is easy if it is a **routine task** that you have done a thousand times before. Simply keep a note of how long it takes you, on average.

13: Planning and organising personal work

With **non-routine tasks**, particularly substantial ones, it can be far more difficult to determine how long to allow. You can ask someone with more experience than you, or you might be able to break the new task down into smaller stages whose duration you can more easily estimate. The important thing is to be realistic.

4.7 Time schedules can be determined by different methods.

(a) **Forward scheduling** can be used, starting with a given start time/date and working through estimated times for each stage of the task (allowing for some which may be undertaken simultaneously, by more than one person or machine) to the estimated **completion** time/date. This method can be used, for example, when completing routine accounting tasks.

(b) **Reverse scheduling** is where you start with a **completion** time/date or deadline, and work **backwards** through estimated times for each stage of the task, determining **start times** for each stage – and for the task as a whole – which will enable you to meet the deadline. This method can be used to meet deadlines, for example, for a report to be prepared, for office relocation, and many other projects which have a set completion date.

Activity 13.5

Georgette works in the correspondence department of a large building society. She has made a list of all the tasks that she has to do today.

(a) Read and deal with first post
(b) Finish filing yesterday's work
(c) Attend staff meeting at 2.30pm
(d) Chase up replies to previous correspondence
(e) Read and deal with afternoon post
(f) Try to complete work outstanding from earlier days
(g) File today's work

How should Georgette organise her day?

4.8 Various aids to **scheduling** – and to **monitoring progress against schedule** – are available, and we will discuss these now.

5 PLANNING AIDS

Lists

5.1 Lists are a useful way of identifying and remembering what needs to be done, and of monitoring how far you've got. You should work from a list of 'Things to do' all the time. If you don't do this already, try this approach once and you will be hooked. What's more, your daily productivity will shoot up.

- ☐ **Plan the whole of the coming week**. It is best to do this when you are free from the pressures and distractions of actually being at work.

- ☐ **Make a list every day before you start work**. Again, it is probably best to do this the night before.

- ☐ **On the day itself refuse to do anything that is not on your list**. Every new task that arises has to be added to your list.

☐ **Every time you finish something on your list, cross it off.** This is the really satisfying part of making lists!

☐ **At the end of the day take all the items that are still on the list and transfer them to your list for the next day.** Don't skip this part and just staple today's unfinished list to tomorrow's unstarted one. The physical act of writing tasks down on paper is an important part of the process. They will not be channelled through your mind if you just look at them.

Activity 13.6

Make a list **now** of everything you have to do for the rest of the day today **or** the whole day tomorrow.

Checklists

5.2 A checklist is simply a list which allows for **ticking or checking off** each task as it is completed (such as that in paragraph 5.1 above). Again, it may or may not reflect the order in which you actually perform the tasks. You may simply have a column to put ticks against each task, or you may want to have a space for times/dates on which you started or finished the activity, or even for stages of the activity (for example, where a particular document is at a given date) – or elements of all of these.

5.3 As an example, here is a checklist for an accounts manager preparing deadlines for sending a number of job advertisements to press.

Ad	Due date	Writer	Designer	Photographer	Film	Print	Proofed	Sent?
Times	3/9	21/8	22/8	24/8	30/8	–	2/9	☑
Standard	3/9	22/8	23/8	26/8	30/8	–	2/9	☑
A5 classified	7/9	29/8	30/8	–	–	–	4/9	☑
Leaflet A	12/9	10/8	12/8	15/8	–	2/9		☐
Leaflet B	13/9	2/9	3/9	–				☐

Activity 13.7

You are the accounts manager's assistant at Modus Operandi Ltd. Mrs Tancredi has fallen ill on the 5th September, and has asked you to take over the ad and leaflet production. 'I've left you my work checklist,' she says. 'You can work from that.' You find on her desk the checklist given as our example above.

(a) What can you tell from the checklist?
(b) What does this suggest about the usefulness of checklists?

Action plans

5.4 **Action plans** set out a programme of work or action, including time scheduling. Our example of a checklist above was a kind of action plan.

13: Planning and organising personal work

The following is another example, for the writing of a report.

Activity		Days before due date	Target date	Date begun	Date completed
1	Request files	6	3/9		
2	Draft report	5	4/9		
3	Type report	3	6/9		
4	Approve report	1	8/9		
5	Signature	1	8/9		
6	Courier	0	9/9		

Precedence networks

5.5 If you are having trouble converting your list or checklist into a workable **sequence** of actions, a fairly simple approach to working it out is to 'map' it, using what is called a **precedence network**. A simple precedence network shows which activities need to be completed before others. The circles or 'nodes' denote activities, and the arrows show logical progression and precedence.

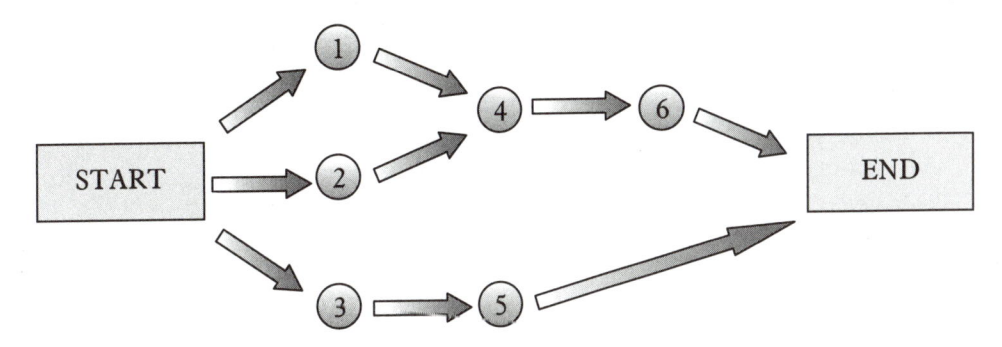

5.6 Consider the network above as a plan for going away on holiday, say.

Key

Activity 1 = Reserving your holiday place by phone

Activity 2 = Booking travel insurance

Activity 3 = Renewing your passport

Activity 4 = Sending in a completed booking form. (This follows a reservation and requires details of insurance cover.)

Activity 5 = Obtaining a travel visa. (This can't be done until you have a valid passport.)

Activity 6 = Collection of tickets (for which you need to have made a written booking).

And you're off! The advantage of such a method is that (unlike a checklist) it allows you to show where a number of activities need to be done at roughly the same time (like activities 1, 2 and 3 above).

Timetables and diaries

5.7 The information and dairies for your action plan could be formatted as a timetable or diary entry. You may already be using such methods to timetable your studies – and/or your social life! Timetables and diaries are designed to do three things.

(a) Remind you of key times and dates

(b) Remind you to undertake advance preparations or subsequent follow-up actions

Part D: Individual effectiveness at work

(c) Help you allocate and co-ordinate your time effectively – no 25-hour days or clashing appointments

5.8 A variation on the diary system is the more sophisticated **personal organiser**. Benefits of a personal organiser system include the following.

(a) **You can store names, addresses, telephone numbers** and other basic information so that it is readily accessible, wherever you are.

(b) **You can set down tasks, goals and task priorities**, using a goal planning or **do today** framework. It will also act as a **schedule** and **checklist** to ensure that you complete all tasks at the right time.

(c) **You will record appointments, day-to-day and in the longer term** if required. This will not only help to ensure that you do not forget them but will help you to plan ahead so that:

   (i) You do not waste unnecessary time and energy travelling back and forth when you could fit in several tasks at the same time

   (ii) You can prepare, and have to hand any files or other information required;

   (iii) You can see where peak and slack periods fall, for planning other tasks.

(d) **You can take notes of ideas, meetings and plans** in a single, convenient format. (Portable electronic organisers also have 'notepad' facilities, albeit limited.) Keeping everything together – in flexible loose-leaf or (electronically) accessible format – will keep personal 'files' organised.

(e) **You will follow up tasks**. Uncompleted work, future action required, expected results or replies can be scheduled for the appropriate time as a memory jog.

5.9 **Potential problems of the system** include the following.

(a) The system requires a **time commitment** in itself. You may spend so much time filling in the sections of the personal organiser or using all of its functions (if it is electronic) that you lose work time.

(b) Just having a personal organiser is no guarantee of being suddenly organised. **Time management involves techniques which may only be acquired through training.**

(c) It is easy to grow very **dependent** on a personal organiser, to the point where its loss or destruction creates total chaos.

Activity 13.8

On the following page is shown an extract from the diary kept by the finance manager of Modus Operandi Ltd, Cynthia Cillie, who has just had an accident and who will therefore be off work for some time.

You have been asked to stand in for Cynthia while she is away.

What will you have to do over the next week and what further information do you need?

13: Planning and organising personal work

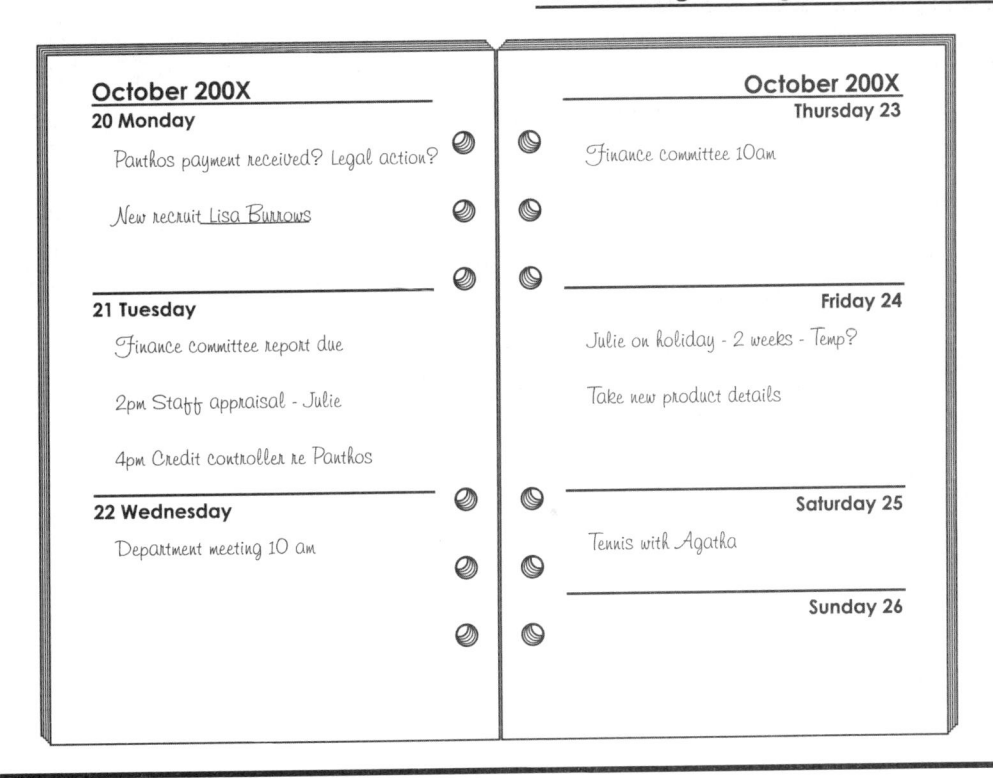

October 200X
20 Monday
Panthos payment received? Legal action?
New recruit Lisa Burrows

21 Tuesday
Finance committee report due
2pm Staff appraisal - Julie
4pm Credit controller re Panthos

22 Wednesday
Department meeting 10 am

October 200X
Thursday 23
Finance committee 10am

Friday 24
Julie on holiday - 2 weeks - Temp?
Take new product details

Saturday 25
Tennis with Agatha

Sunday 26

5.10 Many scheduling and diarising functions are now available on **electronic personal organisers** (EPOs) or **personal digital assistants** (PDAs). These may take the form of small hand-held computers (such as the Palm Pilot or IBM Workpad) or desktop computer software (such as Palm Desktop or Microsoft Outlook).

Charts

5.11 Longer-term schedules may be more conveniently read using charts, peg-boards or year-planners. These can be used to show:

- The length of time to be taken for scheduled events or activities
- The relationship between events or tasks
- The relationship between planned and actual task duration or output

Bar charts

5.12 The following is a simple example, which you may have seen used, of a year planner; in this case, a general plan for a fashion retail outlet.

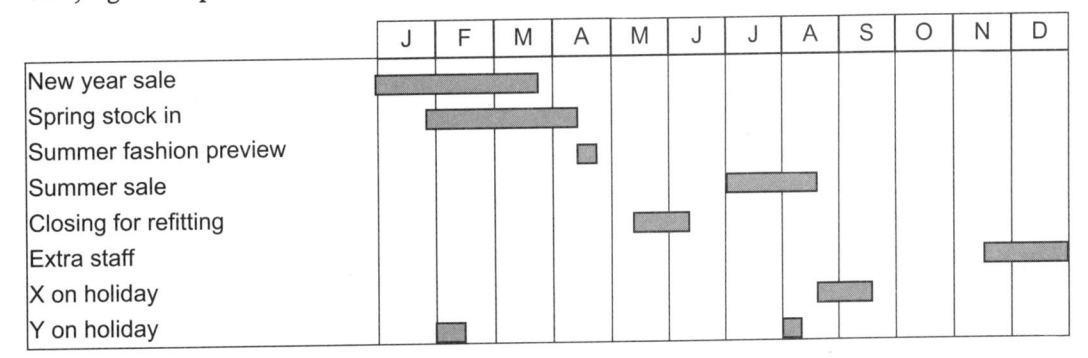

	J	F	M	A	M	J	J	A	S	O	N	D
New year sale	▬	▬	▬									
Spring stock in		▬	▬	▬								
Summer fashion preview				▪								
Summer sale							▬	▬				
Closing for refitting					▪							
Extra staff											▬	
X on holiday								▪				
Y on holiday		▪										

Part D: Individual effectiveness at work

Gantt charts

5.13 Another widely-used form of chart, which is used to show **progress** as well as schedule, is the Gantt chart.

A Gantt chart is like the horizontal bar chart used above, but each division of space represents both an amount of **time** and an amount of **work** to be done in that time. Lines or bars drawn across the space indicate how much work is scheduled to be done and/or how much work has actually been done; the more work, the longer the line or bar.

5.14 The advantage of such a chart is that you can see the relationship between time spent and amount done or produced. You can compare amounts produced in one week or month, say, with those in another (by the relative lengths of the bar or line). You can, similarly, compare amounts scheduled to be done with those actually done.

5.15 The following information, about planned work and actual progress, is set out in the following Gantt chart.

Day	Daily schedule (units)	Cumulative schedule (units)	Work done in the day (units)	Cumulative work done (units)
Monday	100	100	75	75
Tuesday	125	225	100	175
Wednesday	150	375	150	325
Thursday	150	525	180	505
Friday	150	675	75	580

Daily schedule and work actually done

Monday	Tuesday	Wednesday	Thursday	Friday
100	125	150	150	150
75	100	150	180	75

Work done ⟶

Scheduled work ┄┄┄▶

Activity 13.9

Look at the chart above.

(a) What information is clearly shown by the chart? (Is it more obvious how production is doing on the chart than on the tabulated data from which it was drawn?)

(b) What further Gantt chart might be helpful for the manager of this work, which can be drawn from the data given?

(c) Draw the Gantt chart you have suggested.

(d) What information is most usefully provided by this new chart?

Bring forward systems

5.16 On an individual level, **control over work** must be maintained to ensure that jobs do in fact reach completion, and if those jobs involve various tasks over varying periods, planning will be necessary to keep track of future events, deadlines, results and so on.

13: Planning and organising personal work

5.17 Systems which provide for this are called **bring forward** or **bring up** systems. Anything which needs action at a later date (and therefore may get forgotten) should be processed in this way, for example:

- Checking on progress of an operation
- Checking completion when the deadline is reached
- Checking payments when they fall due
- Retrieving files relevant to future discussions, meetings, correspondence

5.18 Checklists are useful, as we suggested earlier, for monitoring what has been done and what hasn't. Diary systems may also be used.

Some **computer-based schedule/diary systems** (including Microsoft Outlook) issue **alert messages** when the scheduled event or completion time approaches. These may be visual (diary entries highlighted) and/or audible (a warning bell or bleep).

Activity 13.10

Alison's section, in the data processing department of Modus Operandi, is divided into teams of three people, a senior, Alison, an intermediate, Kathryn, and a junior, Margaret. Everybody has a steady stream of their own work to be getting on with but the section also engages in special work to get specific jobs done.

On Friday afternoon Alison's team is allocated some special work which the section leader wants completed by Tuesday week, although Friday week is the latest date by which it must be completed.

Alison has divided the work up into the following steps.

	Job	Experience level	Time required
1	Information extraction	Junior	2 days
2	Information analysis	Senior	1 day
3	Data entry	Junior	2 days
4	Interpretation of results	Senior	1 day
5	Liaison with production department	Senior	1 day
6	Correspondence	Intermediate	1 day

Senior and intermediate staff are able to do the work of lower levels although this is to be avoided where possible, especially because it does not save time. Junior and intermediate staff gain new experience by doing work at the next level up. This doubles the time normally required for the work and the work is then subject to review by a person at the next level which takes an additional half day. Staff development is encouraged. None of the tasks can be done before the previous task is complete, and sharing individual tasks generally proves to be inefficient.

Alison's team members are available as follows over the next two weeks.

	M	T	W	T	F
S	–		–		
I				–	–
J	–	–			

	M	T	W	T	F
S					
I		–	–	–	
J					

The dashes indicate days when the team member is committed to working on other matters.

Tasks

(a) Alison has asked you to help her plan how the special work can best be achieved by her team in the time available.

(b) What is the first matter that Alison should attend to, so as to be sure that the plan can be implemented?

(c) Margaret seems to be showing signs of developing flu. Should Alison take any action?

Part D: Individual effectiveness at work

6 MANAGING RESOURCES

What resources do you use?

6.1 With every task, and every moment you spend at work, you are using the organisation's resources.

(a) Your own **time**, which is paid for

(b) The **time of your colleagues**, superiors and subordinates (as you deal with them, use their services or affect their work flow)

(c) **Information**

(d) **Materials**, consumables and power: electricity, paper, stationery, forms, ink

(e) **Equipment**: pens and pencils, telephones, calculators, fax machines, photocopiers, computers

(f) **Money**: the cost of all the above to the organisation, as well as any expenditure you incur or authorise as part of your job

Managing resources

6.2 Part of managing your workload is being responsible for **obtaining**, **organising**, **maintaining** and **mobilising** the resources you use in the course of your work.

(a) **Obtaining resources**

(i) Identifying appropriate resources required to meet work demands

(ii) Requisitioning resources in time to maintain work flow and meet deadlines

(iii) Monitoring the usage rate of resources, in order to re-supply without interruption to work flows

(iv) Following appropriate requisitioning and authorisation procedures for obtaining resources

(b) **Organising resources**

(i) Ensuring that regularly used resources are conveniently accessible

(ii) Clearly labelling, indexing and separating similar resources (eg forms or files), for ease of identification

(c) **Maintaining resources**

(i) Storing, using and cleaning resources (as relevant) in such a way as to preserve efficient working and longevity

(ii) Monitoring the condition of resources and replacing or repairing those which are no longer fit for their purpose

(d) **Mobilising** resources

(i) Allocating the right resources to the right processes at the right time to meet work demands efficiently and effectively

(ii) Sharing or co-ordinating resources to meet the needs of others

(iii) Adjusting resource allocations in the face of new demands, changed priorities or difficulties in meeting deadlines

Activity 13.11

List the basic resources you use regularly at work:

(a) Tools and stationery
(b) Information/reference resources: technical, organisational, personal
(c) Machine time (eg printers, photocopiers, fax)
(d) Staff time (eg word processing, filing, information services)

How do you obtain these resources?

How can you organise, maintain and mobilise these resources effectively?

Key learning points

- **Personal effectiveness** is determined in the context of: your job descriptions (defining the tasks and responsibilities of your position); the policies, procedures and practices of your organisation and department; and the requirements of co-ordination with the work of others.

- Effective **workload organisation** involves deciding when and in what order to do your work, and making sure you have all the information and physical resources that you need.

- Effective **time management** involves attention to:
    - goal or target setting
    - action planning
    - prioritising
    - focus
    - urgency and
    - organisation

- **Prioritising** tasks involves ordering tasks in order of preference or priority, based on:
    - The relative consequences of timely or untimely performance
    - Importance
    - Dependence of other people or tasks
    - Urgency
    - Defined deadlines, timescales and commitments

- **Work planning** includes the following basic steps
    - Establishing priorities
    - Loading: allocation of tasks
    - Sequencing of tasks
    - Scheduling: estimating the time taken to complete a task and working forwards or backwards to determine start and target finish times

- **Planning and scheduling aids** include: lists and checklists, precedence networks, action plans, timetables, diaries or personal organisers and charts.

- **Follow-up systems** are required to signal when checks should be made to ensure that performance is proceeding according to plan.

Part D: Individual effectiveness at work

Quick quiz

1. List six elements of effective time management.

2. Which of the following necessarily makes a piece of work high priority?

    A   Importance
    B   Urgency
    C   Importance and urgency
    D   Other people want you to do the work by a given deadline

3. A list of activities in the order in which they must be completed is the product of task loading. True or false?

4. When scheduling routine accounting tasks, are you most likely to use forward scheduling or reverse scheduling?

5. List the three key purposes of a timetable or diary system.

6. In a Gantt chart, each division of space represents both an amount of (1) .... and an amount of (2) .... output scheduled or actually done.

7. A system which provides for keeping track of future events, deadlines and follow-up action required is called a:

    A   Bring back system
    B   Bring forward system
    C   Back up system
    D   None of the above

Answers to quick quiz

1. Goals; action plans; priorities; focus; urgency; organisation

2. C. An important point: work may be urgent-but-not-important or important-but-not-urgent. You may have paused over D – but this is an assertiveness issue: if someone else 'wants' you to do something, you still have a right to consult your own priorities and commitments, assess their right to ask and so on.

3. False: it is a product of task sequencing. Task loading is allocating tasks to people or machines.

4. Forward scheduling. Reverse scheduling is more suitable for scheduling tasks for which you already have a completion date or deadline.

5. Remind you of key times and dates; remind you to take advance or follow-up action; help you allocate and co-ordinate your time.

6. (1) time; (2) work

7. B: bring forward (or bring up)

Answers to activities

Answer 13.1

Own research.

Answer 13.2

Examples might include:

(a) Logic of the task: routine task sequences such as petty cash systems or preparing invoices/ ledger balances/ management reports.

(b) Law and regulation: data security measures, retention of financial records, drafting financial statements/tax computations, complying with health and safety provisions.

13: Planning and organising personal work

(c) Policy: making (or defending) disciplinary complaints, non-discriminatory conduct, submitting leave requests, obeying smoking/alcohol rules.

(d) Formal instruction: carrying out any task as requested by a team leader or manager.

(e) Informal customs: taking smoking breaks 'out the back'; by-passing known blockages in the communication system; skipping certain forms or procedures accepted as redundant and so on.

Answer 13.3

Own self-assessment.

Answer 13.4

Delay on your part delays other people from getting on with their work, and creates a bad impression of you and the organisation you work for.

If you are late in producing a piece of work then you will tend to hurry it as the deadline draws near or passes, and its quality will suffer.

You will have less time to do your next piece of work. That too will be late or below standard.

You may get a reputation as someone who misses deadlines, and may not be trusted with responsibility in future.

Answer 13.5

We would suggest that the first post should be read first (assuming that it arrives before Georgette starts work) in case it contains anything that needs to be attended to urgently. If the post has not arrived yet Georgette could get on with clearing the backlog of filing while waiting.

Once the post arrives, any item that can be dealt with quickly should be dealt with straight away – for example redirecting correspondence that is normally dealt with by someone else to that person. Other items will require information to be obtained which may cause some delay. At this point Georgette needs to take stock of work outstanding from earlier days and new work that has just arrived, and determine the priorities.

Chasing up replies should probably wait until after the second post has been received and read: some of the replies may have come in, in which case the effort will have been wasted.

The staff meeting needs to be worked around. It would be better not to start a lengthy task just after lunch if it is going to be interrupted by the meeting in half an hour's time. If possible Georgette should try to find out how long the meeting will last and how big a chunk it will take out of her normal day.

Here is a suggested schedule.

9am to 9.30	Get on with yesterday's filing until first post arrives.
9.30 to 10.00	Look through first post and identify priorities. Forward any items that will be dealt with by others.
10.00 to 1.00	Complete each task or progress it as far as possible according to priorities identified. File completed work as soon as it is completed rather than adding to yesterday's pile.
1.00 to 2.00	Lunch.
2.00 to 2.30	Read afternoon post and adjust priorities as necessary. Forward non-relevant items.
2.30 onwards	Attend meeting.
3.30 (say)	Chase up replies to previous correspondence.
4.00 to 5.00	Complete tasks as far as possible according to priorities identified.
5.00	Go home, if both yesterday's filing and all of today's filing is done. Stay a few minutes late to get this out of the way if not.

Part D: Individual effectiveness at work

Answer 13.6

Own activity: just do it!

Answer 13.7

(a) Studying the manager's checklist shows that you don't need to worry about the ads: they are finished and sent off. Leaflet A is at the printers, and has been for 3 days: it still needs to be proofed and sent off before the 12th – a week to go. Leaflet B seems to be at the designers – with just over a week to go: it is clearly falling behind and will need watching: in particular, the photography seems to be held up and will have to be dealt with first.

(b) Checklists are particularly helpful in the event that you have to hand a task over to someone else for completion.

(c) You might have suggested shopping lists or things to do in general – or points to be covered in an essay (a very useful planning habit to get into!).

Answer 13.8

On Monday you will have to check the situation on the Panthos account. It looks as though this is a slow paying customer and that legal action is being considered if payment has not been received by the 14th. It seems that your boss was due to have a meeting about this on Tuesday with the credit controller, but it may be worth bringing this forward, or at least contacting the credit controller to get the full story and find out exactly what you should do. You may not have the authority to institute legal action and the credit controller may wish to take over responsibility here.

There is also a new person joining the department on Monday, and she will need some induction. Having been new once yourself, you will have some idea of what is required, but you should check to see whether anything specific was planned: a tour of the department, a meeting with personnel staff, signing of forms and so on. This is an ongoing task, not just something that will take five minutes on Monday morning. Over the next few days you will frequently need to make sure that the new person is being 'looked after', given work to do, receiving on-the-job training and so on.

On Tuesday your boss was due to submit a report for Thursday's finance committee meeting. You will need to find out how near this is to completion as soon as possible. Was the deadline Tuesday morning or Tuesday last thing? Will you be able to complete the report or will you need help from others? Where do you have to send the report when it is finished? Does it usually have some kind of covering letter or memo?

On Tuesday afternoon Cynthia was due to conduct a staff appraisal with a member of staff called Julie. Assuming that it would not be appropriate for you to conduct the appraisal yourself, can this be delayed until after your boss's return to work? Or can another manager conduct it instead? Does a pay rise depend on the outcome of the appraisal? Note that Julie is going on holiday for two weeks starting on Friday: it may be demotivating to make her wait for her appraisal. You need to find out the background before making a decision and discussing the matter with Julie herself.

Note also that Cynthia was considering employing a temp in Julie's absence: the diary entry about this is on Friday, but you may have to decide whether a temp will be needed (and if so when and for how long) before then, to allow time to recruit one. This is another good reason for having a discussion with Julie early in the week, to find out what her current and anticipated workload is.

On Wednesday the only thing scheduled is a departmental meeting. What was this about? Will you be expected to lead it in Cynthia's absence? Do you have all the information you need to do so?

What else will you be doing on Wednesday? Who is doing your work while you are standing in for Cynthia?

On Thursday there is the finance committee meeting, for which the report was due on Tuesday. Are you expected to attend the meeting? Will you be expected to comment on the report?

On Friday Cynthia has made a note to herself which presumably means 'take home and read the details about one of the company's new products'. Do you know which new product(s) she had in mind, and why she particularly wanted to familiarise herself with the details over the weekend? Perhaps there is some kind of meeting about this or some work on the new product has to be submitted by next week. In other words you need to look ahead in the diary to see what is coming up: you cannot just take one week at a time.

Answer 13.9

(a) The Gantt chart shows clearly that production is slightly behind schedule on Monday and Tuesday, spot on Wednesday, better than planned on Thursday, but well short on Friday.

(b) It would be helpful to see how the cumulative production measured against the cumulative schedule, since daily comparisons are up and down.

(c)

Monday	Tuesday	Wednesday	Thursday	Friday
100	225	375	525	675
75	175	325	505	580

(d) It is easy to see that the final weekly total output is well down on schedule.

Answer 13.10

(a)

Day	Task (level)	Performed by (level)	Comments
Monday	Extraction (J)	Kathryn (I)	Junior staff not available
Tuesday	Extraction (J)	Kathryn (I)	
Wednesday	Analysis (S)	Kathryn (I)	Staff development, but takes all day
Thursday (Half)	Review	Alison (S)	Review of Wednesday's work
Thursday (Half)	Data entry (J)	Margaret (J)	After review, data entry can commence
Friday	Data entry (J)	Margaret (J)	–
Monday (Half)	Data entry (J)	Margaret (J)	–
Monday (Half)	Interpretation (S)	Alison (S)	–
Tuesday	Liaison (S)	Alison (S)	–
Wednesday	Correspondence (I)	Margaret (J)	Staff development, but task takes twice as long
Thursday	Correspondence (I)	Margaret (J)	–
Friday (Half)	Review	Kathryn (I)	–

(b) Alison should speak to somebody in the production department to make sure that it will be possible to carry out the task that requires their input on the day planned and to make them aware of the overall deadlines so that they can organise any preparatory work that they need to do.

(c) If Margaret is ill and is not back at work by Thursday, the whole job will be delayed. Alison should mention this matter to her section leader, who may be prepared to accept a revision of the final deadline or be able to arrange for help from another junior in the section.

Answer 13.11

The solution should apply to your own work role and organisation in regard to:

(a) The resources you use

- Tools and stationery include: pens and pencils, staplers, hole punches, floppy disks, mouse mats and ink cartridges; analysis sheets; notepads (memo pads, telephone message pads etc); cash books, vouchers and authorisation forms (journal vouchers, petty cash vouchers etc); forms; letter heads and so on.

- Information resources include: technical (reference books; product/service brochures; procedure, policy and instruction manuals; legal updates); organisational (policy and procedure manuals; staff planning charts; forms and reports); personal (diaries, expense sheets, timesheets, training/appraisal information, your portfolio of evidence of competence; any personal documents you may occasionally need to refer to eg doctor, bank details).

Part D: Individual effectiveness at work

- Machine time: access to printers, photocopiers, fax machines, shredders etc (all of which may be have to be shared and scheduled with others)
- Staff time: staff under your authority (to whom you can delegate tasks), support staff (to whom you can give tasks – often shared and scheduled with others: eg typists, office assistants), service departments (from whom you can requisition services: eg maintenance, cleaning, information technology support).

(b) How you obtain these resources. You may need the authorisation of your supervisor or manager; stores requisition forms (to obtain physical resources); job requisition forms (to request staff time or services); telephone/e-mail requests to stationery or service departments and so on.

(c) How you can best organise, maintain and mobilise the resources you use. Issues in organisation and maintenance (for items within your control) are fairly clear cut. Mobilising resources is often more difficult: what authorisation or procedures are required to get extra time on a machine; reallocate staff to different duties; acquire extra resources to push through a high-priority job?

Now try Question 12 in the Exam Question Bank

Chapter 14 Constructive relationships

Chapter topic list

1. Work relationships
2. Interpersonal skills at work
3. Communication
4. Communication methods
5. Communication styles
6. Managing dissatisfaction and conflict

The following study sessions are covered in this chapter:

Syllabus reference

15(a)	Recognise the importance of good communication and interpersonal skills	4(b)
15(b)	Identify and describe the main methods and attributes of effective communication	4(b)(i)
15(c)	Distinguish between verbal and non-verbal forms of personal communication	4(b)(i)
15(d)	Define the term 'interpersonal skills' in the context of effective management practice	4(b)
15(e)	Explain the importance of developing effective working relationships	4(b)
15(f)	Identify appropriate ways of gaining commitment from individual staff members	4(b)(ii)
15(g)	Describe methods and procedures for dealing with disagreement and conflict	4(b)(iii)

Part D: Individual effectiveness at work

1 WORK RELATIONSHIPS

What are working relationships?

1.1 How might you describe a good working relationship?

(a) **Good working**

A good working relationship allows or facilitates work **transactions**, the completion of **tasks** and the fulfilment of **objectives**, eg prompt and willing service, co-operation and co-ordination, communication, expertise, teamworking skills and mutual reward or benefit.

(b) **Good ... relationships**

A good working relationship allows or facilitates ongoing and mutually satisfying **interpersonal relations**. For example, politeness, friendliness, trust, openness, the ability to resolve conflict and respect.

1.2 A working relationship can be established with anyone with whom you come into contact for the fulfilment of a transaction or task: colleagues, suppliers, customers or clients.

1.3 Any group of people at work has relationships, roles and communication, even if they are not deliberately planned or developed.

Roles

1.4 **Roles** are sometimes described as parts that people play or hats that people wear.

(a) People adopt different roles in different circumstances.

(b) Roles define 'who a person is' in these circumstances and in relation to others. (The people you relate to in a particular role are called a **role set**.)

(c) Roles have certain signs or characteristics associated with them, so that a style of behaviour is expected of a person in a given role. (These are called **role signs**.)

1.5 In the accounts department, you adopt your **work role**, as opposed to your roles as student, member of a family or sports enthusiast. Within your work role may be more specific roles, such as payroll clerk, assistant to your superior or colleague to your peers – depending on what function you are performing and what other people in that context (your role set) require and expect from you.

Activity 14.1

Choose one role in which your regularly interact with other people. (The role of 'student', say?)

(a) Identify your role set and role signs.

(b) Identify any areas of ambiguity, compatibility or conflict the role presents. What could be done about each (if anything)? Could the other members of your role set help?

1.6 An important skill in working with others is being able to identify two things.

- What roles other people are in, and **what your role should be** in relation to them
- The **behaviours and role signs** expected of you in a given role

This will help you to **avoid inappropriate behaviours** such as over-familiarity in a professional context, lack of leadership in an authority role or insubordination in a

14: Constructive relationships

subordinate role, discussing matters irrelevant to the situation in hand or dressing inappropriately.

Structural relationships

1.7 Roles exist **in relation to each other**. In the work environment, there are three basic relationships between roles.

- **Subordinate role.** You work for and report to others.
- **Equal or peer role.** You work with others towards a shared goal.
- **Authority role.** Other people work for and report to you.

1.8 **Authority** and **functional** relationships are built into the **formal structure**, communication and procedures of the organisation. Its **culture** influences how these relationships are regarded and expressed. Some organisations (or departments within them) are laid-back, informal and democratic, and some are formal and strictly hierarchical. You will need to judge the appropriate **relational style** in your own department and organisation.

Interpersonal relationships

1.9 Overlaid on structural factors in relationships, there are interpersonal or human factors: individual **personalities**; interpersonal **skills**; whether people have **rapport**; personal **differences, attitudes and values**; **perceptions** (and misperceptions); **communication** and communication barriers; **group** behaviour.

1.10 When we talk about **building relationships** in this chapter, we are mainly talking about developing **rapport, trust and effective communication**, which are essentially interpersonal skills.

2 INTERPERSONAL SKILLS AT WORK

What are interpersonal skills?

> **KEY TERM**
>
> **Interpersonal skills** are skills used in interactions and relationships between two or more people.

2.1 Interpersonal skills include:

(a) Building **rapport** or a sense of 'being in tune with' another person, which draws them into a relationship

(b) Building **trust** and **respect,** so that the relationship is maintained and co-operation facilitated

(c) Managing **conflict** in such a way that the relationship is preserved.

(d) **Persuading** or **influencing** another person to do what you want them to do or to share your beliefs

(e) **Negotiating** or bargaining in order to reach mutually acceptable or compromise solutions to problems

(f) Communicating **assertively**, so that you uphold your rights and get your needs met – without violating the rights or ignoring the needs of others

(g) Communicating **informatively**, so that you give (and receive) relevant and timely information

(h) Communicating **supportively**, so that you encourage the other person and gain their commitment

These are essentially communication skills. We discuss many aspects of communication in this chapter.

Why are interpersonal skills important?

2.2 You need interpersonal skills in order to:

(a) Understand and manage the **roles, relationships, attitudes** and **perceptions** operating in any situation in which two or more people are involved

(b) **Communicate** clearly with other people

(c) Achieve your **aims** from any interpersonal encounter (ideally, allowing the other parties to emerge satisfied as well).

2.3 In a business context, interpersonal skills are particularly important for processes such as:

(a) **Motivation**: persuading and inspiring employees to committed performance (often identified with 'leadership')

(b) **Teamworking and team-building**: building trust, encouraging communication, forming co-operative relationships and managing conflict

(c) **Customer care** (including internal customers): winning trust, managing conflict, exchanging information and persuading

(d) **Human resource management**: negotiating, interviewing, conducting appraisals, managing formal disciplinary and grievance procedures

(e) **Negotiation**: maintaining relationships despite conflicting interests, working towards mutually acceptable solutions

(f) **Workload management**: being able to delegate effectively, negotiate assistance, say 'no' assertively

(g) **Career development**: demonstrating networking, communication and leadership skills – increasingly essential for managerial roles

Activity 14.2

Using the following grid, monitor all the various conversations or interactions you have at work in the course of one day. For each one, put a tick in the appropriate column.

14: Constructive relationships

	Technical/ work-related with colleagues	Technical/ work-related with customers/ clients/ enquirers	Organisational team/ 'membership'	Giving advice/ support/ challenge	Getting advice/ support/ challenge	Non work-related: just friendly/ courteous
During work time						
During breaks/ lunch/after work etc						
	Total:	Total:	Total:	Total:	Total:	Total:

What does this information tell you about the contexts in which your interpersonal skills are required?

3 COMMUNICATION

> **KEY TERM**
>
> **Communication** is – at its most basic – the transmission or exchange of information.

3.1 Communication underpins everything you do at work. It is so basic to our lives that you may never have thought about what is actually going on when we communicate. There is no need to go too deeply into the theory, but it is worth examining **why** we communicate and **what has to happen** for effective communication to take place.

Why we communicate

3.2 The general purpose of most communications will be as follows.

(a) **To inform**: to give people data that they require

(b) **To persuade**: to get somebody to do something

(c) **To request**: to ask for something

(d) **To confirm**: to check that information is correct and that both parties have the same understanding of it

(e) **To build the relationship**: giving information in such a way as to acknowledge and maintain the relationship between the sender and receiver – mutual trust, loyalty, respect and benefit

3.3 In addition, you may have a specific purpose for communicating. Think in terms of the **outcome** that you want from the communication event: what do you want to happen, and when? Knowing the **purpose of your communication** – what you want to achieve – is the first step in planning any message.

The communication process

3.4 Effective communication is a **two-way process**, often shown as a 'cycle'. Signals or messages are sent by the communicator and received by the other party who sends back some form of confirmation that the message has been received and understood.

Part D: Individual effectiveness at work

Key

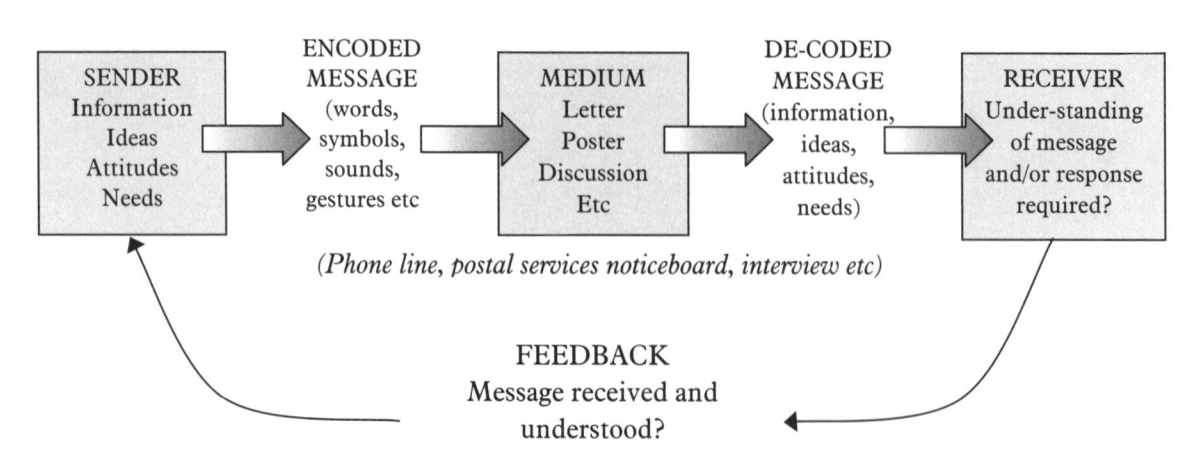

```
                              CHANNEL

                ENCODED                      DE-CODED
                MESSAGE                      MESSAGE
  SENDER        (words,      MEDIUM          (information,    RECEIVER
  Information   symbols,     Letter          ideas,           Under-standing
  Ideas    →   sounds,   →  Poster      →   attitudes,   →   of message
  Attitudes     gestures etc  Discussion     needs)           and/or response
  Needs                       Etc                             required?

              (Phone line, postal services noticeboard, interview etc)

                              FEEDBACK
                          Message received and
                              understood?
```

3.5 Encoding and decoding

Words are only symbols or stand-ins for your ideas or intentions in communicating. In other situations a gesture, pictures, symbols or numbers will be the most appropriate code to use. The important thing is that both parties understand the code.

3.6 **Feedback** is the reaction of the receiver which indicates to the sender that the message has (or has not) been received and enables him to assess whether it has been understood and correctly interpreted.

Feedback can range from a smile or a nod to a blank look or a shrug, or from the desired action being taken to no action or the wrong action being taken.

Activity 14.3

Give five examples each of what you would interpret as:

(a) Negative feedback (a sign that your message was not having its desired effect); and
(b) Positive feedback (a sign that your message was received and understood).

3.7 Media

The choice of an appropriate medium for communication depends on a number of factors.

(a) **Speed.** A phone call, for example, is quicker than a letter

(b) **Complexity.** A written message, for example, allows the use of diagrams, figure working etc and time for perusal at the recipient's own pace, repeated if necessary.

(c) **Need for a written record**: eg for the confirmation of business or legal transactions

(d) **Need for interaction** or the immediate exchange of information or questions and answers. Face-to-face and phone discussion is often used to resolve conflicts, solve problems and close sales for this reason.

(e) **Confidentiality** (eg a private interview or sealed letter) or, conversely, the **need to disseminate** or spread information widely and quickly (eg via a notice board, public meeting or Web site).

(f) **Cost**: for the best possible result at the least possible expense.

Activity 14.4

Suggest the most effective medium for communication in the following situations.

(a) New printer cartridges are urgently required from the office goods supplier.
(b) The managing director wants to give a message to all staff.
(c) Fred Bloggs has been absent five times in the past month and his manager intends to take action.
(d) You need information quickly from another department
(e) You have to explain a complicated operation to a group of people.

Communication flows

3.8 Formal channels in an organisation may run in three main directions.

(a) **Vertical**: ie up and down the scalar chain.

   (i) **Downward** communication is very common, and takes the form of instructions, briefings, rules and policies and the announcement of plans, from superior to subordinate.

   (ii) **Upward** communication is rarer – but very important for the organisation. It takes the form of reporting back, feedback and suggestions. Managers need to encourage upward communication to take advantage of employees' experience and know-how, and to be able to understand their problems and needs in order to manage better.

(b) **Horizontal or lateral**: between people of the same rank, in the same section or department, or in different sections or departments. Horizontal communication between 'peer groups' is usually easier and more direct then vertical communication, being less inhibited by considerations of rank.

   (i) **Formally:** to co-ordinate the work of several people, and perhaps departments, who have to co-operate to carry out a certain operation

   (ii) **Informally:** to furnish emotional and social support to an individual

(c) **Diagonal**. This is interdepartmental communication by people of different ranks. Departments in the technostructure which serve the organisation in general, such as Human Resources or Information Systems, have no clear 'line authority' linking them to managers in other departments who need their involvement. Diagonal communication aids co-ordination, and also innovation and problem-solving, since it puts together the ideas and information of people in different functions and levels. It also helps to by-pass longer, less direct channels, avoiding blockages and speeding up decision-making.

Barriers to effective communication

3.9 General problems which can occur in the communication process include the following.

(a) **Distortion**. The technical term for a process through which the meaning of a message is lost in the coding or decoding stages. Misunderstandings may arise from technical or ambiguous language, misinterpretation of symbols and tones of voice.

(b) **Noise**. Interference in the environment of communication which prevents the message getting through clearly. This may be:

- Physical noise (eg passing traffic)
- Technical noise (eg a bad Internet connection)
- Social noise (eg differences in personalities, status or education)
- Psychological noise (eg anger or prejudice distorting what is heard)

(c) **Misunderstanding** due to lack of clarity or technical jargon

(d) **Non-verbal signs** (gesture, facial expression) contradicting the verbal message

(e) Failure to give or to seek **feedback**

(f) '**Overload**' - a person being given too much information to digest in the time available

(g) **People** hearing only what they want to hear in a message

(h) **Differences** in social, racial or educational background

(i) **Poor communication skills** on the part of sender or recipient

3.10 Additional difficulties may arise from the work context

(a) **Status** (of the sender and receiver of information)

(i) A senior manager's words are listened to closely and a colleague's perhaps discounted.

(ii) A subordinate might mistrust his or her superior and might look for 'hidden meanings' in a message.

(b) **Jargon.** People from different job or specialist backgrounds (eg accountants, personnel managers, IT experts) can have difficulty in talking on a non-specialist's wavelength.

(c) **Suspicion.** People discount information from those not recognised as having expert power.

(d) **Priorities.** People or departments have different priorities or perspectives so that one person places more or less emphasis on a situation than another.

(e) **Selective reporting.** Subordinates giving superiors incorrect or incomplete information (eg to protect a colleague, to avoid 'bothering' the superior); also a senior manager may only be able to handle edited information because he does not have time to sift through details.

(f) **Use.** Managers who are prepared to make decisions on a 'hunch' without proper regard to the communications they may or may not have received.

(g) **Timing.** Information which has no immediate use tending to be forgotten.

(h) **Opportunity.** Mechanisms, formal or informal, for people to say what they think may be lacking, especially for upward communication.

(i) **Conflict.** Where there is conflict between individuals or departments, communications will be withdrawn and information withheld.

(k) **Cultural values** about communication. For example:

(i) **Secrecy.** Information might be given on a need-to-know basis, rather than be considered as a potential resource for everyone to use.

(ii) **Can't handle bad news.** The culture of some organisations may prevent the communication of certain messages. Organisations with a 'can-do' philosophy may not want to hear that certain tasks are impossible.

14: Constructive relationships

Activity 14.5

Before reading on, what problems are suggested by the following?

(a) [On the noticeboard] 'P Brown. Your complaint about the behaviour of your colleague S Simms is being looked into. Manager.'

(b) 'Prima facie, I would postulate statutory negligence, as per para 22 Sec three et seq. Nil desperandum.' 'Eh?'

(c) 'Smith - you've been scratching your head and frowning like mad ever since I started the briefing half an hour ago. I've tried to ignore it but - have you got fleas or something?'

(d) 'Sorry, this line's terrible - *how* many? *how* much? - what was that? NO, it's OK: I'll remember it all. We'll deliver on Monday - no, MONDAY: no, MONday ...'

(e) Date: 11 March. Report on communication for staff meeting 12 March. 463 pages.

(f) 'Look. Nobody pays you to think: leave that to us professionals. Just do your job.'

Improving the communications system

3.11 Depending on the problem, measures to improve communication may be as follows.

(a) **Encourage, facilitate and reward** communication. Status and functional barriers (particularly to upward and inter-functional communication) can be minimised by improving opportunities for formal and informal networking and feedback.

(b) **Give training and guidance** in communication skills, including consideration of recipients, listening and giving feedback.

(c) **Minimise the potential for misunderstanding**. Make people aware of the difficulties arising from differences in culture and perception, and teach them to consider others' viewpoints.

(d) **Adapt technology, systems and procedures** to facilitate communication: making it more effective (clear mobile phone reception), faster (laptops for e-mailing instructions), more consistent (regularly reporting routines) and more efficient (reporting by exception).

(e) **Manage conflict and politics** in the organisation, so that no basic unwillingness exists between units.

(f) **Establish communication channels and mechanisms** in all directions: regular staff or briefing meetings, house journal or intranet and quality circles. Upward communication should particularly be encouraged, using mechanisms such as inter-unit meetings, suggestion schemes, 'open door' access to managers and regular performance management feedback sessions.

3.12 Communication between superiors and subordinates will be improved when **interpersonal trust** exists. Exactly how this is achieved will depend on the management style of the manager, the attitudes and personality of the individuals involved, and other environmental variables. Peters and Waterman advocate 'management by walking around' (MBWA), and **informality in superior/subordinate relationships** as a means of establishing closer links.

Part D: Individual effectiveness at work

4 COMMUNICATION METHODS

4.1 We will now go on to look at some of the main methods of communication used in the work context.

- Written (verbal) communication
- Oral (verbal) communication
- Non-verbal communication

Written communication

4.2 Written communication has been a primary method of formal business communication for hundreds of years. Although supplanted by the advent of the telephone, it is now making a comeback in the form of e-mail.

4.3 The advantages and disadvantages of written communication can be summarised as follows.

Advantages	Disadvantages
• Permanent record (eg of a transaction or agreement) for confirmation, processing and legal evidence	• Can take time to produce and transmit
	• Lack of interactivity: feedback, questions and answers etc are not immediately available
• Provide confirmation and back-up of oral conversations and messages	
• Easily duplicated and sent out to numerous recipients, ensuring consistency	• Inflexibility: once sent, the message cannot immediately be altered or recalled.
• Capable of relaying complex ideas, aided by suitable layout and visual aids	• Can come across as formal and inflexible: not ideal for situations requiring interpersonal tact, support etc.
• Allow lengthy or repeated perusal if necessary	

Skills in written communication

4.4 **Skills in effective written communication** include the following.

(a) **Use of appropriate structures and layouts**. For example:

(i) **Formal reports** have strict requirements and conventions, with typical section headings such as:

- Title
- Terms of reference/Introduction/Background (aims and context of the report)
- Procedure/Method (how the research was carried out)
- Findings/Analysis (the body of the report information)
- Summary/Conclusions/Recommendations (based on the report: as requested by the person commissioning the report)

(ii) **Memoranda** and **emails** have standard 'header' information, kept clear from the body of the message and allowing for effective transmission to the right person.

- To: (the target recipient)
- From: (the writer)

14: Constructive relationships

- Date: (of the message)
- Subject: / 'Re:' (the main topic of the message)
- Cc:/Copies to: (other recipients to whom the message has been sent)

(iii) **Letters** have conventions of layout and style, with certain standard elements.

- Letterhead (containing details of the sender, often with a logo and conforming to corporate identity or style guidelines)
- Recipient address (the name and address of the target recipient)
- Date (of the message)
- Salutation (Dear Sir, Dear Mr/Mrs/Ms X)
- Subject line (referring to the main reason for writing)
- Main body of the letter (set out in logical paragraphs:)
- Complimentary close (Yours Faithfully, Yours Sincerely)
- Signature and typed name (to identify the sender)
- Copy (cc) and enclosure (enc) references (to signal other copies sent or other items enclosed with the letter)

(b) **Observance of 'house style'**; organisations often have their own rules and guidelines for communication, set out in formal or informal guidelines.

(c) **Consideration of the sender's purpose and the recipient's needs**. The structure, language and style of the message should be adapted to:

(i) The sender's purpose: informing, persuading, supporting, explaining, getting action

(ii) The recipient's needs and capabilities: what information he needs (and has already), what his concerns and interests are, what language he is likely to understand, what the effect of the message will be.

A useful framework for message planning is: PASS. **Purpose, Audience, Structure, Style.**

(d) **Attention to the 'Five Cs' of effective communication**:

- Clear
- Concise
- Complete
- Correct
- Courteous

Written formats

4.5 Written communications formats commonly used in business include the following.

Letters	• Used for interpersonal communication via the external mail system (eg from the organisation to external stakeholders)
	• Flexible for use in a wide variety of situations
	• Often used to provide 'covering' or confirming details
	• May be used within the organisation for confidential or personal matters

Part D: Individual effectiveness at work

Memoranda	• Equivalent of a letter in internal communications within the organisation
	• Flexible for use in a wide variety of work situations
	• Efficient, especially where pre-printed stationery or e-mail formats are used
	• Can be overused, where a phone call or note would suffice
Reports	• Enable a number of people to review complex facts and arguments, for decision-making
	• Should be objective in content and impersonal in style
	• May be formal (subject to strict structural conventions) or informal (in the form of a memo or e-mail)
Emails	• Popular alternative to paper-based media such as letters, memos and reports: can be overused!
	• Instant transmission throughout the world, 24 hours a day
	• Must be used properly: problems include lack of security; liability for harassing, offensive or libellous content; impersonality (coming across as abrupt); and instant transmission (without time for second thoughts!).
Handbooks and journals	• Used for employee communications
	• Can be used to set out work-relevant information, policies and regulations, procedures
	• Can be used to brief and update employees on performance, results, staff news, meetings

Activity 14.6

Which written formats do you use most often in interpersonal communication (a) with colleagues or team members, (b) with your superiors and (c) with friends at work?

- What do you find most convenient about each of these formats?
- What factors or guidelines do you have to bear in mind when using them?

Oral communication

KEY TERM

Oral communication is communication 'by speech'. It is sometimes also called 'verbal communication': communication in spoken words.

4.6 Oral or verbal communication is the most basic and generally-used way of sending a message to another person: think of all the people you talk to in a day, in person or on the phone.

4.7 The same process occurs in oral communication as in written: a message is conceived, encoded, transmitted, decoded, interpreted and acknowledge by feedback. However, in oral communication there is:

14: Constructive relationships

(a) **More immediate interaction**: you switch between 'sending' (speaking) and 'receiving' (listening) very quickly, as you ask and answer questions and exchange information.

(b) **More going on**! In addition to the meaning of the words themselves, there is an additional **non-verbal** element to the communication process. You will be sending and receiving messages through tone of voice and (if you are communicating face-to-face) through facial expressions, gesture and appearance. These 'signals' are collectively known as '**body language**' (discussed below).

4.8 The advantages and disadvantages of oral communication, compared to written communication, may be summarised as follows.

Advantages	Disadvantages
• Speed of transmission (eg by telephone, briefing)	• Interference from various sorts of noise
• Interactivity: immediate interchange of feedback, questions and answers etc.	• Lack of confirmation/record (without written follow-up)
• Allows multiple interactive input from a number of people (eg in a meeting): good for ideas generation, shared decision-making and conflict resolution	• Interactivity gives less time for message planning: may lead to lack of tact, misunderstanding etc
• Immediate feedback (including non-verbal messages) minimises misunderstanding	• Non-verbal messages may complicate or undermine verbal ones
• Interpersonal immediacy (ability to adjust to feedback and use non-verbal cues): effective for persuasion, counselling etc	• Interpersonal immediacy: personalities may get in the way of clear communication
	• If large numbers of people are involved, difficult to organise and control

Skills in oral communication

4.9 **Skills in effective oral communication** include the following.

(a) **Clear speaking**: paying attention to factors such as:

- Clear articulation of words
- Suitable pace, with pauses to enable others to take in what you've said
- The use of emphasis and tone of voice to reinforce your message.

(b) **Message organisation**. Spoken messages 'flow' past the listener: the communicator must work harder to help the listener grasp the structure and content of the message. This involves techniques such as:

(i) Preparing in advance (as far as possible) for telephone and face-to-face discussions: knowing what you want to say, and how

(ii) Using introductions (summarising what you're about to say) and conclusions (summarising what you've just said) to help your listeners follow your argument

(iii) Using repetition, examples and explanations to highlight and clarify key points

(c) **Giving and seeking feedback**: checking and confirming constantly that messages have been correctly received and understood, in both directions.

(d) **Using non-verbal communication** to hold your listener's attention (eg keeping eye contact, or using emphasis in your tone of voice) and to reinforce your message (eg by appropriate gestures and facial expressions). We discuss this further below.

(e) **Active listening**: co-operating with the person talking to you: staying attentive; using questions and feedback to aid concentration and understanding.

Listening skills

4.10 **Listening skills** are particularly important for managers.

(a) They enable you to tap a quick, direct **source of information** – and to obtain information from unexpected sources.

(b) They enable you to **maximise interpersonal interactions**, by allowing you to ask questions, adjust your message to the interests/needs of the other person, interpret messages more accurately.

(c) They enable you to **build relationships** and **resolve problems**, by encouraging communication and demonstrating willingness to take another person's feelings and point of view into account.

4.11 The following are some basic guidelines on being a good listener.

(a) **Be prepared to listen**. Put yourself in an attentive frame of mind.

(b) **Maintain your interest**. Don't soak up a message like a sponge: make it interesting for yourself by asking questions: how is this information relevant to me and how can I use it?

(c) **Keep an open mind**. Don't let your prejudices and opinions get in the way of grasping the other person's points. A useful communication technique is to feed back to the person what you think they've said (briefly) in your own words. (This is a way of demonstrating 'empathy': you make sure you've heard the person correctly - and allow them to feel 'heard'.)

(d) **Use your critical faculties**. While being open-minded, you should still make a note of questions, doubts, weak points in the argument or the need for supporting evidence.

(e) **Concentrate**. Don't switch off or be distracted by irrelevancies: stay active by giving feedback, noting questions.

(f) **Be patient**. Don't interrupt (wait until a suitable opening) and don't be so pre-occupied with how you're going to respond that you forget to listen to what is said in the meantime. Write down any questions or points you want to make (briefly, in order to avoid distraction).

(g) **Co-operate**. Be prepared to give feedback, ask for clarification or repetition or whatever else it takes to get a good grasp of what the speaker is saying.

Oral communication media

4.12 Oral communication skills will be applied in a number of organisational settings.

- Telephone calls
- Informal discussions
- Meetings
- Interviews (for selection, appraisal, counselling, discipline, grievance and so on)
- Presentations

Activity 14.7

Using the material on oral communication given above (and your own experience and/or organisational guidelines) draft some simple guidelines for staff on using the **telephone** effectively.

Non-verbal communication

> **KEY TERM**
>
> **Non-verbal** communication is, as its name implies, communication without words, or other than by words: for example, by tone of voice.

4.13 When people interpret what we say, they attach much more importance to how we say it (tone of voice, body language) than they do to the actual words – especially if the two don't match!

4.14 We can **control and use non-verbal behaviour**:

   (a) **Instead** of words (eg storming out of a room or pointing something out)

   (b) To **confirm or add** to the meaning of our words (eg nodding and saying 'yes', or pointing something out and saying 'look')

   (c) To give appropriate **feedback** to another communicator (eg yawning, fidgeting or applause)

   (d) To **create a desired impression** (smart dress, firm handshake)

   Be aware, though, that body language can also **undermine** our spoken messages (eg wearing a grim expression while saying 'Everything's fine') – and studies show that people believe the body language more then the words!

4.15 If you can be aware of **other people's body language**, and **interpret** its meaning, you can:

   (a) Receive **feedback** from listeners and modify your message accordingly

   (b) Recognise people's **real feelings** when their words are constrained by politeness or dishonesty

   (c) Recognise **interpersonal problems** (eg an angry silence, refusal to look someone in the eye)

   (d) Read situations so you can **modify your communication/response strategy**. (Is the boss irritated by a delay? Reassure – and hurry. Is a colleague on the point of tears? Support and soothe.)

4.16 **What is it that we see and interpret** when we say 'He looked upset', 'I could tell he was nervous', or 'She didn't say anything, but I could tell she was pleased'?

Sign	Meaning and interpretation
Facial expression	The eyebrows, eyes, nose, lips and mouth, jaw and head position all contribute to the expression on someone's face: lips can be tight or slack, eyes narrowed or widened, the eyebrows lowered or raised, the whole face moving or still, pale or flushed.
Gestures	People make gestures unconsciously: jabbing a finger in the air for emphasis, tapping the fingers when impatient. They also make conscious gestures – and not only impolite ones: a finger against the lips for silence, a jerk of the head to indicate a direction, a shrug to indicate indifference.
Movement	Watch how people move, at what pace, and to what effect. Someone who walks briskly conveys determination; someone who shuffles along, laziness or depression; someone who can never sit still, nervousness or impatience.
Positioning	You will probably find you sit closer to the people you like and trust, face them directly, or even lean towards them. You may keep a 'respectful' distance between yourself and someone with whom you have a more formal relationship.
Contact	Shaking hands is acceptable for transmitting greeting in most contexts but, for example, nudging or prodding for emphasis, or clapping on the back, implies familiarity and ease.
Posture	Consider the way you sit and stand. Lounge, hunch or sit/stand up straight and you convey relaxation, negativity or alertness. Lean forward when you listen to someone, and you transmit interest: lean well back and you convey weariness or boredom.
Sounds	A sceptical grunt, a sympathetic murmur and a delighted whoop are useful non-verbal feedback signals.

4.17 Be aware that no non-verbal cue **by itself** is enough to make an accurate diagnosis of someone's meaning or mental state! A frown may be caused by irritation *or* perplexity *or* a headache! Consider the **whole body language** of the person, take the context into account – and test out your theories before acting on them!

You should also be aware that body language **means different things in different cultures**. An assertive level of steady eye contact, for a Westerner, would be regarded as aggressive and offensive to some Eastern cultures – just to give one example. Beware of making assumptions!

Activity 14.8

How might you interpret (or use) the following non-verbal cues?

(a) A clenched fist
(b) Stroking the chin slowly, with furrowed brow
(c) Head in hands
(d) Sitting elbow on knee, chin resting on fist
(e) Tapping toes
(f) Turning or leaning away from another person while talking
(g) A sigh, whole facial muscles relax and mouth smiles
(h) A sigh, while body sags and face 'falls'

5 COMMUNICATION STYLES

Informing

5.1 The following are some general guidelines on giving information to others.

(a) Consider the **information needs and priorities** of others: what do they need and want to know (which may not be the same thing)?

(b) Consider how much others **know already**: what background or explanation will (or will not) be required? Some people will be familiar with your subject matter, and some will not.

(c) **Avoid 'jargon'**: technical terminology which you use in your specialism, but may not mean anything to others.

(d) Communicate as **clearly, simply** and **directly** as possible – even (or especially) if the topic is complex.

(e) Use **visual aids** if this will help to make points more appealing, accessible or understandable.

(f) Provide an appropriate **volume** of information. This means:

(i) Not **overloading** people with information they will not be able to get through or take in, in the time available.

(ii) Not giving people more information than is **relevant** to them (or you).

(iii) Not giving people **less** information than they need, or you want them to have

(g) Consider the degree of **accuracy** required. All information should be accurate in the sense of **correct** – without falsehood – but need not be minutely detailed: a summary or average figure may be all that is needed.

(h) Present factual information **objectively**: without emotional colour, exaggeration or bias.

Influencing

5.2 Types of influencing strategy.

Push	Pull
1. Identify the problem/opportunity and propose your solution.	1. State your view of the problem/opportunity.
2. Invite reactions.	2. Clarify how the other person sees the situation.
3. Check that you understand each other's arguments.	3. Work towards agreement on the nature of the problem/opportunity.
4. Deal with objections: – by persuasion (if you want commitment) – by authority (if you only need compliance)	4. Look for solutions, using as many of the other person's ideas as possible.
5. Agree on the outcome and action plan.	5. Come to joint agreement on outcome and action plan.

Part D: Individual effectiveness at work

Push	Pull
• Directive	• Supportive/collaborative
• Effective where you are clear about problem/solution	• Effective where consensus, input desired
• Quick decisions where authority works to secure compliance, or where decision routine	• Slower decisions, but secures commitment
• **Can appear authoritarian**	• **Can appear weak**

Being assertive

> **KEY TERM**
>
> **Assertive behaviour** is a considered response to a problem which seeks to **satisfy the wants and needs of all parties involved** in the situation – and to **preserve the relationship** between them.

5.3 Assertive communication involves:

(a) Standing up for **your own rights** – but in such a way that you do not violate another person's rights.

(b) Expressing your **needs, wants, opinions, feelings** and **beliefs** in direct and honest – but appropriate – ways.

5.4 Examples of assertive communication include:

(a) Asking **specifically and directly** for what you want: not assuming that others will know, or work it out from hints.

(b) **Acknowledging your feelings**, using 'I' statements instead of blaming ('I feel let down' *not* 'You let me down')

(c) Using **specific statements instead of exaggeration**, especially when giving criticism ('I feel let down when you deliver work late, as you did on Tuesday' *not* 'You *always* let me down)

(d) **Sticking to statements**, repeating them as often as necessary until you feel heard, without raising your voice or entering into arguments. ('I have booked a day off... Yes, I realise you're under staffed, but I have booked a day off.')

(e) **Defusing criticism** by accepting what is valid, without becoming defensive ('You're right: I've been late twice this month' *not* 'I am not late all the time! I come in on time more than *you* do!')

(f) **Saying 'no', when you need to**, without being apologetic ('My schedule is full right now' *not* 'Oh, I'm sorry, I'm not sure... well, I suppose I *could*... if you were really desperate... But... Oh, well, never mind...)

5.5 An example of an assertive response to an inconvenient demand by a supervisor, for example, might be:

'I appreciate that you would like this task done immediately. [**Show respect for the other person's needs**] However, I would prefer to complete the project I'm working on first. [**Clearly stating own wants in the matter.**] Will tomorrow morning work for you?

14: Constructive relationships

[Inviting the other person to work with you in coming up with a solution that will satisfy you both]'

5.6 Assertive behaviour must be carefully distinguished from:

(a) **Aggressive behaviour**, a 'fight' reaction which takes the form of a verbal or physical attack:

- Standing up for your rights in such a way that you violate the rights of others
- Ignoring or dismissing the needs, wants, feelings or viewpoints of others
- Expressing your own needs, wants and opinions in inappropriate ways

An example of an aggressive response in the circumstances cited above might be: 'I'm not going to disrupt my work just because you've left the job late. Get someone else to do it!'

(b) **Passive or non-assertive behaviour**, a 'flight' reaction which takes the form of giving in to others' demands:

- Failing to stand up for your rights, or allowing others to disregard them
- Expressing your needs, wants, opinions and feelings apologetically or vaguely
- Failing to express honestly your needs, feelings and opinions

An example of a non-assertive response in the circumstances cited above might be, 'Well, I'm very busy at the moment ... but I suppose I could work late and fit it in, if you really want me to.'

Activity 14.9

What can you see as the (a) immediate or apparent benefits ('payoffs') and (b) the actual longer term results of:

- Behaving passively or non-assertively?
- Behaving aggressively?
- Behaving assertively?

Negotiating

5.7 **Negotiating** is a process of:

(a) **Purposeful persuasion**: each party attempts to persuade the other to accept its case, by marshalling persuasive arguments.

(b) **Constructive compromise**: each party accepts the need to move closer towards each other's position, so that they can explore common ground and areas where concessions and compromises can be made while still meeting the key needs of both parties.

5.8 Negotiation is a **problem-solving** technique. Its objective is that both parties reach **agreement**, so that they both go away with a **decision they can live with** – without damaging the **relationship** between them.

This is not just a useful skill for purchasing departments! You can use it as a style of communication to reach agreement and solve problems in all kinds of areas: asking your boss for permission to decorate your work space; asking your tutor for more time to complete an assignment; sorting out the demands of different people asking you to do things at the same time.

Part D: Individual effectiveness at work

5.9 A basic 'win-win' approach to negotiating (using the example of a purchasing negotiation, for relative simplicity) is as follows.

Step 1. Map out, in advance, what the needs and fears of both parties are. This outlines the psychological and practical territory.

Step 2. Define your desired outcome and estimate the worst, realistic and best case scenarios. ('If I can pay £500, it would be ideal, but I'd settle for £600. Above £700, it's just not worth my while.') Start with the best case and leave room to fall back to the realistic case. Keep your goal in sight.

Step 3. Look for mutual or trade-off benefits. How might you both gain (for example, by getting a higher discount in return for prompt or direct-debit payment). What might be cheap for you to give that would be valuable for the other party to receive or vice versa?

Step 4. Spell out the positive benefits to the other party and support them in saying 'yes' to your proposals by making it as easy as possible. (Offer to supply information or help with follow-up tasks, for example.) Emphasise areas of agreement and common ground.

Step 5. Overcome negativity by asking questions such as:

- 'What will make it work for you?'
- 'What would it take to make this possible?'

Step 6. Overcome side-tracks by asking questions such as: 'How is this going to get us where we need/want to go?'

Step 7. Be hard on the issue/problem but soft on the person. This is not personal competition or antagonism: work together on problem solving (eg by using flip chart or paper to make shared notes). Show that you have heard the other person (by summarising their argument) before responding with your counter argument.

Step 8. Be flexible. A 'take it or leave it' approach breaks relationships. (However, saying 'no' repeatedly to sales people is a good way of finding out just how far below the list price they are prepared to go!) Make and invite, reasonable counter offers.

Step 9. Be culturally sensitive. Some markets thrive on 'haggling'. Some cultures engage in a lot of movement up and down the bargaining scale (eg Asian and Middle Eastern), while others do their homework and fix their prices.

Step 10. Take notes, so the accuracy of everyone's recollection of what was proposed and agreed can be checked.

Step 11. Summarise and confirm the details of your agreements to both parties (by memo, letter, contract) and acknowledge a mutually positive outcome.

Counselling

KEY TERM

Counselling can be defined as 'a purposeful relationship in which one person helps another to help himself. It is a way of relating and responding to another person so that that person is helped to explore his thoughts, feelings and behaviour with the aim of reaching a clearer understanding. The clearer understanding may be of himself or of a problem, or of the one in relation to the other.'

14: Constructive relationships

5.10 The need for workplace counselling can arise in many different situations.

- During appraisal
- In grievance or disciplinary situations
- Following change, such as promotion or relocation
- On redundancy or dismissal
- As a result of domestic or personal difficulties
- In cases of sexual harassment or violence at work

5.11 Effective counselling is not merely a matter of pastoral care for individuals, but is very much in the organisation's interests. Counselling can:

(a) **Prevent underperformance,** reduce labour turnover and absenteeism and increase commitment from employees

(b) Demonstrate an organisation's **commitment** to and concern for its employees

(c) Give employees the confidence and encouragement necessary to take responsibility for self and career development

(d) Recognise that the organisation may be contributing to the **employees' problems** and therefore it provides an opportunity to reassess organisational policy and practice

5.12 The checklist below contains much useful advice for meeting and interviewing people generally, not merely in counselling situations.

Counselling checklist

Preparation

- Choose a place to talk which is quiet, free from interruption and not open to view
- Research as much as you can before the meeting and have any necessary papers readily available
- Make sure you know whether the need for counselling has been properly identified or whether you will have to carefully probe to establish if a problem exists
- Allow sufficient time for the session. (If you know you must end at a particular time, inform the individual of this)
- Decide if it is necessary for the individual's department head to be aware of the counselling and its purpose
- Give the individual the option of being accompanied by a supportive colleague
- If you are approaching the individual following information received from a colleague, decide in advance the extent to which you can reveal your source
- Consider how you are going to introduce and discuss your perceptions of the situation
- Be prepared for the individual to have different expectations of the discussion, eg the individual may expect you to solve the problem - rather than come to terms with it himself/herself
- Understand that the individual's view of the facts of the situation will be more important than the facts themselves and that their behaviour may not reflect their true feelings

Format of discussion

- Welcome the individual and clarify the general purpose of the meeting
- Assure the individual that matters of confidentiality will be treated as such
- The individual may be reticent through fear of being considered somewhat of a risk in future and you will need to give appropriate reassurances in this regard
- Be ready to prompt or encourage the individual to move into areas he/she might be hesitant about

Part D: Individual effectiveness at work

- Encourage the individual to look more deeply into statements
- Ask the individual to clarify statements you do not quite understand the individual and which you both might prefer to avoid
- Recognise that some issues may be so important to the individual that they will have to be discussed over and over again, even though this may seem repetitious to you
- If you sense that the individual is becoming defensive, try to identify the reason and relax the pressure by changing your approach
- Occasionally summarise the conversation as it goes along, reflecting back in your own words (not parrot phrasing) what you understand the individual to say
- Try to take the initiative in probing important areas which may be embarrassing/emotional to the interviewee
- Sometimes emotions may be more important than the words being spoken, so it may be necessary to reflect back what you see the individual feeling
- At the close of the meeting, clarify any decisions reached and agree what follow-up support would be helpful

Overcoming dangers

- If you take notes at an inappropriate moment, you may set up a barrier between yourself and the individual
- Realise you may not like the individual and be on guard against this
- Recognise that repeating problems does not solve them
- Be careful to avoid taking sides
- Overcome internal and external distractions. Concentrate on the individual and try to understand the situation with him/her
- The greater the perceived level of listening, the more likely the individual will be to accept comments and contributions from you
- Resist the temptation to talk about your own problems, even though these may seem similar to those of the individual

Source: *IPD Statement on Counselling in the Workplace*

6 MANAGING DISSATISFACTION AND CONFLICT

How does conflict arise?

6.1 **Conflict** is the clash of opposing 'forces', including the personalities, interests, opinions or beliefs of individuals and groups. Conflict often arises within and between teams, because of a number of factors.

(a) **Power and resources** are limited (and sometimes scarce) in the organisation. Individuals and groups **compete** for them, fearing that the more someone else has, the less there is to go around.

(b) Individuals and teams have their own **goals, interests and priorities** – which may be incompatible.

(c) There may be differences and incompatibilities of **personality** between individuals, resulting in 'clashes'.

(d) There may be differences and incompatibilities of **work methods, timescales and working style**, so that individuals or teams frustrate each other with apparent lack of co-ordination (especially if one person's task depends on the other's).

6.2 **Difference** and **competition** by themselves do not lead directly to conflict: they can even be positive forces, helping people to solve problems or to lift their performance.

However, they can **escalate** or **deteriorate** into destructive conflict if:

(a) There is **poor or limited communication**: assumptions go unchallenged, misunderstandings go unclarified, and feelings are left undealt with.

(b) There is **poor co-ordination**: working relationships are not managed or structured, and so are subject to interpersonal problems or unchecked competition

(c) There are **status barriers**: problems in the relationship are glossed over by the superior asserting authority ('do it because I said so'), or hidden by the subordinate feeling powerless or threatened ('it's more than my job's worth to say anything').

(d) Work demands put pressure on individuals and teams: competition may escalate, feelings may become less manageable under stress, and there may be little time allowed for interpersonal problem-solving.

Activity 14.10

Suggest how conflict may be (a) positive or constructive and (b) negative or destructive.

Managing your own interpersonal conflicts

6.3 Conflicts and sources of dissatisfaction can be managed informally in several ways. If you have a problem working with someone – for any of the reasons mentioned above – you might attempt the following.

(a) **Communicate**

The first step in any conflict or difficulty should be **direct, informal discussion** with the person concerned.

(i) Where there is a **personality or style clash**, this gets the problem out in the open and gives an opportunity to clear up any misunderstandings and misperceptions.

(ii) Problems of **incompatible working styles** or **excessive work demands** are matters which can be taken, informally, to your supervisor: (s)he will best be able to help you develop solutions to the problem.

(iii) If your dissatisfaction is with someone in authority over you, or about your own **status**, you may have to discuss the matter with someone higher up in the organisation: this is probably best handled using more formal channels.

(b) **Negotiate**

Where interests or styles are genuinely incompatible, or work demands are unmanageable, you may need to work together to explore a range of options that will at least partially satisfy both parties. You may have to make a concession in order to gain a concession: this is called **compromise**. However, the best approach is to attempt to find a mutually satisfying solution: a **win-win**.

(c) **Separate**

If personality clash is the main source of conflict, you may have to arrange (or request) a way of dealing with the other person as little as possible. It may be within your power to simply walk away from potential conflicts, rather than allow yourself to participate.

Part D: Individual effectiveness at work

If the problems persist, you may need to initiate formal conflict resolution proceedings: to have a third party mediate – or to physically separate you in different areas, duties or departments.

Managing conflict in the team

6.4 **Management responses to the handling of conflict** (not all of which are effective).

Response	Comment
Denial/withdrawal	'Sweeping it under the carpet'. If the conflict is very trivial, it may indeed blow over without an issue being made of it, but if the causes are not identified, the conflict may grow to unmanageable proportions.
Suppression	'Smoothing over', to preserve working relationships despite minor conflicts.
Dominance	The application of power or influence to settle the conflict. The disadvantage of this is that it creates all the lingering resentment and hostility of 'win-lose' situations.
Compromise	Bargaining, negotiating, conciliating. To some extent, this will be inevitable in any organisation made up of different individuals. However, individuals tend to exaggerate their positions to allow for compromise, and compromise itself is seen to weaken the value of the decision, perhaps reducing commitment.
Integration/ collaboration	Emphasis must be put on the task, individuals must accept the need to modify their views for its sake, and group effort must be seen to be superior to individual effort.
Encourage co-operative behaviour	Joint problem-solving team, goals set for all teams/departments to follow.

Activity 14.11

In the light of the above consider how conflict could arise, what form it would take and how it might be resolved in the following situations.

(a) Two managers who share a secretary have documents to be typed.

(b) One worker finds out that another worker who does the same job as he does is paid a higher wage.

(c) A company's electricians find out that a group of engineers have been receiving training in electrical work.

(d) Department A stops for lunch at 12.30 while Department B stops at 1 o'clock. Occasionally the canteen runs out of puddings for Department B workers.

(e) The Northern Region and Southern Region sales teams are continually trying to better each others results, and the capacity of production to cope with the increase in sales is becoming overstretched.

A win-win approach

6.5 One useful model of conflict resolution is the **win-win model**. This states that there are three basic ways in which a conflict or problem can be worked out.

Method	Frequency	Explanation
Win-lose	This is quite common.	**One party gets what (s)he wants at the expense of the other party**: for example, Department A gets the new photocopier, while Department B keeps the old one (since there were insufficient resources to buy two new ones). However well-justified such a solution is (Department A needed the facilities on the new photocopier more than Department B), there is often lingering resentment on the part of the 'losing' party, which may begin to damage work relations.
Lose-lose	This sounds like a senseless outcome, but actually **compromise** comes into this category. It is thus very common.	**Neither party gets what (s)he really wanted**: for example, since Department A and B cannot both have a new photocopier, it is decided that neither department should have one. However 'logical' such a solution is, there is often resentment and dissatisfaction on *both* sides. (Personal arguments where neither party gives ground and both end up storming off or not talking are also lose-lose: the parties may not have lost the argument, but they lose the relationship ...) Even positive compromises only result in half-satisfied needs.
Win-win	This may not be common, but working towards it often brings out the best solution.	**Both parties get as close as possible to what they really want**. How can this be achieved?

6.6 It is critical to the **win-win approach** to discover **what both parties really want** – as opposed to what they **think**:

- They want (because they have not considered any other options)
- They can **get away with**
- They need in order to **avoid an outcome they fear**.

Department B may want the new photocopier because they have never found out how to use all the features (which do the same things) on the old photocopier; because they just want to have the same equipment as Department A; or because they fear that if they do not have the new photocopier, their work will be slower and less professionally presented

6.7 The important questions in working towards win-win are:

- What do you want this for? and
- What do you think will happen if you don't get it?

These questions get to the heart of what people really need and want.

In our photocopier example, Department A says it needs the new photocopier to make colour copies (which the old copier does not do), while Department B says it needs the new copier to make clearer copies (because the copies on the old machine are a bit blurred). Now there are options to explore. It may be that the old copier just needs fixing, in order for Department B to get what it really wants. Department A will still end up getting the new copier – but Department B has in the process been consulted and had its needs met.

Part D: Individual effectiveness at work

6.8 **Win-win** is not always possible: it is **working towards it** that counts. The result can be mutual respect and co-operation, enhanced communication, more creative problem-solving and – at best – **satisfied needs all round**.

Activity 14.12

Suggest a (i) win-lose, (ii) compromise and (iii) win-win solution in the following scenarios.

(a) Two of your team members are arguing over who gets the desk by the window: they both want it.

(b) You and a colleague both need access to the same file at the same time. You both need it to compile reports for your managers, for the following morning. It is now 3.00pm, and each of you will need it for two hours to do the work.

(c) Manager A is insisting on buying new computers for her department before the budgetary period ends. Manager B cannot understand why, since the old computers are quite adequate. She will moreover be severely inconvenienced by such a move, since her own systems will have to be upgraded as well in order to remain compatible with department A (the two departments constantly share data files). Manager B protests, and conflict erupts.

The limits of your ability and authority to resolve relationship issues

6.9 Resolving difficulties in working relationships may be:

(a) **Beyond your authority**

Difficulties arising from work demands, work methods and status, for example, may require the intervention of someone who has the authority to change work schedules, re-organise work – and discipline unco-operative subordinates and colleagues (or even superiors) if necessary.

(b) **Beyond your ability**

You may have done your best to resolve personality clashes or to solve other problems, but the situation or relationship may just not be improving. It may require a wider perspective, more developed interpersonal skills, or special expertise in conflict resolution.

In these cases, you may need to mobilise organisational procedures for **formal grievance handling**.

Formal grievance procedures

KEY TERM

A **grievance** occurs when an individual thinks that he or she is being wrongly treated by their colleagues or supervisors, that is, when working relationships break down.

6.10 The individual may consider that he or she is being picked on, being given an unfair workload, unfairly appraised in the annual report or unfairly blocked for promotion, or discriminated against.

6.11 When an individual has a grievance he or she should be able to pursue it and ask to have the problem resolved.

6.12 If one-to-one discussion has not worked, a more formal approach will be needed. A typical **grievance procedure** provides for the following steps.

Step 1. The grievance should be carefully explained to the aggrieved **individual's immediate boss** (unless he is the subject of the complaint, in which case it will be the next level up). Employees have the right to be accompanied by a colleague or representative to such an interview, if they feel they need support or a witness.

Step 2. If the immediate boss or other person cannot resolve the matter, or an employee is otherwise dissatisfied with the first interview, the case should be referred to the **next level of management** (and if necessary, in some cases, to an even higher authority).

Step 3. Cases referred to a higher manager should also be reported to the **personnel department**, for the assistance/advice of a personnel manager in resolving the problem.

6.13 All complaints should be thoroughly investigated, so if you do find that you have to go through a formal grievance procedure it is important that **you are honest and fair**. Records should be kept of all interviews and actions taken – and these should be confidential.

Activity 14.13

Check what the grievance procedures are in your organisation! If there is nothing set out in your job description or procedures manual, ask the Personnel Department.

6.14 A Code of Practice issued by the **Advisory Conciliation and Arbitration Service** (ACAS) in September 2000 underlines the importance of all workers being made aware of grievance procedures and all supervisors, managers and worker representatives being trained in their use.

Part D: Individual effectiveness at work

Key learning points

- A **constructive working relationship** is one that allows the purpose of transactions to be fulfilled without either party being deterred from entering into further transactions. Relationships in work organisations are both structural (based on authority and function) and interpersonal (based on human factors).

- **Interpersonal skills** are essential for maintaining effective communication and co-ordination and for building and maintaining relationships. They include rapport building, influencing, negotiating, assertive communication, and managing conflict.

- **Communication** is the transmission or exchange of information. It is a two way process: **feedback** is the signal returned from the recipient of a message, indicating whether (and how accurately) the message has been received.

- **Communication methods** include a variety of media involving written, oral and non-verbal communication. Each of these may be appropriate for different applications and requires a different mix of skills.

- **Verbal communication** uses words (spoken or written). **Non-verbal communication** uses a variety of signals including tone of voice and body language.

- It is important to **adapt the content and style of communication** to your purpose and the likely response of others. Different styles of communication include: informing; influencing; negotiating; assertion and counselling

- Key approaches to **managing disagreements and conflicts** include:
    - understanding the problem and the personalities involved
    - encouraging those involved to discuss the problem
    - exploring possibilities for mutual satisfaction (win-win)
    - negotiating compromise where required
    - using formal grievance procedures where necessary

Quick quiz

1 Label the numbers in the following diagram of the communication process.

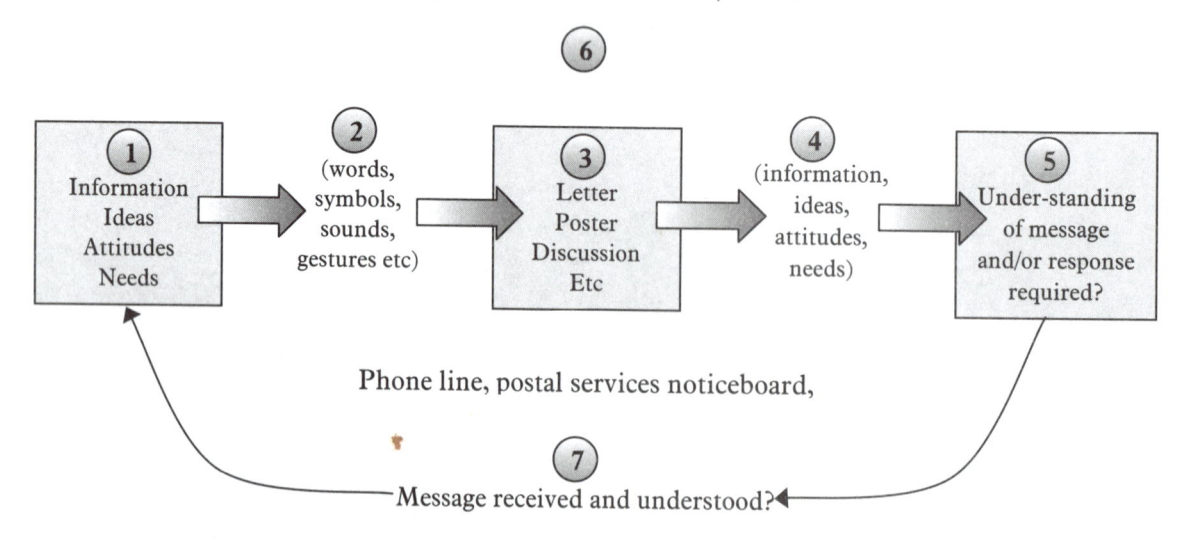

```
                                    (6)

     (1)              (2)            (3)           (4)            (5)
  Information      (words,         Letter      (information,   Under-standing
    Ideas          symbols,        Poster          ideas,       of message
  Attitudes        sounds,        Discussion     attitudes,     and/or response
    Needs         gestures etc)       Etc          needs)         required?

                    Phone line, postal services noticeboard,

                                    (7)
                    Message received and understood?
```

2 Effective listening means not thinking your own thoughts until the other person has finished speaking. True or false?

3 Your manager comes to you late on a Friday afternoon and tells you that she needs a piece of work from you 'urgently'. You are in the middle of something else. You say (loudly): 'There's no way I can do it now: I'm busy. Get someone else to do it!'

14: Constructive relationships

This would be defined as:

- A An assertive response
- B A non-assertive response
- C An aggressive response
- D An informative response

4 The best means of conveying bad news to someone is via e-mail. True or false?

5 Give five examples of non-verbal communication, and suggest what they might be used to indicate.

6 Communication between two members of a project team from different functions, but the same level of authority, is:

- A Upward
- B Downward
- C Lateral
- D Diagonal

7 Which of the following describes the advantages and disadvantages of a 'push' style of influencing and which describes a 'pull' style?

- A Is quick and effective where the solution is clear-cut, but can appear authoritarian and lose genuine commitment.
- B Is supportive/collaborative and secures genuine commitment, but tends to be slower and can appear weak.

8 The people who relate to you in a particular role are called:

- A Role signs
- B Role models
- C Role set
- D Role play

9 List four common sources of conflict in organisations.

10 You have gone to your supervisor with a complaint about a colleague and you don't feel the matter has been satisfactorily resolved. In order to appeal to higher authority, you will need to implement:

- A Disciplinary procedures
- B The internal customer concept
- C Equal opportunities procedures
- D Grievance procedures

11 (a) What are the possible outcomes of any conflict, according to the 'win-win' model?
   (b) What are the two most important questions in the 'win-win' model?

Answers to quick quiz

1 (1) Sender, (2) Encoded Message, (3) Medium, (4) De-coded message, (5) Receiver, (6) Channel and (7) Feedback.

2 False. You may have had to think carefully about this. The point is not to distract yourself or interrupt the other person with your thoughts (or your impatience to say them). However, you need to keep thinking: consider whether what you are hearing is true/relevant, come up with questions, further information requests, feedback signals etc.

3 C. Many people confuse 'assertive' with 'aggressive': make sure you know the difference!

4 False, in general. Face-to-face would be preferable, allowing sensitivity and supportive communication. If the news was very urgent, a telephone call would still be preferable to e-mail, which can come across as very cold and abrupt.

5 A nod of agreement; a smile to encourage; a frown to disapprove; a yawn to show boredom; turning away to discourage.

6 C

7 A: push, B: pull.

8 C – but the others are all useful terms, too: make sure you know what they mean!

Part D: Individual effectiveness at work

9   Poor relationships/co-ordination; poor communication; competition for power and resources; clashes of personality.

10 D. Many people confuse disciplinary procedures (used to investigate, punish, deter or otherwise manage unacceptable or illegal behaviours by employees) and grievance procedures (used to investigate and resolve employee complaints or disputes).

11 (a) Win-lose, lose-lose, win-win.
    (b) What do you want it for? What do you fear will happen if you don't get it?

Answers to activities

Answer 14.1

Your answer might be along the following lines.

(a) If you chose 'student' your role set would consist of fellow students, lecturers, library and administrative staff. Your role signs may include dressing and acting informally with your colleagues, but being rather more formal with others.

(b) Lecturers who dress and act informally with their students may cause problems. Mature students with partners and children may find role incompatible when study interferes with personal life.

Answer 14.2

Your answer will reflect your interpersonal activities on the day you chose: no two answers will be alike.

What could you learn from this data? You would expect technical/work-related conversations to dominate during work time, and friendly/courteous conversations during breaks. (If not, are you wasting the organisation's time? Or becoming a workaholic?)

You would expect to ask for advice and help sometimes, but not as a large proportion of your interactions. (If not, are you avoiding seeking help when you ought to do so? Or are you constantly in crisis, or asking for help needlessly?)

You would expect to receive some supportive and encouraging words occasionally. (If not, where can you get some?)

Answer 14.3

Positive feedback		Negative feedback	
1	Action taken as requested	1	No action taken or wrong action taken
2	Letter/memo/note confirming receipt of message and replying in an appropriate way	2	No written response where expected
3	Accurate reading back of message	3	Incorrect reading back of message
4	Statement: 'Yes, I've got that.'	4	Request for clarification or repetition
5	Smile, nod, murmur of agreement	5	Silence, blank look, frown etc

Answer 14.4

(a) Telephone, confirmed in writing later (order form, letter) – or e-mail order (if both parties have access)

(b) Noticeboard (or employee Web page, if available) or general meeting: depending on the sensitivity of the topic and the need for staff to ask questions.

(c) Face-to-face private conversation – but it would be a good idea to confirm the outcome in writing so that records can be maintained.

(d) Telephone, email or face-to-face (if close by).

14: Constructive relationships

(e) Face-to-face, supported by clear written notes. You can then use visual aids or gestures to help explain. This will also give you the opportunity to check the group's understanding – while the notes will save the group having to memorise what you say, and enable them to focus on understanding.

Answer 14.5

Problems suggested by the statements made may be summed up as follows.

(a) A complete lack of tact and diplomacy. it may be that the manager is deliberately alerting 'S Simms' to the complaint by 'P Brown' but, of course, by putting the information on the notice board the whole department will be aware of it too.

(b) Here is someone from a specialist background talking in a jargon which will mean virtually nothing to the average recipient.

(c) At least the speaker has noticed Smith's body language! Even if the suggestion about fleas is an attempt to be facetious, the speaker appears to have misunderstood the nature of feedback: Smith is giving clear signals that (s)he is perplexed by the briefing.

(d) Technical 'noise', plus a further problem, which you may have spotted: the speaker has chosen an inappropriate medium, since he is not writing down the details which are clearly important and will require reference and confirmation later.

(e) A 463 page report to be read for the following day sounds like overload; (and since it's on 'communication', it sounds like a contradiction in terms!).

(f) Status differentials (real or imagined) are the principal source of difficulty here, the speaker evidently wishing to 'put down' the listeners and 'keep them in their place'. S(he) is potentially losing valuable contributions.

Answer 14.6

Your own observations.

Answer 14.7

Some brief suggestions include:

Plan the call: know whom you want to speak to, what you want to say, what you will do if the person is not available. Have all relevant information to hand.

When making calls:

- Greet the other person by name, identify yourself and explain the context of your call
- Pace your message so that the other person can refer to information or take notes
- Seek constant feedback, to ensure that the other person has heard and understood
- Speak clearly, spell out proper names, use emphasis and tone of voice to reinforce the message
- Close the call effectively: emphasise any action your require and check that your information or expectations have been understood
- Be concise – but courteous!

When taking calls:

- Give a courteous greeting and identify yourself appropriately
- Identify and note the caller's name and organisation
- Listen actively throughout the call, taking notes as required
- Check your understanding: ask for repetition, clarification or spelling as required
- Speak clearly and remember that you may be the first impression of your organisation to someone outside it!

Part D: Individual effectiveness at work

- Make sure you have agreed on any follow-up action before closely the call courteously

Answer 14.8

(a) Anger or tenseness
(b) Perplexity or thoughtfulness
(c) Despair or exhaustion
(d) A rather negative (tired? bored?) attempt to show attention
(e) Impatience
(f) Unease or coldness, even hostility
(g) Relief, relaxation
(h) Sadness, wistfulness

Answer 14.9

You may have come up with some of the following points. Note that assertiveness is an effective strategy for interpersonal relations!

Passive behaviour

Apparent/immediate payoffs: you avoid conflict and unpleasantness; you get to feel good for sacrificing your needs to others; people may like you.

Longer-term results: you do not get our needs met; you may feel angry and resentful later; others may lose respect for you; dominant people may feel they can exploit you whenever they wish

Aggressive behaviour

Apparent/immediate payoffs: you get your way; you may enjoy dominating people; you can let off some steam or anger; you may be respected for your 'forthrightness'.

Longer-term results: others may resent or fear you; others may withdraw from relationship with you; if others are equally dominant, conflict may escalate; you may feel guilty later; you may suffer anger-related problems such as high blood pressure.

Assertive behaviour

Apparent/immediate payoffs: you get your needs met; you have the satisfaction of expressing your feelings; you don't need to feel guilty or resentful later; interpersonal relationships are maintained or improved; new solutions to problems can be reached.

Longer-term results: as apparent/immediate payoffs, precisely because assertive behaviour takes this into consideration in deliberately managing communication for long term benefits.

Answer 14.10

Conflict is constructive, when its effect is to:

- Introduce different **solutions** to problems
- **Define power relationships** more clearly
- Encourage **creativity**, the testing of ideas
- **Focus attention** on individual contributions
- **Bring emotions** out into the open
- **Release of hostile feelings** that have been, or may be, repressed otherwise

Conflict is destructive when its effect is to:

- Distract attention from the task
- Polarise views and 'dislocate' the group
- Subvert objectives in favour of secondary goals
- Encourage defensive or 'spoiling' behaviour
- Force the group to disintegrate
- Stimulate emotional, win-lose conflicts, ie hostility

14: Constructive relationships

Answer 14.11

(a) Both might need work done at the same time. Compromise and co-ordinated planning can help them manage their secretary's time.

(b) Differential pay might result in conflict with management - even an accusation of discrimination. There may be good reasons for the difference (eg length of service). To prevent conflict such information should be kept confidential. Where it is public, it should be seen to be **not arbitrary**.

(c) The electricians are worried about their jobs, and may take industrial action. Yet if the engineers' training is unrelated to the electricians' work, management can allay fears by giving information. The electricians cannot be given a veto over management decisions: a 'win-lose' situation is inevitable, but both sides can negotiate.

(d) The kitchen should plan its meals better - or people from both departments can be asked in advance whether they want puddings.

(e) Competition **between** sales regions is healthy as it increases sales. the conflict lies between sales regions and the production department. In the long-term, an increase in production capacity is the only solution. Where this is to possible, proper co-ordination methods should be instituted.

Answer 14.12

(a) (i) **Win-lose**: one team member gets the window desk, and the other does not. (Result: broken relationships within the team.)

 (ii) **Compromise**: the team members get the window desk on alternate days or weeks. (Result: half satisfied needs.)

 (iii) **Win-win**: what do they want the window desk for? One may want the view, the other better lighting conditions. This offers options to be explored: how else could the lighting be improved, so that both team members get what they really want? (Result: at least, the positive intention to respect everyone's wishes equally, with benefits for team communication and creative problem-solving.)

(b) (i) **Win-lose**: one of you gets the file and the other doesn't.

 (ii) **Compromise**: one of you gets the file now, and the other gets it later (although this has an element of win-lose, since the other has to work late or take it home).

 (iii) **Win-win**: you photocopy the file and **both** take it, or one of your consults his or her boss and gets an extension of the deadline (since getting the job done in time is the real aim – not just getting the file). These kind of solutions are more likely to emerge if the parties believe they **can** both get what they want.

(c) (i) **Win-lose**: Manager A gets the computers, and Manager B has to upgrade her systems.

 (ii) **Compromise**: Manager A will get some new computers, but keep the same old ones for continued data-sharing with Department B. Department B will also need to get some new computers, as a back-up measure.

 (iii) **Win-win**: what does Manager A want the computers for, or to avoid? Quite possibly, she needs to use up her budget allocation for buying equipment before the end of the budgetary period: if not, she fears she will lose that budget allocation. However, that may not be the case, or there may be other equipment that could be more usefully purchased – in which case, there is no losing party.

Answer 14.13

Your own observations.

Now try Question 13 in the Exam Question Bank

Chapter 15 Performance appraisal

Chapter topic list

1. Performance management
2. The purpose of appraisal
3. The process of appraisal
4. The appraisal interview
5. Barriers to effective appraisal
6. Evaluating the appraisal system

The following study sessions are covered in this chapter:

		Syllabus reference
17(a)	Explain the process of competence assessment	4(c)
17(b)	Outline the purpose and benefits of the staff appraisal process	4(c)
17(c)	Describe the barriers to effective staff appraisal	4(c)
17(d)	Identify the management skills involved in the appraisal process	4(c)
17(e)	Describe the roles of the appraiser and appraisee in the appraisal process	4(c)
17(f)	Explain the process of preparation for an appraisal interview	4(c)
17(g)	Recognise the importance of feedback from the appraisal interview	4(c)
17(h)	Explain the link between the appraisal process and effective employee development	4(c)

1 PERFORMANCE MANAGEMENT

> **KEY TERM**
>
> **Performance management** is: a means of getting better results by managing performance within an agreed framework of goals, standards and competence requirements. It is a process to establish a shared understanding about what is to be achieved, and an approach to managing and developing people in order to achieve it.

1.1 This definition highlights key features of performance management.

Aspect	Comment
Agreed framework of goals, standards and competence requirements	The manager and the employee agree about a standard of performance, goals and the skills needed.
Performance management is a process	Managing people's performance is an on-going activity, involving continual monitoring, discussion and adjustment.
Shared understanding	The goals of the individual, unit and organisation as a whole need to be integrated: everyone needs to be 'on the same page' of the business plan.
Approach to managing and developing people	Managing performance is not just about plans, systems or resources: it is an **interpersonal** process of influencing, empowering, giving feedback and problem-solving.
Achievement	The aim is to enable people to realise their potential and maximise their contribution to the organisation's success.

1.2 In Sections 2-6 of this chapter, we discuss the process of **appraisal** or **competence assessment**: the measurement and evaluation of the individual's performance in relation to given plans and criteria. You should be aware that this is part of a broader process of:

- Goal setting
- Performance monitoring
- Feedback giving and
- Performance adjustment

The process of performance management

1.3 A systematic approach to performance management might include the following steps.

Step 1. From the **business plan**, identify the requirements and competences required to carry it out.

Step 2. Draw up a **performance agreement**, defining the expectations of the individual or team, covering standards of performance, performance indicators and the skills and competences people need.

Step 3. Draw up a **performance and development plan** with the individual. These record the actions needed to improve performance, normally covering development in the current job. They are discussed with job holders and will cover, typically:

Part D: Individual effectiveness at work

- The areas of performance the individual feels in need of development
- What the individual and manager agree is needed to enhance performance
- Development and training initiatives

Step 4. **Manage performance continually throughout the year,** not just at appraisal interviews done to satisfy the personnel department. Managers can review actual performance, with more informal interim reviews at various times of the year.

(a) High performance is reinforced by praise, recognition and increasing responsibility. Low performance results in coaching or counselling

(b) Work plans are updated as necessary.

(c) Deal with performance problems, by identifying what they are, establish the reasons for the shortfall, take control action (with adequate resources) and provide feedback

Step 5. **Performance review**. At a defined period each year, success against the plan is reviewed, but the whole point is to assess what is going to happen in future.

Activity 15.1

What are the advantages to employees of introducing such a system?

Goal setting

1.4 People are 'purposive': that is, they act in pursuit of particular goals or purposes. The goals or objectives of an individual influence:

(a) What (s)he **perceives**, since we filter out messages not relevant to our goals and objectives and select those which are relevant

(b) What (s)he **learns**, since learning is a process of selecting and analysing experience in order to take it into account in acting in future, so that our goals and objectives may be more effectively met

(c) What (s)he **does**, since people behave in such a way as to satisfy their goals. This is the basis of motivation, since organisations can **motivate** people to behave in desirable ways (effective work performance) by offering them the means to fulfil their goals.

1.5 In order for learning and motivation to be effective, it is essential that **people know exactly what their objectives are**. This enables them to do the following.

(a) **Plan and direct their effort** towards the objectives

(b) **Monitor their performance** against objectives and adjust (or **learn**) if required

(c) Experience the **reward of achievement** once the objectives have been reached

(d) Feel that their tasks have **meaning and purpose**, which is an important element in job satisfaction

(e) Experience the **motivation of a challenge:** the need to expend energy and effort in a particular direction in order to achieve something

(f) Avoid the **de-motivation** of impossible or inadequately rewarded tasks. As we have discussed in the chapter on motivation, there is a calculation involved in motivated performance. If objectives are vague, unrealistic or unattainable, there may be little incentive to pursue them: hence the importance of SMART objectives.

1.6 Some principles for devising performance measures are as follows.

Principle	Comment
Job-related	They should be related to the actual job, and the key tasks outlined in the job description
Controllable	People should not be assessed according to factors which they cannot control
Objective and observable	This is contentious. Certain aspects of performance can be measured, such as volume sales, but matters such as courtesy or friendliness which are important to some businesses are harder to measure
Data must be available	There is no use identifying performance measures if the data cannot actually be collected

Activity 15.2

A senior sales executive has a job which involves: 'building the firm's sales' and maintaining 'a high degree of satisfaction with the company's products and services'. The firm buys sports equipment, running machines and so on, which it sells to gyms and individuals. The firm also charges fees to service the equipment. Service contracts are the sales executive's responsibility, and he has to manage that side of the business.

Here some possible performance indicators to assess the sales executive's performance in the role. What do you think of them?

(a) Number of new customers gained per period
(b) Value of revenue from existing customers per period
(c) Renewal of service contracts
(d) Record of customer complaints about poor quality products
(e) Regular customer satisfaction survey

Giving feedback

> **KEY TERM**
>
> **Feedback** is communication which offers information to an individual or group about how their performance, results or behaviours are perceived or assessed by others.

1.7 There are two main types of feedback, both of which are valuable in enhancing performance and development.

(a) **Motivational feedback**: used to reward and reinforce positive behaviours and performance by praising and encouraging the individual, and allowing him or her to celebrate positive results, progress or improvements. Its purpose is to increase **confidence** and **motivation**.

(b) **Developmental feedback**: given when a particular area of performance needs to be improved, helping the individual to identify what needs to be changed and how this might be done. Its purpose is to increase **competence** and aid **learning**.

Part D: Individual effectiveness at work

1.8 Feedback is a crucial tool in managing people – as in any control system.

(a) Positive feedback acts as a **reinforcer** or reward, which (as we saw in Chapter 12) aids motivation and commitment.

(b) Negative feedback – delivered constructively – provides information for **learning** processes: it supports goal-setting and improvement planning.

(c) Feedback on performance **enriches work** by giving it meaning. It helps to integrate individual goals with team and organisational goals, adding to employees' satisfaction and commitment by giving them a sense of how their work is contributing to the whole.

(d) Feedback on progress helps employees to manage and adjust their **performance**; they know 'where they are' in relation to standards and targets.

(e) Ongoing feedback contributes to an effective **management style**. Rewards, sanctions and corrections are perceived to be more fair (and are less stressful for employees) if they are based on known performance standards and attainments. Feedback empowers employees to diagnose and solve their own performance problems.

1.9 **Constructive feedback** is designed to widen options and support development. This does not mean giving only encouraging or positive feedback when a person has done something well: feedback about undesirable behaviours or performance shortfalls, given skilfully, is in many ways more useful to the individual.

1.10 Giving constructive feedback is an important leadership skill. It requires:

(a) **Assertiveness.** You must be prepared to give difficult messages and confront difficult issues where required.

(b) **Respect for others**. While being honest about other peoples' development/ improvement needs, you must consider their right to be treated with respect.

(c) **Skill.** Giving effective feedback is a complex interpersonal skill.

1.11 The following are some general guidelines for giving constructive feedback.

(a) **Choose the right time**. Feedback should be given close to the event, so that the details are fresh in both parties' minds – but with sensitivity to the appropriate time and setting. Feedback is best given calmly and confidentially.

(b) **Start with positives**. People will more readily accept criticism as constructive if it is balanced with acknowledgement of positive aspects.

(c) **Focus on the behaviour**. Feedback needs to refer clearly to behaviours, actions and results – not the person or their personality. ('Tough on the problem, soft on the person' is a good general rule.)

(d) **Be accurate**. Feedback needs to be specific, avoiding vague and global statements (Eg not 'you're always late!' but 'on two occasions this week you have been more than fifteen minutes late for work') and avoiding inferences and assumptions.

(e) **Don't tackle everything at once**. Give the person one or two priority areas to deal with at a time.

(f) **Close with encouragement**. Balance negative feedback with positive encouragement that change is possible and will be supported by you and the organisation.

Activity 15.3

Consider how easy or difficult you find it to receive feedback. See if you can come up with some guidelines for yourself on how to receive (possibly negative) feedback assertively, and how to make use of it constructively for your learning and development.

2 THE PURPOSE OF APPRAISAL

2.1 The general purpose of any appraisal system is to improve the efficiency of the organisation by ensuring that the individuals within it are performing to the best of their ability and developing their potential for improvement.

(a) **Reward review**. Measuring the extent to which an employee is deserving of a bonus or pay increase as compared with his or her peers.

(b) **Performance review**, for planning and following-up training and development programmes, ie identifying training needs, validating training methods and so on.

(c) **Potential review**, as an aid to planning career development and succession, by attempting to predict the level and type of work the individual will be capable of in the future.

2.2 **Objectives of appraisals**, and related procedures, may include the following.

(a) Establishing the **key or main results** which the individual will be expected to achieve in the course of his or her work over a period of time.

(b) **Comparing the individual's level of performance against a standard**, to provide a basis for remuneration above the basic pay rate.

(c) Identifying the individual's improvement, training and development **needs** in the light of actual **performance**.

(d) Identifying **potential candidates for promotion.**

(e) Establishing an **inventory of actual and potential performance** within the undertaking, as a basis for human resource planning.

(f) Monitoring the undertaking's **initial selection procedures** against the subsequent performance of recruits, relative to the organisation's expectations.

(g) **Improving communication** about work tasks between different levels in the hierarchy.

2.3 Most managers would say that they gather performance evaluations and give feedback to employees on an ad hoc basis all the time. So why is there a need for a **formal appraisal system**?

(a) Managers and supervisors may obtain **random impressions** of subordinates' performance (perhaps from their more noticeable successes and failures), but rarely form a coherent, complete and objective picture.

(b) They may have a fair idea of their subordinates' shortcomings - but may not have devoted **time and attention** to the matter of improvement and development.

(c) Judgements are **easy to make**, but **less easy to justify** in detail, in writing, or to the subject's face.

(d) **Different assessors** may be applying a **different set of criteria**, and varying standards of objectivity and judgement. This undermines the value of appraisal for comparison, as well as its credibility in the eyes of the appraisees.

Part D: Individual effectiveness at work

(e) Unless stimulated to do so, managers rarely give their subordinates adequate **feedback** on their performance.

2.4 **Three basic problems**

(a) The **formulation and appreciation of desired traits and standards** against which individuals can be consistently and objectively assessed.

(b) **Recording assessments**. Managers should be encouraged to utilise a standard and understood framework, but still allowed to express what they consider important, and without too much form-filling.

(c) **Getting the appraiser and appraisee together,** so that both contribute to the assessment and plans for improvement and/or development.

> **Exam alert**
>
> Questions on topics such as appraisal, training and development and other HR initiatives often ask you to consider their purposes and benefits from the point of view both of the organisation **and** the individual. Look out for such detailed instructions in exam questions – and be sure to obey them precisely! (In this case, make sure you attempt Activity 15.1.)

Activity 15.4

List four disadvantages to the **individual** of not having a formal appraisal system.

3 THE PROCESS OF APPRAISAL

3.1 **A typical appraisal system** would consist of the following steps.

Step 1. **Identification of criteria** for assessment, perhaps based on job analysis, performance standards and person specifications.

Step 2. The preparation by the subordinate's manager of an **appraisal report**. In some systems both the appraisee and appraiser prepare a report. These reports are then compared.

Step 3. An **appraisal interview,** for an exchange of views about the appraisal report, targets for improvement and solutions to problems.

Step 4. **Review of the assessment** by the assessor's own superior, so that the appraisee does not feel subject to one person's prejudices. Formal appeals may be allowed, if necessary to establish the fairness of the procedure.

Step 5. The preparation and implementation of **action plans** to achieve improvements and changes agreed.

Step 6. **Follow-up:** monitoring the progress of the action plan.

3.2 This can be depicted as a control system, as follows.

15: Performance appraisal

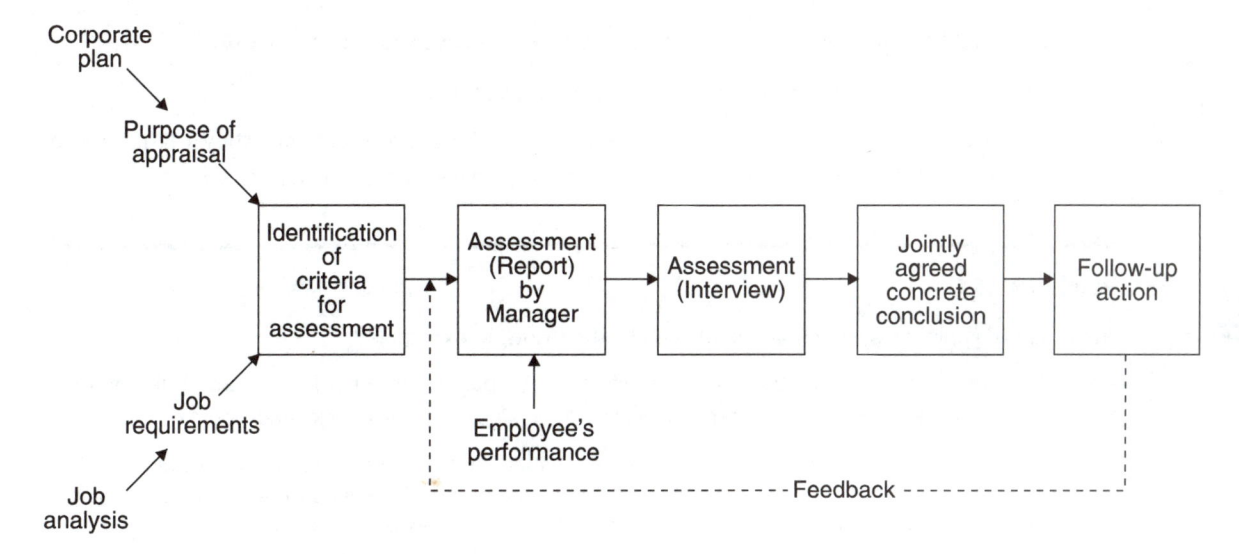

```
Corporate
  plan
      ↓
  Purpose of
   appraisal
       ↘
        Identification      Assessment                        Jointly
           of                (Report)       Assessment        agreed         Follow-up
         criteria      →       by        →  (Interview)  →    concrete   →    action
           for                Manager                         conclusion
        assessment ↑              ↑
       ↗           ¦              ¦
Job               ¦          Employee's
requirements      ¦          performance
   ↑              ¦
 Job              └ - - - - - - - - - - - - - - - - Feedback - - - - - - - - - ┘
analysis
```

What is appraised?

3.3 Assessments must be related to a **common standard**, in order for comparisons to be made between individuals: on the other hand, they should be related to **meaningful performance criteria**, which take account of the **critical variables in each different job**.

Activity 15.5

Identify specific competences which may be relevant to some jobs of your choice.

3.4 A variety of **appraisal techniques** can be used to measure and describe different criteria in different ways.

(a) **Overall assessment**. The manager writes in narrative form his judgements about the appraisee. There will be no guaranteed consistency of the criteria and areas of assessment, however, and managers may not be able to convey clear, effective judgements in writing.

(b) **Guided assessment**. Assessors are required to comment on a number of specified characteristics and performance elements, with guidelines as to how terms such as 'application', 'integrity' and 'adaptability' are to be interpreted in the work context. This is more precise, but still rather vague.

(c) **Grading**. Grading adds a comparative frame of reference to the general guidelines, whereby managers are asked to select one of a number of levels or degrees to which the individual in question displays the given characteristic. These are also known as **rating scales**.

Numerical values may be added to ratings to give rating scores. Alternatively a less precise **graphic scale** may be used to indicate general position on a plus/minus scale.

(d) **Behavioural incident methods**. These concentrate on **employee behaviour**, which is measured against typical behaviour in each job, as defined by common **critical incidents** of successful and unsuccessful job behaviour reported by managers.

(e) **Results-orientated schemes**. This reviews performance against specific **targets and standards** of performance agreed in advance by manager and subordinate together.

   (i) The subordinate is more involved in appraisal because he/she is able to evaluate his/her progress in achieving jointly-agreed targets.

Part D: Individual effectiveness at work

(ii) The manager is relieved of a critic's role, and becomes a counsellor.

(iii) Clear and known targets help modify behaviour.

The effectiveness of the scheme will depend on the **targets set** (are they realistic and clearly defined?) and the **commitment** of both parties to make it work.

Activity 15.6

What sort of appraisal systems are suggested by the following examples?

(a) The Head Teacher of Dotheboys Hall sends a brief report at the end of each term to the parents of the school's pupils. Typical phrases include 'a satisfactory term's work', and 'could do better'.

(b) A firm of auditors assess the performance of their staff in four categories: technical ability, relationships with clients, relationships with other members of the audit team, and professional attitude. On each of these criteria staff are marked from A (= excellent) to E (= poor).

(c) A firm of insurance brokers assesses the performance of its staff by the number of clients they have visited and the number of policies sold.

Who does the appraising?

3.5 Modern appraisal techniques recognise that appraisal has traditionally been seen as a process of top-down 'judgement' of subordinates by superiors. This perception has created resistance on the part of subordinates and reluctance on the part of appraisers. Modern approaches focus on a **wider range of sources of feedback**.

Self-appraisal

3.6 Self-appraisal occurs when individuals carry out their own self-evaluation as a major input into the appraisal process.

(a) **Advantages**

(i) It **saves the manager time**.

(ii) It offers **increased responsibility** to the individual, which may improve motivation and involvement.

(iii) This helps to integrate the goals of the individual and the organisation: the individual may be able to identify problems and recommend improvements in work systems or conditions.

(iv) It encourages individuals to focus on their specific job demands, skill gaps and development opportunities making the process more relevant for the organisation and individual alike.

(v) It turns the appraisal process into a collaborative, problem-solving exercise – rather than a 'judgement' with individuals undertaking ongoing self-evaluation.

(b) **Disadvantage**

People are often not the best – or most honest – judges of their own performance.

Upward appraisal

3.7 A notable modern trend is **upward appraisal**, whereby employees are not rated by their superiors but by their subordinates. The followers appraise the leader.

(a) **Advantages of upward appraisal**

15: Performance appraisal

      (i) Upward appraisal allows evaluation of people management, teamworking and influencing skills by the people who experience them.

      (ii) As multiple subordinates rate each manager, these ratings tend to be more reliable.

      (iii) Subordinates' ratings have more impact because upward feedback is perceived as unusual.

      (iv) It encourages upward communication in general, which may help co-ordination, innovation and employee involvement.

(b) **Problems** with this approach include:

      (i) Subordinates' fear of reprisals, should they give a negative appraisal.

      (ii) Limited power (or the perception that subordinate feedback will not be taken seriously).

Customer appraisal

3.8 In some companies part of the employee's appraisal process must take the form of **feedback from customers** (whether internal or external). This may be taken into account as a factor in remuneration. This is a valuable development in that customers are the best judges of customer service, which the appraisee's boss may not see.

360 degree appraisal

3.9 A comprehensive approach may include **360 degree appraisal** (or **multi-source feedback**): collecting feedback on an individual's performance from:

- The immediate superior
- People who report to the appraisee
- Peers/co-workers
- Customers
- The appraisee

4 THE APPRAISAL INTERVIEW

4.1 The process of the interview can be summarised as follows.

Step 1. **Prepare**

- Plan: place, time and environment
- Review employee's history
- Consult other sources of feedback
- Give appraisee time to prepare/self-appraisal

Step 2. **Interview**

- Listen to employee.
- Encourage employee to talk, identify problems and solutions
- Be fair

Step 3. **Gain commitment**

- Agree plan of action
- Summarise to check understanding
- Complete appraisal/improvement/development report

Part D: Individual effectiveness at work

> *Step 5.* **Follow up**
> - Take action as agreed
> - Monitor progress
> - Keep employee informed

Interview approaches

4.2 There are three types of approach to appraisal interviews.

(a) **The tell and sell method**. The manager tells the subordinate how he/she has been assessed, and then tries to 'sell' (gain acceptance of) the evaluation and the improvement plan. This requires unusual human relations skills in order to convey constructive criticism in an acceptable manner, and to motivate the appraisee to alter his/her behaviour.

(b) **The tell and listen method**. The manager tells the subordinate how he/she has been assessed, and then invites the appraisee to respond. The manager therefore no longer dominates the interview throughout, and there is greater opportunity for **counselling** as opposed to pure **direction**.

   (i) The employee is **encouraged to participate** in the assessment and the working out of improvement targets and methods: it is an accepted tenet of behavioural theory that participation in problem definition and goal setting increases the individual's commitment to behaviour and attitude modification.

   (i) This method does not assume that a change in the employee will be the sole key to improvement: the manager may receive helpful feedback about how job design, methods, environment or supervision might be improved.

(c) **The problem-solving approach**. The manager abandons the role of critic altogether, and becomes a helper. The discussion is centred not on the assessment, but on the employee's **work problems**. The employee is encouraged to think solutions through, and to commit himself to the recognised need for personal improvement. This approach encourages intrinsic motivation through the element of self-direction, and the perception of the job itself as a problem-solving activity. It may also stimulate creative thinking on the part of employee and manager alike, to the benefit of the organisation's adaptability and methods.

Activity 15.7

What approach was taken at your last appraisal interview? Could it have been better?

Follow-up

4.3 After the appraisal interview, the manager may complete the report, with an overall assessment, assessment of potential and/or the jointly-reached conclusion of the interview, with **recommendations for follow-up action**. The manager should then discuss the report with the counter-signing manager (usually his or her own superior), resolving any problems that have arisen in making the appraisal or report, and agreeing on action to be taken. The report form may then go to the management development adviser, training officer or other relevant people as appropriate for follow-up.

4.4 **Follow-up** is essential if the whole process is to be taken seriously. It may include:

(a) **Informing appraisees of the results** of the appraisal, if this has not been central to the review interview

(b) **Carrying out agreed actions** on training and promotion

(c) **Monitoring the appraisee's progress** and checking that he/she has carried out agreed actions or improvements

(d) Taking necessary steps to **help the appraisee to attain improvement objectives,** by guidance, providing feedback, upgrading equipment or altering work methods

---

Activity 15.8

What would happen without follow-up?

4.5 The appraisal can also be used as input to the employee's **personal development plan** (See Chapter 16).

5 BARRIERS TO EFFECTIVE APPRAISAL

Problems in practice

5.1 In theory, such appraisal schemes may seem very fair to the individual and very worthwhile for the organisation, but in practice the **appraisal system often goes wrong**. Appraisal barriers can be identified as follows.

Appraisal barriers	Comment
Appraisal as confrontation	Many people dread appraisals. In this kind of climate: • There is a lack of agreement on performance levels. • The feedback is subjective: in other words the manager is biased, allowing personality differences to get in the way. • The feedback is badly delivered. • Appraisals are based on 'yesterday's performance' not on the whole year. • There is a lack of attention to appraisees' development needs and potential.
Appraisal as judgement	The appraisal 'is seen as a one-sided process in which the manager acts as judge, jury and counsel for the prosecution'. This puts the subordinate on the defensive. Indeed, the process of performance management 'needs to be jointly operated in order to retain the commitment and develop the self-awareness of the individual.'
Appraisal as chat	The appraisal is conducted as if it were is a friendly chat 'without ... purpose or outcome ... Many managers, embarrassed by the need to give feedback and set stretching targets, reduce the appraisal to a few mumbled "well dones!" and leave the interview with a briefcase of unresolved issues.'

Part D: Individual effectiveness at work

Appraisal barriers	Comment
Appraisal as bureaucracy	Appraisal is a form-filling exercise, to satisfy the personnel department. Its underlying purpose, improving individual and organisational performance, is forgotten.
Appraisal as unfinished business	Appraisal should be part of a continuing future-focused process of performance management, not a way of 'wrapping up' the past year's performance issues.
Appraisal as annual event	Many targets set at annual appraisal meetings become irrelevant or out-of-date. Feedback, goal adjustment and improvement planning should be a continuous process.

Appraisal and pay

5.2 Another problem is the extent to which the appraisal system is related to the **pay and reward system**. Many employees consider that the appraisal system should be definitely linked with the reward system, on the ground that extra effort should be rewarded. Although this appears, superficially, a 'common sense' and fair view, there are major drawbacks to it.

(a) **Funds available** for pay rises rarely depend on one individual's performance alone: the whole company has to do well.

(b) **Continuous improvement** is always necessary: many firms have 'to run to stand still'. Continuous improvement should be expected of employees as part of their work, not rewarded as extra.

(c) In low-inflation environments, **cash pay rises are fairly small**.

(d) Performance management is about a lot more than pay for past performance: it is often **forward looking**.

Appraisal, management expertise and empowerment

5.3 In organisations where **empowerment** is practised and employees are given more responsibility:

(a) Many **managers may not have the time** to keep a sufficiently close eye on individual workers to make a fair judgement.

(b) In some jobs, **managers do not have the technical expertise** to judge an employee's output.

(c) Employees depend on **other people** in the workplace/organisation to be effective - in other words, an individual's results may not be entirely under his/her control. A person's performance is often indirectly or directly influenced by the **management style** of the person doing the appraisal.

Activity 15.9

This activity shows some of the problems of operating appraisal schemes in practice.

It is time for Pauline Radway's annual performance appraisal and Steve Taylor, her manager, has sought your advice on two problem areas which he has identified as 'motivation' and 'the organisation's systems'.

15: Performance appraisal

The appraisal system has a six point rating scale:

1 Excellent
2 Outstanding
3 Competent
4 Acceptable
5 Room for improvement
6 Unacceptable

The annual pay increase is determined, in part, by the overall rating of the employee.

Pauline was recruited into Steve's section 18 months ago. She took about five months to learn the job and achieve competence. Accordingly, at last year's appraisal she and Steve agreed that an overall rating of '4' was appropriate.

Over the next six months Pauline worked hard and well and in effect developed her job so she was able to accept more responsibility and expand her range of activities into areas which were both interesting and demanding.

During the last six months the section has been 'rationalised' and the workforce has been reduced (although the workload has increased). Steve is under pressure to contain costs - particularly in the area of salary increases.

Steve now has to rely on Pauline performing her enriched job which, taking the past six months as a whole and given the increased pressure, she performs 'satisfactorily' rather than 'outstandingly'; there are aspects of her performance in this enriched job which she could improve.

When Steve met Pauline to agree the time for the appraisal interview she said - only half jokingly - 'I warn you, I'm looking forward to a respectable pay rise this year.

Task

(a) Outline the problems for Steve that arise from the above scenario:

　(i)　in relation to Pauline's feelings;
　(ii)　in relation to the organisation's systems.

(b) Suggest how Steve should proceed.

6 EVALUATING THE APPRAISAL SYSTEM

6.1 Evaluating the appraisal system can involve the following.

Measurement	Evaluating what?
Asking appraisers and appraisees how they felt about the process	Is the appraisal system taken seriously?
	Is the system perceived to be fair and useful?
	Are appraisers able to be honest/constructive?
	Do appraisees feel threatened/judged or supported and involved in performance improvement?
Monitoring performance results	Has appraisal resulted in problem-solving and development with the effect of enhanced performance by individual employees/groups and the organisation as a whole?
Monitoring training provision and results	Has appraisal resulted in identification and take-up of training/development opportunities?
Monitoring other human resource indicators, such as attitudes, staff turnover and absenteeism, disciplinary actions.	Has appraisal resulted in employee motivation and a culture of continuous improvement?

Part D: Individual effectiveness at work

Measurement	Evaluating what?
Monitoring succession and promotion processes	Has appraisal identified promotable individuals and resulted in development for smooth promotion from within the organisation?
Measuring the time and costs spent on appraisal against perceived benefits in performance improvement	Is the system efficiently organised and cost-efficient?

6.2 However, firms should not expect too much of the appraisal scheme. Appraisal systems, because they target the individual's performance, concentrate on the **lowest level of performance feedback**. They ignore the organisational and systems context of that performance.

Activity 15.10

Look up the procedures manual of your organisation, and read through your appraisal procedures. Also get hold of any documentation related to them; the appraisal report form and notes, in particular.

How effective do you think your appraisal procedures are? Measure them against the criteria given above. How do you feel about appraisal interviews?

If you can get hold of an appraisal report form, have a go at filling one out for yourself - a good exercise in self-awareness!

Key learning points

- **Appraisal** is part of the system of **performance management**, including goal setting, performance monitoring, feedback and improvement planning.
- Appraisal can be used to **reward** but also to identify **potential**, and to plan training, development and improvement programmes.
- A variety of appraisal **techniques** can be used to measure different criteria in different ways.
- **New techniques** of appraisal aim to monitor the appraisee's effectiveness from a number of perspectives, including self appraisal, upward appraisal and 360-degree feedback.

Quick quiz

1. What are the purposes of appraisal?
2. What bases or criteria of assessment might an appraisal system use?
3. Outline a results-oriented approach to appraisal, and its advantages.
4. What is a 360-degree feedback, and who might be involved?
5. When a subordinate rates his or her manager's leadership skills, this is an example of:

    A   Job evaluation
    B   Job analysis
    C   Performance management
    D   Upward appraisal

6. What follow-up should there be after an appraisal?
7. How can appraisals be made more positive and empowering to employees?

15: Performance appraisal

8 What kinds of criticism might be levelled at appraisal schemes by a manager who thought they were a waste of time?

9 What is the difference between performance appraisal and performance management?

10 The most empowering style of appraisal interview is the 'tell and listen' approach. True or false?

Answers to quick quiz

1 Identifying performance levels, improvements needed and promotion prospects; deciding on rewards; assessing team work and encouraging communication between manager and employee.

2 Job analysis, job description, plans, targets and standards.

3 Performance against specific mutually agreed targets and standards.

4 Refer to Paragraph 3.9 for a full answer.

5 D. (A is a technique for grading jobs for salary-setting purposes. B is the process of analysing jobs for job evaluation and job description. Make sure you know what C is!)

6 Appraisees should be informed of the results, agreed activity should be taken, progress should be monitored and whatever resources or changes are needed should be provided or implemented.

7 Ensure the scheme is relevant, fair, taken seriously, and co-operative.

8 The manager may say that he has better things to do with his time, that appraisals have no relevance to the job and there is no reliable follow-up action, and that they involve too much paperwork.

9 Appraisal on its own is a backward-looking performance review. But it is a vital input into performance management, which is forward-looking.

10 False. The most empowering style is 'problem solving'.

Answers to activities

Answer 15.1

The key to performance management is that it is forward looking and constructive. Objective-setting gives employees the security in knowing exactly what is expected of them, and this is agreed at the outset with the manager, thus identifying unrealistic expectations. The employee at the outset can indicate the resources needed.

Answer 15.2

These measures do not all address some of the key issues of the job.

(a) **Number of new customers**. This is helpful as far as it goes but omits two crucial issues: how much the customers actually spend and what the potential is. Demand for this service might be expanding rapidly, and the firm might be increasing sales revenue but losing market share.

(b) **Revenue from existing customers** is useful - repeat business is generally cheaper than gaining new customers, and it implies customer satisfaction.

(c) **Renewal of service contracts** is very relevant to the executive's role.

(d) **Customer complaints about poor quality products**. As the company does not make its own products, this is not really under the control of the sales manager. Instead the purchasing manager should be more concerned. Complaints about the service contract are the sales executive's concern.

(e) **Customer satisfaction survey**. This is a tool for the sales manager to use as well as a performance measure, but not everything is under the sales executive's control.

Part D: Individual effectiveness at work

Answer 15.3

The following are just some suggestions.

- Stay open: listen actively and demonstrate your willingness to be receptive.

- Clarify and test your understanding of what is being said. Feedback may be non-specific, ambiguous or unfair. You need to find out exactly what the problem (learning opportunity) is, by asking questions: 'What do you mean by...?', 'Could you give me some specific examples?'

- Don't be too quick to reject or deny. It will be your choice whether you act on the feedback or not: you can afford to hear and reflect on it first.

- Don't be too quick to defend or justify: remember it is to your benefit to learn how your behaviour or performance is perceived by others, whether or not you think it fair.

- Monitor your feelings. We usually react to negative (and sometimes positive) feedback as a threat to our self image and competence: be aware that you may feel refusal, anger and defensiveness before you move on to acceptance and problem-solving.

- Thank the person for the feedback. Giving feedback is a tough job!

Answer 15.4

Disadvantages to the individual of not having an appraisal system include: the individual is not aware of progress or shortcomings, is unable to judge whether s/he would be considered for promotion, is unable to identify or correct weaknesses by training and there is a lack of communication with the manager.

Answer 15.5

You might have identified such things as:

(a) Numerical ability applicable to accounts staff, say, more than to customer contact staff.
(b) Ability to drive safely, essential for transport workers - not for desk-bound ones.
(c) Report-writing (not applicable to manual labour, say).

Answer 15.6

(a) Overall assessment of the blandest kind.
(b) This is a grading system, based on a guided assessment.
(c) Results orientated scheme.

Answer 15.7

Answer from your own experience

Answer 15.8

The appraisal would merely be seen as a pleasant chat with little effect on future performance, as circumstances change. Moreover the individual might feel cheated.

15: Performance appraisal

Answer 15.9

(a) **Steve's problems**

   (i) *Pauline's feelings*

   Pauline, not unreasonably, makes a connection between performance and reward. She feels she has worked hard and that this should be recognised in financial terms. Steve, on the other hand, is under pressure to keep costs under control. In fact, one of the reasons for Pauline's increased responsibility is the rationalisation of the department.

   Pauline, however, does make a crude assumption that effort equals performance. She is highly motivated at the moment, but her performance is not outstanding. Her performance is only satisfactory in her changed job, and therefore it would not be appropriate to tell her otherwise. However, using expectancy theory, we can assert that a pay increase for her is an important motivating factor to get her to work hard.

   Steve is thus faced with a dilemma. If she is not rewarded, it is likely that she will make less effort to perform well, and this would be suggested by expectancy theory. Steve will suffer, as the rationalised department depends on her continual hard work. In short, this is a hygiene factor.

   Another factor is fairness. Pauline cannot expect special treatment, when compared to other workers, who may have made an equal effort. Over-rewarding average performance, despite the effort, might demotivate other staff who will accuse Steve of favouritism.

   (ii) *The organisation's systems*

   It is clear that Steve is having to negotiate the requirements and failings of four different systems here.

   (1) The budgetary control system, restricting pay rises.
   (2) The appraisal system, which conflates effort and performance.
   (3) The remuneration system, by which pay rises are awarded.

   Finally, Pauline's job is very different from what it was when she first started.

   The source of the problem is the failure to recognise that Pauline is now doing a different job. Her job should have been re-evaluated. If this were the case, Steve could assess her reward on the basis of the performance in this re-evaluated job. She would have higher pay, commensurate with her enhanced responsibilities, but not an unfairly favourable grading.

   However, Steve realises that the appraisal system is the one over which he has most direct control. He is in a position to reward her effort, but this would be anomalous as her performance in the new job is not exceptional. Her rating would not be appropriate to her performance. Yet her enhanced responsibilities need to be recognised somehow, although Steve, under pressure from the budgetary control system, may not be able to reward it financially.

   There is little Steve can do about the budgetary factors, apart from stating to Pauline that everybody is in the same boat. There might be non-financial rewards that he can offer her. Pauline might like to have her own separate office space, for example, if it were available, or Steve might be able to offer her increased annual leave or a unique job title.

   Pauline might also resent waiting for the outcome of a job re-evaluation exercise, as, from her point of view, that is the organisation's problem, not hers.

(b) **What Steve should do**

   Steve has a choice either to overrate Pauline, according to the appraisal system, in recognition of her efforts rather than her performance in the changed job, or, alternatively, to try and negotiate a job re-evaluation first, with the risk that Pauline will become demotivated.

   Steve needs to consider the effects of an unfairly favourable appraisal grading on the other staff. There are good reasons to believe that, while it might let him off the hook immediately, it would have bad long term repercussions, as it would send the wrong signals to Pauline about her current performance. Next year, for example, if her performance had not improved, he would have to downgrade her.

   He will have to try and persuade Pauline of the complexities of the situation.

   Pauline is obviously strongly motivated by money. Steve has to give some guarantee that her efforts will be recognised. While a low pay rise may be a negative hygiene factor, Steve should try and invoke motivator factors to counterbalance this effect.

Part D: Individual effectiveness at work

Steve can promise Pauline that the job will be re-evaluated. This might be a long term objective. He can promise Pauline that he will be supportive in the re-evaluation exercise, and involve her in any input to it.

Steve can also suggest new targets for Pauline to achieve in her changed job, to give her something to aim for. This might still motivate her, providing Steve can explain to her the slightly difficult situation he is in.

He might give her formal recognition of her status, and allow her more autonomy in planning her work, if she is sufficiently competent.

Obviously he cannot guarantee the result of the job evaluation system, but he can make some effort to solve the problem.

Answer 15.10

Your own research.

> **Now try Question 14 in the Exam Question Bank**

Chapter 16 Training and development

Chapter topic list

1 Training and development
2 Identifying training needs
3 Personal development planning
4 Methods of training and development
5 Evaluating training
6 The learning process
7 Supporting individual and organisational learning

The following study sessions are covered in this chapter:

		Syllabus reference
16(a)	Distinguish between training and development	4(c)
16(b)	Explain the importance of training and development to the organisation and the individual	4(c)
16(c)	Explain the roles and responsibilities of a training manager	4(c)
16(d)	Explain the methods used to analyse training needs	4(c)
16(e)	Suggest ways in which training needs can be met	4(c)
16(f)	Compare and contrast the various methods used in developing individuals in the workplace	4(c)
16(g)	Describe methods of staff evaluation and follow-up	4(c)

Part D: Individual effectiveness at work

1 TRAINING AND DEVELOPMENT

What are training and development?

> **KEY TERMS**
>
> **Development** is 'the growth or realisation of a person's ability and potential through the provision of learning and educational experiences'.
>
> **Training** is 'the planned and systematic modification of behaviour through learning events, programmes and instruction which enable individuals to achieve the level of knowledge, skills and competence to carry out their work effectively'.
>
> (Armstrong)

1.1 The overall purpose of employee development is:

- To ensure the firm meets current and future performance objectives by...
- Continuous improvement of the performance of individuals and teams, and...
- Maximising people's potential for growth (and promotion)

Activity 16.1

Note down key experiences which have developed your capacity and confidence at work, and the skills you are able to bring to your employer (or indeed a new employer!).

1.2 Organisations often have a **training and development strategy**, based on the overall strategy for the business. Development planning includes the following broad steps.

Step 1. Identify the **skills and competences** are needed by the business plan or HR plan.

Step 2. Draw up the **development strategy** to show how training and development activities will assist in meeting the targets of the corporate plan.

Step 3. **Implement** the training and development strategy.

Benefits of training

1.3 Training offers some significant benefits for the organisation.

Benefit	Comment
Minimise the learning costs of obtaining the skills the organisation needs	Training supports the business strategy.
Lower costs and **increased productivity**, improving performance	Some people suggest that higher levels of training explain the higher productivity of German as opposed to many British manufacturers
Fewer accidents, and better health and safety	EU health and safety directives (enacted into legislation require a certain level of training.
Less need for detailed supervision	If people are trained they can get on with the job, and managers can concentrate on other things. Training is an aspect of **empowerment**.

Benefit	Comment
Flexibility	Training ensures that people have the **variety** of skills needed – multi-skilling is only possible if people are properly trained.
Recruitment and succession planning	Training and development attracts new recruits and ensures that the organisation has a supply of suitable managerial and technical staff to take over when people retire.
Retention	Training and development supports an internal job market (through transfer and promotion). It also helps to satisfy employees' self-development needs internally, without the need to change employers for task variety and challenge.
Change management	Training helps organisations manage change by letting people know why the change is happening and giving them the skills to cope with it.
Corporate culture	(1) Training programmes can be used to build the corporate culture or to direct it in certain ways, by indicating that certain values are espoused. (2) Training programmes can build relationships between staff and managers in different areas of the business
Motivation	Training programmes can increase commitment to the organisation's goals, by satisfying employees' self-actualisation needs (discussed in Chapter 9).

1.4 Bear in mind, however, that training cannot do everything. It cannot, for example, automatically **improve performance problems** arising out of:

- Bad management
- Poor job design
- Poor equipment, factory layout and work organisation
- Other characteristics of the employee (eg intelligence)
- Motivation – training gives a person the ability but not necessarily the willingness to improve
- Poor recruitment

Activity 16.2

Despite all the benefits to the organisation, many are still reluctant to train. What reasons can you give for this?

1.5 For the **individual employee**, the benefits of training and development are more clear-cut, and few refuse it if it is offered.

Benefit	Comment
Enhances portfolio of **skills**	Even if not specifically related to the current job, training can be useful in other contexts, and the employee becomes more attractive to employers and more promotable. (This is called 'employability'.)
Psychological benefits	The trainee might feel reassured that (s)he is of continuing value to the organisation. A perception of competence also enhances self-esteem and confidence.

Part D: Individual effectiveness at work

Benefit	Comment
Social benefit	People's social needs can be met by training courses: they can also develop networks of contacts
The job	Training can help people do their job better, thereby increasing job satisfaction, promotion and earning prospects.

A systematic approach to training

1.6 In order to ensure that training meets the real needs of the organisation, larger firms adopt a planned approach to training. This has the following steps.

Step 1. Identify and define the **organisation's skill requirements**. It may be the case that recruitment might be a better solution to a problem than training

Step 2. **Define the learning required** – in other words, specify the knowledge, skills or competences that have to be acquired. For technical training, this is not difficult: for example all finance department staff will have to become conversant with a new accounting system.

Step 3. **Define training objectives** – what must be learnt and what trainees must be able to do after the training exercise

Step 4. **Plan training programmes** – training and development can be structured in a number of ways, employing a number of techniques, as we shall discuss in Section 3. This covers:

- Who provides the training
- Where the training takes place
- What methods of training will be used

Step 5. **Implement the training programme**

Step 6. **Monitor, review and evaluate** training. Has it been successful in achieving the learning objectives?

Step 7. Go back to Step 2 if more training is needed.

Exam alert

Seven marks were available in the Pilot Paper for this syllabus for outlining the 'main steps in the training process': make sure you have a clear grasp of these kind of systematic approaches. The question also noted that training and development add value to staff both **individually** and **collectively**. We deal with collective training planning and with individual learning and self-development. As you read on, think about the benefits and limitations of each approach.

Case example: training standards

Training for quality

The British Standards for Quality Systems (BS EN ISO 9000) which many UK organisations are working towards (often at the request of customers, who perceive it to be a 'guarantee' that high standards of quality control are being achieved) includes training requirements. As the following extract shows, the Standard identifies training needs for those organisations registering for assessment, and also shows the importance of a systematic approach to ensure adequate control.

16: Training and development

The training, both by specific training to perform assigned tasks and general training to heighten quality awareness and to mould attitudes of all personnel in an organisation, is central to the achievement of quality.

The comprehensiveness of such training varies with the complexity of the organisation. The following steps should be taken:

1. Identifying the way tasks and operations influence quality in total
2. Identifying individuals' training needs against those required for satisfactory performance of the task
3. Planning and carrying out appropriate specific training
4. Planning and organising general quality awareness programmes
5. Recording training and achievement in an easily retrievable form so that records can be updated and taps in training can be readily identified

1.7 We will now look at the stages of the training and development system in more detail.

2 IDENTIFYING TRAINING NEEDS

2.1 Some training needs will **emerge** in the course of work and **workplace changes**.

(a) If forthcoming **legislation or regulation** is likely to affect your work role, you will need to get information on the provisions and their implications for your work.

(b) If new **technology or equipment** is introduced in your organisation, you may need to learn how to use it.

(c) If your organisation is seeking accreditation for its training scheme, or is seeking a British or International Standard (say, for quality systems, ISO 9000), it will have certain **training requirements** imposed on it by the approving body.

Training needs analysis

2.2 Training needs analysis identifies the gap between the individual's and/or organisation's current results and skill/competence base and those required by its corporate plan.

Current state	Training gap	Desired state
Organisation's current results		Desired results, standards
Existing knowledge and skill		Knowledge and skill needed
Individual performance		Required standards

2.3 **Training surveys** combine information from a variety of sources.

(a) The **business strategy** and Human Resource Plan, which should set out current and future skill requirements.

(b) **Appraisal and performance reviews** (see Chapter 15): training may be recommended as a result of performance planning.

(c) **Training needs surveys**, self-administered by employees, asking them what training they think they need or would like

(d) **Evaluation of existing training** programmes and ongoing identification of further opportunities or needs.

(e) **Job analysis**. Researchers can pay attention to:

(i) Reported difficulties people have in meeting the skills requirement of the job

(ii) Existing performance weaknesses, of whatever kind, which could be remedied by training

(iii) Future changes in the job

The job analysis can be used to generate a **training specification** covering the knowledge needed for the job, the skills required to achieve the result and the attitudinal changes required.

Setting training objectives

2.4 If it is considered that training would improve work performance, training **objectives** can then be defined. They should be clear, specific and related to observable, measurable targets, ideally detailing:

- **Behaviour** - What the trainee should be able to do
- **Standard** - To what level of performance?
- **Environment** - Under what conditions (so that the performance level is realistic)?

2.5 For example:

'At the end of the course the trainee should be able to describe ... or identify ... or distinguish x from y ... or calculate ... or assemble ...' and so on. It is insufficient to define the objectives of training as 'to give trainees a grounding in ...' or 'to encourage trainees in a better appreciation of ...': this offers no target achievement which can be measured.

2.6 Training objectives link the identification of training needs with the content, methods and technology of training. Some examples of translating training needs into learning objectives are given in *Personnel Management, A New Approach* by D Torrington and L Hall.

Training needs	Learning objectives
To know more about the Data Protection Act	The employee will be able to answer four out of every five queries about the Data Protection Act without having to search for details.
To establish a better rapport with customers	The employee will immediately attend to a customer unless already engaged with another customers.
	The employee will greet each customer using the customer's name where known.
	The employee will apologise to every customer who has had to wait to be attended to.
To assemble clocks more quickly	The employee will be able to assemble each clock correctly within thirty minutes.

2.7 Having identified training needs and objectives, the manager will have to decide on the best way to approach training: there are a number of types and techniques of training, which we will discuss below.

3 PERSONAL DEVELOPMENT PLANNING

> **KEY TERMS**
>
> A **personal development plan** is a clear developmental action plan for an individual which incorporates a wide set of developmental opportunities, including formal training.
>
> **Self development** may be defined as: 'personal development, with the person taking primary responsibility for his or her own learning and for choosing the means to achieve this.' (Pedler, Burgoyne & Boydell)

3.1 **Personal development** implies a wide range of activities with the objectives of:

(a) Improving performance in an existing job

(b) Improving skills and competences, perhaps in readiness for career development or organisational change

(c) Planning experience and pathways for career development and/or advancement within the organisation

(d) Acquiring transferable skills and competences for general 'employability' or change of direction

(e) Pursuing personal growth towards the fulfilment of one's personal interests and potential

---

Activity 16.3

What mechanisms and programmes are there in your organisation to help you:

(a) Assess your job requirements, current competence and training requirements?
(b) Identify and plan relevant training and development activities?
(c) Access or implement training resources?

How do you mobilise these procedures?

How far are you encouraged to get actively involved in the process of development?

A systematic approach to personal development planning

3.2 A systematic approach to planning your own development will include the following steps.

Step 1. Select an **area for development**: a limitation to overcome or a strength to build on. Your goals might be based on your need to **improve performance** in your current job and/or on your **career goals**, taking into account possible changes in your current role and opportunities within and outside the organisation. You might carry out a personal SWOT (strengths, weaknesses, opportunities, threats) analysis. One helpful tool is an interest/ aptitude and performance matrix, on which you can identify skills which you require (don't do well) but for which you can build on your aptitudes and interests (like).

Part D: Individual effectiveness at work

		Performance	
		High	Low
Aptitude/ interest	High	Like and do well	Like but don't do well
	Low	Dislike but do well	Dislike and don't do well

Step 2. Set a SMARTER (specific, measurable, agreed, realistic, time-bounded, evaluated and reviewed) **learning objective**: what you want to be able to do or do better, and in what time scale.

Step 3. Determine how you will move towards your objective:

- **Research** relevant learning resources and opportunities
- **Evaluate** relevant learning resources and opportunities for suitability, attainability and cost-effectiveness
- Secure any **support or authorisation** required from your manager or training development

Step 4. Formulate a comprehensive and specific action plan, including:

- The SMARTER objective
- The learning approaches you will use, described as **specific actions** to take. (Ask a colleague to provide feedback; watch a training video; enrol in a course.) Each action should have a **realistic time scale** or schedule for completion.
- A **monitoring and review plan**. Precisely how and when (or how often) will you assess your progress and performance, against your objectives? (Seek feedback? review results? pass an end-of-course test?)

Step 5. Secure **agreement** to your action plan (if required to mobilise organisational support or resources)

Step 6. **Implement** your action plan.

3.3 The following is an example of a completed Personal Development Action Plan for someone who is focusing on improving his interpersonal skills.

Activity 16.4

Draw up an action plan sheet, using the columns show in in our example.

Select one immediate training need for yourself (perhaps related to this syllabus?) and formulate an action plan.

Exam alert

Six marks were available in the Pilot Paper for this syllabus, for outlining the stages in preparing a PDP. A useful reminder not to neglect your study and revision in what may appear to be 'soft' syllabus topics!

Objective	Methods	Timescale	Monitoring and review
To be able to utilise a range of influencing strategies and styles to achieve successful outcomes: by end December.	*Reading*: Gillen 'Agreed: Improve your powers of influence'	End March	Review progress in June and December with manager
	Coaching: Meet with manager. Discuss key decision makers in the organisation. Identify examples of successful strategies.	By end March	Monthly meetings with mentor
	Project: Take responsibility for agreeing timescales for delivery of budget reports with department heads	Agreement reached by October	Seek feedback on influencing style from colleagues
	Reflect on day-to-day influencing experiences: note in Personal Development Journal and discuss with mentor.	Monthly	
To remain calm when faced with aggressive behaviour (not raise voice, use sarcastic tone or make uncontrolled gestures): by end August	Meet with John before next accounts meeting: ask him to observe and give feedback on my behaviour. At accounts meeting, try to implement assertiveness skills (broken record, count to 10) if Paula becomes aggressive.	Meet with John by end April	Seek regular meeting with John for on-going feedback.
	Meet with John after the meeting to get feedback. Identify from this meeting further action points.	Further action points by mid May	Reflect on accounts meetings in PDJ: evaluate results of assertiveness behaviours.

4 METHODS OF TRAINING AND DEVELOPMENT

4.1 There is a huge menu of learning resources and opportunities available, including:

- Courses, workshops and information seminars
- Books, quality newspapers, professional journals and technical publications
- Videos, CDs and computer software
- Websites (for obtaining information *and* accessing training courses and materials)
- The knowledge and expertise of other people at work
- Your own daily experience, from which you can also learn, if you know how

4.2 Training can be divided into two types.

- **On the job** training: carried out in the workplace, based on learning while performing the job itself.

- **Off the job** training: carried out in-house (but in separate training/education areas) or externally (at a training centre or home), based on learning relevant to – but separate from – the job itself.

On the job training

4.3 **On-the-job training** methods include the following.

Observation	You watch experienced colleagues at work, and model or imitate their effective procedures, techniques and behaviours.
	• This may be done informally as you work with someone.
	• Alternatively, a formal period of observation may be arranged: 'shadowing' someone in their role, or watching them demonstrate procedures or techniques and then trying them yourself (under supervision, if necessary).
Information and advice from colleagues	Relevant specialist advisers are available in your organisation (the legal compliance officer or IT support person, say) – but do not forget or underestimate your own manager and colleagues as a learning resource!
	You should be able to ask for any information or guidance required to do your job better, using appropriate communication channels and methods.
Job instruction by colleagues	A more expert colleague or trainer explains and/or demonstrates a technique or procedure, and supervises as you attempt it yourself.
Coaching by colleagues	• A colleague or trainer explains and demonstrates procedures or techniques.
	• You then try them yourself, with the coach's guidance, advice and correction.
	• The coach helps you identify problems or further learning needs and encourages you to keep doing this.
	This is essentially a more collaborative process than instruction.
Work experience	Changing roles can offer you new, more varied or higher-level experience, challenges and opportunities to learn from others. Examples include:
	• Project or committee work
	• Secondments to other departments
	• Temporary 'assistant to' positions
Mentoring by a colleague	A more experienced or senior member of the organisation accepts a role as your teacher/coach, adviser, counsellor, role model, challenger, feedback-giver, encourager and supporter – as appropriate to your needs. Mentoring is aimed at empowering you to take responsibility for your own long-term personal and career development.
Experiential learning	Deliberately learning lessons from your own work experience, successes and failures. (We discuss this process further below.)

16: Training and development

4.4 The advantages and disadvantages of on-the-job training may be summarised as follows.

Advantages	Disadvantages
• Takes account of job context: high relevance and transfer of learning	• Undesirable aspects of job context (group norms, corner-cutting) also learned
• Suits 'hands on' learning styles: offers 'learning by doing'	• Doesn't suit theorist/reflective learning styles
• No adjustment barriers (eg anti-climax after training) to application of learning on the job	• Trial and error may be threatening (if the organisation has low tolerance of error!)
• Develops working relationships as well as skills	• Risks of throwing people in at the deep end with real consequences of mistakes
	• Distractions and pressures of the workplace may hamper learning focus

Off the job training

4.5 **Off-the-job training** methods include the following.

Formal training courses	• Lectures • Workshops • Information briefings, seminars or conferences These may be provided within your organisation (by its own training department) or by external training providers: colleges, universities and adult education centres; private sector colleges and training centres; and individual trainers and training consultants. They may involve different time commitments: day release, evening classes, or full-time (short or long) courses.
Self-study courses	• Computer-based training or assessment packages • Video- or Interactive Video-based training packages • Open or distance learning materials (which you study at home at your own pace, sometimes with an added face-to-face taught component)
Visits and tours	• To work sites where procedures and practices are demonstrated • To clients or suppliers, to broaden awareness of customer/supply-side issues • To other departments or branches of your organisation, to broaden awareness of business processes and differences in practice and culture
Research assignments	• Information search (discussed further below) • Preparation of a written project, report or presentation

4.6 The advantages and disadvantages of off-the-job training may be summarised as follows.

Advantages	Disadvantages
• Allows exploration/experimentation without the risk of consequences for actual performance	• May not be directly relevant or transferable to the job and/or job content
• Allows focus on learning, away from distractions and pressures of work	• May be perceived as a waste of working time
• Allows standardisation of training	• Immediate and relevant feedback may not be available (eg if performance is assessed by exam)
• Suits a variety of learning styles (depending on the method used)	
• May confer status, implying promotability	• Tends to be more theoretical: does not suit 'hands on' learning styles
	• May represent a threat, implying inadequacy

Activity 16.5

Which of the above might be most appropriate (or high on your list of methods to research), if you wanted to:

(a) Learn a detailed administrative procedure for employee record keeping which has recently been developed by the human resources department

(b) Improve your negotiation skills

(c) Learn about changes to equal opportunities law arising from the adoption of EU directives

(d) Learn how your work in accounts affects the production department (as production staff always claim...).

Induction training

4.7 Induction is the process whereby a person is formally introduced and integrated into an organisation or system. The purposes of induction are:

(a) To help new recruits to find their bearings

(b) To begin to socialise new recruits into the culture and norms of the team/organisation

(c) To support recruits in beginning performance

(d) To identify on-going training and development needs

(e) To avoid initial problems at the 'induction crisis' stage of the employment lifecycle, when frustration, disorientation and disappointment may otherwise cause new recruits to leave the organisation prematurely

4.8 The immediate supervisor should commence the **on-going process of induction**.

Step 1. Pinpoint the areas that the recruit will have to learn about in order to **start the job**. Some things (such as detailed technical knowledge) may be identified as areas for later study or training.

Step 2. Introduce the recruit to the work premises and facilities, so (s)he can get his or her bearings.

16: Training and development

Step 3. Briefing by the HR Manager on relevant policies and procedures: conditions of employment, sickness and holiday absences, health and safety and so on.

Step 4. Introduce the recruit to key people in the office: co-workers, health and safety officers, etc. One particular colleague may be assigned to the recruit as a **mentor**, to keep an eye on them, answer routine queries, 'show them the ropes'.

Step 5. Introduce work procedures, systems, rules, reporting structures and so on.

Step 6. Plan and implement an appropriate **training programmes** for whatever immediate technical or practical knowledge is required.

Step 7. Monitor initial progress, as demonstrated by performance, as reported by the recruit's mentor, and as perceived by the recruit him or herself. This is the beginning of an on-going cycle of feedback, review, problem-solving and development planning.

4.9 Note that induction is an **on-going process**, embracing mentoring, coaching, training, monitoring and so on. It is not just a first day affair! After three months, six months or one year the performance of a new recruit should be formally appraised and discussed with them. Indeed, when the process of induction has been finished, a recruit should continue to receive periodic appraisals, just like every other employee in the organisation.

Methods of development

4.10 As we noted at the beginning of this chapter, **development** is a 'wider' approach to fulfilling an individual's potential than training. Development may include training, but may also include a range of learning experiences whereby:

(a) Employees **gain work experience** of increasing challenge and responsibility, which will enable them to perform more senior jobs in due course

(b) Employees are given **guidance, support and counselling** to help them to formulate personal and career development goals

(c) Employees are given suitable **education and training** to develop their skills and knowledge

(d) Employees are facilitated in **planning their future** and identifying opportunities open to them in the organisation

4.11 Approaches to development include the following.

Approach	Comment
Management development	'An attempt to improve managerial effectiveness through a planned and deliberate learning process' (Mumford). This may include the development of management/leadership skills (or competences), management education (such as MBA programmes) and planned experience of different functions, positions and work settings, in preparation for increasing managerial responsibility.
Career development	Individuals plan career paths. The trend for delayered organisations has reduced opportunities for upward progression: opportunities may be planned for sideways/lateral transfers, secondments to project groups, short external secondments and so on, to offer new opportunities.

Approach	Comment
Professional development	Professional bodies offer structured programmes of continuing professional development (CPD). The aim is to ensure that professional standards are maintained and enhanced through educational, development and training self-managed by the individual. A CPD approach is based on the belief that a professional qualification should be the basis for a career lifetime of development and adherence to a professional code of ethics and standards
Personal development	Businesses are increasingly offering employees wider-ranging development opportunities, rather than focusing on skills required in the current job. Personal development creates more rounded, competent employees who may contribute more innovatively and flexibly to the organisation's future needs. It may also help to foster employee job satisfaction, commitment and loyalty.

5 EVALUATING TRAINING

KEY TERMS

Validation of training means observing the results of the programme and measuring whether the training objectives have been achieved.

Evaluation of training means comparing the actual costs of the programme against the assessed benefits which are being obtained. If the costs exceed the benefits, the programme will need to be redesigned or withdrawn.

5.1 From the point of view of the **organisation**, training may be evaluated as follows:

(a) Measuring **what the trainees have learned** on the course, by means of a test or assessment of competence linked to training needs and objectives.

(b) Measuring **changes in job behaviour** following training: studying the subsequent behaviour of the trainees in their jobs, to assess how the training scheme has altered the way they do their work in line with training needs and objectives.

(c) Measuring the **correlation** between training and other indicators (error/wastage rates, accident rates, absenteeism, labour turnover, disciplinary actions and so on), to assess how training may have impacted on areas such as **quality** and **employee morale**.

(d) Measuring the correlation between training and the achievement of **organisational goals and objectives**, to assess bottom-line effectiveness.

(e) Measuring all the above in relation to the **costs** of training.

5.2 From the point of view of the **individual**, training may be evaluated as follows:

(a) Measuring what trainees have learned on the course, by means of a test or **assessment of competence** linked to departmental training needs and objectives. (This is an element in individual trainee motivation and learning, as well as organisational effectiveness).

(b) Measuring what trainees have learned and the **qualifications** they have obtained against their personal aspirations, goals and personal development plans

(c) Measuring trainee **reactions** to and **perceptions** of training: using Feedback Forms and Attitude Surveys, for example, to ask the trainees whether they thought the training programme was relevant to their work, effectively implemented, suitable for their learning style

(d) Measuring individual **post-training attainment** and trainee satisfaction against the costs of training.

Activity 16.6

Outline why it is important to evaluate and validate a training programme.

---

6 THE LEARNING PROCESS

6.1 There are different schools of learning theory which explain and describe how people learn.

(a) **Behaviourist psychology** concentrated on the relationship between stimuli (input through the senses) and responses to those stimuli. 'Learning' is the formation of new **connections between stimulus and response**, on the basis of conditioning. We modify our responses in future according to whether the results of our behaviour in the past have been good or bad.

(b) The **cognitive approach** argues that the human mind takes sensory information and imposes organisation and meaning on it: we interpret and rationalise. We use feedback information on the results of past behaviour to make rational decisions about whether to maintain successful behaviours or **modify unsuccessful behaviours** in future, according to our goals and our plans for reaching them.

6.2 Whichever approach it is based on, learning theory offers certain useful propositions for the design of **effective training programmes**.

Proposition	Comment
The individual should be **motivated** to learn	The advantages of training should be made clear, according to the individual's motives - money, opportunity, valued skills.
There should be clear **objectives and standards** set, so that each task has some meaning	Each stage of learning should present a challenge, without overloading the trainee or making them lose confidence. Specific objectives and performance standards for each will help the trainee in the planning and control process that leads to learning, and providing targets against which performance will constantly be measured.
There should be timely, relevant **feedback** on performance and progress	This will usually be provided by the trainer, and should be concurrent - or certainly not long delayed. If progress reports or performance appraisals are given only at the year end, for example, there will be no opportunity for behaviour adjustment or learning in the meantime.
Positive and negative **reinforcement** should be judiciously used	Recognition and encouragement enhance an individuals confidence in their competence and progress: punishment for poor performance - especially without explanation and correction - discourages the learner and creates feelings of guilt, failure and hostility

Part D: Individual effectiveness at work

Proposition	Comment
Active **participation** is more telling than passive reception (because of its effect on the motivation to learn, concentration and recollection).	If a high degree of participation is impossible, practice and repetition can be used to reinforce receptivity. However, participation has the effect of encouraging 'ownership' of the process of learning and changing - committing the individual to it as their own goal, not just an imposed process.

Individual differences in learning

6.3 The way in which people learn best differs according to individual psychological preferences, which have been categorised as distinct **learning styles**. Peter **Honey** and Alan **Mumford** have drawn up a popular classification of four learning styles.

(a) **Theorists**

   Prefer to understand principles

   - Take an intellectual, 'hands-off' approach
   - Learn best from programmed and structured training which allows time for analysis
   - Learn best from teachers who share their preference for concepts and analysis

(b) **Reflectors**

   Prefer to think things through first

   - Observe phenomena, think about them and then choose how to act
   - Need to work at their own pace
   - Find learning difficult if forced into a hurried programme
   - Produce carefully thought-out conclusions after research and reflection
   - Tend to be fairly slow, non-participative (unless to ask questions) and cautious

(c) **Activists**

   Prefer to try things 'hands on'

   - Deal with practical, active problems and do not have patience with theory
   - Require training based on hands-on experience
   - Are excited by participation and pressure, such as new projects
   - Flexible and optimistic, but tend to rush at something without due preparation

(d) **Pragmatists**

   Prefer to work with real tasks/problems

   - Only like to study if they can see its direct link to practical problems
   - Good at learning new techniques in on-the-job training
   - Aim is to implement action plans and/or do the task better
   - May discard good ideas which only require some development

6.4 Training programmes should ideally be designed to accommodate the preferences of all four styles, or to suit individual trainees. (This is one advantage of individual, as opposed to collective training programmes: the needs and preferences of the individual learner can be taken into account.)

Activity 16.7

With reference to the four learning styles drawn up by Honey and Mumford, which of these styles do you think most closely resembles your own? What implications has this got for the way you learn?

The learning cycle

6.5 '**Experiential learning**' is the term given to 'learning by doing'. Honey and Mumford (building on the work of David Kolb) have produced a simple model called the **learning cycle**, which shows how individuals can turn everyday work into learning opportunities.

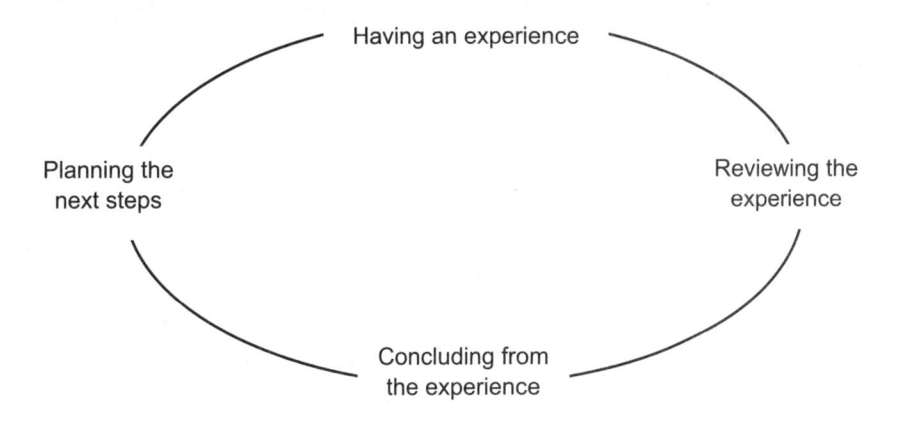

```
              Having an experience
           /                          \
    Planning the                    Reviewing the
    next steps                       experience
           \                          /
              Concluding from
              the experience
```

6.6 Learning from experience is a process of:

(a) **Having an experience**: being fully involved in an action or interaction, utilising your current knowledge and skills. (*Not* distracting your attention from the job to consider its 'training' implications.)

(b) **Reviewing the experience**: afterwards, looking back at what happened, describing it, reflecting on how effective you were and what you could do better or differently. You may use a Personal Development Journal (PDJ) to write about events and interactions, to help you to reflect on these matters.

(c) **Concluding from the experience**: forming general principles or theories that suggest how you might do something different next time in order to achieve different results

(d) **Planning the next steps**: planning specific opportunities to apply and test your conclusions in action – which provides a new experience with which to start the cycle again...

6.7 Say you are negotiating work sharing with a colleague *(having an experience)*: you are fully engaged in the activity, on the job. Afterwards, however, you are able to think more objectively about the interaction: reflecting on your failure to get the assistance you wanted, in your PDJ, you realise that you were not very assertive in your communication style *(reviewing the experience)*. You think that perhaps a more assertive style would enable you to secure co-operation *(concluding from the experience)*. You decide to try out some specific assertive behaviours in your next discussion with the colleague *(planning the next steps)*.

Part D: Individual effectiveness at work

7 SUPPORTING INDIVIDUAL AND ORGANISATIONAL LEARNING

Organisational learning

7.1 **Pedler, Burgoyne and Boydell** are the main proponents in the UK of the idea that some organisations are better adapted to continuous learning than others.

> **KEY TERM**
>
> The **learning organisation** is an organisation that facilitates the acquisition and sharing of knowledge, and the learning of all its members, in order continuously and strategically to transform itself in response to a rapidly changing and uncertain environment.

7.2 The key dimensions of a learning organisation are:

- The generation and transfer of knowledge
- A tolerance for risk and failure as learning opportunities
- A systematic, on-going, collective and scientific approach to problem-solving

7.3 **Garvin** suggests that '**learning organisations**' are good at certain key processes.

(a) **Experimentation.** Learning organisations systematically search for and test new knowledge. Decision-making is based on 'hypothesis-generating, hypothesis-testing' techniques: the plan-do-check-act cycle. Application of information and learning is key. Innovation is encouraged, with a tolerance for risk.

(b) **Learning from past experience.** Learning organisations freely seek and provide feedback on performance and processes: they review their successes and failures, assess them systematically and communicate lessons to all employees. Mistakes and failures are regarded as learning opportunities.

(c) **Learning from others.** Learning organisations recognise that the most powerful insights and opportunities come from looking 'outside the box' of the immediate environment. They encourage employees to seek information and learning opportunities outside the organisation as well as inside.

(d) **Transferring knowledge quickly and efficiently throughout the organisation.** Information is made available at all levels and across functional boundaries. Education, training and networking opportunities are constantly available.

7.4 According to Peter **Senge**, there are also sources of **learning disability** in organisations, which prevent them from attaining their potential - which trap them into 'mediocrity', for example, when they could be achieving 'excellence'.

(a) '**I am my position**'. When asked what they do for a living, most people describe the tasks they perform, not the purposes they fulfil; thus they tend to see their responsibilities as limited to the boundaries of their position.

(b) '**The enemy is out there**'. If things go wrong it is all too easy to imagine that somebody else 'out there' was at fault.

(c) **The illusion of taking charge.** The individual decides to be more active in fighting the enemy out there, trying to destroy rather than to build.

(d) **The fixation on events.** Conversations in organisations are dominated by concern about events (last month's sales, who's just been promoted, the new product from our competitor), and this focus inevitably distracts us from seeing the longer-term patterns of change.

16: Training and development

(e) **The parable of the boiled frog.** Failure to adapt to gradually building threats is pervasive. (If you place a frog in a pot of boiling water, it will immediately try to scramble out; but if you place the frog in room temperature water, he will stay put. If you heat the water gradually, the frog will do nothing until he boils: this is because 'the frog's internal apparatus for sensing threats to survival is geared to sudden changes in his environment, not to slow, gradual changes'.)

(f) **The delusion of learning from experience.** We learn best from experience, but we never experience the results of our most important and significant decisions. Indeed, we never know what the outcomes would have been had we done something else.

(g) **The myth of the management team.** All too often, the management 'team' is not a team at all, but is a collection of individuals competing for power and resources.

Activity 16.8

How far do Senge's seven learning disabilities apply to your own organisation, or to some other significant organisation with which you may be familiar?

7.5 For individuals, additional barriers to learning may be:

- 'A waste of time': people see no personal benefit from training
- Training programmes employ the wrong techniques for people's learning styles
- Unwillingness to change

The training manager

7.6 The training manager is a member of staff appointed to arrange and sometimes run training. The training manager generally reports to the **human resources** or **personnel director**, but also needs a good relationship with line managers in the departments where the training takes place.

7.7 Responsibilities of the training manager include:

Responsibility	Comment
Liaison	With HRM department and operating departments
Scheduling	Arranging training programmes at convenient times
Skills identifying	Discerning existing and future skills shortages
Programme design	Develop tailored training programmes
Feedback	The trainee, the department and the HR department

The role of line managers

7.8 Line managers bear some of the responsibility for training and development within the organisation by identifying:

- The training needs of the department or section
- The current competences of the individuals within the department
- Opportunities for learning and development on the job
- When and how supportive feedback, counselling, coaching and mentoring can be given.

Part D: Individual effectiveness at work

Key learning points

- In order to achieve its goals, an organisation requires a **skilled workforce**. This is partly achieved by training.

- The main purpose of training and development is to **raise competence and therefore performance standards**. It is also concerned with **personal development**, helping and motivating employees to fulfil their potential.

- A thorough analysis of **training needs** should be carried out as part of a systematic approach to training, to ensure that training programmes meet organisational and individual requirements. Once training needs have been identified, they should be translated into **training objectives**.

- Individuals can incorporate training and development objectives into a **personal development plan**.

- There are different schools of thought as to how people learn. Different people have different **learning styles** (Honey and Mumford). They can also learn from everyday work experience, using the **learning cycle** (Kolb).

- There are a variety of **training methods**. These include:
    - Formal (off-the-job) education and training
    - On-the-job training

- **Development** includes a range of learning activities and experiences (not just training) to enhance employees' or managers' portfolio of competence, experience and capability, with a view to personal, professional or career progression.

- The **learning organisation** is an organisation that facilitates the learning of all its members (Pedler, Burgoyne, Boydell).

Quick quiz

1. List examples of development opportunities within organisations.

2. List how training can contribute to:
    (a) Organisational effectiveness
    (b) Individual effectiveness and motivation

3. According to ISO 9000, what are the main steps to be adopted in a systematic approach to training?

4. The formula 'required level of competence *minus* present level of competence describes _____ _____'.

5. How should training objectives be expressed?

6. What does learning theory tell us about the design of training programmes?

7. Which of the following is not one of the learning styles defined by Honey and Mumford?

    A Pragmatist
    B Theorist
    C Abstractor
    D Reflector

8. List the four stages in Kolb's experiential learning cycle.

9. List the available methods of on-the-job training.

10. What are the levels of training validation/evaluation?

16: Training and development

Answers to quick quiz

1   Career planning, job rotation, deputising, on-the-job training, counselling, guidance, education and training.

2   (a) Increased efficiency and productivity; reduced costs, supervisory problems and accidents; improved quality, motivation and morale.

    (b) Demonstrates individual value, enhances security, enhances skills portfolio, motivates, helps develop networks and contacts.

3   Identify how operations influence quality; identify individual training needs against performance requirements; plan and conduct training; plan and organise quality awareness programmes; record training and achievement.

4   Training needs.

5   Actively - 'after completing this chapter you should understand how to design and evaluate training programmes'.

6   The trainee should be motivated to learn, there should be clear objectives and timely feedback. Positive and negative reinforcement should be used carefully, to encourage active participation where possible.

7   C: the correct 'A' word (you may like to use the acronym PART or TRAP to remember the model) is 'Activist'.

8   Concrete experience, observation/reflection, abstraction/generalisation, application/testing.

9   Induction, job rotation, temporary promotion, 'assistant to' positions, project or committee work.

10 Reactions, learning, job behaviour, organisational change, ultimate impact.

Answers to activities

Answer 16.1

Few employers throw you in at the deep end – it is far too risky for them! Instead, you might have been given induction training to get acclimatised to the organisation, and you might have been introduced slowly to the job. Ideally, your employer would have planned a programme of tasks of steadily greater complexity and responsibility to allow you to grow into your role(s).

Answer 16.2

Cost: training can be costly. Ideally, it should be seen as an investment in the future or as something the firm has to do to maintain its position. In practice, many firms are reluctant to train because of poaching by other employers – their newly trained staff have skills which can be sold for more elsewhere. While some organisations encourage this 'employability' training, recognising their inability to offer employees long-term job security, others may experience it as a resource drain. In addition, it must be recognised that training by itself is not the solution to performance problems: it must be effectively planned and managed, as we will see later in this chapter.

Answer 16.3

Specific to your organisation, but examples include:

(a) Job analysis, job descriptions, role definitions, job and personnel specifications (for recruitment), competence definitions, training needs analysis, self-appraisal, performance appraisal (performance management, 360-degree feedback, peer appraisal etc), informal feedback from others

(b) Training and development planning, appraisal reports and interviews, performance management programmes, coaching/mentoring schemes

(c) In-house resource library, access to Internet for training purposes, in-house training centres and activities, sponsorship of training, day-release or training sabbaticals.

Part D: Individual effectiveness at work

Answer 16.4

Just do it, using our example as a guide!

Answer 16.5

(a) Administrative procedure: possibly best learned by on-the-job demonstration, instruction and supervised practice by a member of the HR department. Written notes may be used for the instruction phase, and as an aide-memoire.

(b) Negotiation: observation and modelling of an experienced negotiator; off-the-job learning and practice eg through a workshop allowing negotiation role plays. Possibly followed by experiential learning: attempting negotiations, reflecting on your performance and results, and adjusting where necessary in an ongoing cycle.

(c) Off-the-job information search, update bulletin or information seminar. This is mainly factual knowledge, which may be taken in better away from the demands of the job.

(d) Site visit to the production department; project or committee work involving accounts and production staff.

Answer 16.6

Validation of a new course is important to ensure that objectives have been achieved. Evaluation of it is more difficult, but at least as important because it identifies the value of the training programme to the organisation.

Answer 16.7

Depending on your answer you will learn most effectively in particular given situations. For example, the theorist will learn best from lectures and books, whereas the activist will get most from practical activities.

Answer 16.8

Your own observations.

Now try Question 15 in the Exam Question Bank

Part E
Health, safety and security in the working environment

Chapter 17 Health and safety in the workplace

Chapter topic list

1. The importance of health and safety
2. Responsibility for health and safety at work
3. Law and regulation on health and safety
4. Workplace hazards and safety procedures
5. Fire prevention
6. Emergency procedures
7. Reporting procedures

The following study sessions are covered in this chapter:

		Syllabus reference
19(a)	Outline the main provisions of relevant legislation on health and safety	5(a)
19(b)	Identify possible sources of danger to health and safety of individuals within the workplace	5(a)
19(c)	Suggest appropriate preventative and protective measures	5(a)
19(d)	Discuss the role of training in raising awareness of safety issues	5(a)
19(e)	Describe safe working conditions and identify potential hazards	5(a)
19(f)	Outline the role and responsibility of management in promoting health and safety	5(a)

Part E: Health, safety and security in the working environment

1 THE IMPORTANCE OF HEALTH AND SAFETY

Why is health and safety important?

1.1 Health, safety and well-being at work are important for several reasons.

(a) Employees should – as human beings – be **protected** from needless pain and suffering.

(b) Employers and employees both have **legal obligations** to take reasonable measures to promote healthy and safe working. (We'll discuss these in Section 3 below.)

(c) Accidents, illness and other causes of employee absence and/or impaired performance **cost** the employer money.

(d) A business's **corporate image** may suffer if its health and safety record is bad.

(e) A business's **employer brand** (its reputation as an employer) may suffer if its health and safety record is bad. This may make it difficult to attract and keep qualified staff.

1.2 People need jobs. Historically, this has put employers in a strong position: workers have often had to put up with difficult and dangerous working conditions, believing that they had no choice. Greater affluence, better education and more competitive labour markets have gradually stimulated study and debate about issues such as:

(a) Workplace health and safety hazards (such as dangerous machinery and substances)

(b) The protection of vulnerable groups of workers (such as pregnant women, young workers and night shift workers) and

(c) What workers are entitled to expect in the way of 'quality of working life'.

1.3 In 1972, a UK Royal Commission on Safety and Health at Work reported that unnecessarily large numbers of work days are lost each year through industrial **accidents**, **injuries** and **diseases**, because of the '**attitudes**, **capabilities** and **performance** of people and the efficiency of the organisational **systems** within which they work'.

1.4 Since the 1970s, increasingly complex **legislation** and **regulation** has been brought into effect, specifying the **rights** and **responsibilities** of workers and employers in regard to health and safety in different work contexts.

At the same time, employers themselves have recognised the benefits of protecting their workers – and the costs of not doing so – and have begun to establish health and safety policies above the legal minimum.

1.5 EXAMPLE: THE INTERNATIONAL DIMENSION

While most of the material in this chapter covers UK health and safety law, Health and safety concerns are obviously not confined to the UK. The International Labour Organisation (ILO) published a report entitled 'Safe Work and Safety Culture' to mark World Day for Safety and Health at Work on 28 April 2004. It is felt that there is a need for a new 'safety culture' to reduce and prevent occupational accidents and disease. For example, workers worldwide suffer approximately 270 million occupational accidents each year, and fall victim to some 160 million incidents of occupational disease. In the United States in 2002, approximately two million workers were victims of workplace violence (357,000 in the UK).

To quote the ILO

> 'The ILO has never accepted the notion that injury and disease 'go with the job'. Prevention works. In the course of the 20th century, industrialised countries saw a clear decrease in serious

17: Health and safety in the workplace

injuries, not least because of real advances in making the workplace healthier and safer. The challenge is to extend the benefits of this experience to the whole working world.

Experience has shown that a strong safety culture is beneficial for workers, employers and governments alike. Various prevention techniques have proven themselves effective, both in avoiding workplace accidents and illnesses and improving business performance. Today's high safety standards in some countries are a direct result of long-term policies encouraging tripartite social dialogue, collective bargaining between trade unions and employers, and effective health and safety legislation backed by potent labour inspections.'

The ILO has issued more than 30 Codes of Practice on Occupational Health and Safety. For more information:

www.ilo.org/safework
www.ilo.ru/osh

The cost of accident and illness

1.6 More than 700,000 people are reported injured in the UK every year, and the Health and Safety Executive estimates that the real cost of work-related ill health, accidents and injury equates to between five and ten percent of the UK's gross trading profit every year: an average of £170- £360 per employed person.

1.7 Costs to the employer may include the following.

  (a) **Productive time lost** by the absent employee, and by other employees who (through choice or necessity) stop work at the time of, or following, the accident

  (b) A proportion of the cost of employing **first aid and medical staff**

  (c) The cost of **disruption** to operations at work

  (d) The cost of any **damage to equipment**, including subsequent **modifications** to make it safer

  (e) The cost of any **compensation payments** or **fines** resulting from legal action following an accident or illness

  (f) The costs of **increased insurance premiums**

  (g) Possible **reduced output** from the employee on return to work

  (h) Possible reduced output, increased absenteeism or increased labour turnover as a result of **low morale** among workers in an environment which has been shown to be unsafe or unhealthy

  (i) The cost of **recruiting** and **training** a replacement for the absent employee

Activity 17.1

What might be the cost to you, the *employee*, of a serious accident or illness at work?

What's so dangerous about an office?

1.8 We'll be looking at a number of health and safety hazards that the law identifies (in Section 3 below) and that you might encounter yourself (in Section 4). But if you are to appreciate the relevance of health and safety to your workplace, it is important not to associate risk only with building sites, factories and coal mines!

Part E: Health, safety and security in the working environment

Take a look around you, where you are right now, and see if you can see any health or safety risks.

How about these (just for starters)?

(a) Slippery or uneven floors, frayed carpet or trailing cables and wires (which you might trip over)

(b) Obstacles such as boxes, files, books or open desk drawers (which you might bang into)

(c) A cup of coffee or other liquids placed where they might spill (causing damage or slippery surfaces)

(d) Objects placed too high to reach, so you're tempted to stand on a chair (even a swivel chair)

(e) Heavy items which you may have to lift (without necessarily knowing how to do so safely)

(f) Electrical or other equipment which you're not really sure how to use properly

(g) Chemicals (such as glue, solvent or insect repellent) which require special handling or ventilation

(h) Taking insufficient work breaks, or sitting with poor posture, creating mental and physical strain or stress

2 RESPONSIBILITY FOR HEALTH AND SAFETY AT WORK

Who's responsible for health, safety and security in your workplace?

2.1 Your organisation may have **dedicated departments, managers or staff** in charge of health and safety security. These may include specialists such as:

(a) A first aid or medical officer

(b) An employee counsellor and/or health promotion officer

(c) A fire prevention officer

(d) Security guards

(e) A building manager, sanitation officer, equipment manager and others with responsibility for different aspects of the work environment

The role of these people is to make and implement relevant **policies and procedures**, to listen to employee **concerns** and to respond to any **problems and emergencies.**

2.2 In addition, a number of **employee health and safety representatives** may be appointed by the trade unions or staff associations in your workplace, by agreement with your employer. Their role is to listen to employees' concerns and to consult with the employer on their behalf. Know who these people are in your organisation!

Activity 17.2

Who should you call in the event of:

(a) A photocopier explosion which injures a co-worker?
(b) A co-worker suddenly feeling ill at work?
(c) An unidentified chemical substance appearing to leak from a container in a storage area?

Compile a Health and Safety Directory for yourself: a phone or e-mail contact list for use in emergencies, or when questions arise.

17: Health and safety in the workplace

What is your own responsibility?

2.3 In a general sense, everyone in the workplace is responsible for health and safety.

2.4 In order to contribute to a healthy, safe and secure work environment, you may need to:

(a) **Be alert** to potential hazards as you go about your work

(b) **Take responsibility** for your own behaviour in the workplace, in order to protect yourself and others

(c) **Co-operate** with your employers' health and safety measures: read instructions, follow procedures, perform drills and so on

(d) **Keep yourself informed** about health and safety issues relevant to your workplace. You may need regular training.

(e) **Warn people** who may be at immediate risk as a result of hazardous conditions or behaviours (for example, if you see someone about to electrocute themselves, trip over or set fire to something!)

(f) Take steps, within the scope of your authority, to **minimise hazards** (for example, by clearing your own work area of obstructions, or reminding co-workers of smoking bans and other safety rules)

(g) Take steps, within the scope of your authority, to **mobilise appropriate response procedures** (for example, by sounding emergency alarms, or calling a first aid officer in the event of an accident)

(h) **Inform** appropriate people of identified hazards and the need for corrective action which is beyond the scope of your own authority.

This just gives a flavour of what it might mean to take responsibility for health and safety.

2.5 According to the ILO (see the example earlier in the chapter), the following are vital tools in promoting a **safe and healthy working culture**:

(a) **Participation** from governments, workers' and employers' organisations
(b) **Implementation** of clear working procedures
(c) **Provision** of training and information to workers
(d) **Inspection** activities.

3 LAW AND REGULATION ON HEALTH AND SAFETY

The role of law and regulation

3.1 In the UK, several major Acts of Parliament apply to workplaces, including:

- The **Offices, Shops and Railway Premises Act 1963**
- The **Health and Safety at Work Act 1974**
- The **Fire Precautions Act 1971** and **Fire Safety and Safety of Places of Sport Act 1987**

3.2 In recent years, the UK has also implemented a number of **EC Directives** on various aspects of health and safety by issuing **Regulations** and **Codes of Practice** to supplement the existing legislation.

Part E: Health, safety and security in the working environment

Regulations are legally enforceable. Codes of Practice are not enforceable in themselves, but failure to comply with them may suggest failure in the legal duty to provide a safe and healthy place of work.

3.3 You are not expected to have a detailed knowledge of health and safety law in all its aspects, but you do need to demonstrate that you are aware of, and can comply with, the provisions that affect **your place of work**. This will not necessarily be in the UK. These may be set out in:

- Relevant legislation and regulations
- Associated publications by health and safety authorities
- Your own organisation's health and safety policies, procedures and rules
- Specific procedures and instructions relevant to your job and the equipment you use

The point of being aware of general health and safety principles and provisions is that, if they are not currently set out clearly in your organisation's own documentation and procedures, you will nevertheless be aware of potential risks – and perhaps be able to make constructive recommendations.

3.4 As you read on, bear in mind that 'the law is a floor': it is only meant to set out the **minimum standards** of protection required for ethical practice. '**Best practice**' among employers is likely to be:

(a) More scrupulous in enforcing safeguards

(b) More committed to providing consultation, information and training on health and safety

(c) More wide-ranging in its attempt to promote positive health and well-being (rather than just minimising ill-health and injury).

3.5 Bear in mind, too, that health and safety is not just a legal or procedural matter. Everyday working practices, the working environment and the behaviour of people can put you and others at risk. As well as looking out for hazards such as unsafe machinery or poorly lit staircases (for which employers are clearly responsible), you need to remember that you are responsible for your own **behaviour at work**. Carelessness, foolishness, practical jokes and 'cutting corners' in work practices can have unforeseen consequences!

Your health and safety responsibilities

3.6 You have a general legal responsibility **not to cause harm** to other people or property wherever you are: walking down the street, attending a lecture, working at your desk or sitting at home in front of the TV.

3.7 As an employee, you are obliged under the Health and Safety at Work Act:

(a) To take **reasonable care** to avoid injury to yourself and others

(b) To **co-operate** with your employers to help them comply with their legal obligations (including enforcing safety rules)

3.8 Under the Management of Health and Safety at Work Regulations 1992, you have more specific responsibilities to:

(a) Use all equipment, machinery, safety devices (and so on) provided by your employers **properly** and in accordance with the **instructions** and **training** you received

(b) **Inform your employers,** or another employee who has specific responsibility for health and safety in your workplace, of any perceived shortcoming in safety arrangements or any serious and immediate dangers to health and safety which you identify.

3.9 If you **break safety regulations** (whether or not an accident actually occurs as a result), you can be prosecuted, fined or (in very serious cases) imprisoned. If you are injured, you may be refused compensation because you brought the injuries upon yourself. Even if such a case does not go before the courts, you lay yourself open to disciplinary action by your employer.

Your employer's health and safety responsibilities

3.10 The Health and Safety at Work Act 1974 (and related regulations) impose general duties upon **employers** to make sure that:

- All **systems** (work practices) are safe
- The **work environment** is safe and healthy (well-lit, warm, ventilated and hygienic)
- All **plant and equipment** is kept up to the necessary standard.

On-going risk management

3.11 **Information, instruction, training** and **supervision** should be directed towards safe working practices. Under the Management of Health and Safety at Work Regulations 1992, employers must:

(a) Carry out **risk assessment,** generally in writing, of all work hazards on a continuous basis.

(b) Introduce **controls** to reduce risks.

(c) Assess the **risks to anyone else** affected by their work activities (such as suppliers, customers, visitors)

(d) **Share hazard and risk information** with other employers, including those on adjoining premises, other site occupiers and all subcontractors coming onto the premises

(e) **Revise safety policies** in the light of the above – or initiate safety policies if none were in place previously

(f) Identify **employees who are especially at risk** (such as pregnant women or night shift workers)

(g) Provide up-to-date and appropriate **training in safety matters**

(h) Provide **information to employees** (including part-time and temporary workers) about health and safety

(i) Employ **competent health and safety advisers**

Activity 17.3

Consider the health and safety programme(s) at your place of work or study.

(a) How well aware are you of any rules, procedures and information regarding health and safety? (Think about how well instructed you are in the safe use of office equipment, for example, or how clear you are about what to do in the event of a fire or other emergency.)

(b) Who is responsible for *making* you aware of such matters? Where is the information available, and how easily is it accessed?

Information and consultation

3.12 You may have noticed how important **information**, **awareness** and **consultation** are in health and safety provisions. Employees must be told clearly what the risks are, and how to minimise them, in order to be (and feel) safe at work.

The employees themselves may be in the best position to put forward this information, and must be listened to. They may also require some support in making sure that their concerns are heard and met by management.

3.13 Under the Safety Representatives and Safety Committees Regulations 1977 and the Health and Safety (Consultation with Employees) Regulations 1996, employers must consult employees on health and safety matters such as the planning of health and safety training or any change in equipment or procedures which may significantly affect their health and safety at work.

3.14 The regulations require employers to:

(a) Produce, and bring to the attention of all employees, a **written statement of safety measures**. (Only employers with less than five employees are exempt from this requirement.)

(b) Consult with **safety representatives**, appointed by recognised trade unions (where applicable), with a view to maintaining adequate safety measures.

(c) Appoint a **safety committee**, at the request of the safety representatives, to keep safety measures under review.

Health and safety policy

3.15 There will be several elements to a health and safety policy, whatever the specific needs and hazards of a particular workplace.

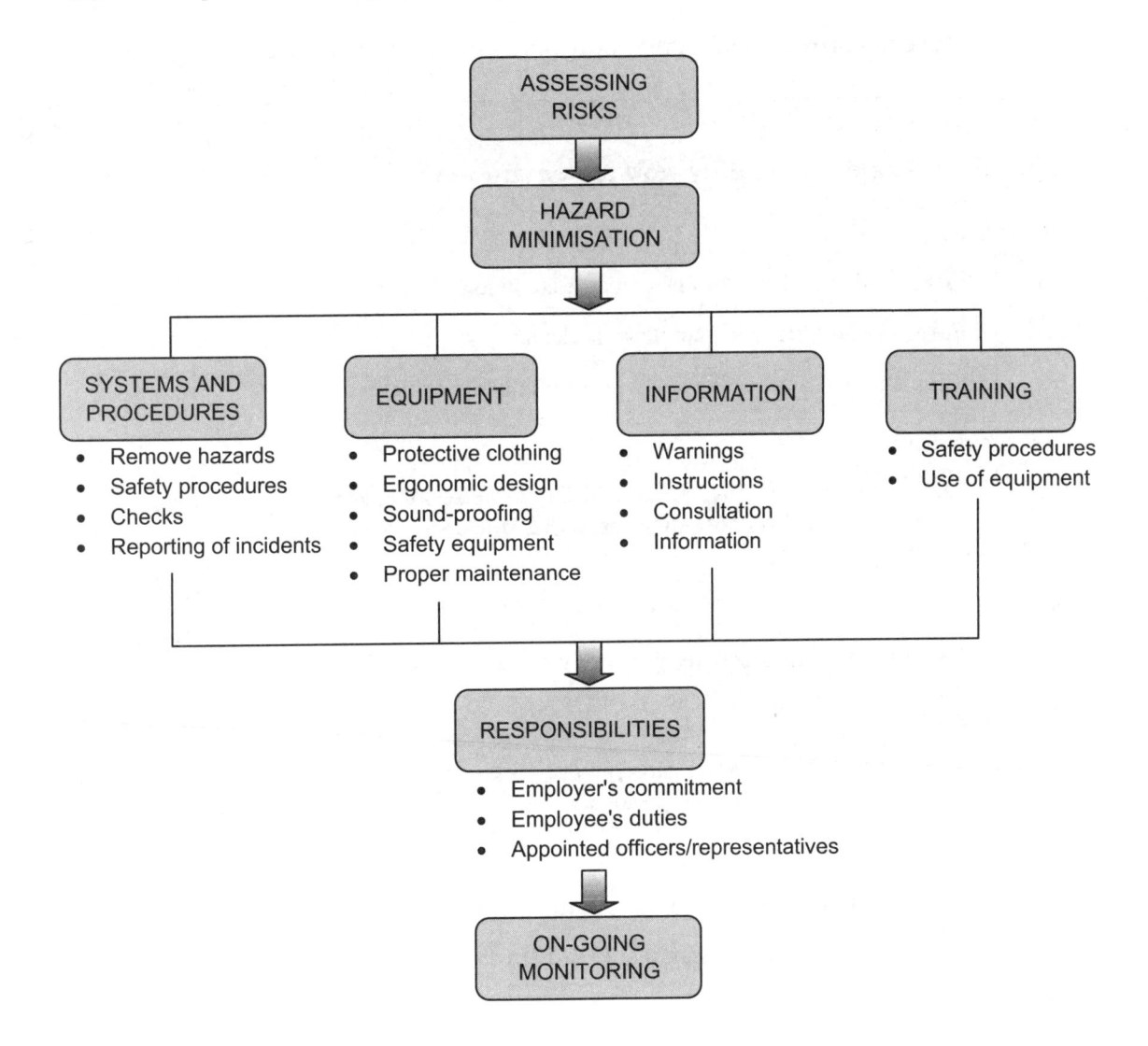

```
                    ASSESSING
                      RISKS
                        ↓
                     HAZARD
                   MINIMISATION
                        ↓
    ┌───────────────┬──────────────┬──────────────┐
  SYSTEMS AND    EQUIPMENT     INFORMATION    TRAINING
  PROCEDURES
```

- **SYSTEMS AND PROCEDURES**
  - Remove hazards
  - Safety procedures
  - Checks
  - Reporting of incidents

- **EQUIPMENT**
  - Protective clothing
  - Ergonomic design
  - Sound-proofing
  - Safety equipment
  - Proper maintenance

- **INFORMATION**
  - Warnings
  - Instructions
  - Consultation
  - Information

- **TRAINING**
  - Safety procedures
  - Use of equipment

```
                  RESPONSIBILITIES
```
- Employer's commitment
- Employee's duties
- Appointed officers/representatives

```
                  ON-GOING
                  MONITORING
```

Health and safety training

3.16 Training is required on an ongoing (and individual) basis for technical updates on health and safety law, when changing roles or areas of work, new work methods and new equipment. The amount and types of training required should be assessed according to individual employee needs.

Example

Croner (the professional information and publications company) has a PC-based 'Interactive Safety Trainer' to prepare and test employees on areas including:

- Office health and safety
- Display screen equipment
- Fire safety
- Manual handling

Go to www. healthandsafety – centre.net for more information.

Part E: Health, safety and security in the working environment

A safe and healthy work environment

3.17 The Workplace (Health, Safety and Welfare) Regulations 1992 provide for health and hygiene in a number of areas.

3.18 We have summarised some of the key requirements in the following table.

Checklist: A safe and healthy working environment

Cleanliness

☐ Floors and steps must be cleaned at least once a week.

☐ Furniture and fittings must be kept clean.

☐ Rubbish must not be allowed to accumulate in work areas.

Overcrowding

☐ Each person should have at least 11 cubic metres of space. (This may sound like quite a lot of space, but it is not much more than the space occupied by a desk and chair, plus a gangway for access.)

Ventilation

☐ There must be an adequate supply of fresh or purified air in circulation.

Temperature

☐ A reasonable temperature (not below 16°C where people are sitting down) must be maintained, except for brief periods.

Lighting and windows

☐ There must be adequate natural or artificial light.

☐ Windows must be kept clean inside and out.

Toilets

☐ There must be enough suitable toilets. (Broadly, a male and female WC for every 15 to 20 employees.)

☐ They must be properly ventilated and lit, kept clean and properly maintained.

Washing facilities

☐ These should be provided on the same scale as toilets.

☐ They should have clean hot and cold water, soap and towels (or equivalent)

Drinking water

☐ Adequate drinking water must be provided together with cups or a fountain.

Seating

☐ Where work can or must be done sitting down, seats must be suitable in design, construction and size.

Lifts
- [ ] Lifts must be safe, and examined by a competent engineer at least every 6 months.

Floors, passages and stairs
- [ ] These should be soundly constructed and maintained: without holes, slip-free and kept free from obstruction.
- [ ] Stairs should have hand-rails and any floor openings fenced round.

Traffic routes
- [ ] These should have regard to the safety of pedestrians and vehicles alike.

Machinery and equipment
- [ ] All equipment should be properly maintained.
- [ ] Dangerous parts of machines should be fenced.
- [ ] No person under the age of 18 should be required to clear machinery if this involves risk.
- [ ] No person should be allowed to operate a machine specified as dangerous unless fully instructed of the dangers.

Heavy lifting
- [ ] People should not be required to lift, carry or move a load likely to cause injury.

Falls or falling objects
- [ ] These should be prevented by erecting effective physical safeguards (fences, safety nets, ground rails and so on)

Fire precautions
- [ ] Appropriate fire-fighting equipment should be provided.
- [ ] There must be adequate means of escape.
- [ ] Business premises should generally have a valid fire certificate from the local fire authority (depending on the size of the premises and the number of people).
- [ ] Fire exits should be clearly marked.
- [ ] Escape routes should be kept unobstructed.
- [ ] Fire alarms should be provided and tested periodically.
- [ ] People working in the building should be familiar with the escape drill.

First aid
- [ ] A first aid box or cupboard, under the charge of a responsible person, should be provided for every 150 employees or fraction thereof (ie there should be two, if there are 160 employees).
- [ ] Where there are more than 150 employees, the responsible person should be trained in first aid and should be available to attend to accidents during working hours.
- [ ] Where there are more than 400 employees, there should be a first aid room.

Part E: Health, safety and security in the working environment

> ☐ Even if you are **working at home**, you are still an employee: your employers are required to provide you with a safe place of work, just as they are to those employees working at corporate premises.

Activity 17.4

Use the above checklist to appraise your own working environment.

Other health and safety regulations

3.19 Many more specific regulations exist in the UK for a range of workplace health and safety issues, including:

(a) The minimising of hearing impairment, stress and distraction from **noise**: The Noise at Work Regulation 1989

(b) The safe handling and storage of **chemicals** and other potentially dangerous substances: Control of Substances Hazardous to Health Regulations 1994

(c) Equipment and techniques for safely lifting **heavy objects**: Manual Handling Operations Regulations 1992

(d) The provision and use of safety **equipment** (where required) and the safe use of all equipment at work: The Provision and Use of Work Equipment Regulations 1992, the Personal Protective Equipment at Work Regulations 1992

(e) Healthy hours, techniques and safeguards when using **computers**: Health and Safety (Display Screen Equipment) Regulations 1992

(f) Managing added health risks for **pregnant women**: Management of Health and Safety at Work (Amendment Regulations) 1994

(g) Controlling **working hours** and rest breaks (particularly for at-risk groups like night-shift workers): Working Time Regulations 1998

(h) Requirements and restrictions for the content and use of **first aid** boxes: The Health and Safety (First Aid) Regulations 1981

(i) **Reporting** problems and incidents: Reporting of Injuries, Diseases and Dangerous Occurrences Regulations (RIDDOR) 1995

3.20 In March 2002, the European Commission issued its Five Year Plan for health and safety. Proposals included:

(a) Legislation on repetitive strain injury, or RSI

(b) A new directive on ergonomics: the design of workplace equipment, furniture and environments to minimise strain on human users

(c) An update on the display-screen directive, to cover increased use of computer mice, laptop computers and handheld ('palm pilot') computers

(d) Amendments to the manual handling directive to cover not just heavy lifting, but the repetitive lifting of small loads

3.21 Health and safety is very much on the agenda of policy-makers: keep your eyes and ears open for proposals and changes that affect your workplace.

4 WORKPLACE HAZARDS AND SAFETY PROCEDURES

Workplace hazards

4.1 A **hazard** is something that is likely to cause injury, or a point of exposure to risk of accident, injury or illness.

As we noted in Section 1, it is easy to assume that 'work hazards' apply mainly to building sites, factories or coal mines. So what are the health and safety hazards that affect people working in an administrative role, and how can the risk be minimised?

Office equipment

4.2 Many items of equipment used in an administrative role:

(a) are **electrical**, carrying a risk of electric shock or electrical fire (if misused)

(b) contain **moving or heated** parts, carrying a risk of injury or burns (if misused)

4.3 The key phrase is: 'if misused'. All equipment should be used in accordance with the **operating instructions** and any **induction** or technical **training** you receive in your workplace.

So, for example, you will probably be shown how to use office equipment like the photocopier, fax machine and computer printers in your first days in an office. Even so, it is worth reading the instructions to ensure that office practice complies with them: people often develop 'short cuts' when doing routine jobs, and these may not be safe (especially for those who are less experienced).

Electrical equipment

4.4 The following checklist (adapted from a photocopier instruction manual) is designed to demonstrate the kind of **precautions** that should be taken when operating any electrical equipment.

(a) Never place **heavy objects** on the equipment, or subject it to shocks.

(b) **Insert the plug fully** into the electrical socket. Do not use damaged plugs or sockets.

(c) **Do not remove or open any covers** while using the equipment.

(d) If the equipment becomes **jammed**, follow the instruction manual for unjamming: be sure to turn the equipment off (if required) and look out for warning signs and symbols (eg of sharp or heated parts)

(e) Never **unplug or turn off** the equipment while it is in operation.

(f) When unplugging the power cord, do not pull on the cord. **Grasp the plug** and pull it out.

(g) If the plug or socket get hot, **switch off at the socket**, pull out the plug and call a qualified electrician.

(h) Never use any **magnetised object, inflammable aerosols** or **liquids** near the equipment.

(i) Be careful not to drop **small objects** (paper clips, staples) into the equipment.

(j) If the equipment produces smoke, becomes unusually hot or produces abnormal noises, turn it off, unplug it and **report the fault**.

Part E: Health, safety and security in the working environment

(k) Turn the equipment off **at the end of the work day** or during a power blackout.

(l) Do not plug the equipment into the **same power outlet** used for other electrical equipment.

(m) Watch out for **exposed wires**: stress points like the base of the plug and the point where the flex enters the equipment are particularly dangerous.

Electric shock

4.5 If the worst happens and someone receives an electric shock, stop the current, if possible, by switching off at the wall or pulling out the plug.

If this is not possible, make sure that you are standing on a dry surface (a piece of wood or newspaper is ideal) and knock the part of the victim's body clear of the source of the electricity, using something non-conductive like a piece of wood, or a rolled up newspaper – *not* metal.

Avoid anything wet and do not touch the person's body with your own until the current is switched off.

Mechanical equipment

4.6 Basic **office tools** also require care.

(a) Devices designed to puncture or cut paper or plastic are just as good at making holes and gashes in flesh! Be aware of the risks when using guillotines, hole punches, binding machines, franking machines and shredders. Do not try to clear paper jams or faults unless you are fully familiar with the machine!

(b) Electricity and moving parts generate heat: a machine that is left ticking over all day may get hot enough to burn.

(c) Be particularly careful with personal effects like necklaces, bracelets or other jewellery, ties and scarves: they can get trapped in machines with moving parts. Long hair can also be a hazard: you may prefer to tie it back in some way if you feel it is particularly at risk because of machinery you use.

Activity 17.5

List the items of equipment – manual, electric, mechanical or computerised – that you use regularly in your role.

(a) What potential hazards can you see in each? (Think about what might happen if it was used irresponsibility or improperly, not properly maintained, or left unattended or in the wrong place?)

(b) What could you do *immediately* to protect yourself and others from each of these hazards?

(c) What would you need to know more about, or have instruction in, in order to do this?

Workplace chemicals

4.7 Some common office equipment and machinery requires liquid or powder consumables. Beware of:

(a) Substances marked with symbols or warnings: **toxic** (poisonous), **corrosive** (acidic, eats into flesh or materials), combustible or **flammable** (easily catches fire), or otherwise hazardous to health

17: Health and safety in the workplace

(b) Substances such as **spirits** and **oils** that are generally flammable

(c) Substances that give off fumes or may otherwise be harmful if **inhaled** (including glue and other solvents, and potentially asthma-inducing substances like dust)

(d) Substances that are harmful if **swallowed** or exposed to **skin** or **eyes**.

4.8 If you or your organisation regularly use a potentially harmful substance, you should:

(a) Report any shortcomings in **control measures** (such as lack of warning notices, ventilation, product labelling or secure storage).

(b) Ensure that you wear and look after any **protective clothing** provided (gloves, masks).

(c) Ensure that you comply with all **procedures** and **instructions**

Heavy lifting

4.9 More than a quarter of accidents reported each year are associated with manual handling, back injuries being the most common.

4.10 There may be specifically trained and equipped personnel whose job it is to lift heavy loads such as deliveries or furniture: check whether your organisation has dedicated porters. If you are required to lift heavy or awkward weights yourself:

(a) Check the load for information about its **weight** and **weight distribution** (if one side or part is heavier than another) before you attempt to lift it.

(b) Get advice (or obey instructions) on proper **lifting technique**. Make sure you have a secure and well-balanced hold on the object. Keep your spine straight. Bend from the knees.

(c) Inform your manager if you believe you are **at risk** eg because of an existing back condition or hand injury.

(d) Use any back braces, hand strapping or other **supportive devices** that are available.

(e) If in doubt, ask your health and safety officer for a risk assessment.

Computer workstations and VDUs

4.11 Most administrative roles today involve the use of a computer.

If you have ever worked for a long period at a computer terminal, you may personally have experienced some **discomfort**: back ache, eye strain and stiffness of the neck, shoulders, arms or hands, say.

4.12 Some of the problems associated with computer use are to do with **work practices**: insufficient breaks and poor seating posture, which leads to muscles being starved of oxygen, the build up of waste products in the body and the compression of nerves.

Other problems come from the design of **workstations** themselves: visual glare and flicker from the screen (the Visual Display Unit or VDU), or poorly designed tables and chairs contributing to poor posture and physical strain and so on.

4.13 **RSI (repetitive strain injury)** is the collective term for the various disorders associated with working at computers. It now accounts for a high proportion of all work-related injuries, and is to be the specific focus of forthcoming health and safety initiatives.

Part E: Health, safety and security in the working environment

Ergonomics

KEY TERM

Ergonomics is the scientific study of the relationship between a human being and the working environment. It explores the mental and physical demands that can arise from a working environment, and the capabilities of people to meet those demands.

4.14 Ergonomic data is used to design **equipment**, **furniture** and **working systems and conditions** which – apart from functioning well – minimise the worker's expenditure of energy and experience of physical strain.

The following diagram shows the recommended way of sitting at a workstation and positioning the equipment for maximum efficiency and minimum strain.

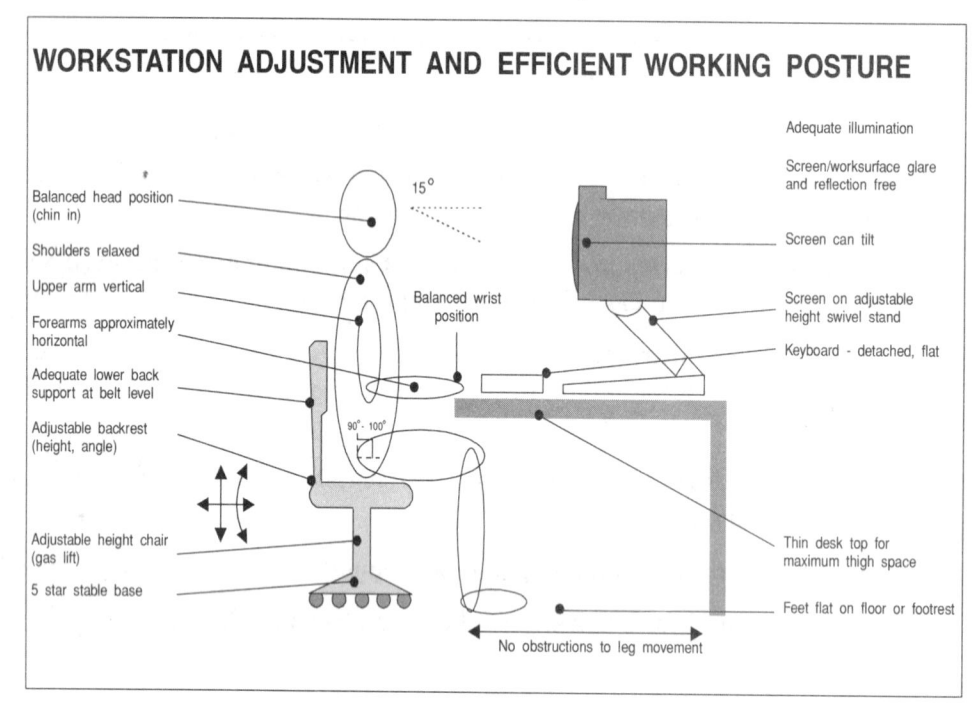

WORKSTATION ADJUSTMENT AND EFFICIENT WORKING POSTURE

- Balanced head position (chin in)
- Shoulders relaxed
- Upper arm vertical
- Forearms approximately horizontal
- Adequate lower back support at belt level
- Adjustable backrest (height, angle)
- Adjustable height chair (gas lift)
- 5 star stable base
- 15°
- Balanced wrist position
- 90° - 100°
- No obstructions to leg movement
- Adequate illumination
- Screen/worksurface glare and reflection free
- Screen can tilt
- Screen on adjustable height swivel stand
- Keyboard - detached, flat
- Thin desk top for maximum thigh space
- Feet flat on floor or footrest

Activity 17.6

A scene from everyday office life at Hazzard Limited is shown below. Note down anything that strikes you as being dangerous about this working environment.

17: Health and safety in the workplace

Employee behaviour at work

4.15 Many workplace hazards are caused or aggravated not by objects or systems – but by the people who use them. We have already mentioned some obvious examples, such as:

  (a) failing to read or comply with usage instructions and health warnings
  (b) failing to comply with routine safety procedures
  (c) risky behaviour, such as standing on swivel chairs or leaving objects in gangways

4.16 Such behaviours represent a deliberate choice to take risks. Why would people do such a thing? They might take safety for granted: 'nothing's ever happened *before*...' They might be playing a practical joke. They might be in a hurry. There may even be a culture in the office which is 'macho' about health and safety, showing off about being tough and taking risks. Whatever the reason, risk-taking behaviours are irresponsible: everything's fine – *until* someone is seriously injured.

Workplace stress

4.17 As well as physical health and safety, increasing attention is being paid to mental well-being at work. Despite pressure to enhance performance, many companies are realising that increasing workloads and longer working hours are in fact counter-productive. **Stress** – and related physical and mental illnesses – is now a primary cause of lost work hours.

4.18 Stress can be caused by a wide range of factors:

  (a) **Work overload**: excessive workload or pressure; insufficient regular breaks and time off for rest, relaxation, exercise and non-work activities

  (b) **Work 'underload'**: boredom, monotony and lack of meaning in the work

  (c) Poor **management style**: lack of clear instructions or targets, unpredictable moods and so on, which make team members feel insecure

  (d) **Isolation**: lack of constructive relationships with colleagues; politics, competition, cliques and so on

Part E: Health, safety and security in the working environment

(e) **Bullying, harassment** or **discrimination**: on-going physical or verbal intimidation, hostility, insult or injustice

(f) **Uncertainty** and **insecurity**: changes at work over which the individual has no control

(g) **Personality** factors: ambitious, inflexible and perfectionistic people are more prone to stress

(h) **Non-work factors**: bereavement, illness, financial or relationship difficulties and so on

4.19 Some stress is stimulating and positive. The signs of **harmful stress** include: irritability and mood swings; sleeplessness; skin and digestive disorders and other physical symptoms; withdrawal; abuse of drugs or alcohol; apathy and low confidence; and changes in behaviour at work (such as poor timekeeping or error rates).

Activity 17.7

(a) Using the above lists of causes and symptoms of stress, assess whether you – or your colleagues – might be at risk (or already suffering) from harmful stress.

(b) Who would be the appropriate person to ask about managing workplace stress in your organisation (or outside it)? Selecting an appropriate communication method, request information on how to manage stress.

(c) Which of the *causes* of stress are within your own control? What could you do immediately to reduce your exposure to stress?

5 FIRE PREVENTION

Fire hazards in the workplace

5.1 The main causes of fire in the workplace are as follows.

(a) **Electrical** appliances (especially portable heaters) and tools which create sparks

(b) **Smoking**

(c) Flammable **materials** (such as waste paper, chemical-soaked rags, clothing and some furniture materials) particularly where these are likely to come into contact with heaters or cigarettes

(d) Flammable **substances** (such as chemicals, or aerosol cans left in direct sunlight)

(e) Poor **housekeeping**. Well organised and carefully maintained premises lessen the likelihood of fire breaking out and enable it to be more readily controlled if it does.

Fire prevention

5.2 The Fire Precautions (Workplace) Regulations 1997 require employers to:

(a) Provide the appropriate number of **fire extinguishers** and other means of fighting fires

(b) Install **fire detectors** and **fire alarm systems** where necessary

(c) Take whatever measures are necessary for **fighting fire** (eg the drawing up of a suitable emergency plan of action) and nominate a sufficient number of workers to implement these measures and ensure that they are adequately **trained** and **equipped** to carry out their responsibilities.

17: Health and safety in the workplace

(d) Provide adequate **emergency routes and exits** for everyone to escape quickly and safely.

(e) Ensure that protective equipment and facilities (including fire doors, fire notices, fire alarms, fire extinguishers and sprinklers) are **regularly maintained** and that any faults found are rectified as quickly as possible.

5.3 **Fire precautions** in the workplace may include the following matters.

(a) **Cleanliness/tidiness**
- Keeping premises clear of combustible waste and refuse
- Keeping separate receptacles for waste and special hazards (such as flammable liquids)

(b) **Storage**
- Ensuring that fire doors, exits, fire equipment and fire notices are unobstructed at all times
- Keeping storage areas accessible to fire fighters

(c) **Building maintenance**
- Keeping points of entry secure against intruders (limiting the risk of arson)
- Ensuring that gangways, exit routes and fire doors are clear and in good repair
- Keeping windows, doors and other ventilation openings shut unless required
- Switching off or unplugging electrical equipment when not in use

(d) **Flammable liquids and gases**
- Keeping flammable substances away from possible sources of ignition
- Posting appropriate warning notices and labels

(e) **Machinery**
- Regularly maintaining all machinery and equipment
- Ensuring adequate cleaning, lubrication and clearing of vents (to prevent overheating)
- Ensuring safe and proper usage

(f) **Heating and lighting**
- Restricting the use of unauthorised heaters
- Keeping safe distance from combustible materials

(g) **Smoking**
- Prohibiting smoking in all but designated smoking areas
- Enforcing non-smoking regulations

(h) **Fire protection equipment**
- Keeping fire doors free for emergency access (*never* locking or blocking them!)
- Ensuring that fire doors can be closed in the event of fire (*not* wedging them open)
- Ensuring that they are fitted with effective self-closing devices
- Ensuring that they are clearly labelled 'Fire Door: Keep Shut'
- Ensuring that *any* door on an escape route can be opened easily and immediately without a key

Fire door keep shut

(i) **Warning notices**

- Displaying prominent warning notices on hazardous substances and equipment
- Clearly identifying fire doors, fire alarm call points and exit routes
- Posting emergency evacuation procedures (including details of safe rendezvous/roll call points outside the building)
- Posting fire exit signs where they can be clearly seen, and including a pictogram (eg showing a person running through a door with a directional arrow)

(j) **Staff training**

- Instructing all new staff in fire procedures and escape routes during induction
- Appointing and training fire wardens
- Training staff in the correct use of fire-fighting equipment

(k) **Damage control**

- Keeping duplicate copies of important records and computer disks in another building
- Drawing up contingency plans to enable work to recommence as soon as possible after a fire.

Activity 17.8

As with identifying hazards in your work area, see if you are up to speed with fire safety in your office.

Question	Answer	Plan to acquire further information (if required)
What should you do if fire breaks out in your workplace?		
Would you recognise the sound of a smoke or fire alarm?		
Where is the nearest fire extinguisher to your work area?		
How do you set off the fire alarm?		
Where is the nearest fire exit?		
Where is your department's meeting point in the event of evacuation?		

17: Health and safety in the workplace

Question	Answer	Plan to acquire further information (if required)
Should you leave doors open or shut in the event of fire?		
Who knows at any given time whether you are (or are not) in the building, and how?		
Who is the Fire Safety officer in your building?		

6 EMERGENCY PROCEDURES

Illness and accident

6.1 As with any other emergency, there should be clear procedures laid down for health emergencies in the organisation's **Occupational Health and Safety plan**: as a first step, make sure you know what those procedures are. Health emergencies may include such events as these given below.

(a) **Workplace injury** (including dislocations, sprains, strains, fractures, burns, eye injuries, bleeding from wounds)

(b) **Electric shock** or heat exhaustion

(c) **Fainting** or collapse

(d) **Poisoning** or allergic reaction to gases or toxic substances

(e) Manifestations of **illness** or chronic conditions suffered by individuals: heart attack, diabetic shock, epileptic fits and so on

The scope and limits of your responsibility

6.2 In the area of health emergency, it is particularly important to recognise the limits of your authority and expertise – however powerful your desire to be helpful. The most valuable things you can do are as follows.

Step 1. **Stay calm** – and avoid personal danger (eg in the event of electric shock or gas poisoning).

Step 2. **Call for help**. Ensure that you can identify the trained first aiders and appointed persons (who are nominated to take charge in the event of health emergency), and that you know how they can be contacted. In case of serious emergency, it is the appointed person who should arrange to call an ambulance (discussed further below). Emergency phone numbers should be posted in conspicuous places near or on telephones.

Step 3. Do not attempt to administer **first-aid** yourself unless you are trained to do so.

- Keep the victim still: do not move unless absolutely necessary to ensure safety
- Stop arterial bleeding (bright red, spurting) immediately, using a pressure pad or bandage: do not touch wounds with your fingers
- Clear blocked airways (mouth and throat) if safe to do so

Remain with the ill or injured person until help arrives.

Step 4. **Take careful note** of what happened immediately before and during the emergency (what the victim was doing, how he or she looked, whether he or she was unconscious and for how long and so on): this may be helpful to medical staff.

6.3 You should also ensure that your employers (and/or medical staff) are informed of any medical conditions that *you* suffer from that may affect you at work: any medication you regularly take, any substances to which you are allergic and so on.

General principles in dealing with emergencies

6.4 Safety procedure in the case of emergencies will obviously depend upon what has happened. Quite often it will mean evacuating the building according to fire safety procedures as we have just seen, but in the case of, say, armed intruders it might mean ensuring that certain doors are locked. In **any emergency situation** you should do the following.

Step 1. Stay calm.

Step 2. Avoid personal danger.

Step 3. Call for help: contact the company's first-aider or security staff as appropriate or, if no-one is available, call the emergency services. (Check that you know who your first-aider, fire officer and security officer are, and how to contact each of them.)

Step 4. Help others to avoid danger if possible.

Step 5. In no circumstances move injured people unless it is more dangerous not to do so. Remove the source of danger instead, if possible.

Step 6. Do not attempt to administer first-aid yourself unless you are trained to do so.

Evacuating the building

6.5 One of the most common reasons for evacuating staff from a building is the outbreak of **fire**. Other reasons include **bomb threats**, and the discovery of **unsafe structures or substances** (such as asbestos in the building fabric, or suspected anthrax in mailed packages).

6.6 Every organisation should have a set of **procedures** that should be followed when the building needs to be evacuated. These should be clearly displayed in the workplace and staff manuals.

6.7 Evacuations are generally notified and managed by a **safety officer or fire officer**. They should have some sort of formal training by the local fire brigade or by the Health and Safety Executive, and are responsible for making sure that everyone known to be in a building at the time of evacuation:

(a) gets safely out of the building and
(b) can be accounted for.

6.8 A typical evacuation procedure would include the following steps.

Step 1. When requested to do so, everyone in the building should leave as quickly as possible, using the quickest and safest route. (In the event of fire, for example, do not use lifts.)

Step 2. Consistent with swift departure, carry out any preventative/containing measures. (In the event of fire, for example, close all windows and doors and ensure that designated fire doors are shut.)

Step 3. Employees should meet at a designated meeting place outside the building. They should direct any visitors (or others who do not know where to go) to the correct meeting place.

Step 4. The fire or safety officer, or designated supervisors, should call a register (picked up as they leave the building) to ensure that all people logged as being in the building are accounted for.

Step 5. Only when the fire or safety officer declares an 'all clear' should people return to the building.

Step 6. Regular evacuation drills should be held and performance reviewed to identify any shortcomings in the procedures or the way in which they are carried out.

6.9 All employees must ensure that they are familiar with the organisation's evacuation procedures and official meeting places, and that someone is aware (or they are formally signed in) when they are in the building.

Activity 17.9

Following your previous helpful recommendations to the management of Hazzard Ltd, you have been asked to post appropriate 'Fire Action' notices in your office, covering key actions for:

(a) Any person discovering a fire
(b) Everyone hearing the fire alarm
(c) Exiting the building safely

Make your notice simple and direct enough to act as a quick emergency prompt for staff.

General principles of emergency evacuation

6.10 In the event of an evacuation, you need to attend to **your own safety** and to **the safety of others**.

Respond promptly and swiftly	Don't stop to gather personal belongings or finish tasks.
	Use the nearest designated escape route.
Respond calmly and efficiently	Don't panic, and encourage others to be calm if necessary.
	Move fast – but with care. (Do not run, especially on stairs)
	Move quietly: you may need to hear instructions.
Guide people who are not familiar with the emergency plan (eg customers or visitors)	Inform others of escape routes and meeting points
	Warn others of risks (eg using lifts in the event of fire)
Help people with special needs (restricted mobility, poor hearing, poor sight) as far as it is safe to do so.	Inform yourself about special evacuation arrangements (safe lifts, fire-safe refuges where people can wait for assistance)
	Pass on alerts and warnings to those who do not appear to be aware of them (eg hearing impaired people)
	Look out for people who appear to be in difficulty

Part E: Health, safety and security in the working environment

7 REPORTING PROCEDURES

Reporting accidents

7.1 You may have an accident yourself, or you may witness one and be asked to make a report. No matter how minor an accident may seem at the time, there may be complications later, so it is important that the facts are recorded accurately as soon as possible after the incident.

7.2 If you have an accident, follow any procedures laid down by your organisation. They would typically require you to do the following.

Step 1. Get first aid (from someone properly qualified to give it!)

Step 2. **Report** the incident as soon as possible to someone in authority. You may be asked to fill in a form.

Step 3. If your organisation employs more than ten people, it should by law keep an **accident book**. See that your accident is accurately recorded in the book: read the entry for yourself, if it is made by someone else.

Step 4. If you are injured to the extent that you cannot immediately check the entry, **write** a letter or memorandum to your employer (or get somebody to write on your behalf) setting out your version of events.

Step 5. If anybody else witnessed the accident, get **signed statements** from them, including their names and addresses.

Obviously, not all of these measures will be necessary for a small cut or bruise, but you should be aware of the need to protect your own interests and that of other potential victims, in the case of a serious accident.

Accident book

7.3 The illustration below shows the format of a typical accident book. The one used by your organisation may be laid out differently, or may consist of loose-leaf sheets.

TO BE COMPLETED BY THE INJURED PARTY OR A WITNESS			TO BE COMPLETED BY FIRST AID OFFICER		TO BE COMPLETED BY SAFETY OFFICER
Date	Name	Details of accident (include time, place and names of any witnesses)	First aid treatment	Report to HSE	Preventative action taken

Notifiable accidents and diseases

7.4 In the UK, certain accidents, dangerous occurrences and cases of disease must be notified to the relevant authorities: the environmental health department of the employer's local authority, or the Health and Safety Executive.

(a) A '**reportable major injury**' includes fractured limbs (not fingers or toes); amputation; temporary or permanent loss of sight; and injuries resulting in hospitalisation for more than 24 hours.

(b) A '**reportable dangerous occurrence**' is a 'near miss' that might have caused major injuries: electrical short circuits causing fire or explosion; collapse of building structures and many others.

(c) '**Reportable diseases**' include certain poisonings, occupational asthma, asbestosis, hepatitis and many others.

7.5 The Reporting of Injuries, Diseases and Dangerous Occurrences Regulations (RIDDOR) 1995 require employers to do the following.

(a) **Notify the enforcing authority immediately** (eg by telephone) if there is an accident resulting in death or major injury, the hospitalisation of a member of the public, or a dangerous occurrence.

(b) **Leave the site of a major accident or dangerous occurrence undisturbed** (if safe to do so) to facilitate investigation.

(c) **Send a completed accident report form** (within ten days) to:

 (i) **confirm** the telephone report

 (ii) **notify** any injury which stops someone doing their normal job for more than three days

 (iii) **report** certain work-related diseases

Activity 17.10

Review the scene from office life at Hazzard Ltd (shown in Activity 17.6).

As the observer – and assuming that you have by now had one of the many accidents possible in this working environment – fill out a report in the Accident Book page shown below.

Part E: Health, safety and security in the working environment

Accident book

Full name, address and occupation of injured person (1)	Signature of injured person or other person making this entry* (2)	Date when entry made (3)	Date and time of accident (4)	Room/place in which accident happened (5)	Cause and nature of injury † (6)
1					
2					
3					
4					
5					
6					
7					
8					
9					
10					

* If the entry is made by some person acting on behalf of the employee, the address and occupation of that person must also be given
† State clearly the work or process being performed at the time of the accident

17: Health and safety in the workplace

Key learning points

- Health, safety and security at work are **important** primarily to protect employees from harm, suffering and disruption and to protect the assets of the business (including data) from theft and sabotage.
- **Employees** have responsibilities to:
    - take reasonable care to avoid injury
    - co-operate with their employers in complying with health and safety requirements
    - use all equipment properly and in accordance with instructions and training
    - inform appropriate authorities of any perceived dangers to health and safety
- Employers have general responsibility to:
    - provide a healthy and safe work environment
    - make sure that all systems are safe
    - ensure that plant and equipment is kept up to the necessary standard
    - issue a written statement of safety measures and the means used to implement them
    - consult with employee safety representatives and appoint a safety committee (if requested)
    - carry out on-going monitoring, policy-making, information sharing, consultation and training in safety matters
- There are specific provisions in the UK relating to workplace health and safety, including those under the Health and Safety Act 1974 and subsequent Regulations. (You should familiarise yourself with the equivalents in your own country of study and work, if not the UK.)
- Common health and safety hazards in an administrative role include:
    - Electrical and mechanical equipment
    - Chemicals
    - Heavy lifting
    - Computer/VDU usage and poor ergonomics
    - Irresponsible behaviour and poor workplace maintenance
    - Mental stress or strain
- General rules for dealing with emergencies
    - Respond swiftly but calmly to alarms
    - Avoiding personal danger, remove the source of danger if possible
    - Call for help
    - Administer first aid (only if you are trained to do so)
    - Follow any accident, emergency and evacuation procedures and instructions
    - Help others, especially those with special needs

Quick quiz

1. List five reasons why health and safety at work are important.

2. Which of the following might be identified as a hazard in an office?

    A   A swivel chair
    B   A co-worker's sense of humour
    C   A photocopier
    D   All of the above

3. Fill in the gaps in the following sentences.

    'As an employee, you are obliged under the Health and Safety at Work ....:

    'To take .... care to avoid injury to yourself and ....

    'To co-operate with your .... to help them comply with their .... obligations.

Part E: Health, safety and security in the working environment

'To use all equipment provided by your employers .... and in accordance with the .... and training you received.'

4 Individuals appointed by a recognised trade union to consult with employers on maintaining adequate safety measures are called:

  A Safety Representatives
  B Safety Committees
  C Health and Safety Commission
  D Health and Safety Executive

5 List any five items provided for in the Workplace (Health, Safety and Welfare) Regulations 1992 in regard to a healthy and hygienic work environment.

6 List five causes of stress at work

7 Fill in the blanks in the following sentences about using electrical equipment.

  When unplugging a power cord, grasp the .... – not the .... - and pull it out. Watch out for .... wires. Never use .... aerosols or liquids near the machine. If a plug or socket gets hot, ... the machine at the socket, pull out the ....and call an electrician.

8 Which of the following may be considered an issue in fire safety?

  A How tidy your desk is at the end of the day
  B Where you keep an aerosol can
  C Which doors you leave open, shut or locked
  D All of the above

9 In the event of an evacuation, you should use the nearest exit and stay near that exit once you are outside. True or false?

10 Which of the following would not be immediately notifiable under RIDDOR 1995?

  A A broken arm, as a result of a fall down the office stairs
  B Concussion (by a box falling off a shelf) resulting in 36 hours in hospital
  C Electrical overload causing a small fire at an office power point
  D A broken finger as a result of a slamming photocopier lid

Answers to quick quiz

1 Responsible protection of employees
   Compliance with legal obligations
   Costs of accidents, illness and other absences
   Corporate image
   Employer brand

2 D (A is the most obvious risk, but B may lead to 'horse-play' or 'practical jokes' which can be hazardous, and C may be dangerous if the person using it has failed to read or obey the instructions)

3 Act; reasonable; others; employers; legal; properly; instructions

4 A

5 See the checklist in Section 4 for a full list.

6 Work overload or underload; poor management style; isolation; insecurity; harassment/discrimination; personality factors; non-work circumstances.

7 Plug; cord; exposed; flammable/combustible; switch off; plug

8 D (A may be a surprise, but if your desk is untidy, it is less likely that waste paper will be cleared away)

9 False: you should go to the designated meeting/roll-call point for your department

10 D

Answers to activities

Answer 17.1

(a) At worst, a serious accident may render you permanently unable to work.

(b) You may be forced to stay away from work for a considerable period. Employers generally allow a period of weeks or months on full pay, perhaps followed by a further period on half pay. The period is probably not as long as you think – check your contract of employment. Thereafter you will only receive state benefits.

(c) Your career or training will be interrupted. You might miss a sitting of professional exams, putting you back six months!

Answer 17.2

Remember, this exercise is specific to your workplace. Depending on its procedures and structure, and on the severity of the circumstances in each case, the appropriate person may be (suggestions only):

(a) First aid officer. Emergency services: ambulance and/or fire. Health and safety officer. The departmental manager and/or the victim's line manager.

(b) First aid officer. Health and safety officer (if the illness is work related). Ambulance (if serious). The victim's line manager.

(c) Health and safety officer. Local fire brigade. Stores manager. Technical specialist (to identify substance).

Keep such a directory where you will access it readily: by the phone or computer terminal.

Answer 17.3

You should have answered from your own workplace experience. Note that the issue of communication and awareness is crucial: the best safety policy in the world is no good unless people know about it!

Answer 17.4

Bear in mind that health and safety regulations are much more detailed than this, and that specific provisions and exemptions may apply in the case of your workplace: the checklist is only a general guide. However, if you do identify shortcomings in areas you consider important, it will be worth noting them.

Answer 17.5

You probably use a wide range of equipment at work, from calculators and staplers to more complex machines such as photocopies and faxes, right up to fairly dangerous machines such as document shredders and binders.

(a) Each has its own hazards: remember that even a stapler or letter opener can be dangerous if misused; a fax machine may be subject to electrical faults; a photocopier uses chemicals; and any heavy object is hazardous if dropped or thrown!

In addition, knowing this Unit is about security as well as safety, you might have thought about security risks of leaving a computer on and unattended (who has access to your data)?

(b) What you can immediately do to minimise risks includes: obeying all warnings and instructions; following organisational procedures for maintenance, storage, use and reporting of faults; behaving responsibly yourself and encouraging others to do so; warning others if they are about to do something potentially dangerous.

(c) If you have identified something you need to know more about, or have instruction in: follow it up! Make an action plan to obtain the instruction manual, get advice or a demonstration, get a key for your desk drawer – or whatever it might be.

Part E: Health, safety and security in the working environment

Answer 17.6

You should have spotted the following hazards.

(a) Heavy object on high shelf
(b) Standing on swivel chair
(c) Lifting heavy object incorrectly
(d) Open drawers blocking passageway
(e) Trailing wires
(f) Electric bar fire
(g) Smouldering cigarette unattended
(h) Overfull waste bin
(i) Overloaded socket
(j) Carrying too many cups of hot liquid
(k) Dangerous invoice 'spike'

If you think you can see others, you are probably right.

Answer 17.7

Some of the causes of stress may be within your control. You may have suggested:

(a) Taking more regular work breaks (to which you are entitled)

(b) Being more assertive in negotiating your workload, saying 'no' and asking for help (if you suffer from overload)

(c) Being more assertive in negotiating more varied tasks, responsibility or information (if you suffer from underload)

(d) Being more assertive in asking for clear instruction and targets (poor management)

(e) Being more assertive in making your needs and rights clear, and initiating grievance procedures if necessary (bullying, harassment, discrimination)

(f) Learning better relaxation techniques to make use of your breaks and leisure time

(g) Seeking workplace or private counselling for help with stress or underlying problems

Answer 17.8

We've already given general guidelines in the Text: this activity is designed to make you aware of your own organisation's specific procedures, provisions and sources of information.

Answer 17.9

Fire action

Any person discovering a fire
1. Sound the alarm.
2. [Receptionist] to call fire brigade.
3. Attack the fire if possible using the appliances provided.

On hearing the fire alarm
4. Leave the building by [nearest route]
5. Close all doors behind you.
6. Report to assembly point.
   [Rear car park]

Do not take risks.
Do not return to the building for any reason until authorised to do so.

Do not use lifts.

Part E: Health, safety and security in the working environment

Answer 17.10

Accident book

	Full name, address and occupation of injured person (1)	Signature of injured person or other person making this entry* (2)	Date when entry made (3)	Date and time of accident (4)	Room/place in which accident happened (5)	Cause and nature of injury † (6)
1	Constantine Larousse, 14 North Street, Islington (Office Junior)	C Larousse	14/8/X8	10.30 14/8/X8	Rm 74	Tripped over trailing wire & bruised knees and elbows whilst carrying cups of coffee for fellow workers
2						
3	Marcus Davis, 17 Albert Sq, Acton London W3 (Accounting Technician)	M Davis	=	=	=	Attempted to prevent injury to Constantine. Suffered minor scalding to chest from hot coffee and punctured hand on letter spiker. Obtained first aid
4						
5						
6						
7	Percy Lal, 247 East Street, Finchley	M Davis (as above)	=	=	=	Percy was standing on a chair trying to put a box on the shelf. It appears that he was alarmed by the above incident, banged his head on the shelf, dropped the box and fell off the chair. He has been taken to hospital.
8						
9						
10						

* If the entry is made by some person acting on behalf of the employee, the address and occupation of that person must also be given
† State clearly the work or process being performed at the time of the accident

---

Now try Question 16 in the Exam Question Bank

Chapter 18 Security in the workplace

Chapter topic list

1. Security
2. Security risks
3. Security procedures and devices
4. Data security
5. Responsibility for workplace security

The following study sessions are covered in this chapter:

Syllabus reference

20(a) Describe possible sources of security breaches within the organisation — 5(b)

20(b) Outline measures for preventing security breaches — 5(b)

Part E: Health, safety and security in the working environment

1 SECURITY

What is security?

1.1 In a business setting, **security** generally involves preventing or dealing with *commercial threats:* theft, espionage (spying) or sabotage, and unauthorised access to premises or confidential data. However, you should also be alert to other kinds of security risk, such as violent or disruptive conduct (eg by disgruntled individuals or interest groups), or even terrorist threats or attacks.

This syllabus is concerned with the security of the **workplace**: the building where you work and the people, physical objects and confidential data within it.

Why is security important?

1.2 Security, like health and safety, is important for a number of reasons.

(a) To protect **employees** and others on the premises from danger and fear.

(b) To protect the **assets** of the business, and save costs of repair or replacement (in the event of sabotage or theft)

(c) To prevent or minimise **disruption** to normal working from unexpected intrusions (even if harmless)

(d) To protect **confidential and sensitive information** from unauthorised access and its potential consequences.

Activity 18.1

Think of the various types of people or items in your organisation that might be the focus of attempted theft, sabotage, espionage, disruption or attack. Which items or people might you consider most at risk?

We'll start your list with some examples.

(a) Cash and cheques
(b) Vehicles
(c) Moveable/saleable items such as computers, laptops, TV/video equipment, mobile phones
(d) Staff who have direct access to assets (eg counter staff in banks)

Carry on…

Data security

1.3 **Information** is an item at risk of security breach. It can be damaged, lost or stolen in the same way that equipment and valuables can. People may seek to sabotage or steal information from organisations for:

- Monetary/sale value
- Competitive advantage
- Pure nuisance value

1.4 Certain types of data may be particularly at risk.

(a) Information integral to the business's **standing** and **competitive advantage**: for example, unique product formulae, designs and prototypes, marketing plans and some financial information.

(b) **Personal and private** information relating to employees and customers: for example, grievance and disciplinary reports; employee medical details; customer credit ratings. (Some of this information is protected by law.)

(c) Information related to the **security** of the organisation: for example, details of access codes, computer passwords, banking/delivery schedules.

(d) Information integral to the **outcome of dealings**, which would be affected by public knowledge – for example, legal or financial details of intended mergers, takeovers or redundancies.

Principles of security

1.5 Effective security is a combination of **delay**, **checking** and **alarm**.

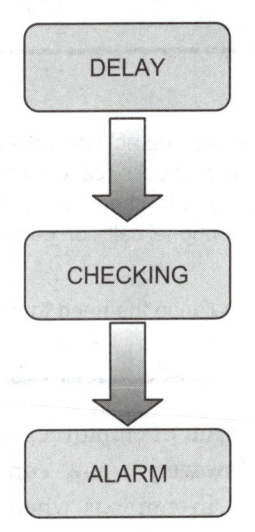

DELAY

Lines of defence before vulnerable areas and items can be reached
- Outer doors to the main building
- Reception area where visitors
- Lockable/guarded offices
- Lockable filing cabinets and safes

CHECKING

Procedures for authorised access to vulnerable areas or items
- Identification of authorised staff
- Checking/signing in/escorting visitors
- Challenging unauthorised individuals
- Computerised/personal passwords
- Checking authorisation before access to files allowed

ALARM

Procedures for alerting those responsible for responding to security breaches
- Electronic security alarms
- Individual alertness and response
- Computerised warning of file access attempts

Data protection issues

1.6 You should be aware that there are legal issues in security, particularly in regard to **data protection** and **personal privacy**.

(a) Under the **Data Protection Act 1998**, there are restrictions on the kinds of data which can be kept on employees, and to whom that data can and must be disclosed on request. (Confidential references, legally privileged documents and so on should never be disclosed.)

(b) The **Human Rights Act 1998** gives individuals the right to respect for their private life. This restricts employers from disclosing employees' sickness information or medical records. It also restricts certain types of security checks, such as random drug testing.

Privacy issues

1.7 A Code of Practice entitled '**Monitoring at Work**' (part of the Employment Practices Data Protection Code) covers workers' privacy rights. It states that:

'Workers have a right to expect a degree of trust from their employers, and to be given reasonable freedom to determine their own actions without constantly being watched or listened to.'

Part E: Health, safety and security in the working environment

(a) Staff must be informed when and why monitoring at work is taking place (eg for performance, or to check compliance with company rules) and how data obtained through monitoring will be used. This information could be set out in staff policies or handbooks.

(b) Covert (hidden) monitoring should only be used if criminal activity is suspected. The police need to be involved if the surveillance is specifically to check for criminal activity (such as drug-taking) in places where workers have high expectations of privacy, such as toilets or private offices.

(c) Organisations wishing to monitor staff at work must, where possible, avoid monitoring any information likely to be of a private nature: eg private e-mail messages. However, the latest draft of the code gives employers the right to open personal staff e-mails in 'appropriate circumstances': eg if the member of staff is suspected of criminal activity.

Activity 18.2

How do workplace security measures affect your daily activity? What areas and activities are monitored by your employers (if any)? Some may be obvious: security passes and checks, security cameras in certain areas and so on. Others may be less obvious, and you may need to check the staff manual, policy statements or specific warnings: monitoring or recording of telephone calls or e-mails (eg for quality purposes).

Consider **why** these measures are in place. How does your employer balance the need to protect your privacy – and the need to protect the business (including you…)?

1.8 In general, you employer has no right to insist on **physical search** of employees or visitors entering or leaving premises without their **consent**. However, some contracts of employment include a clause giving the employer this right, in contexts where theft of stock, components or files is an identified risk or problem.

The right to search visitors can be secured simply by displaying a notice informing them (before they enter the premises) that they are liable to be searched. (This is often the approach of retail outlets, to deter shoplifting.)

Keeping informed

1.9 Remember to keep your eyes and ear open! Try *People Management* journal (www.peoplemanagement.co.uk) or www.dataprotection.gov.uk for updates on your individual rights – and your organisational responsibilities.

2 SECURITY RISKS

Vulnerable items and people

2.1 Security aims to prevents others from taking away or doing damage to things that belong to your organisation and/or the people who work in it. What type of belongings or people are particularly at risk? Here are some suggestions.

(a) Items that are **valuable** *and* **portable/movable**: cash and cheques, stocks, ownership documents (such as share certificates or title deeds), vehicles, small equipment (including computers)

(b) Potentially valuable **information** in portable form (paper files, floppy disks and CDRoms)

18: Security in the workplace

(c) **Security** devices: pass cards, keys

(d) Staff in the **front line**: security guards, reception staff

(e) Staff with **custody of assets**: counter staff in banks, say

(f) **Key personnel,** who may be kidnapped or intimidated to obtain assets or security codes

Vulnerable points in premises and systems

2.2 What are the most **exposed** or **vulnerable** areas of an organisation? Here are some suggestions, but think what others might apply in your own organisation.

(a) **Public or open areas,** such as entrances, hallways, parking areas, toilets, stairways and lifts – particularly if these are unattended or inadequately attended for the volume of traffic.

(b) **Points of entry and exit**: doors, windows, gates and lifts. By definition, these are points where intruders may attempt to gain access. Pay attention to open, unsecured or broken windows and doors – especially in unattended areas.

(c) **Unattended areas**: store rooms or back stairs, where there are not always people about.

(d) **Ill-lit areas**: car-parks or stair wells.

(e) **Reception areas**: if an unauthorised person can talk, trick or slip his way past reception, he may be much harder to identify as a stranger (and locate within the premises) later.

(f) **Areas where at-risk items and data are concentrated,** such as store rooms, computer rooms, offices, file stores and so on – especially if they are located near points of entry/exit or busy public areas.

(g) **Points of transit or storage** outside the organisation's premises. Valuable items taken out of the office (for banking, delivery, work at home or whatever) may be particularly vulnerable.

Activity 18.3

Back at Hazzard Ltd, what security risk(s) can you identify in the following scenes from office life, and what could be done in each case to minimise the risk?

(a) There is one person on the reception desk in a busy entrance area, and she is dealing with five impatient people trying to get visitors' tags and direction, plus two couriers trying to deliver packages.

(b) It is very hot in the office, so the back door (at the end of the corridor by the storerooms) has been propped open to allow air to circulate.

(c) A visitor has been shown into your supervisor's office and asked to wait: he is early for an appointment, and your supervisor has not yet returned from lunch. Nobody else knew about the appointment. The visitor says he does not wish to be in the way, and shuts the office door.

Part E: Health, safety and security in the working environment

3 SECURITY PROCEDURES AND DEVICES

Controlling access

3.1 Controlling access will usually involve a combination of devices and procedures for:

(a) controlling people's ability physically to **open points of access**, such as gates, doors and windows

(b) **identifying people** as authorised or unauthorised to be given access to the premises, particular areas or data

3.2 The following procedures and devices may be used to control access.

(a) **Doors** can be closed and locked

(b) **Windows** can be closed and locked. Sensitive areas may also have strengthened glass or bars.

(c) **Swipe cards** (and more sophisticated equivalents, such as voice recognition systems) may allow only authorised individuals to trigger the opening of doors.

(d) **Combination locks** (in the form of electronic keypads) may control the opening of the doors: only authorised individuals are given the entry code number, which should be periodically changed.

(e) **Video** and **entry phone systems** may be used so that would-be entrants can be identified by those inside, before the door is opened.

(f) **Cabinets, cupboards** and **drawers** can be protected by means of locks.

(g) Some items should be kept in a **strongbox** or **safe**, cash being the most obvious example. Safes may be opened by combination (to which only authorised personnel have access) or electronically-controlled time locks (as in a bank).

(h) **Computers** and **computer files** can be protected using electronic passwords and access codes.

Security procedures

3.3 Most organisations of any size have to have some **formal security measures**, if only to satisfy their insurers. The extent of the measures will depend on the risks involved in the business.

3.4 If your organisation has a formal **security procedures manual**, get hold of a copy and read it carefully. It is likely to have the following procedures.

Procedure for	Examples
Identifying regular staff	If the procedures state that you should wear your **identity badge** at all times, then you must do so, no matter how well known you are to the security staff.
	If the procedures state that you should **show your pass** to the security guard whenever you enter the building, you should do so, and you should not be allowed access if you do not do so.
	Likewise if you are required to **sign in and out**, don't forget to do so.

18: Security in the workplace

Procedure for	Examples
Vetting non staff members	If somebody is coming to visit you on business then you may be required to go down to reception and accompany them to the place where you work. If you have not met them before you may have to ask them to produce some further means of identification: a letter inviting them to a meeting or the like.
Non business visitors	Say a friend is meeting you for lunch. Some organisations will not let such visitors past reception at all. Others allow free access to non-sensitive areas. Make sure your friend does not unwittingly break the rules.
Protecting the building	A particular door may have to be kept locked at all times. It may be the individual's responsibility to ensure that all windows in his or her working area are closed and locked at the end of the day.
Protecting the organisation's assets	You might be expected to lock away items like calculators in your desk drawer at night, for example.
Protecting documents and information	Locking away files and ledgers, or not leaving your computer terminal in a state where it can be used by someone without the password, are typical of measures of this sort. Other aspects of your work may be sensitive, and there may even be a confidentiality clause in your contract of employment: check.
Protecting the procedures	It ought to go without saying that you should not reveal your computer password to others and there is no point in having doors or safes with combinations if the combination is given to anyone who asks for it. Likewise there should be procedures to control keys – such as a list of authorised keyholders and instructions about where keys should be kept. There is no point in locking doors if the keys are accessible to all. In fact, do not discuss your organisation's security procedures with *anyone* outside the organisation: if an outsider asks persistently about security, report this as suspicious.
Explaining what to do in the event of a breach of security	The names and numbers should be available of the people to ring, and of the information they will need to be told: location of the intruders, time of entry, how many there are, items missing or damaged, and so on.

Activity 18.4

Choose any one area of security (personal identification, entry and exit, security equipment, data security, breach of security and so on) and design a notice or poster, suitable for posting on a departmental noticeboard, outlining the procedure *and/or* communicating its importance to staff.

If your notice accurately and effectively communicates a real procedure in your office, consider seeking authorisation to post it on a noticeboard – and keep a copy for your portfolio.

3.5 We will now discuss **data security**, specifically, in more detail.

Part E: Health, safety and security in the working environment

4 DATA SECURITY

> **Exam alert**
>
> A full 20-mark compulsory question was set in the Pilot Paper for this syllabus. It covered a range of topic areas: why data protection is important; the main risks for data security; how staff can help prevent loss, damage and compromise to data; and examples of systems and products used to do this.

Data security

4.1 **Information** is an item at risk of security breach. It can be damaged, lost or stolen in the same way that equipment and valuables can. People may seek to sabotage or steal information from organisations for:

(a) Monetary/sale value
(b) Competitive advantage
(c) Pure nuisance value

4.2 Certain types of data may be particularly at risk.

(a) Information integral to the business's **standing** and **competitive advantage**: for example, unique product formulae, designs and prototypes, marketing plans and some financial information.

(b) **Personal and private** information relating to employees and customers: for example, grievance and disciplinary reports; employee medical details; customer credit ratings. (Some of this information is protected by law.)

(c) Information related to the **security** of the organisation: for example, details of access codes, computer passwords, banking/delivery schedules.

(d) Information integral to the **outcome of dealings**, which would be affected by public knowledge – for example, legal or financial details of intended mergers, takeovers or redundancies.

The importance of data security

4.3 You should be aware, however, that the loss, damage or corruption of data files of a less sensitive nature can also have an impact on the organisation.

(a) Information is critical to all business activities and systems. Even 'routine' transaction data are used – not just to process transactions – but:

(i) To support marketing strategy, customer communications and customer relationship management (eg by providing information on customer preferences and buying habits)

(ii) To support efficient materials management (eg by allowing Just-In-Time supply and other strategies to maximise the use of resources and to facilitate supplier relationships)

(iii) To support the control and use of funds

(iv) To enable the organisation to comply with the requirements of business ethics, corporate governance and legislation in its dealings with customers, suppliers

18: Security in the workplace

and investors and in the storage and accessibility of financial and product information.

(b) Potentially sensitive data now flows more freely than at any time in history between the organisation and:

 (i) Its employees: with legislation and social trends towards worker consultation and involvement at a strategic level. Many organisations facilitate employee communication through media such as an **intranet**: a mini-Internet on the corporate computer network for employee message boards, Web pages and e-mail.

 (ii) Its other stakeholders: with trends towards customer relationship marketing and supply chain management, as well as statutory requirements for information to shareholders. Many organisations deliberately increase the availability of information to stakeholder groups, for example through the use of **extranets**: areas of the corporate Web site available only to authorised users, such as customers, members, suppliers and business partners.

 (iii) Its macro environment, with the global information explosion of the World Wide Web and **Internet**. A Web presence opens the organisation to global access.

(c) Information and Communications Technology (ICT) has enabled the gathering, storage and use of much larger amounts of data than has been possible previously.

 (i) Organisations routinely gather and hold in databases – for a variety of strategic and operational purposes – data on customers, suppliers, competitors, markets, inventory and employees.

 (ii) Increasingly, transactions are conducted via the Internet, through e-Commerce and the direct networking of business systems for supply chain management. Huge amounts of personal, business and transactional information – and funds are transmitted electronically.

4.4 The protection of data is therefore vital:

(a) To support business decisions and transactions with reliable, accurate and complete data and information

(b) To support ethical and legal dealings in regard to individual privacy and the disclosure of information (discussed below).

The Data Protection Act

4.5 Especially with the advent of computer records systems, fears have arisen with regard to:

(a) Access to personal information by unauthorised parties

(b) The likelihood that an individual could be harmed by the existence of data which was inaccurate, misleading or sensitive (eg medical details)

(c) The possibility that personal information could be used for purposes other than those for which it was requested and disclosed.

4.6 The Data Protection Act 1998 (and related Codes of Practice still in the process of publication) address these concerns. The legislation is an attempt to protect:

(a) **Individuals** (not corporate bodies)

Part E: Health, safety and security in the working environment

(b) In regard to the gathering, storage and use of **personal data** (information about a living individual, including facts and expressions of opinion)

(c) Which are **processed** (mechanically or manually) so that records can be systematically used to access data about the individual

(d) By **data controllers**: organisations or individuals who control the contents and use of files of personal data.

4.7 Data controllers and computer bureaux have to register with the Data Protection Commissioner. They must limit their use of personal data to the uses registered, and must abide by Data Protection Principles.

DATA PROTECTION PRINCIPLES

(1) The information to be contained in personal data shall be obtained, and personal data shall be processed, fairly and lawfully. (In particular, information must not be obtained by deception.)

(2) Personal data shall be held only for one or more specified (registered) and lawful purposes.

(3) Personal data shall be adequate, relevant and not excessive in relations to its purpose or purposes.

(4) Personal data shall be accurate and, where necessary, kept up to date. ('Accurate' means correct and not misleading as to any matter of *fact*. An *opinion* cannot be challenged.)

(5) Personal data shall not be kept for longer than is necessary for its purpose or purposes.

(6) An individual shall be entitled:

   (i) to be informed by any data controller whether he/she holds personal data of which that individual is the subject

   (ii) to be informed of the purpose or purposes for which personal data is held

   (iii) to have access to any such data held by a data controller and

   (iv) where appropriate, to have such data corrected or erased.

(7) Appropriate security measures shall be taken against unauthorised access to, or alteration, disclosure or destruction of, personal data and against accidental loss or destruction of personal data. The prime responsibility for creating and putting into practice a security policy rests with the data controller.

(8) Data may not be exported outside the European Economic Area, except to countries where the rights of data subjects can be adequately protected.

4.8 There are some important **exemptions** from these provisions.

(a) **Unconditional exemptions**: personal data essential to national security, required to be made public by law or concerned *only* with the data controller's own personal, family or household affairs.

(b) **Conditional exemptions**: including:

- Personal data held for payroll and pension administration

- Data held by unincorporated members' clubs, relating only to club members

- Data held only for distribution of articles or information to the data subjects, and consisting only of their names and addresses or other particulars necessary for the distribution

(c) **Exemptions from 'subject access' provisions**: data held for the prevention or detection of crime, or assessment or collection of tax; data to which legal professional

18: Security in the workplace

privilege could be claimed (eg that held by a solicitor); data held solely for statistical or research purposes

(d) A special exemption for **word processing operations** performed only for the purpose of preparing the text of documents. (A manager who uses a word processor to automatically insert employee data into a letter or report will not as a result become a data controller. If he intends to used the database to access employee records, he must register as a data controller.)

4.9 Your organisation should have a **data protection co-ordinator,** whose responsibility it is to arrange registration and set up systems; to monitor compliance with the Data Protection Principles; to meet subject access requirements; and to amend the registered entry whenever there is a change in the nature or purpose of the data being held and used by the organisation.

Activity 18.5

Are the following examples permissible under the Data Protection Act, or not?

(a) You demand your right to access any personal data held by the Inland Revenue on your tax affairs.

(b) Your personnel file contains an appraisal report by your supervisor which states: 'In my opinion, [your name] appears to display a negative attitude towards supervision, which may account for recent disciplinary proceedings'. You do not, in fact, have a negative attitude towards supervision: the disciplinary proceedings were caused by factors outside your control. You demand compensation for loss caused to you (since you were not promoted, as expected, following this appraisal) as a result of this inaccurate data.

(c) You discover that your employee record contains a mention of a conviction for drink-driving – which you have never had. You had wondered why you were always refused access to the pool car at work. You claim compensation for the loss caused as a result of this inaccurate data, and ask for it to be wiped from the file.

(d) The Accounts Manager has compiled a recruitment file on a candidate for the position of his assistant. He hired an investigation agency to access her bank records (without her knowledge) in an effort to vet her character and circumstances, in the interest of the firm's security. The report is held on your database.

Risks to data

4.10 **Main risks to data:**

(a) **Human error.** Individuals lose, damage or incorrectly input or store data.

(b) **Technical malfunction or error.** Systems, equipment or software fails, resulting in loss, damage, corruption or inability to access data.

(c) **Catastrophic events.** Natural disasters (such as flood, earthquake or hurricane) and – less rarely – accidents such as fire or burst water pipes, can disrupt organisational activity, break communication systems and/or destroy data storage and transmission facilities.

(d) **Malicious damage.** Individuals within or outside the organisation deliberately attempt to disrupt the organisation's activities by damaging or tampering with data (eg through 'hacking' or viruses)

(e) **Industrial espionage or sabotage.** Individuals within or outside the organisation deliberately attempt to steal (espionage) or damage (sabotage) data, with a view to commercial gain (eg to sell plans to a competitor, or delay a product launch on their behalf)

(f) **Dishonesty.** As discussed in Chapter 6, dishonest individuals may wish to access information, or steal funds, for personal gain.

4.11 When data are transmitted over a **network** or a **telecommunications line** (especially the Internet) there are numerous security dangers.

(a) Corruptions such as viruses on a single computer **can spread through the network** to all of the organisation's computers.

(b) Unless care is exercised it is **easy to overwrite somebody else's data**.

(c) **Disaffected employees** have much greater potential to do deliberate damage to valuable corporate data or systems because the network could give them access to parts of the system that they are not really authorised to use.

(d) If the organisation is linked to an external network, persons outside the company (**hackers**) may be able to get into the company's internal network, either to steal data or to damage the system. Intranets can have **firewalls** (which disable part of the telecoms technology) to prevent unwelcome intrusions into company systems, but a determined hacker may well be able to bypass even these.

(e) Employees may download **inaccurate information** or imperfect or virus-ridden software from an external network. For example 'beta' (free trial) versions of forthcoming new editions of many major packages are often available on the Internet, but the whole point about a beta version is that it is not fully tested and may contain bugs that could disrupt an entire system.

(f) Information transmitted from one part of an organisation to another may be **intercepted**. Data can by encrypted in an attempt to make it unintelligible to eavesdroppers, but there is not yet any entirely satisfactory method of doing this.

(g) The **communications link** itself may break down or distort data.

Basic principles of data security

4.12 Extending the principles of premises security to confidential and sensitive information, you should consider the following – alongside any rules and procedures set by your own organisation.

(a) Do not leave **paper files** or **computer disks** where they are generally accessible. (Preferably, lock them away.)

(b) **Lock** safes, strongboxes and filing cabinets when you have finished with them.

(c) Use **passwords,** where advised, to secure computers and computer files.

(d) Do not **share** passwords, combinations or keys with unauthorised people.

(e) Do not **copy** or **transmit** confidential information without specific authorisation and appropriate security measures.

(f) Select **appropriate communication** channels and media to protect confidentiality. (There is a big difference between a memo posted on a staff noticeboard, or a conversation in an open office, and a sealed letter or memo clearly marked 'Private and Confidential' or 'For addressee's eyes only'.) Remember that e-mail is neither secure nor confidential.

(g) Avoid **careless talk** or gossip about sensitive work-related matters with, or in the hearing of, unauthorised people. (This includes mobile phone conversations in public!)

(h) Respect the **privacy** of others – and assertively request them to respect yours.

4.13 In addition, specific precautions can be taken against each of the categories of risk outlined in Paragraphs 4.10 and 4.11.

(a) Risks of human error can be reduced by checks and controls, systematic procedures and employee training and supervision.

(b) Risk of technical error and malfunction can be minimised by regular system testing and the use of backup systems (discussed below).

(c) Risk of malicious damage and industrial espionage/sabotage can be minimised by controlling access, both physically (using locks, security checks and so on) and electronically (using passwords, strong encryption of data, anti-virus software and so on).

(d) Risks of disaster are difficult to foresee, but contingency plans may be made, including off-site backup storage of files, emergency power generators and adequate insurance for any loss or damage to data and associated systems.

(e) Risks of dishonesty can be minimised by a range of checks and controls, discussed in Chapter 6.

Back-up systems

4.14 Many organisations ensure that a **minimum of two copies** is always held in addition to the original data. If the original data is lost, the back-up becomes the master copy.

4.15 The **grandfather-father-son** technique is used on systems where the main data storage is on replaceable magnetic media such as tape. Data on the grandfather tape is updated with transactions and the update stored on the father tape. When further transactions are processed, the father tape is used and output stored on the son tape. When the next batch of transactions is processed, the output is stored on the grandfather tape, which thus becomes the new son tape and the other two generations move up one stage. There are thus 3 generations available at anytime, plus all the transactions relating to them.

4.16 A different approach will be used with PCs and smaller network servers using hard disks. One technique is to make backups daily using a set of weekly media, one for each working day in the week. These are thus re-used once each week. A further set of backups may then be made of each month-end with the media being reused annually. Finally, a backup is taken at year end and kept permanently. Once again, it is necessary to store the transaction inputs if it is to be possible to re-create data.

4.17 Back-up copies should be stored in a different place from the original file and preferably in a fire-proof safe.

4.18 The backing-up of data is a critical requirement for systems security. However, data on a back-up file will not itself be entirely secure unless some additional measures are used. If there is a **hardware fault** which causes data loss or corruption the fault must be diagnosed and corrected before the correct data is put at risk in the system.

Part E: Health, safety and security in the working environment

4.19 The back-up data should also be **isolated from the operations staff** so that it is not too readily available. Back-up data which is easily available could be used before system errors have been fully corrected and may then become corrupted too. An organisational policy which dictates the systems tests necessary prior to the loading of back-up data is vital for ensuring that the back-up data is itself protected against system and human faults.

Passwords and user profiles

4.20 Email, intranets and the internet means that computer systems are increasingly connected over telecommunications lines. These are rarely completely secure, and an expert **hacker** can easily enter the system.

> **KEY TERMS**
>
> A **password** is a unique code a person uses to enter the system. A **user profile** in a networked system only allows certain people access to particular files, but does not involve a password.

4.21 Hackers may programme their own computers to try many combinations of characters in the hope of finding a password by a process of elimination. Keeping track of these attempts can alert managers to repeated efforts to break into the system; in these cases the culprits might be caught, particularly if there is an apparent pattern to their efforts.

4.22 **User profiles** can prevent people accessing the **system at all** without a password. They may, alternatively, allow a person access to a system, but with **restrictions** to the files that can be used.

   (a) Computer files marked 'restricted access' might only be accessed by a few people with appropriate profiles. This is very important for database or network systems.

   (b) Data and software will be classified according to the **sensitivity and confidentiality** of data.

   (c) Records can be kept of access to files, so that a 'trail' can be left of unauthorised attempts at entry.

4.23 **Passwords** ought to be effective in keeping out unauthorised users, but they are by no means foolproof. By experimenting with possible passwords, an unauthorised person can gain access to a programme or file by guessing the correct password. This is not as difficult as it may seem when too many computer users specify 'obvious' passwords for their files or programmes. Someone who is authorised to access a data or programme file may tell an unauthorised person what the password is, perhaps through carelessness.

4.24 For a password system to be effective, passwords should be:

- Changed regularly
- Difficult to guess
- Confidential
- Hidden

Activity 18.6

What passwords do you use on computer and other systems (such as bank ATMS or video store memberships)?

- How easy might they be to guess or get hold of by other means, should a dishonest or malicious person wish to do so?
- What could they do with this information in each case?
- What could you do to increase your security?

Viruses

4.25 A virus is a computer program that infects a computer system and replicates itself within it, much in the same way as a human being catches a cold. Some viruses can destroy data and files; other just display messages. The best way to deal with viruses is to **avoid infection** in the first place.

4.26 It is difficult for the typical user to identify the presence of a virus.

(a) **Anti-virus software** such as Dr Solomon's is capable of detecting and eradicating a vast number of viruses before they do any damage. Upgrades are released regularly to deal with new viruses. The software will run whenever a computer is turned on and will continue to monitor in the background until it is turned off again.

(b) Organisations must guard against the introduction of unauthorised software to their systems. Many viruses have been spread on **pirated versions** of popular computer games or possibly the Internet.

(c) **Check any disk received from the outside is virus-free** before the data on the disk is downloaded.

(d) Any flaws in a widely used program should be rectified as soon as they come to light.

(e) Do not open email attachments without virus checking.

5 RESPONSIBILITY FOR WORKPLACE SECURITY

5.1 As with health and safety, your organisation may have dedicated departments, managers or staff in charge of security, including:

- Security guards
- Data security specialists (IT officers and Data Protection officers)
- Industrial security consultants

The role of these people is to make and implement relevant **policies and procedures**, to **listen** to employee concerns and to **respond** to any problems and emergencies.

5.2 There will obviously be a limit to the responsibility that *you*, as an accountant, have for the security of your organisation, its premises, belongings and staff. Find out exactly what your responsibilities are in this respect – and where they stop.

5.3 **Follow the rules** that affect your own behaviour directly.

(a) If you see **doors, windows or drawers** of filing cabinets left open (or unlocked if they are supposed to be locked) when the area is unattended: close or lock them.

Part E: Health, safety and security in the working environment

(b) If you have **keys** to a filing cabinet, or the **password** to a computer, use them responsibility and keep them safe.

(c) Follow **secure access procedures**. Even if the person on reception knows you so well that he doesn't need to see your pass, there is no harm in showing it to him anyway. It reminds him of part of *his* job and helps him to do it more effectively when strangers enter the building.

(d) Obey **security warnings** and **reporting procedures**. These may relate to suspicious strangers on the premises, or the handling of suspicious packages. What are you required and authorised to do? To whom should you report the matter?

(e) Take commonsense measures to **protect yourself**. If you are going out to meet a client or supplier for the first time off your premises, make sure somebody in the office knows where you are going, whom you are going to meet, what time you are expected back and (if possible) a contact number.

5.4 **Notify the appropriate person** if you become aware of a security problem outside your authority to deal with.

(a) Know who the **appropriate person** is in your organisation or department.

(b) **Report security risks** which you identify, but which are outside your ability to fix or authority to get fixed: for example, broken locks or windows, or evidence that someone has divulged a security code or password, so that it needs to be changed. Workplace changes may not have been thought about by others from the security angle: a new procedure for handling cash, say, or moving the safe over to a desk by a ground floor window while the offices are being decorated. You may be able to make timely recommendations or warnings.

(c) **Report security breaches** (eg suspicious strangers or packages, or evidence of theft or vandalism) to those who are more qualified to deal with them and/or who have the authority to initiate appropriate response measures. Are you authorised to call the police yourself – or do you need to go through your supervisor or security officer?

(d) If **other people** in the department do not appear to know or adhere to security procedures, tactfully draw their attention to them. If breaches continue, you may need to approach their supervisor.

(e) **Don't be a hero.** If you find yourself in a dangerous situation, remember: your organisation can replace its belongings: the safety of people comes first.

Key learning points

- **Security** generally involves preventing or dealing with commercial threats: theft, espionage or sabotage, and unauthorised access to premises or confidential data. It may also involve other kinds of risk, such as violent or disruptive conduct or even terrorist threats or attacks.

- Legal issues in security focus on employee privacy and data protection.

- **Security** procedures require
    - the control of access to premises, people, confidential information and assets/resources
    - the immediate reporting of security breach (unauthorised access, theft or vandalism)
    - the securing of security data (passwords, combinations) and devices (keys, passes)
    - the awareness and responsible co-operation of all employees and visitors

- **Data security** is vital in the information age. Key risks to data security include: human error, technical malfunction, catastrophic events, malicious damage, industrial espionage/sabotage and dishonesty.

Quick quiz

1. List three reasons why people may seek to sabotage or steal information from an organisation.
2. An employer has the right to monitor employees' activities, without informing them, in order to check compliance with the organisation's security procedures. True or false?
3. List three ways of keeping confidential information secure.
4. If you are confronted by a potentially dangerous intruder, your first responsibility is to protect your employer's assets. True or false?
5. If a back-up copy of data is taken, is the data then secure? (Several points should be made in your answer.)
6. What are passwords used for?

Answers to quick quiz

1. Monetary/sale value; competitive advantage; nuisance value
2. False: covert monitoring is only allowed to check specifically for suspected criminal activity.
3. Computer passwords. Locked file cabinets. Avoiding careless talk.
4. False: your first responsibility is for your own safety and that of others.
5. The data is more secure than if no copy is taken, but there are still potential problems.
    (a) The data is not really secure if it is the only other copy: if the original data is lost the single back-up becomes the only version in existence.
    (b) It is not secure if it is stored on the same site as the original, or somewhere else where it is liable to get damaged.
    (c) If there is a hardware fault which causes data loss or corruption the fault must be diagnosed and corrected before the correct data is put at risk in the system. The usefulness of data on back-up would be entirely negated if it were fed mindlessly into a faulty system.
    (d) The back-up data may also be at risk if it is too readily available to operations staff. Back-up data which is easily available could be used before system errors have been fully corrected and may then become corrupted too.

    For all of these reasons it is better to keep two back-up copies.

6. Passwords are used to deny access to the system entirely and to restrict access to particular files.

Part E: Health, safety and security in the working environment

Answers to activities

Answer 18.1

You may have included such things as:

- Stocks
- Confidential files and documents (on paper, computer disk, CD ROM)
- Stationery, small components etc ('petty' theft is a bigger problem in most organisations than major theft)
- Ownership documents like share certificates, title deeds and so on
- Technical, marketing or business plans (of value to competitors)
- Security passes and devices (eg pass cards allowing access to restricted areas)
- Staff in the front line (eg security guards)
- Staff who work late, or in isolated areas, with fewer people around
- Key personnel (eg who may be tricked or forced into divulging information)

Answer 18.2

This exercise is designed to heighten your awareness of your organisation's security procedures, since you may be on the 'receiving end' more than performing security tasks yourself. Even so, this is part of your responsibility for security: to co-operate with your employers' measures to keep the workplace secure (by following file security procedures, wearing and showing identification/passes if required, keeping computer passwords secure, locking drawers/safes/doors responsibly and so on).

If – having given full value to the need for security – you have concerns about matters such as when or why your work or activities are being monitored (by security cameras, call recording or e-mail vetting), who might you talk to about it?

Answer 18.3

(a) The receptionist's attention is overloaded. It would be easy, in the general to-and-fro, for an unauthorised person to get past her into the offices without the appropriate checks and procedures – whether intentionally or unintentionally. It might also be a temptation to let the couriers deliver direct to the offices – again, a risk if they are unescorted and unlogged. To minimise the risk, reception should – permanently, or on a temporary 'at need' basis – be manned by extra personnel: a 'back-up' reception person might be kept 'on call'.

(b) It is surprisingly quick work to slip through an open door, gather a bag, or armful of valuable items, and slip out again! It can be done – swiftly – right under the nose of unwary occupants, and in this case, there is added risk since the door and storerooms are (i) close together and (ii) out of the way of office traffic. A further risk exists of the door being forgotten at the end of the day, if it is not usually left unlocked. The only way to minimise this risk is not to open the back door, or to allow it to be opened on a security chain or with a security gate or grill.

(c) The risk is that the visitor is not bona fide – nobody has checked – and has been left alone and unobserved in the office, where he has unchallenged access to anything left lying around. Ways of minimising such a risk include: vetting such visitors at reception and giving proof (such as a visitor's card) that this has taken place; requiring visitors to wait at reception or in other open areas until the visitee is available; people who are expecting visitors warning others in the office and describing/naming the visitor so they can cross-check the visitor's identity informally – especially if the visitee might not be available; having someone escort and stay with a visitor at all times, tactfully; and, as a last resort, ensuring that the door to the supervisor's office is kept open, and the visitor is visible to staff until the supervisor's return.

Answer 18.4

Your answer will obviously depend on your choice of topic, your organisation's specific procedures, and your imagination and communication style. You may have chosen to outline the steps in the procedure (without simply copying them from the Procedures Manual!), or you may have opted for a reminder/warning poster such as (at its simplest) the following.

18: Security in the workplace

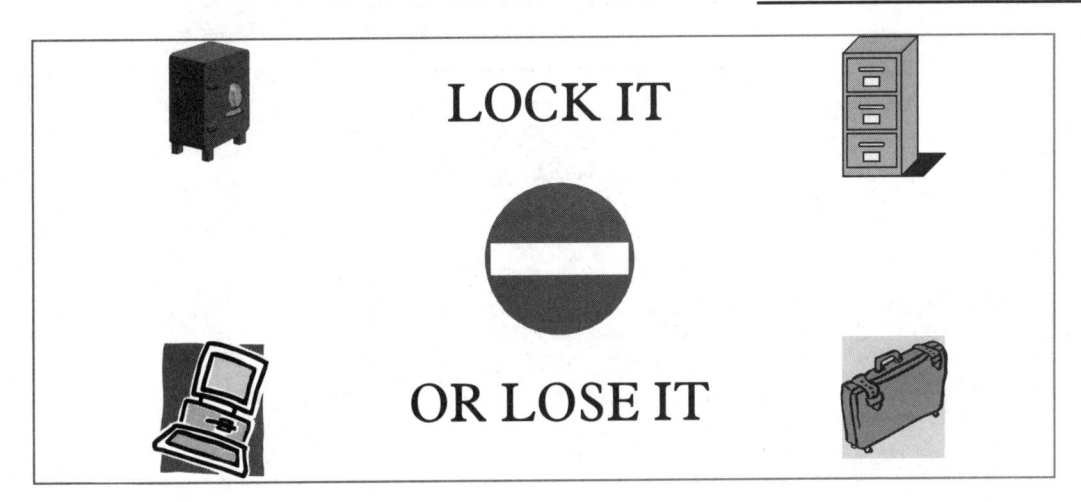

LOCK IT

OR LOSE IT

Answer 18.5

(a) No: this is an exemption from the 'subject access' provisions.
(b) No: an opinion cannot be challenged on these grounds.
(c) Yes: this is your right.
(d) No: data must be obtained 'fairly and lawfully'.

Answer 18.6

It is important that you think through this issue for yourself, although the material in the chapter will be a useful guide.

Now try Question 17 in the Exam Question Bank

Question bank

Question bank

1 BUSINESS ENVIRONMENT

(a) Why is the degree of uncertainty in an organisation's environment so important for business strategy? (4 marks)

(b) Explain the segments into which the business environment can be analysed. (8 marks)

(c) Discuss in what sense government, as a segment of the environment, may be regarded both as an aid and as an impediment to business. (8 marks)

(20 marks)

2 TALL AND FLAT STRUCTURES

Business organisations vary considerably in their choice of management structures.

Required

(a) Define a tall organisation and flat organisation giving one real life example of an industry or organisation for each type. (4 marks)

(b) Identify and explain the key business and environmental factors affecting the height and width of a business organisation. (8 marks)

(c) Briefly discuss the advantages and disadvantages of a flat organisational structure compared with a tall organisational structure. (8 marks)

(20 marks)

3 PLANNING PROCESS

Sean Turner has recently been appointed as the head of a new section.

This section will be responsible for work not previously undertaken by the organisation. Sean has been told that the necessary resources will be available to him. He has a reputation for achieving impressive results, although he has always worked within the context of an existing operation. Sean is very keen to succeed in his new job and has asked you for your thoughts on how he should get things started.

During your discussions you have mentioned: '... the planning process - from defining aims through to feedback on performance ...' Sean has now asked you to explain this.

Required

(a) Outline a structure for the planning process. (6 marks)

(b) Describe the individual steps in the planning process. (12 marks)

(c) Suggest those steps to which Sean should pay particular attention in establishing his new section. (2 marks)

(20 marks)

4 JONES AND JONES LTD

Jones and Jones Limited is a firm of electrical contractors. The Directors, George and his sister Alice, are responsible for estimating, tendering and contracting for jobs and for the supervision of the workforce. The firm does not have an accounts department; responsibility for the accounts is shared among its office staff.

John keeps records of all purchases and expenses. He also makes out cheques for the directors' signatures and records them in the cash book.

Joyce maintains records of jobs done. She sends out invoices and statements, looks after the sales ledger, records receipts in the cash book and prepares a monthly balance which she does not reconcile with the bank.

Betty calculates the wages, draws an appropriate amount of money from the bank, makes them up and distributes them among the firm's employees. She is also responsible for petty cash for which she periodically draws £100 from the bank.

Question bank

You are required to produce a report to the directors in which you advise them on what you see as weaknesses in the internal control of the firm's accounts and recommend ways of securing effective control of the accounts.

(20 marks)

5 IDENTIFYING AND PREVENTING FRAUD

Fraud costs businesses and their shareholders a vast amount of money and resources, and seems to be on the increase.

Required

(a) Identify and briefly describe the three broad prerequisites for fraud. (6 marks)

(b) Explain what systems and procedures an organisation should have to prevent and detect fraud.

(14 marks)

(20 marks)

6 FUNDRAISING EVENT

The chairman of the board of directors has recently joined the committee of a charity which is organising a fund raising event. This will be a day long festival, with a parade through the town to the local park where a carnival will be held. Funds will be raised through collections on the parade, admission charged to the carnival and income and donations from trade and charity stalls. Payments will have to be made for various expenses including the entertainers at the carnival and gifts for the TV celebrity opening the event. Your chairman has offered your services as a senior accounting technician to look after the receipts and payments for the event. Similarly the local bank manager has nominated a senior member of his staff with whom you will liaise.

Required

(a) Explain the control procedures you would introduce for both receipts and payments. (15 marks)

(b) Outline the assistance you would expect from your bank colleague. (5 marks)

(20 marks)

7 INFORMATION USES

Cheap 'n Cheerful is a supermarket chain that is looking to improve the quality of its management information. As part of this initiative, it is thinking about introducing a customer loyalty card scheme.

(a) What information could be collected by this scheme, and what might it indicate? (8 marks)

(b) Describe the areas of management activity where information such as that collected by supermarket loyalty cards might be used, ie for planning, control and decision making. (12 marks)

(20 marks)

8 SUPERVISORS, MANAGERS AND LEADERS

Management roles within organisations range from supervising to possessing ultimate executive power over the strategic, financial and operational direction of a business organisation. The function of management between these levels can vary significantly, as would the qualities required of those working as managers at these levels.

Required

(a) Describe the main duties and capabilities of a supervisor within a typical accounting system, using examples. (6 marks)

(b) Briefly describe the role of a manager within a typical accounting system, using examples.

(6 marks)

(c) Explain why it is necessary for management at the highest levels within an organisation to have leadership qualities to support their managerial capabilities. (8 marks)

(20 marks)

Question bank

9 INDIVIDUAL BEHAVIOUR

Individual behaviour is different from group behaviour.

Required

(a) Explain the impact on work behaviour of:

    (i) Personality factors   (7 marks)
    (ii) Attitudes   (7 marks)

(b) In what ways might individual work contribution be more effective than group or team working?

     (6 marks)

(20 marks)

10 PROJECT TEAM

You have been placed in charge of a cross-functional project team. It comprises half a dozen members who are unknown to each other and to you. The team will not only have to work together co-operatively but also deliver high quality results.

Required

Using your concepts from team building and group behaviour outline how you would ensure the team welded together to become an effective unit. **(20 marks)**

11 MOTIVATION THEORIES

An understanding of motivation in the workplace is an essential part of a supervisor's role. There are two basic theories of motivation: content theory and process theory.

Required

(a) Explain the 'content theory' of motivation.   (5 marks)
(b) Maslow is a content theorist. Describe the problems with Maslow's hierarchy.   (7 marks)
(c) Explain the 'process theory' of motivation.   (5 marks)
(d) Vroom is a process theorist. Describe his expectancy theory.   (3 marks)

(20 marks)

12 HARRY IBBOTSON

It was getting to the end of Harry Ibbotson's appraisal interview. He was pleased with it so far. His boss, Fiona Glencross, had been complimentary about his year's work.

'Now for what I see as a problem area,' said Fiona. 'Time management. Not yours, Harry, but Julie Kent's.' Julie was one of the supervisors in the department of which Harry was manager.

Fiona continued, 'Over the past three months I've noticed that:

(a) Julie always seems to have a mound of paper in her in-tray;

(b) Despite this she spends most of her time on the telephone or typing away at her electronic mail keyboard;

(c) She submitted a report to me the other day - 14 pages of well researched work, very well presented. It must have taken her days to produce the report - but it concerned only a minor part of her job and I'd emphasised to her when briefing her that I only wanted a half-page opinion;

(d) She's submitted annual appraisal reports on two of her staff which have been over a week late;

(e) I've checked her holiday records - she's not taken a major holiday for 12 months, and did you notice that last week she struggled in every day despite being obviously ill?'

'I know,' said Harry, 'I've already spoken to her about this. I confirm everything you say. I told her to sort herself out but she's made no effort. She says she has no way of knowing how much work will hit her desk on any one day. Do you think I should reprimand her?'

'Harry, is it you or Julie who's at fault?' said Fiona. 'You selected her, we both agreed she was the right person for the job. Have you identified what's wrong with her time management? Have you given her guidance or support or advice?'

'No', said Harry.

Required

(a) Explain what aspect of poor time management each of Julie's symptoms suggests.

(b) What suggestions could Harry make to Julie to help her overcome her time management difficulties?

(20 marks)

13 COMMUNICATION SKILLS

You have attended recently a week long course to improve and develop your communication skills. Part of the course emphasised the importance of 'questioning and listening' as key skills for managers. You are about to conduct an appraisal interview with one of your staff.

Required

Suggest how the development of these skills will help you to more effectively carry out the appraisal interview.

(20 marks)

14 PERFORMANCE MANAGEMENT

Recent developments in Human Resource Management have seen a change of emphasis. The traditional management activity of simply giving instructions has changed into a more supportive style of management, aimed at individual and organisational development. This has become known as 'performance management', a process linking organisational and individual objectives. Your manager is aware of this idea and has asked you to explain it in more detail.

Required

(a) Briefly explain what is meant by 'performance management.' (5 marks)

(b) Describe the process or steps involved in performance management. (10 marks)

(c) List the advantages to employees of the organisation adopting a performance management process. (5 marks)

(20 marks)

15 TRAINING AND DEVELOPMENT

Systems of training and personal development planning are key areas where organisations can add value to staff individually and collectively in order to provide economic benefits to the organisation as a whole.

Required

(a) Briefly describe the main steps of the training process. (7 marks)

(b) Identify and explain the key stages in preparing a personal development plan (6 marks)

(c) Outline advantages and disadvantages of individual training and development compared with collective training and development from the perspective of both the individual and the organisation. (7 marks)

(20 marks)

Question bank

16 SAFETY AT WORK

According to the ILO, in 2002 there were 357,000 incidents of workplace violence in the UK. Many of these are assaults on staff by members of the public.

If you were in a position that regularly required you to deal with members of the public in situations that could potentially become unpleasant, what would you do to protect yourself, and what would you expect your employer to do?

(20 marks)

(Concentrate on interview situations (for example working in a benefit office), not situations that are prone to crime of other sorts such as robbery.)

17 DATA SECURITY

The importance of data security and protection in the workplace may sometimes be underestimated by management and staff within an organisation.

Required

(a) Explain why data protection is important and identify the main risks to data security within the organisation. **(10 marks)**

(b) Explain how organisations and their staff can help prevent possible loss, damage or compromise to their data and give examples of systems and products available to the organisation to protect it in this area. **(10 marks)**

(20 marks)

Answer bank

WARNING! APPLYING THE ACCA MARKING SCHEME

If you decide to mark your paper using the ACCA marking scheme (reproduced at the end of each BPP suggested solution) you should bear in mind the following points.

1 Our answers are not definitive: we have applied our own interpretation of the marking scheme to our solutions to show how good answers should gain marks, but there may be more than one way to answer the question. You must try to judge fairly whether different points made in your answers are correct and relevant and therefore worth marks.

2 If you have a friend or colleague who is studying or has studied this paper, you might ask him or her to mark your paper for you, thus gaining a more objective assessment. Remember you and your friend are not trained or objective markers, so try to avoid complacency or pessimism if you appear to have done very well or very badly.

Before marking your exam, you should read the guidance given by the examiner to markers of this paper, which is reproduced below. This should aid your own marking process. It is most important that you analyse your solutions in detail and that you attempt to be as objective as possible.

> **ACCA note to marking scheme**
>
> The marking scheme is used as a guide only to markers in the context of the suggested answer. Given the practical nature of the paper, scope is given to markers to award marks for alternative approaches to a question, including relevant comment, and where well-reasoned conclusions are provided.

Answer bank

1 BUSINESS ENVIRONMENT

(a) A large part of business strategy consists of making the organisation's **interaction with its environment** as efficient as possible, by ensuring a good 'fit'. The more complex or dynamic the environment is, the more uncertain it is, and the greater the strategic challenge. An uncomplicated and stable environment can be dealt with as a matter of routine, but when the environment is **dynamic**, the management approach must emphasise **flexibility**.

The strategic **environment** of the firm, discussed in more detail in part (b), consists of **economic, political, legal, social** and **technological** factors which influence the ability of the organisation to survive and make profits.

Examples of **environmental variables** with which a 'fit' must be achieved include:

- The changing **tastes** of customers
- Developments in the **market demand** for a product
- The likely **trend** of interest and exchange rates

(b) **The environment of a business**

(i) **Politico-legal** factors include political changes (eg change in government, openness of political institutions to business influence) and legal developments (eg health and safety legislation, developments in company law).

(ii) **Economic factors** include overall economic growth levels, interest and exchange rates and the effects of the government's fiscal and monetary policies.

(iii) **Social factors** include the country's demographic profile (eg age structure), the class system and trends in consumer tastes and wants.

(iv) **Technological factors** include new product technologies, new materials and new techniques in production.

(c) **Government as an aid or impediment to business**

The government's overall conduct of its **economic policy** affects all companies operating in its region of authority. The **government can aid business** by providing a more **stable** operating environment and by direct financial **assistance**.

(i) Setting or targeting appropriate **interest and exchange rates**

(ii) Providing **education and training** relevant to business

(iii) **Economic planning** of key industrial areas

(v) Acting as a **customer** to the private sector, for example when purchasing from the aerospace and defence industries

(vi) Giving incentives for **capacity expansion**, for example investment grants

(vii) Giving support to **emerging business**

(viii) Creating **entry barriers** by restricting the activities of foreign businesses

Conversely, the government can act as an impediment to business.

Governments may be the source of **instability** and lead to costs, in addition to **tax**, being incurred by organisations.

(i) Creation of legal **regulations** which are costly to comply with

(ii) **Uncertainty and volatility** in financial markets occur when governments change their policies in response to political pressure

Answer bank

    (iii) Imposition of **restrictions** such as monopolies and mergers controls and equal opportunities legislation may limit business activities

    (iv) Acting solely on behalf of **vested interests**

Marking scheme	Marks
(a) 1.5 marks for consideration of environmental fit, and 1.5 marks for consideration of uncertainty. Examples to be given. Maximum of 4 marks in total.	4
(b) 2 marks per category of factor, involving definition and explanation. Up to a maximum of 8 marks in total	8
(c) 1 mark each for examples of aids and impediments. Up to a maximum of 8 marks in total	8
Maximum for question	20

2 TALL AND FLAT STRUCTURES

Tutorial note. This question should be straightforward, if you have revised this area of the syllabus. It shows how questions for this paper may feature multiple parts on related topic areas: make sure that you read the topic and instruction key words carefully and answer the exact question set for each part. With 20 marks available for just one aspect of the syllabus topic 'organisational structure', this question is also a useful guide to the level of detail required in your study and revision across all syllabus areas. Note that you were only required to cite *one* example of each structure in part (a): we have given a few alternatives for revision purposes.

(a) **Tall and flat organisation**

A tall organisation is one which has a large number of managerial layers in what Mintzberg called the 'middle line' of its organisation hierarchy. These layers are created by the flow of direct authority down the 'scalar chain' of command (Fayol) in relatively small increments (ie authority is fairly centralised and the differentials in authority between the levels is fairly small), together with a narrow span of control, whereby managers have direct responsibility over relatively few subordinates and relatively specialised task areas.

Tall organisations tend to be large, bureaucratic organisations. Examples in 'real life' might include public sector bodies such as local authorities or the National Health Service, and large traditional corporations such as Barclays Bank.

A flat organisation is one which as a relatively small number of managerial layers in its 'middle line'. Managers at each level have a wider span of control (with more employees reporting to them over a wider range of tasks), and there is a higher degree of delegation or decentralisation of authority to lower levels of the organisation. This often creates wider differentials of authority and responsibility between each level of the middle line.

Flat organisations tend to be smaller, more progressive organisations in competitive and fast-changing environments. Examples in real life include Virgin Airways, software development firms and management consultancies such as McKinseys.

(b) **Influences on organisation height and width**

A number of business and environmental factors affect the 'shape' of the organisation.

    (i) The size of the organisation. As organisations grow over time, they tend to become more formalised and to divide labour by specialisation, creating narrow spans of control and taller structures. Smaller, newly-established organisations tend to be flatter, because they are less formalised, and are structured to respond to modern competitive conditions and trends.

(ii) The business environment. Tall organisations are efficient and technically competent (as recognised by Weber), only in relatively static or highly regulated markets such as the public sector. Flat organisations have a competitive advantage in high-technology and customer-sensitive environments, where they can respond flexibly to changing demands.

(iii) The nature of the task. Complex and varied tasks usually require narrower spans of control, in order to provide closer support and supervision. Where tasks are more highly structured, repetitive or automated, wider spans of control are possible.

(iv) The skills, knowledge and personality of staff. Tall organisations imply closer supervision and less delegation, based on the needs of staff for managerial support and co-ordination. Flat organisations take advantage of the willingness and ability of staff to accept responsibility and work independently on their own initiative, to allow wider spans of control.

(v) Communication systems. Tall organisations involve chains of formal vertical communication. Networked systems of fast multi-directional communication, especially supported by the use of Information and Communications Technology, allow wider spans of control and delayering (with more direct access to decision support information by the strategic apex and operating core).

(c) **Advantages and disadvantages of flat organisation**

Advantages of flat organisation, compared to tall organisation, include the following.

(i) Greater opportunity for delegation and empowerment of staff. This in turn is said to have benefits for employee morale and motivation, the harnessing of initiative and ideas, and employee development (through growth in the job)

(ii) Savings in administration and overhead (managerial) costs, with fewer levels of supervisory management

(iii) More efficient use of managerial time, which can be devoted to higher-level, non-supervisory roles (planning, entrepreneurial activity, staff development)

(iv) Faster communication and decision-making chains between the strategic apex and operating core, with particular benefits for customer service

(v) Increased organisational flexibility, by empowering lower levels of staff, encouraging initiative and keeping the strategic apex close to the 'front line'.

Disadvantages include the following.

(i) Loss of supervisory control, through wider spans of management. This may have negative consequences where conditions require close control and co-ordination

(ii) Wide spans of management may overtax the capabilities of managers (especially if they are not effective delegators)

(iii) Increased delegation may not be effective: eg if subordinates are not capable or objectives are not made clear

(iv) There are fewer steps on the managerial 'ladder' for internal promotions: capable managers may seek career development outside the organisation, or may become demotivated

(v) There may be some dis-integration of objectives, without the middle line to interpret strategic plans at a detailed, operational level

Answer bank

Official ACCA Marking scheme	Marks
(a) 1.5 marks each for defining flat and tall organisations, and 1.5 marks forgiving an example of each (3 × 2). Up to a maximum of 4 marks in total.	4
(b) 2 marks per valid business and environmental factor affecting the shape of an organisation up to a maximum of five (2 × 5). Up to a maximum of eight marks in total.	8
(c) Up to 5 marks each for advantages and disadvantages of flat or tall organisations (2 × 5). Up to a maximum of 8 marks in total.	8
Maximum for question	20

3 PLANNING PROCESS

Tutorial note. Answering this question in itself requires careful planning because you could be tempted to write too much in part (a) and not have enough to say in part (b). In addition, in part (c) you should be careful to apply the theory specifically to Sean, not continue describing the nature of steps in the planning process.

(a) **Structure for the planning process**

1	Define aims of the section
2	Define the key tasks of the section
3	Set standards
4	Identify information required for control
5	Identify short-term goals and develop action plans
6	Choose which plan is best and implement it
7	Feedback - review performance

(b) (i) **Define aims**

The aims for which the new section has been set up should be defined as its specific aims.

Once the short-term goals have been set, detailed action plans can be drawn up to meet them. These will set out the very specific tasks which must be performed (eg interview 3 staff with 3 GCSEs and keyboard skills) and by when (eg staff to be on board at the beginning of Month 2). Action plans must take into account any restrictions on the use or availability of resources and any known time restraints - eg staff cannot be recruited until a supervisor is employed.

Sean Turner should make sure that he knows exactly what is expected of this new section. It may be that he is heading up a new product line, is involved in a new geographical market or is responsible for the computerisation of previously manual tasks. Whatever it is he should know what the aim is - for instance, to achieve 20% return on capital, to achieve 10% reduction in costs or to provide better information to the workforce.

(ii) **Define key tasks**

In order to achieve these aims, certain things will have to be done and these are the section's key tasks. Identifying them allows plans to be based on completing specified tasks, so nothing is forgotten, everything is done on time and no backlog develops - the aims can thus be achieved. Most importantly, the plans are thereby precise enough to be followed in practice.

(iii) **Set standards**

The project should be planned so that it is possible for the tasks to be done well enough for the aims to be met. Setting standards for performance allows Sean to plan the resources which will be necessary to meet those standards (eg having staff with the right qualifications) and allows control action to be taken if the standards are not met.

Well-designed standards are precise and directly applicable to the tasks in hand. They must be practicable and stated in such a way that actual performance can be measured.

(iv) **Information required for control**

Standards an the achievement of the section must be measured so that they can be compared. It is therefore vital to identify what information must be gathered in order to carry out the comparisons.

When identifying what information needs to be available to him, Sean will have regard not only to the tasks to be done and the terms in which standards are set, but also to the qualities of good information:

(1) Accuracy
(2) Timeliness
(3) Clarity and sufficiency (excessive amounts are counter-productive)
(4) Relevance and comprehensiveness

Finally, he should not overlook how much it costs to gather and use the information.

(v) **Short-term goals and action plans**

The aims of the section can be seen as its long-term goals. It is necessary as well to set short-term goals so that the path to the aim is marked by identified achievements. With a new section, short-term goals may be as follows.

(i) To obtain the required staff at the right time

(ii) To ensure that people within and outside the organisation know what the section is doing

(iii) To achieve 50% of planned full capacity within 3 months

The goals should be as precise and measurable as possible - for instance, the second goal above may be achieved by doing a survey within the organisation after a few months as to whether people know of the section.

(vi) **Choose plan**

Depending on the nature of the section's work, it is likely that there will be more than one way of achieving the short-term goals and hence more than one action plan. Making a choice between them will depend on how well each seems likely to achieve the goals in the quickest, cheapest and best way.

(vii) **Feedback**

Actual results achieved from implementing the action plans should be measured and compared against the standards. It is also necessary to ensure that the information obtained fulfils what was expected of control information at stage 5 and whether any items have been omitted which could be used.

The comparison of actual to expected should be evaluated and it should be decided whether further action is necessary to ensure the plan is achieved. This

Answer bank

may mean changes to the plans, to the types of information obtained or to the level of standards set.

Reasons for departures from plan should be carefully analysed - it may be that outside circumstances have changed, that the task is impossible or that the staff lack motivation or training. Corrective action may then be taken.

(c) Although it is true to say that all steps in the planning process are important, Sean Turner should probably pay particular attention to the early stages since the whole section is new. If his short-term goals or action plans are wrong they can be corrected easily, but if he makes wrong assumptions about the section's aims and key tasks the whole section will be built on shifting sand.

Marking scheme		**Marks**
(a)	Correct outline of structure – marks to a maximum of 4	4
(b)	2 marks per step, including a clear description of its features	14
(c)	1 mark per valid point made, up to a maximum of two	2
Maximum for question		20

4 JONES AND JONES LTD

Date: 30 June 200X
To: George and Alice Jones, Directors, Jones and Jones Limited
From: Accounting Technician
Subject: Internal control

You have asked me to advise on weaknesses in the internal controls of your firm's accounting systems, and to recommend ways in which effective control may be secured. My report has been based upon discussing the established work practices with the staff of Jones and Jones Limited, and observing these work practices in operation. I have also reviewed the company's books.

Findings

Three members of your office staff, John, Joyce and Betty, are responsible for maintaining the accounting records. Unfortunately little attention has been paid to internal control, with the result that there are virtually no **internal checking procedures** and any discrepancy to arise (either deliberately or accidentally) would almost certainly escape detection.

(a) John keeps the record of all purchases and expenses but also makes out cheques for the directors to sign and records these payments in the cash book. He is thus in a prime position either to pay fictitious expenses or to pay twice against the same invoice without either transaction being queried.

(b) Joyce is responsible for recording all work done but also for receiving payment and for credit control. If she fails to invoice a customer, or to record a cash receipt, this would not be picked up.

(c) Betty could steal from the firm simply by drawing more money than she needs from the firm's bank account and altering the wage records to hide what she had done. She could also overpay members of staff without this being detected.

The fact that no fraud appears to have taken place so far is attributable entirely to the honesty of your staff who are being given every opportunity to steal from your firm, should they wish. The errors I discovered in the accounts were all small ones, but they had not been spotted previously and could have been very much larger. In short, your internal control system requires a radical overhaul if it is to be effective.

Recommendations

The changes outlined below are designed to ensure that the tasks of preparing and handling initial documents (such as sales invoices and suppliers' invoices), preparing records and handling cash are reallocated, as far as possible, between different employees and to introduce a proper internal checking procedure. However, I recognise that prior consultation with your office staff will be necessary if these improvements are to be implemented successfully.

(a) **Expenses and purchases**

John can continue to be responsible for maintaining trade creditor records. However, Joyce should check all suppliers' invoices against purchase orders before they are given to John for recording. The responsibility for preparing cheques should fall to Betty, who would draw cheques against suppliers' invoices passed to her by John. As directors, you should ensure that invoice(s) and cheque match before you sign each cheque.

(b) **Debtor balances**

Joyce should retain her present function of maintaining the sales ledger. However, the responsibility for initiating sales invoices should pass to John and the responsibility for receiving cash should pass to Betty. This is not ideal, though it is probably the best arrangement which can be achieved given the very small numbers of staff.

(c) **Cash payments and receipts**

Betty should be responsible for maintaining the cash book, recording both amounts paid and received. She would also be required to handle cheques received from debtors. The cash book must be reconciled with the bank statements. Preferably, this would be done by someone other than Betty. Joyce would be the most appropriate candidate for this task.

For petty cash payments, an imprest system would be appropriate. John or Joyce could pay claims as they were submitted, recording them in a petty cash book. This would be submitted to Betty when reimbursement was required.

(d) **Wages**

Wages represent a substantial expense item for the business. The procedures for calculating, checking and paying wages should be as secure as possible. Betty could calculate the wages due using the employee time records. Her figures could be checked by John, who would then record them in the wages book. It might be worthwhile to consider paying all employees by cheque, which would avoid some of the security problems associated with paying wages in cash. Wages cheques made out to individual employees could be submitted to yourselves for signature, along with the wages book. Alternatively, a single wages cheque could be presented. After signature by yourselves, this would be taken to the bank by Joyce and Betty, who would make up the wages ready for paying out by you.

(e) **General supervision**

To ensure that these arrangements are working properly, you should regularly inspect the accounting records yourselves to ensure that the operations of the business are being recorded in a timely and accurate manner.

Answer bank

Marking scheme	Marks
(a) Appropriate report layout	2
(b) Overview of findings	3
(c) Recommendations – 3 marks for identification and explanation of each point	15
Maximum for question	20

5 IDENTIFYING AND PREVENTING FRAUD

Tutorial note. This question should be straightforward, if you have revised this area of the syllabus, although you might have struggled with part (a) if the word 'prerequisite' was unfamiliar. Make sure you check the meaning of such words as you revise topics. There are various terms for 'conditions supporting', 'causes of', 'effects of', 'influences on' and so on – and these are often used as topic key words in questions, specifying exactly what aspect of a topic the examiner wants you to address. This question is also a useful example of the need for time management in line with the mark allocations for question parts: check the balance of your answer between part (a) for 6 marks and part (b) for 14 marks.

(a) **Three pre-requisites for fraud**

There are three broad pre-requisites or 'pre-conditions' that must exist in order to make fraud a possibility: dishonesty, motivation and opportunity.

Dishonesty is an individual's general pre-disposition or tendency to act in ways which contravene accepted ethical, social, organisational and legal norms for fair and honest dealing. This tendency may arise from personality factors (such as a competitive desire to gain advantage over others, or low respect for authority) or cultural factors (national or familial values, which may be more 'flexible' or anti-authority than the law and practice prevailing in the organisation).

Motivation. In addition to a willingness to act dishonestly, the individual needs a motivation to do so. The goal or motive for fraudulent behaviour may be: financial needs or wants, or envy of others; a desire to exercise power over those in authority; or a desire to avoid punishment (in the case of cover ups, say). Individuals weigh up the potential rewards of fraudulent action compared to the risks of being caught and the sanctions that would be applied.

Opportunity. A dishonest and motivated individual must find an opportunity or opening to commit fraud: a 'loophole' in the law or control system that allows fraudulent activity to go undetected, or that makes the risk of detection acceptable, given the rewards available.

An individual will have a high incentive to commit fraud if (s)he is predisposed to dishonesty *and* the rewards for the particular fraud are high *and* there is an opportunity to commit fraudulent action with little chance of detection *or* with insignificant sanctions if caught.

(b) **Systems and procedures for preventing and detecting fraud**

A primary aim of any system of internal controls should be to prevent fraud. However, recognising the difficulties of prevention, it is also important to have systems for detecting fraud if it does occur.

Most of the systems and procedures for preventing and detecting fraud will be aimed at identifying and reducing *opportunity*. Examples include the following.

(i) **Systematic risk assessment.** A systematic attempt should be made to asses external factors (business environment, industry risks and so on) and internal factors (such as new personnel, changes in information systems, lack of segregation of duties and so on) which may heighten the risk of fraud.

(ii) **Physical controls.** These are the most basic method of discouraging theft. They include keeping tangible assets under lock and key, identifying all office equipment (and/or bolting hardware to desks).

(iii) **Segregation of duties.** Staff who have responsibility for a range of tasks have more scope for committing and concealing fraud. By segregating duties, it is more likely that other people will become aware of discrepancies.

(iv) **Standard procedures.** Standard procedures should be defined clearly for normal business operations and made clear to all staff so that any deviations from the norm become visible. Examples include the investigation of new customer credit histories, the authorisation of all payments and the collection of wage/pay slips in person.

(v) **Authorisation procedures.** Written authorisations by management (eg making payments, signing cheques, validating time/expenses sheets) increase accountability and makes it harder to conceal fraudulent transactions.

(vi) **Computer controls,** to minimise tampering with data inputs and outputs. Passwords and user profiles may be used to prevent unauthorised access to data or areas of the system. 'Firewalls' can be used to prevent the transmission or receipt of unauthorised electronic files.

In addition, organisations may give attention to reducing *dishonesty* and *motivation*.

(vii) **Screening employees.** Pre-disposition to dishonesty is likely to show up in the conduct, employment history or CV of prospective employees, in the form of dishonest claims or past incidents. Employees should be appropriately screened and checked (within privacy guidelines) for the level of trust that will be given them.

(viii) **Removing inequities.** Unfair terms and conditions, or unequal access to benefits, is one motivation for fraud: equitable reward systems and employee counselling (to identify and address attitude, personal or financial problems) are two methods of reducing the risks.

Official ACCA Marking Scheme	Marks
(a) 1.5 marks each for identifying three pre-requisites of fraud and 1.5 marks each for briefly explaining what they are (3 × 3). Up to a maximum of 6 marks in total.	6
(b) 1 mark for identifying and 1 mark for explaining up to eight systems for protection from and detection of fraud (8 × 2). Up to a maximum of 14 marks in total.	14
Maximum for question	20

Answer bank

6 FUNDRAISING EVENT

(a) (i) It will be necessary to introduce three main types of control over receipts. These are:

(1) Controls over who may **receive** money,
(2) Controls over **recording** details of all money received,
(3) **Security arrangements** to prevent any money received from being lost or stolen.

Cash will be received in the form of collections from onlookers in the town, charges for admission to the carnival and income and donations from various stalls. It will be necessary to set up different control procedures for each type of receipt.

Collections are voluntary and should be accepted only by authorised collectors who must be easy for a spectator to identify. This could be achieved by issuing official badges and having all collection boxes clearly labelled as such. The stewards should be given strict instructions not to allow anyone other than an authorised collector to accept donations from members of the public. The collection boxes should be taken to a secure point, such as a room in the carnival office, once the parade through the town is over. This will serve as the cashier's office. Here the money will be counted and a receipt issued to each collector from a pre-numbered receipt book. It must then be taken to be banked as soon as it is practicable to do so.

Admission charges must be paid by everyone (other than the organisers) who enters the park where the carnival is being held. They should be collected by stewards or other authorised official at the gate(s). Enough stewards must be on duty at each entrance to ensure that no one gets in without paying and to bag up the money (out of sight of the crowd) before taking it to the cashier's office, which would ideally be situated near the main entrance. Pre-numbered tickets or other proof of admission should be issued and would have to be produced by anyone claiming that he had already paid. The number of tickets issued would also enable the amount of money received to be checked.

Income from stallholders should be known in advance since the number of different stalls will be known. The responsibility for collecting charges from stallholders should be divided among the different members of the committee. **Donations** are obviously voluntary but should be collected from stall holders at the same time as the compulsory charge. Committee members should be issued with pre-numbered books from which receipts would be issued for any money received.

Money may best be protected against the risk of its being lost or stolen by ensuring that the people involved in collecting money are responsible and that, where possible, they work in pairs. The police should also be present and should be made aware of key points where money is collected or counted.

(ii) All payments should be made by cheque, drawn by a duly appointed cashier, and it should be necessary for two authorised members of the committee to sign each cheque before it can be paid. These committee members should ensure that all cheques are in payment of proper invoices and bills. It may also be convenient for different members of the committee to take on responsibility for different aspects of the carnival (eg catering) and to review all relevant invoices and bills as presented for payment.

It will be necessary to maintain some petty cash. This should be kept to a minimum and will need to be carefully accounted for.

(b) The assistance of a senior bank colleague would be most appropriate. In particular, his help would be needed in:

(i) Setting up a **separate bank account** for the festival, including the forms of authority for cheque signatories.

(ii) Providing facilities for **collecting and paying** in the funds as received.

(iii) Advising on the **adequacy** of the security arrangements.

Marking scheme	Marks
(a) Controls identified and explained in detail – at least five controls identified and properly explained	15
(b) 1-2 marks each for identifying particular areas of assistance	5
Maximum for question	20

7 INFORMATION USES

(a) The people in charge of running a business will wish to be given regular management information, to enable them to make decisions and run the business effectively. They might ask 'How much did we sell last month, and to whom?' 'How much was spent on wages last year?' 'How many staff do we currently employ?'

The question describes the planned introduction of a customer loyalty card by a supermarket chain. Clearly a retail operation of this type would wish to collect, as a minimum, data in the following categories: customer name, customer's address, purchases made, quantities bought, times and dates that the purchases were made. By suitable **processing of this data** it is possible for the supermarket chain to be able to **produce information** that will allow it to predict:

(i) The purchasing patterns of individual customers

(ii) The purchasing patterns of a given store's customers

(iii) The purchasing patterns of the chain's customers on a national and regional basis, identifying purchasing trends such as, say, a shift to low-sugar foodstuffs

(iv) The level of demand for a given product on a daily basis for individual stores, regions and nationally

It may also be desirable for the chain to collect further data such as customer's income level, age, marital status, number of children and so on. Processing this data appropriately would allow the store to gather information that could be used to target in-store offers to a particular group of customers who have a common lifestyle.

(b) In most, if not all organisations, **information is used to control operations** and responses to the current business climate and as an aid to future planning.

It is necessary to make the point that all information must be timely, accurate, complete and relevant to the user. Information that does not fulfil any of these criteria cannot be considered to be good information and will, at best, hinder the decision-making process and, at worst, cause the wrong decisions to be taken. Provided that the data is collected by Cheap 'n' Cheerful in a systematic and thorough manner (with suitable checks and controls used) we may assume that the **data** will be current, accurate and complete. In consequence we can assume that that the **information**

Answer bank

derived from the collected data will also be current, accurate and complete, with the proviso that it must also be relevant and useful to the user.

Planning is concerned with formulating long-term aims and objectives for Cheap 'n' Cheerful. For example, the chain may be attempting to diversify into non-food goods such as clothing and electrical items. This is an example of a strategic decision taken by the organisation. One way that the information gathered could be used to aid decision making at this level is by the identification of the customer base and, hence, suitability of new lines as saleable goods within the chain of shops. Such information can also be used as an aid to marketing new product lines.

Decisions made at the level of management **control** are concerned with providing and allocating resources within the organisation to meet the aims and objectives of the organisation. The information gathered by the chain can be used to identify the needs and wants of customers at a particular store or in a region. Levels of customer satisfaction or dissatisfaction can be also measured and management can take the appropriate action to increase customer satisfaction and, hopefully, sales.

At an **operational level** shopping patterns of customers can be identified to assist in **decision making**. The store manager can then use this information to schedule the number of staff required to serve the expected number of shoppers. Similarly, the demand for a product on a daily, weekly or seasonal basis can be predicted thus allowing the correct quantity to be ordered and storage and shelf space to be allocated.

Marking scheme	**Marks**
(a) Up to 4 marks for identifying types of information, and 4 marks for its possible application (8 marks in total)	8
(b) 4 marks for each area: planning, control and decisions. Clear understanding of each area, and how the information can be used. Maximum of 12 marks.	12
Maximum for question	20

8 SUPERVISORS, MANAGERS AND LEADERS

Tutorial note. The theory of this question is straightforward enough, if you have covered the material. The challenge is to remember to use practical examples from an accounting context! The key aspect of part (a) is the supervisor's role at the interface between managerial and operational staff. For part (b) you might use a number of theoretical frameworks to describe the manager's role: Fayol's functions, for example, or (as we have done) Mintzberg's roles – bearing in mind that only 6 marks are available. (Resist the temptation to write in excessive detail about models you are familiar with.) For part (c), note the instruction key word: you are asked to explain why it is necessary for a senior manager to be a 'leader' – not just to define leadership.

(a) **Duties and capabilities of a supervisor**

A supervisor acts as the interface between managerial and operational staff. (S)he will often perform operational tasks as well as performing managerial functions at a low level, within a small team of individuals with well-defined and specialised responsibilities.

Duties of a supervisor:

(i) **Co-ordinating the work of team members.** In an accounts department, for example, a supervisor might co-ordinate the work of several sales ledger clerks, ensuring that the range of tasks (updating debtor records, invoicing, recording of payments) is efficiently covered between them.

(ii) **Monitoring and checking the work of team members**. The supervisor might, for example, sample the entries made by sales ledger clerks, check outputs and summaries and carry out reconciliations with the control accounts.

(iii) **Performing higher-level tasks within the section**. The supervisor might take responsibility for approving customer credit, say, contacting persistent debtors and preparing management reports.

Capabilities of a supervisor:

(i) **Technical competence**. As a controller and participant in operations, supervisors need to be able to deal with technical work at a detailed technical level. This may be quite specialised, both in terms of a particular area of the accounting system (payroll, sales, purchases, cash and so on) and in terms of the activity, products and systems of the particular organisation.

(ii) **Experience and trustworthiness**. A supervisor has usually been promoted from within the operational section, on the basis of knowledge of the work and ability to take responsibility.

(iii) **Interpersonal skills**. The supervisor is a gatekeeper of information between management and staff (in both directions), and occupies a role as facilitator and coach within the team.

(b) **Role of a manager**

The role of a manager is, broadly, to obtain and deploy human and other resources (information, materials, funds, plant and machinery time) in order to fulfil organisational objectives efficiently and effectively. As the preamble to the question implies, this applies at a wide range of levels, from the strategic to the operational.

Henry Mintzberg categorised the manager's multiple roles as follows.

(i) **Interpersonal roles**. The manager acts as figurehead (eg a senior manager might represent the organisation at a conference); leader (eg hiring, firing and developing staff, communicating goals); and liaison (eg the accounts manager networking with other department managers).

(ii) **Informational roles**. The manager acts as a monitor (receiving information from internal and external networks), spokesperson (eg the accounts manager conveys business plans to staff), and disseminator (eg the accounts manager provides internal and external financial reports and returns).

(iii) **Decisional roles**. The manager acts as entrepreneur (initiating new projects), disturbance handler (eg the accounts manager may need to respond to contingencies such as technical failure, loss of data or new legal provisions), resource allocator (eg the accounts manager authorises expenditure, or introduces new software), and negotiator (eg the accounts manager negotiating department budgets).

It is also possible to view management in more general terms via Fayol's five functions: planning, organising, co-ordinating, controlling and commanding.

(c) **Need for leadership qualities**

According to writers such as Kotter and Zaleznik, management is about maintaining the status quo, deploying resources and coping with complexity to produce order, consistency and predictability. Leadership, on the other hand, is about introducing new approaches and ideas, creating a sense of direction, communicating strategy and coping with change.

At higher levels of management (and arguably, at lower levels as well), managers need to operate at this more strategic, visionary level. Managers need to develop and exercise leadership skills for a variety of reasons.

(i) Energise and support **change**, which is essential for organisational survival in highly competitive and fast-changing business environments. By setting visionary goals and encouraging contribution and commitment, leaders create a flexible, innovation-seeking and learning-tolerant environment.

(ii) Secure **employee commitment**, which is essential in a competitive, customer-focused, knowledge-based business environment. Mobilising the ideas, experience, initiative and involvement of skilled staff contributes to innovation, quality and customer service.

(iii) Set **direction**, which helps teams and individuals to understand their purpose and value to the organisation. This allows the benefits of team-working and empowerment without the loss of co-ordination or direction.

(iv) **Support, challenge** and **develop people,** maximising their contributions to the organisation. Leaders use an influence-based facilitate-and-empower style, rather than a command-and-control style. This is better suited to the expectation of empowered teams, professional staff and managers (which is why it is an important skill for senior management).

(v) Derive **authority** to manage change and implement the vision/mission of the organisation. Managers derive their authority from their position in the organisation, but this may not be enough to carry the organisation forward: leaders derive their authority through interpersonal influence, inspiring willing 'followership'.

Official ACCA Marking Scheme	**Marks**
(a) 1 mark per capability and 1 mark per duty of a supervisor. Up to a maximum of 6 marks in total.	6
(b) 2 marks for each valid factor up to a maximum of four factors (4 × 2). Up to a maximum of 6 marks in total.	6
(c) 2 marks for each valid explanation up to a maximum of six points (2 × 6). Up to a maximum of 8 marks in total.	8
Maximum for question	20

9 INDIVIDUAL BEHAVIOUR

Tutorial note. This is quite a challenging question. Start by defining personality and attitudes, to anchor your answer in specifics. So much emphasis is placed, these days, on teamworking, that it is easy to forget that teams are not always the most suitable option. Part (b) invites you to consider when an individual might function more effectively on his or her own than in a team: think about your own experiences in group decision-making to give you some ideas.

(a) (i) **Personality and work behaviour**

Personality is the total pattern of characteristic ways of thinking, feeling and behaving that constitute the individual's distinctive method of relating to the environment.

If our personality factors affect work behaviour

(1) **Different personality types may suit different types of work.** A person who is inhibited and introverted, for example, may find sales work,

involving a lot of social interactions, intensely stressful – and will probably not be very effective.

(2) **Different personality types may suit different organisational structures, systems and cultures.** Some people hate to be controlled, for example, while others prefer to work in bureaucratic organisations because they prefer the security, predictability and lack of individual responsibility.

(3) Different personality types may 'clash' with each other: a prime source of conflict at work. Perfectionist personalities, for example, may be irritated by more 'laid back' characters (and vice versa).

(4) **Different personality types will have different orientations to work.** Some people will be achievement- or results-oriented, while others will see work primarily as an opportunity for social interaction, satisfying activity, security or the earning of rewards. This will influence the effectiveness of the organisation's strategies for motivation.

(ii) **Attitudes and work behaviour**

Attitudes are mental states (comprised of beliefs, perceptions, feelings, desires and volition) which **predispose individuals** to behave in certain ways in certain contexts. Attitudes may affect work behaviour in the following ways.

(1) **Attitudes to work may be positive or negative.** These will include attitudes to working (as opposed to leisure), work colleagues, working conditions, the task, management, the organisation and so on. They will influence a wide variety of work behaviours: the extent of co-operation or conflict between individuals and groups or between workers and management; the extent of the employees commitment to and contribution to organisational goals; the kinds of incentives and rewards that will motivate the individual and so on.

(2) **Individuals bring all sorts of attitudes about the world to work with them.** These may be attitudes to politics, education, religion, race and so on. They will affect how the individual relates to work colleagues, areas of agreement and conflict, shared perceptions or barriers to communication. Some attitudes may be specifically controlled in the workplace (through legislation and policy on sexual harassment, racial discrimination and so on).

(b) **Individual and group contribution**

Group working has certain advantages for task performance and worker satisfaction: the pooling of skills and resources; opportunities for social interaction; encouraging co-ordination and communication and so on.

However, groups are not always more effective than individual contribution.

(i) Individuals can **make decisions faster than groups** (although not always with the same amount of information and the same degree of acceptability).

(ii) Individuals **can focus on the task**, where groups give energy to relationships, conflicts and group maintenance.

(iii) Individuals can **exercise personal creativity** and flair, where group norms may encourage conformity.

(iv) Individuals are **more cautious in exercising responsibility**, where the shared responsibility in a group can lead to complacent and risky decisions.

Answer bank

Marking scheme	Marks
(a)(i) 2-3 marks for each valid point made about 'personality' and its impact upon work behaviour	7
(a)(ii) 2-3 marks for each valid point about 'attitudes', including explanation of 'predisposition'	7
(b) 1-2 marks for each valid point, up to a maximum of six	6
Maximum for question	20

10 PROJECT TEAM

> *Tutorial note.* A practical situation - but you are specifically asked to use 'concepts' and 'theory' in your answer. Key issues are that the team members do not know each other personally, and that they work in different disciplines in the organisation.

Cross-functional project teams

Team working has become more prevalent, partly because organisations are supposed to be more flexible, and partly because teams are an effective medium of empowerment.

Whilst team working can satisfy people's social needs for companionship, organisations are adopting team based structures because they produce effective work results.

Cross functional teams contain members from different departments in the business. For example, a cross-functional team in charge of implementing a new sales order processing system should ideally contain team members from the sales function, the finance function, and any specialist IT employees.

Effective teams

A group is a collection of people who perceive themselves to be a group, and who can distinguish between members and outsiders. Groups can be formal or informal. A team is a special type of group. A team is formed of people who have to pursue a particular objective (eg install a new IT system, win the cup final). It thus has a purpose. This purpose is, for teams working within organisations, imposed from the outside, as is the case in this question.

Other differences between teams and groups relate to the following.

- The interpersonal relationships - in an effective team, people can be open about work issues and trusting of the others within the team

- People have to learn explicitly how to work as a team. Issues related to the processes of the team have to be worked out overtly rather than covertly.

- Finally teams are formed not in practice to satisfy social needs, although team member satisfaction is an important outcome of teamwork, but to get a task completed. A focus on the task is a characteristic of teams.

Team members

A feature of effective teams is that people can play a number of roles in the dynamics of the team. Belbin identified nine roles.

- Co-ordinator
- Shaper
- Plant
- Monitor/evaluator
- Resource investigator
- Implementer
- Finisher
- Team worker

and, from outside, the specialist

According to Belbin, most people have preference for one of these roles, but team members may find they have to play a different role, to maintain a balance between the roles. In the situation described, this issue is complicated by the fact that the team is a cross-functional project team drawn from different departments. So the roles they play may be determined by their expertise at any one time. For example, the accountant in a cross functional project team might have the job of ensuring the project keeps within financial targets, more of a monitor-evaluator role than say a finisher.

Team development

According to Tuckman, teams are formed in four stages.

Forming. This is when the members of the team are brought together, and the purpose and identity of the team are first defined. The cross functional project team in the question is in this stage of team development. People are still individuals and the prime allegiance of members of the cross functional project team are likely to be the individual department.

Storming involves open conflict, perhaps against the decisions reached in the forming stage. At the forming stage people toe the line, but at the storming stage they begin to assert themselves individually. This stage has the advantage of bringing key issues into the open. However, some teams may get stuck in this stage, and so the successful team builder has to resolve the issues raised.

Norming. The team settles down and establishes a procedures for getting the task done. Decisions are hopefully reached by consensus. In this stage, people might adopt one or more of the roles identified by Belbin.

Performing. The team gets on with the job it is brought together to do.

Building the team

The manager will want to speed up the process of team development to the performing stage - after all time is a scarce resource, and organisations cannot indulge the team too much.

Leadership. The leader of a team must, to be successful, give appropriate attention to the needs of the task, the needs of the team and the needs of the individuals.

Team building involves:

- Building team identity: the team can be given a defined name or role in the confines of the organisation

- Encouraging group loyalty/solidarity, by encouraging interpersonal relationships, controlling conflict and expressing solidarity. The team leader has to build support and trust

- Encouraging commitment to shared objectives. This can be achieved by clearly setting out the team's objectives, involving the team in target setting, giving regular clear feedback, giving positive reinforcement and championing the team within the organisation.

These team building methods must be used against time-wasting blockages to building the team. These blockages include confusion as to roles, excessive competition between group members who are unwilling to share anything.

Action plan

The team leader of the project under consideration should set up an action plan for building the team. The aim of the plan is to get the forming, storming and norming stages over in two meetings, and also to build the team identity and its commitment to the objective.

Answer bank

(a) Clearly identify the task (eg install a new computer system).

(b) Define membership and get the agreement of the participants (and their bosses)

(c) Get resources for the team - eg an office, where necessary, admin backup

(d) At the first team meeting:

   (i) Get the agreement of team members on a timetable for the project (eg the sales system will be set up within six months). This should be realistic - nothing will be gained by underplaying the work involved, and expectations should not be too high.

   (ii) Explain to them the importance of the project, what the firm expects, and why they have been chosen: this is a key opportunity to build team identity.

   (iii) Have a brainstorming or 'get-to-know you' session, perhaps to get early difficulties out of the way (eg sales personnel may not appreciate the cost implications of the project; accounts staff may not appreciate the need for the system to assist the sales unction as well as generate management accounts).

   (iv) Team members should leave the meeting with a task (eg ask them to come up with various ideas).

(e) Second team meeting

   (i) Define and agree objectives in order to achieve the objectives of the team
   (ii) Define methodology - what approaches should be taken
   (iii) Agree how the project will be monitored

(f) Subsequent meetings should deal with the actual work of the team.

Marking scheme

The answer should be based on a sound knowledge of the basis for team building with reference to relevant concepts. These concept should provide a sound framework for the practical nature of the question. Demonstration of a systematic approach to an action plan for practical team building is called for and reflected in the marking scheme.

	Marks
Broad references to the increased awareness of the current need for team building initiatives linked to changes in organisational structures	2

Identification of the need to relate team building to required outcomes
    Effective task achievement
    Team member satisfaction
	2

Differentiation between groups and teams	2
Features of effective teamwork - drawn from following list	4
Balance of roles and skills, honesty and openness, mistakes openly faced, helpful competition support and trust, good relations, pride in success high level of task achievement	
Impact of *Belbin's* team roles on effectiveness	2
Identification of how stage of team development affects practical team building *Tuckman's* stages	2

Answer bank

Marking scheme (Cont.)	Marks
Blockages to, and building blocks for, team building, drawing on *Woodcock* list	4
How the awareness of problems in these areas can waste time and money and lower morale	
Factors to be aware of in practical approach a plan	2
Including clear aims, start modestly, relate to work of organisation, realistic timetables, consult openly, do not raise false expectations	
Maximum for question	20

11 MOTIVATION THEORIES

> *Tutorial note.* This should have been straightforward. Phrases in inverted commas clearly signal a specific theory to be addressed: in this case, you also have named theorists within the specific schools. There are two main pitfalls to avoid here. First, don't waste marks explaining Maslow and Vroom in your answers to parts (a) and (c): save it for parts (b) and (d). Second, note the key word in part (b): you are asked to describe the problems with Maslow's hierarchy, not the hierarchy itself (other than in introductory comments, perhaps).

(a) The **content theory** of motivation asks the question: '**What** are the things that motivate people?'

It is based on the belief that human beings have an innate set of needs or desired outcomes. Behaviour is driven and determined (motivated) by the desire to satisfy those needs or achieve those outcomes. Individuals can therefore be motivated (by others, for example at work) by offering them rewards and incentives which promise to satisfy those needs.

Maslow's hierarchy of needs thus focuses on seven innate needs, each of which motivates human action until it is satisfied. David McClelland formulated a classification of three drives or needs broadly similar to Maslow's, but suggested that people show a predisposition towards power, affiliation or achievement. Frederick Herzberg's two factor theory is based on two basic drives: the avoidance of unpleasantness and the seeking of personal growth.

(b) **Problem's with Maslow's hierarchy of needs model**

Maslow's theory is not very useful in practice for a manager wishing to motivate a team. (It has to be noted that he did not specifically intend his theory to be used in the context of organisations.)

(i) It is difficult to identify where an individual is in the hierarchy: a given behaviour may be motivated by a number of different needs.

(ii) It is difficult to predict behaviour on the basis of where the individual is in the hierarchy: an individual may satisfy a given need in any number of ways.

(iii) It is difficult to design reward systems on the basis of the hierarchy. The place of pay is ambiguous: money is a symbol and stand-in for a wide range of needs. Self-actualisation, too, is notoriously subjective and complex to offer in practice.

(iv) Individual needs, and reactions to those needs, differ.

In addition, the theory has certain internal weaknesses.

(i) It ignores phenomena such as deferred gratification (by which people endure lack of satisfaction at lower levels for the promise of future gratification at higher levels) and altruism (whereby people voluntarily suffer for others).

(ii) The theory is difficult to verify in practice.

(iii) Tests have revealed that the hierarchy may be limited to anglo (US and UK) cultures.

(c) The **process theory** of motivation asks the question: '**How** are people motivated?' or 'How can they be motivated (by others, such as a superior at work)?'

It assumes that people select their goals and appropriate courses of action to reach them, by a conscious or unconscious process of calculation. Process theory thus focuses on the ways in which:

(i) Outcomes become desirable to an individual.

(ii) Individuals select particular behaviours in order to pursue desirable outcomes.

(iii) Individuals calculate whether it is worth implementing and maintaining those behaviours in order to achieve those outcomes.

Process theories such as Vroom's expectancy theory and Handy's motivation calculus thus focus on the information processing required to determine whether to expend energy and effort (which Handy calls 'e' factors) on achieving particular results. This includes concepts such as beliefs, expectations, value attribution and so on.

(d) **Vroom's expectancy theory**

This suggests that people will decide how much they are going to put into their work according to two factors.

(i) **Valence**: the value that they (subjectively) place on a given outcome

(ii) **Expectancy**, or subjective probability: their expectation that the given outcome will in fact result from a certain behaviour

Vroom formulated an equation to model the mental calculation:

$F = V \times E$

Where:

V is valence: the strength of the person's preference for outcome y. This is expressed as a positive number (y is desired), a negative number (y is avoided) or zero (indifference).

E is expectation that doing x will result in y. This is expressed as any number between 0 (no chance) and 1 (certainty).

F is the force or strength of the motivation to do x.

Marking scheme	**Marks**
(a) 1 mark per valid point made. Important to mention '*what* motivates?' and the key writers	5
(b) 1 mark per point made to a maximum of 7: based on lack of practical applicability	7
(c) 1 mark per valid point made. Important to mention '*how* are people motivated?' and the key writers	5
(d) Define 'valence', 'expectancy' and explain the equation	3
Maximum for question	20

12 HARRY IBBOTSON

(a) **Julie's poor time management**

(i) **Mound of paper in the in-tray**

This indicates that Julie is bad at setting priorities. There is obviously a lot of work which she has not even looked at. Some of this perhaps could be delegated. She could also sort the work out into urgent and non-urgent tasks.

(ii) **Telephone and e-mail use**

We do not know the reasons for phone calls and the use of e-mail. Personal calls can obviously be reduced, but if most calls are related to her work it might suggest:

(1) She is searching for information and/or advice herself

(2) People demand to speak to her

(3) She constantly allows herself to be interrupted by the telephone or e-mail

(4) She does not know how to refuse or delay unreasonable or unimportant requests.

Interruptions inevitably mean that other work takes longer to do, as it cannot be tackled in a long stretch. She probably deals with telephone enquiries, as they appear urgent.

This shows a lack of assertiveness, and poor setting of priorities.

(iii) **The over-long report**

A report of 14 pages, rather than a half page memo, would indicate that Julie is not really capable of controlling her work. The issue obviously interested her enough to take care over it, and she probably wanted to impress the supervisor with her diligence and knowledge. It shows a failure to assess priorities.

To summarise, this indicates poor self-control, or even a lack of self-confidence.

(iv) **Late appraisal reports**

A staff appraisal is not an ad hoc request: appraisals take place at regular intervals, and Julie must have had advance knowledge as to when they would be needed. The reports are often in a standard format.

This indicates poor forward planning.

(v) **Overwork**

Overwork can be a sign that there is genuinely too much work for a person to do. In Julie's case, however, she has two assistants to help her, who do not appear to be suffering from the same problem. It is not her section which is overworking but Julie. this can be caused by:

(1) Poor delegation, so that she does too much

(2) Inefficient working

(3) Bad planning

(4) Poor control and prioritisation,

(5) Lack of self-assertiveness, as Julie might be incapable of saying no to a colleague's work demands, even though the request is unimportant.

Answer bank

A final issue is that Julie appears to have been recruited relatively recently, as Fiona and Harry both agreed that she was the right person for the job. It may be that Julie is still climbing a learning curve, and has yet to find her feet. Harry perhaps has been too relaxed in his approach to her.

(b) **What Harry can suggest**

First of all, Harry should take a more active, guiding role, in helping Julie with her work. She may not know what her priorities should be. Other specific suggestions could include the following.

(i) **Identify objectives** and the key tasks which are most relevant to achieving them. Julie should sort out what she must do, from what she could do, and from what she would like to do. 'Urgent' is not always the same as 'important'. This is particularly relevant to phone interruptions.

(ii) **Prioritising and scheduling**. Assess key tasks for relative importance, amount of time required, and any deadlines or time-spans. Routine non-essential tasks should be delegated - or done away with if possible. Routine key tasks should be organised as standard procedures and systems. Non-routine key tasks will have to be carefully scheduled as they arise, according to their urgency and importance. An up-to-date diary with a 'carry forward' system (to check on consequences of decisions, follow-up action and so on) will be helpful to her if it is properly maintained.

(iii) **Planning and control**. She should avoid, where possible, disruption by the unexpected. Schedules should be drawn up and regularly checked for 'slippage': priorities will indicate which areas may have to be set aside for more important or urgent interventions. Information and control systems in the organisation should be utilised so that problems can (as far as possible) be anticipated, and sudden decisions can be made on the basis of readily available information.

(iv) She should do a **personal plan**, in conjunction with detailed goal-planning or target setting for each day.

(v) She should **delegate** tasks to staff who are competent to perform them.

(vi) If **assertiveness** is a problem she could go on an assertiveness training course.

(vii) She should cut down on **time-wasting activities** such as unnecessary or lengthy meetings and paperwork, and interruptions.

(viii) She should ensure that **resources** are available for forthcoming work, in sufficient supply and good condition.

(ix) **Tidiness** is important for efficiency in the office as well as for the organisation's image: files and pieces of work should be easily locatable at all times (and should in any case never be left lying around, as a breach of security, fire hazard etc).

(x) She should **organise work in batches**, while relevant files are to hand, machines switched on and so on, to save time spent in turning from one job to another. Wherever possible one task at a time should be tackled and pursued until it is finished.

(xi) She should work to **plans, schedules, and checklists** rather than relying on memory alone for appointments, events and duties.

(xii) **Large, difficult or unpleasant tasks should not be put off** simply because they are large, difficult or unpleasant.

(xiii) She should take advantage of **work patterns**. Self-discipline is aided by developing regular hours or days for certain tasks: getting into the habit of dealing with correspondence first thing, filing at the end of the day.

(xiv) She should **follow up** tasks, and see them through. Incomplete work, necessary future action, expected results or feedback should be scheduled for the appropriate time and entered in a 'follow-up' file or diary so that she will be reminded to check that the result/action has occurred as promised. **Checklists** are also useful for making sure an operation is completed, marking the stage reached in case it has to be handed over to someone else (because of illness, holiday and so on) or temporarily laid aside because of higher priority interruptions.

Marking scheme	**Marks**
(a) 2 marks for explanation of each symptom	10
(b) 1 mark per suggestion to a maximum of 10 (*the answer above shows more than would be required, for more thorough coverage*)	<u>10</u>
Maximum for question	<u><u>20</u></u>

13 COMMUNICATION SKILLS

> *Tutorial note.* The question actually covers three topics: communication skills in general, questioning and listening skills in particular and their relationship to appraisal.

Communication skills in general

Communication skills are an essential part of the manager's or supervisor's repertoire:

(a) They ensure that information is transmitted throughout the organisation with a minimum of distortion and noise - in other words that the right message gets to the right person in time.

(b) They are part of day to day management. Mintzberg's list of management roles (informational, decisional, interpersonal) suggests many of the communication skills a manager needs. Even in the tasks of planning and co-ordinating, interpersonal skills are needed.

Types of communication employed by managers

Managers use both oral and written communications in different circumstances. Written communication maintains a record, and can be used to transmit information that would be too time consuming or inconvenient to read at one go.

Oral communication is used for an immediate response or request, and is less formal. Oral communication can be more private and informal and has the benefit of being interactive. Also, it is better at conveying information about feelings - there is a rich repertoire of body language which can be used.

Communication is an essential feature of interpersonal behaviour which involves relating to other people, often with an objective in mind. Successful interpersonal behaviour is based on acting and responding to how other people behave and what they say, being aware of one's own presence on the situation.

A model of communication suggests it is a two way process - sending a message and understanding the response via feedback. Listening skills are essential in the process of understanding the response and accepting feedback. Questioning skills are essential to elicit information.

Appraisal interviews

An interview is a discussion between two or more people with some end in mind. It is structured in that the interviewer and interviewee have different roles and expectations about the interview, related to their wider role in the organisation.

The appraisal system is part of the system of *performance management*. Appraisal is the review of the past performance of an individual with a view to improving it in future. In many organisations it is part of the vexed issue of salary and reward - this might be the result of the interview but the content of the interview is primarily about performance. Any serious discussion requires good questioning and listening skills on the part of both participants.

Appraisal is part of the control system of the organisation, by setting standards, monitoring performance and taking corrective action to see that people meet them.

The stages of appraisal interview

Preparation: decide what is going to be discussed. As mentioned above, it may deal with pay. If not, the interviewer may have to have answers ready as to why not. In some appraisal systems, both appraise and appraiser have to fill in forms - employing their skills of clear, concise written communication, in order to describe key challenges in the year and how both view the appraisee's performance.

Performance review. Appraisals are often one-off exercises, on an annual basis. A problem with them is managers rarely look at performance over the whole year. The appraisal interview should take the whole year into account - the manager should have kept records if necessary to gather the right information, to ensure objectivity.

Form-filling

At the interview

Unlike a recruitment interview, the appraiser is not so much seeking to ask questions to gain factual information - he/she should after all be aware of the key issues in the performance.

However, the interviewer may wish to delve deeper as the appraisee may have reasons for particular performance issues. Some cite a 70/30 rule, where at any interview, the interviewee should be speaking for 70% of the time. Whether this is relevant to appraisal depends on the type of appraisal interview chosen. If it follows the 'tell and listen' style where the appraiser simply gives comments then the appraisee will say little. In a discussion you might expect a more equal balance - after all the purpose is to give and respond to feedback.

When information is required, two types of questions might be used.

Open questions ('What do you think went well during the year) allow the appraisee to discuss his or her triumphs, and can be elaborated on, prompting further questions. Closed questions require a definite response (eg 'Do you intend to finish your CAT studies in the next six months?)

In fact both appraiser and appraisee can use open questions, given that the appraisal can be a wide ranging discussion of various performance issues.

Appraiser and appraisee have different levels of power in the interview, even though many try to pretend otherwise, and there are appraisal systems such as upwards appraisal and 360 degrees appraisal in which this applies differently.

Answer bank

The appraiser is trying to concentrate on performance, not on personality, and so a relaxed and open atmosphere will encourage open and honest communication between both sides. The appraiser must also be aware of his/her tendency to bias and stereotype. the interview must be succeeded by **follow-up action**.

Clear communication skills are needed because:

- People can read different meanings into a message
- The interview will have to be summed up and signed by both parties
- Both parties will have to agree on various performance issues and objectives for the future. Listening skills - on both participants in the interview - are essential in this context.

Marking scheme

Good answers will make a link between questioning and listening skills and the part they play in conducting a successful appraisal interview A sound knowledge and understanding of the communication process and its importance to the management's supervisory role is expected. Generally, answers will indicate a satisfactory knowledge of the process of appraisal and, specifically, the value of the appraisal interview in the process.

	Marks
Importance of communication skills	2

Methods of communication
    Formal/informal
    Verbal and written
	2

Link with motivation and feedback	2
Purpose of appraisal process	
Importance of the appraisal interview	2
The part listening and questioning skills play	2

Key stages in the appraisal interview
    Preparation
    Information gathering
    Structure
	3

Interviewing skills	
The importance of questioning and listening	1
Establish rapport/relaxed atmosphere	1
Use of closed/open questions	2
Avoiding stereotyping	1
Avoid subjectivity/emotional responses	1
Review/action plan/future review	1
Maximum for question	20

Answer bank

14 PERFORMANCE MANAGEMENT

> *Tutorial note.* Part (a). 'Performance management' has a clear and distinct meaning in people management. It is a means of establishing a performance framework of objectives shared by employees and the organisation. This part of the question specifically requires a description of the concept.
>
> Part (b). This part of the question clearly asks for the steps involved in performance management. The essence of performance management is that it looks forward, unlike appraisals which look back.
>
> Part (c). This part requires a short and succinct listing of the advantages of performance management. The advantages accruing to an employee though performance management (ie the linking of individual and organisational objectives) must and will be different to those advantages gained through training or successful appraisal.

As business environments have become more competitive and complex, it has been acknowledged that the human resources of the enterprise have an increasing impact on the organisation's success, through their knowledge, creativity, interpersonal skills, flexibility and so on. A sophisticated human resource in a fast-changing environment requires looser managerial control and the willing commitment of the individual to the goals of the enterprise. There is a need to integrate individual and organisational goals, and to support individual performance with feedback information for problem-solving and continuous improvement: performance management is designed to fulfil this need.

(a) **Performance management** is an approach to performance appraisal and development which is designed to integrate individual, team and organisational goals in order to facilitate both employee commitment and business performance. The aim is to enable people to realise their potential and to maximise their contribution to the organisation.

Performance management is based on 'understanding and managing performance within an agreed framework of planned goals, standards and competence requirements' (Armstrong). It is a process of on-going goal-setting and problem-solving communication between performance manager and the individual or team, with a view to establishing a shared understanding of what is to be achieved, what the potential problems and constraints are, and how these can be overcome in order to reach the agreed goals. An alternative to the infrequent, retrospective and potentially judgemental process of performance assessment, performance management is the basis for on-going, collaborative, positive and results-oriented improvement and development planning.

(b) The **process of performance management** may be described as five steps.

Step 1. Identify and describe key functions, competencies, targets and standards required for job performance. This should be derived from the goals and objectives set out for the performance unit, which in turn should be derived from the corporate plan of the business as a whole.

Note: One of the purposes of performance management is to encourage awareness of the mission, goals and objectives of the enterprise: individual performance targets should be based on detailed annual plans underpinned by a clear strategic direction.

Step 2. Define realistic standards and conditions of performance, specific and measurable performance indicators and skill/competency requirements for the job. Taking advantage of input from job-holders as to the nature and requirements of the job, this should result in a mutually acceptable and understood definition of what is expected of the individual or team, in the form of a performance agreement.

Step 3. Draw up a detailed performance and development plan with the collaboration and agreement of the individual or team concerned. This is essentially a problem-solving action plan, detailing:

  (i)   Areas of performance identified as requiring improvement
  (ii) Areas in which the job holder would benefit from training
  (iii) Specific improvements that could be investigated or implemented
  (iv) Areas in which there is potential for future development

Step 4. Monitor, evaluate, discuss and adjust performance on a continual basis. Regular reviews of performance are used as opportunities to exchange feedback, in order to:

  (i)   Identify problems or opportunities and plan control action
  (ii) Reinforce successful performance (with praise, recognition, enlarged responsibility, bonus rewards and so on)
  (iii) Adjust work plans or targets
  (iv) Identify the need for coaching, training or other inputs

Step 5. Review performance at the end of the agreed period (say, annually). Actual performance is evaluated against the agreed performance plan (by methods akin to traditional appraisal: reports, interviews and so on.) However, this is again to be seen as a forward-looking, problem-solving, opportunity-planning activity, centred on on-going improvement.

(c) **Benefits to employees**

Given the constructive, forward-looking and collaborative aspects of performance management, its advantages should be as follows.

  (i)   Security: knowing exactly what is expected, and (having agreed targets) that it is realistically achievable.
  (ii) Opportunity to be involved in problem solving and contribution: source of job satisfaction.
  (iii) Opportunities for learning and development.
  (iv) Managerial commitment to support performance (resources, training, systems improvements etc).
  (v)   Constructive orientation: absence of negative/punitive, judgemental appraisal.

Marking scheme	Marks
(a) Description of 'performance management'	5
(b) Description of process of performance management (2 marks per step of process, five steps altogether)	10
(c) List advantages (1 mark per advantage = 5)	5
Maximum for question	20

Answer bank

15 TRAINING AND DEVELOPMENT

> *Tutorial note.* This question features multiple parts on related topic areas: make sure you read the topic and instruction key words carefully and answer the exact question set for each part. Part (c) is particularly complex: you need to outline both advantages and disadvantages of individual training and development (compared with collective training and development) from the perspective of both the individual and the organisation. This is a useful exercise in structuring your answer: check that you have answered all aspects of part (c) and that you have not run over time for the available mark allocation.

(a) **Steps of the training process**

A systematic approach to training would include the following steps.

(i) **Identify and define the organisation's training needs.** Measure current skills in the work force (or a given section of it) and compare these with the skills and competences required for the achievement of objectives (now and in the future).

(ii) **Define the learning required.** Specify the knowledge, skills or competences to be required, by whom and when.

(iii) **Define training objectives.** Reframe training needs as specific individual and group learning targets and timescales.

(iv) **Plan training programmes.** Decide who provides the training (in-house or external providers); where the training will take place (on the job, in internal training facilities or external venues); and how the training will be delivered (formal teaching, instruction, computer-based training and so on).

(v) **Implement the training programme.** Carry out the training plan and monitor progress to ensure that training objectives are being met.

(vi) **Monitor, review and evaluate training.** Training can be evaluated according to whether objectives have been met, changes in trainees' job performance and behaviour, knock-on changes in performance indicators (such as accidents and errors), and trainee satisfaction.

(vii) Remaining, further or on-going training needs can then be identified and addressed by new or adjusted training programmes.

(b) **Key stages in preparing a PDP**

A personal development plan is a developmental action plan for individual training and development. Three broad stages in preparing such a plan are: analysing the current position, setting goals, and action planning to achieve the goals.

(i) **Analysing the current position.** This may be achieved by personal competence assessment (perhaps using the appraisal system or training needs analysis self-appraisals of the organisation). An alternative approach is to do a personal SWOT (strengths, weaknesses, opportunities, threats) analysis. Another approach is to work through the individual's job description and identify (using a simple matrix), tasks which the employee does/doesn't do well and does/doesn't like or show aptitude for.

(ii) **Setting goals.** Learning goals may be set to cover performance in the existing job (moving tasks from the 'doesn't do well' side of the matrix to the 'does well' side), as well as accounting for anticipated changes in the job role (creating new demands) and for the individual's career aspirations (developing for promotion or career change). Tasks which the individual likes but doesn't do well might suggest priority goals, since the aptitude and motivation are already present for learning.

(iii) **Action planning**. This should involve systematic formulation of specific learning objectives, planning of methods of development (including learning from others and from work experience, as well as training opportunities), setting timescales for review and achievement, and planning monitoring, review and feedback opportunities.

(c) **Individual vs collective training and development**

Individual (as opposed to collective) training offers the following key advantages for the individual.

(i) His or her individual learning preferences or style can be taken into account, making the learning experience both more congenial and more effective. It would be particularly beneficial for learners who prefer a high degree of personal interaction and involvement, and to be able to learn at their own pace.

(ii) His or her particular learning needs and goals can be addressed by the content of the training. Individual strengths and weaknesses can be more flexibly responded to by the trainer, thanks to the greater interactivity of the process.

For the organisation, this has advantages in maximising the learning potential of individuals and the effectiveness of individual training, which may be desirable for senior management and highly specialised positions and tasks.

Individual training also has disadvantages, however.

(i) **Incompatibility with learning style**. Activists, for example, thrive on interaction in groups, which would not be provided by individual learning. Pragmatists thrive on practical application: individual training may pay insufficient attention to work group context.

(ii) **Possible delay of training**. If a number of individuals have to be trained individually, training may be intermittent or delayed for each of them, which may weaken learning and motivation.

For the organisation, the disadvantages of individual training compared to collective training are:

- Greater time required (especially if a number of people are to be trained sequentially)
- Greater cost (because it is more labour intensive)
- Loss of an opportunity to foster team spirit and teamworking through group training programmes

Official ACCA Marking Scheme	Marks
(a) 1.5 marks per step up to a maximum of seven steps Up to a maximum of 7 marks in total.	7
(b) 2.5 marks per stage, up to a maximum of three stages (2.5 × 3). Up to a maximum of 6 marks in total.	6
(c) 1.5 marks per advantage and disadvantage up to a maximum of six (1.5 × 6). Up to a maximum of 7 marks in total.	7
Maximum for question	20

Answer bank

16 SAFETY AT WORK

> *Tutorial note.* Neither of these answers is exhaustive. You may well have thought of other examples from personal experience.

To protect yourself you could take measures such as the following.

(a) Closely follow organisational guidelines about personal safety and security.

(b) Avoid doing things that might provoke people. These could include, for example, being insensitive (wearing a £500 Armani suit to work when you spend much of the day dealing with people living in poverty, say); descending to abusive language if people start swearing at you; allowing yourself to be distracted by telephone calls or other demands on your attention that make the person you are dealing with feel that he or she is not being taken seriously; being inconsistent or showing favouritism (bending the rules for one customer but not for the next).

If you can think of more specific things that would upset the people you deal with in your job, be sure to note them down.

(c) Don't take unnecessary risks. If a customer asks you out for a drink, say, refuse if you are at all unsure of them. If you are tempted to agree, meet in a public place, make sure someone knows you are going, don't give them personal information like your address and phone number until you are sure of them.

(d) Seek assistance from colleagues or security staff if an interviewee starts to become threatening.

(e) Don't be violent or aggressive in manner towards your customer: an obvious point, but worth making.

Your employer could take the following measures.

(a) Provide you with training in dealing with difficult situations.

(b) Provide you with protection by arranging the working environment in such a way that it would be physically difficult to assault you. The obvious example is the counters and screens in banks and post offices. Modern systems have armour plated screens that are not normally on view but which can rise up and seal off staff from the public area in less than a second.

(c) Not place you in situations that are likely to lead to aggression. One example would be abandoning petty bureaucratic rules that just annoy people. Another would be providing whatever it is that people are paying for to the required standard (assaults on public transport staff, for example, may ultimately be due to the failure of the public transport managers to provide a good service).

If you really are in this situation you may be interested to know that the Suzy Lamplugh Trust has produced a *Guide to Personal Safety at Work* which gives advice on developing confidence, assessing and reducing risks, dealing with aggression and physical attack, and travelling safely outside the workplace.

Marking scheme	Marks
Protecting yourself	10
Employer responsibilities	10
Maximum for question	20

17 DATA SECURITY

> *Tutorial note.* This question should be straightforward, if you have revised this area of the syllabus. The main challenge is to structure your answer effectively. In part (a) you must both explain the importance of data protection and identify the main risks to data: make sure you have referred to the three types of risk mentioned in part (b)! In part (b) you must explain security measures and give examples of relevant systems/products.

(a) **Importance of data protection**

The protection of data is vital to support business decisions and transactions with reliable, accurate and complete data and information. It is also required to support ethical and legal dealings in regard to individual privacy and the disclosure of information, as covered by the Data Protection Act.

Information is critical to all business activities and systems. Data stored in organisational systems is constantly needed to support:

- Marketing strategy and customer relationship management (eg data on customer transactions and preferences)
- Efficient materials and supply chain management (eg supplier data, inventory)
- The control and use of funds

Potentially sensitive data now flows more freely than at any time in history between the organisation and its various stakeholders. Trends towards employee consultation and involvement and customer relationship marketing, for example, have increased the availability of potentially sensitive information on corporate intranets and extranets.

Meanwhile, ICT developments have enabled the gathering, storage and use of much larger amounts of data than has been possible previously.

(i) Databased information must be kept secure, both because it is potentially commercially sensitive (eg data on markets and inventory) and because it may be covered by Data Protection provisions (eg data on customers and employees).

(ii) Increasingly, transactions are conducted via the Internet and similar systems. Huge amounts of personal, business and transactional information – and funds – are transmitted electronically, and security is a major concern of e-Commerce users.

Risks to data

(i) **Human error.** Individuals lose, damage or incorrectly input or file data so that it is irretrievable or unusable.

(ii) **Technical malfunction or error.** Systems, equipment or software fails, resulting in loss, damage, corruption or inability to access data.

(iii) **Catastrophic events.** Natural disasters and major accidents can disrupt organisational activity, break communication systems and destroy data.

(iv) **Malicious damage.** Individuals deliberately attempt to disrupt the organisation's activities by damaging or tampering with data. (Examples in a computerised system include 'hacking' into the system or spreading viruses.)

(v) **Industrial espionage or sabotage.** Individuals deliberately attempt to steal or damage data, with a view to commercial gain. (Examples including selling plans to a competitor, or delaying a product launch on their behalf.)

(vi) **Dishonesty.** Dishonest individuals may wish to access information, or steal funds, for personal gain, for example through various forms of fraud.

(b) **Protecting data systems**

Risks of human error can be reduced by the measures below:

- Automation or computerisation of processes (eg input via EFTPOS and similar systems, rather than by manual data entry), checks and controls (eg computer calculation or spell checking)
- Checks and controls on work by procedures and supervision
- The use of systematic procedures to maintain consistency in work practices
- Employee training and supervision

Risk of technical error and malfunction can be minimised by:

- Regular system testing and maintenance
- The use of backup systems. In a computerised system, for example, a 'grandfather-father-son' system may be used to ensure that there are three generations of files available at any time. On a PC or smaller network server, data may be backed up daily onto hard disk, tape or CD-ROM, with the backup media re-used weekly.

Risk of malicious damage and industrial espionage/sabotage can be minimised by controlling access to data, both physically and electronically. Basic control procedures include:

- The use of locked safes and filing cabinets
- The use of passwords to secure access to computer systems and files, supported by user profiles which classify data and software according to sensitivity and confidentiality
- The use of strong encryption of electronic data transmissions
- The use of software for virus checking, 'vaccination' (prevention) and removal (such as Dr Solomon's), with procedures and guidelines for avoiding infection (such as checking of e-mail attachments and external data disks)
- Training staff in the need to keep all passwords, codes and keys secure.

Disasters may be difficult to foresee, but contingency plans should be in place for such matters as:

- Off-site backup storage of files
- Emergency power generators in the event of power failure
- Adequate insurance for any loss or damage to data and associated systems.

Marking scheme	Marks
(a) Up to 6 marks for explaining why data protection is important and 1 mark per risk up to a maximum of six risks (6 + 6). Up to a maximum of 10 marks in total.	10
(b) 1.5 marks per explanation and 1.5 marks per example up to a maximum of 5 explanations and 5 examples (3 × 5). Up to a maximum of 10 marks in total.	10
Maximum for question	20

Key terms & Index

List of key terms

These are the terms which we have identified throughout the text as being KEY TERMS. You should make sure that you can define what these terms mean; go back to the pages highlighted here if you need to check.

Accountability, 131
Activity scheduling, 218
Assertive behaviour, 250
Audit, 14
Authority, 130

Budget, 122
Bureaucracy, 39

Cadbury report, 14
Communication, 237
Control total, 74
Cost centre, 119
Cost code, 119
Counselling, 252
Culture, 162

Delegation, 132
Demography, 10
Development, 286
Discipline, 200
Divisionalisation, 35

Empowerment, 196
Ergonomics, 324
Evaluation of training, 298
External audit, 79

Feedback, 269
Flat organisation, 30
Fraud, 86

Grievance, 258
Group, 158

Incentive, 190
Internal audit, 76
Internal checks, 73
Internal control system, 70
Interpersonal skills, 235

Job description, 210
Job enlargement, 196
Job enrichment, 196
Job rotation, 196

Leadership, 141
Learning organisation, 302

Management information system (mis), 119
Management, 134
Module, 64
Motivation, 188
Motives, 188

Non-verbal communication, 247

Oral communication, 244
Organisation culture, 163
Organisation structure, 23
Organisation, 4

Password, 354
Perception, 156
Performance management, 267
Personal development plan, 291
Personality, 155
Post-list, 74
Pre-list, 74
Prioritising, 215
Procedure, 211

Responsibility, 131
Reward, 190

Self development, 291
SPAM SOAP, 71
Span of control, 28
Stakeholders, 12
Supervisor, 139
System, 6, 210

Tall organisation, 30
Team, 171
Time scheduling, 218
Training, 286
True and fair, 79

List of key terms

User profile, 354

Validation of training, 298

Index

360 degree appraisal, 275

Accident, 311, 329
Accountability, 77, 131, 133
Accounting controls, 70
Accounting packages, 62
Accounts department
    co ordination within, 61
Action plan, 292
Activists, 300
Activity, 5
Administrative controls, 70
Administrative procedures, 211
Administrative system, 210
Aggressive behaviour, 251
Apollo, 165
Applications software, 62
Appraisal, 76
    upward appraisal, 274
Appraisal and pay, 278
Appraisal as annual event, 278
Appraisal as bureaucracy, 278
Appraisal as chat, 277
Appraisal as confrontation, 277
Appraisal as judgement, 277
Appraisal as unfinished business, 278
Appraisal barriers, 277
Appraisal interviews, 276
Appraisal procedures, 272
Appraisal standard, 273
Appraisal techniques, 273
Appraisal, management expertise and
    empowerment, 278
Arithmetical and accounting controls, 72
Artefacts, 163
Ashridge studies, 144
Assertive behaviour, 250
Athena, 165
Audit, 14
    types of, 76
Audit report, 79
Audit trail, 63
Auditing practices board (asb), 14
Auditing regulations, 14
Auditing standards and guidelines, 14
Authorisation, 70, 71, 72, 75, 112
Authorisation and approval, 71
Authority, 72, 130
Authority role, 235

Bad debt policy, 88
Balance sheet, 79
Barriers to communication, 239
Behavioural incident methods, 273
Behaviourist psychology, 299
Behaviours, 234

Beliefs and values, 163
Bench-marking, 58
Blake and mouton's managerial grid, 146
Bogus supply of goods or services, 87
Bring forward, 225
Bring up, 225
Budget, 122
Bureaucracy, 39, 165
Burns and Stalker, 38
Business functions, 22
Business plan, 267

Capital projects, 59
Career development, 297
Cash flow forecast, 121
Centralisation, 32
Changing priorities, 216
Checklists, 219, 225, 253
Chemicals, 322
Closed system, 6
Club culture, 164
Coaching, 294
Codes of practice, 17
Coding, 63
Coding structure, 118
Coding system, 58
Collecting management information, 118
Collusion with customers, 87
Combined code, 15
Communicating, 140
Communication, 235, 237, 255
Communication difficulties, 240
Communication methods, 242
Communication process, 237
Companies Act 1985, 79
Company law, 13, 17
Comparison with budgets, 122
Comparisons, 120
Comparisons with competitors, 123
Comparisons with corresponding periods, 121
Comparisons with forecasts, 121
Comparisons with other organisations, 123
Comparisons with previous periods, 120
Comparisons within organisations, 122
Competition, 255
Competitors, 123
Compliance tests, 77
Compromise, 256
Computer hackers, 93
Computer workstations, 323
Computerised accounting, 62
Content theories, 191
Contingencies, 51
Contingency theory, 26, 28, 148
Continuous improvement, 278

407

Index

Contribution, 122
Contribution as a team member, 162
Contribution as an individual, 162
Contribution patterns, 175
Control, 50, 70, 117
Control total, 74
Controlling, 140
Controls, 102, 106
Controls over payments, 112
Co-ordination, 32, 51, 61, 255
Copyright, 16
Corporate governance, 14
Corporate image, 310
Corresponding period, 121
Cost centres, 118, 119
Cost code, 119
Costing module, 64
Counselling, 252, 276
Courses, 295
Credit terms, 110
Critical, 273
Culture, 28, 133, 162, 163, 235, 240
Customer appraisal, 275
Customer care, 236
Cut-off procedures, 111

Data protection, 16
Data Protection Act 1998, 343, 349
Data protection principles, 350
Data security, 342
Decentralisation, 32
Decision making, 117
Decisional, 138
Decoding, 238
Delayering, 41
Delegation, 132
Demography, 10
Denial/withdrawal, 256
Developing people, 137
Development, 286, 297
Differences, 123, 255
Differentials, 199
Dionysus, 165
Directors, 80
Discharge, 202
Disciplinary layoffs, 202
Disciplinary situations, 201
Discipline, 200
Discrimination, 16
Disposal of assets to employees, 87
Disseminater, 138
Distortion, 239
Disturbance handler, 138
Divisionalisation, 35, 37
Dominance, 256
Dorming, 177
Drucker, 22, 136

E factors, 195
Economic environment, 9
Economic growth, 11
Economic performance, 136
Effective communication, 243
Electric shock, 322
Electrical equipment, 321
Emails, 242, 244
Emergency procedures, 329
Employer brand, 310
Empowerment, 27, 196, 278
Encoding, 238
Entrepreneur, 138
Environment, 28
Environmental influences, 7
Environmental uncertainty, 7
Equal opportunities, 16
Equal or peer role, 235
Equity, 199
Ergonomics, 324
Evacuations, 330
Evaluation of training, 298
Excellence, 166
Existential culture, 165
Expectancy, 194
Expert power, 130
Experts, 165
External audit, 79
External auditors, 79, 80

Facial expression, 248
Fayol, 24, 134
Feedback, 51, 238
Fictitious customers, 87
Fictitious sales, 88
Figurehead, 137
Financial accounting regulations, 13
Financial accounts, 120
Financial controller, 59
Financial information, 117
Financial Reporting Standards (FRSs), 13
Financial statements, 79
Fire hazards, 326
Fire precautions (workplace) regulations 1997, 326
Fire precautions act 1971, 313
Flat organisation, 30
Flexibility, 26
Flexible organisation, 41
Forecasts, 121
Formal groups, 158
Founder, 164
Fraud and error, 74
Functional departmentation, 33
Functional organisation, 33, 36

Index

Garvin, 302
Geographical departmentation, 34
Geographical organisation, 37
Gestures, 248
Grading, 273
Grievance, 258
Grievance procedures, 258
Group, 158
Group behaviour, 159
Group cohesion, 160
Group influence, 159
Group norms, 159
Group process, 160
Group think, 160, 162
Guided assessment, 273

Handbooks, 244
Handy, 148, 164
Harrison, 164
Hawthorne studies, 135
Health and safety, 16
Health and Safety at Work Act 1974, 313
Health and safety policy, 317
Health and safety regulations, 320
Health and safety training, 317
Hersey and Blanchard, 149
Herzberg, 136, 193, 195
Hierarchy, 40
Hierarchy of objectives/goals, 21
High priority, 215
Honey, 300
Horizontal structures, 41
Human relations, 135, 188
Human relations school, 135
Human resources, 28
Human Rights Act 1998, 343
Hybrid structures, 38
Hygiene factors, 193

Identifying the risks, 93
Illness, 329
ILO, 313
Incentive, 190
Independence, 76
Individual performance in the job, 199
Induction, 296
Influences on organisation structure, 28
Influencing, 249
Informal groups, 158
Informal organisation, 41
Informational, 138
Informing, 249
Innovation, 137
Instructions, 211
Integrated accounting system, 120

Integrated software, 64
Integrated system, 113
Integration/ collaboration, 256
Intellectual property, 16
Internal audit
  features of, 76
Internal audit, 76
Independence, 78
Internal audit department, 60
Internal auditors, 80
Internal checks, 73
Internal control, 70, 80
  types of, 70
Internal control system, 70
  characteristics of, 75
Internal control systems, 70
Internal controls, 61, 70
  limitations of, 76
International accounting standards, 13
International Labour Organisation (ILO), 310
Interpersonal, 137
Interpersonal relationships, 235
Interpersonal skills, 235

Janis, 160
Jargon, 240
Job content, 199
Job enlargement, 196
Job enrichment, 196
Job evaluation, 199
Job instruction, 294
Job optimisation, 197
Job satisfaction, 189

Katz and kahn, 142
Kotter, 141

Lack of training within the management team, 93
Leader, 137
Leadership, 141, 164
Leadership style, 143
Learning cycle, 301
Learning disability, 302
Learning from experience, 303
Learning objective, 292
Learning organisation, 302
Learning process, 299
Learning resources, 292
Learning styles, 300
Learning theory, 299
Legislation, 289
Legitimate or position power, 130
Letters, 243

Index

Liaison, 137
Likert, 146
Listening skills, 246
Loading, 218
Long-term trends, 121

MacGregor, Douglas, 197
Management, 141
Management controls, 72
Management development, 297
Management information, 117
Management Information System (MIS), 119
Management of Health and Safety at Work Regulations 1992, 314, 315
Management reports, 64
Management team, 303
Managerial role, 137
Managing conflicts, 255
Manipulation of bank reconciliations and cash books, 87
Manipulation of depreciation figures, 88
Manipulation of year end events, 88
Manual handling, 323
Manuals and handbooks, 211
Market rates, 199
Maslow, 191
Matrix organisation, 37
Matrix structure, 35
Mayo, 135
Mechanistic organisations, 38
Meeting budgets/target performance measures, 87
Memoranda, 242, 244
Mentoring, 294
Middle line, 26
Mintzberg, 25, 137
Misuse of pension funds or other assets, 87
Modules, 64
Monitor, 138
Monitoring and review plan, 292
Monitoring at work, 343
Motivating, 140
Motivation, 188, 236
Motivation calculus, 195
Motivator factors, 193
Motives, 188
Mourning/adjourning, 177
Movement, 248
Multi-skilling, 27
Multi-source appraisal, 275
Mumford, 300
Myers Briggs Type Inventory, 155

Need for ease of access and flexible systems, 93
Negative discipline, 200

Negotiating, 251
Negotiation, 236
Negotiator, 138
Noise, 239
Non-financial information, 117
Non-verbal communication, 247
Norming, 177
Notices, 211

Objectives, 21, 28, 136
Observation, 294
Off the job training, 294
Office equipment, 321
Office tools, 322
Offices, Shops and Railway Premises Act 1963, 313
Official warning, 201
Off-the-job training, 295
On-the-job training, 293, 294
Open system, 6
Operating core, 26
Operating instructions, 321
Operational audits, 77
Operational planning, 49
Oral communication, 244
Oral warning or reprimand, 201
Organisation
    effect on accounts department, 57
Organisation as a control, 72
Organisation charts, 27
Organisation culture, 163
Organisational metaphors, 38
Organising, 139
Organismic organisations, 38
Ouchi, 198
Overall assessment., 273
Over-valuation of stock, 88

Participation, 300
Pay scales, 199
Paying for goods not received, 87
Payroll fraud, 86
Payroll system, 101
Pedler, Burgoyne and Boydell, 291, 302
Perception, 156
Performance agreement, 267
Performance and development plan, 267
Performance management, 267
Performance reports, 60
Performing, 177
Personal development, 291, 298
Personal development plan, 291
Personality, 155, 177
Personality and work behaviour, 156
Personality clashes, 156
Personality traits, 155

Personality types, 155
Personnel controls, 72
PEST, 8
Physical controls, 71
Physical, coercive power, 130
Planning, 50, 117, 139
Plans, 213
Political risk, 9
Positive (or constructive) discipline, 200
Post-list, 74
Posture, 248
Power culture, 164
Pragmatists, 300
Pre-list, 74
Principles of organisation, 24
Priorities, 213
Prioritising, 215
Problem-solving approach, 276
Procedures, 211, 235
Procedures manual, 211
Process theories, 191
Product/ brand organisation, 37
Product/brand departmentation, 34
Professional bodies, 17
Professional development, 298
Profit and loss account, 79
Profit centres, 118
Project management, 41
Project teams, 165
Projects, 118
Providing information, 61
Psychological needs, 136

Quality, 288

Rationality, 40
Reflectors, 300
Regulatory bodies, 17
Relational style, 235
Repetitive Strain Injury (RSI), 323
Reports, 242, 244
Research, 295
Resource allocator, 138
Resource power, 130
Resources, 226
Responsibility, 72, 131
Responsibility without authority, 131
Results-orientated, 273
Reward, 190
Reward system, 278
Rewarding effective teams, 183
Rituals, 163
Role culture, 165
Roles, 234

Safety regulations, 315
Safety representatives, 316
Scalar chain, 25
Scheduling, 218
Security, 342
Security procedures, 346
Segregation of duties, 71, 103, 109, 112
Selective reporting, 240
Self discipline, 201
Self-appraisals, 274
Self-image, 155
Self-study, 295
Semi-closed system, 6
Senge, 302
Situational leadership, 149
Size, 28
Social facilitation, 159
Social loafing, 159
Sources of information, 118
SPAM SOAP, 71, 73
Span of control, 28
Specialisation, 21, 40
Spokesperson, 138
Staff appraisal system, 271
Staff support, 26
Standing data, 101
Statements, 108
Statements of Standard Accounting Practice (SSAPs), 13
Status, 255
Stock Exchange Regulations, 14
Stock module, 64
Storming, 177
Strategic apex, 26
Strategic planning, 49
Stress, 325
Structural relationships, 235
Structure, 235
Substantive tests, 77
Supervision, 139
Supervisor, 139
Supervisors, managers and training, 303
Supervisory controls, 72
Suppression, 256
Suspension, 202
Symbols, 163
Synergy, 21
System, 210
Systems approach, 6
Systems audit, 77

Tactical planning, 49
Tannenbaum and Schmidt, 144
Task culture, 165
Taxation regulations, 14
Team, 156

Index

Team building, 179
Team effectiveness, 181
Team leadership, 178
Team-building, 236
Team-building exercises, 180
Teams, 158
Teamworking, 41
Technology, 11, 28
Techno-structure, 26
Teeming and lading, 87, 112
Tell and listen method, 276
Tell and sell method, 276
Theft from petty cash, 86
Theorist, 300
Theaory X, 197
Theory Y, 197
Training needs analysis, 289
Training objectives, 290
Training requirements, 289
Training surveys, 289
Trait theory, 143
Trompenaars, 162
True and fair, 79
Trust-control dilemma, 133
Tuckman, 177
Two-factor theory, 193

Understating expenses, 88
Unity of command, 25
Unity of direction, 25
Upward appraisal, 274
Urgent Issues Task Force (UITF), 13

Valence, 194
Validation of training, 298
VDUs, 323
Virus, 355
Vroom, 194

Western Electric Company, 135
Whetten and Cameron, 142
Win-win, 252
Woodcock, 179
Work demands, 255
Work environment, 318
Work experience, 294
Work planning, 217
Work role, 234
Working relationship, 234
Working style, 254
Workload, 236
Workplace (Health, Safety and Welfare) Regulations 1992, 318
Workplace changes, 289
Workplace hazards, 321
Written communication, 242

Yukl, 141

Zaleznik, 141
Zeus, 164

See overleaf for information on other
BPP products and how to order

CAT Order

To BPP Professional Education, Aldine Place, London W12 8AW
Tel: 020 8740 2211 Fax: 020 8740 1184
email: publishing@bpp.com
Order online www.bpp.com
website: www.bpp.com

Mr/Mrs/Ms (Full name)
Daytime delivery address

Postcode

Daytime Tel   Email

Date of exam (month/year)

Occasionally we may wish to email you relevant offers and information about courses and products.
Please tick to opt into this service. ☐

POSTAGE & PACKING

Study Texts

	First	Each extra	Online
UK	£5.00	£2.00	£
Europe*	£6.00	£4.00	£2.00
Rest of world	£20.00	£10.00	£4.00
			£10.00

Kits

	First	Each extra	Online
UK	£5.00	£2.00	£
Europe*	£6.00	£4.00	£2.00
Rest of world	£20.00	£10.00	£4.00
			£10.00

CDs

	First	Each extra	Online
UK	£2.00	£1.00	£
Europe*	£3.00	£2.00	£1.00
Rest of world	£8.00	£8.00	£2.00
			£8.00

	6/04 Texts	1/04 Kits	1/04 i-Learn CD	1/04 i-Pass CD	Virtual Campus enrolment
INTRODUCTORY					
Paper 1 Recording Financial Transactions	£17.95 ☐	£9.95 ☐	£29.95 ☐	£19.95 ☐	£80 ☐
Paper 2 Information for Management Control	£17.95 ☐	£9.95 ☐	£29.95 ☐	£19.95 ☐	£80 ☐
INTERMEDIATE					
Paper 3 Maintaining Financial Records	£17.95 ☐	£9.95 ☐	£30.95 ☐	£19.95 ☐	£80 ☐
Paper 4 Accounting for Costs	£17.95 ☐	£9.95 ☐	£30.95 ☐	£19.95 ☐	£80 ☐
ADVANCED CORE					
Paper 5 Managing People and Systems	£17.95 ☐	£9.95 ☐	£30.95 ☐	£21.95 ☐	£80 ☐
Paper 6 Drafting Financial Statements	£17.95 ☐	£9.95 ☐	£30.95 ☐	£21.95 ☐	£80 ☐
Paper 7 Planning, Control & Performance Management	£17.95 ☐	£9.95 ☐	£30.95 ☐	£21.95 ☐	£80 ☐
ADVANCED OPTION					
Paper 8 Implementing Audit Procedures	£17.95 ☐ (12/04 exam)	£9.95 ☐	£30.95 ☐	£21.95 ☐	£80 ☐
Paper 8 Implementing Audit Procedures	£17.95 ☐ (6/05 exam)				
Paper 9 Preparing Taxation Computations (FA2004)	£17.95 ☐ (10/04)	£9.95 ☐ (2/04)	£30.95 ☐	£21.95 ☐	£80 ☐
Paper 10 Managing Finances	£17.95 ☐	£9.95 ☐	£30.95 ☐	£21.95 ☐	£80 ☐
INTERNATIONAL STREAM					
Paper 1 Recording Financial Transactions	£17.95 ☐	£9.95 ☐			
Paper 3 Maintaining Financial Records	£17.95 ☐	£9.95 ☐			
Paper 6 Drafting Financial Statements	£17.95 ☐	£9.95 ☐			
Paper 8 Implementing Audit Procedures	£17.95 ☐	£9.95 ☐			

SUBTOTAL £ ☐

Grand Total (incl. Postage) £ ☐

I enclose a cheque for
(Cheques to *BPP Professional Education*)

Or charge to Visa/Mastercard/Switch

Card Number ☐☐☐☐ ☐☐☐☐ ☐☐☐☐ ☐☐☐☐

Expiry date ☐☐   Start Date ☐☐

Issue Number (Switch Only) ☐

Signature

Register via our website, www.bpp.com/virtualcampus/cat and pay on-line

We aim to deliver to all UK addresses inside 5 working days; a signature will be required. Orders to all EU addresses should be delivered within 6 working days. All other orders to overseas addresses should be delivered within 8 working days. * Europe includes the Republic of Ireland and the Channel Islands.

CAT Paper 5 – Managing People and Systems (6/04)

REVIEW FORM & FREE PRIZE DRAW

All original review forms from the entire BPP range, completed with genuine comments, will be entered into one of two draws on 31 January 2005 and 31 July 2005. The names on the first four forms picked out on each occasion will be sent a cheque for £50.

Name: _____   Address: _____

_____

_____

How have you used this Interactive Text?
(Tick one box only)

☐ Home study (book only)

☐ On a course: college _____

☐ With 'correspondence' package

☐ Other _____

Why did you decide to purchase this Interactive Text? *(Tick one box only)*

☐ Have used BPP Texts in the past

☐ Recommendation by friend/colleague

☐ Recommendation by a lecturer at college

☐ Saw advertising

☐ Other _____

Which BPP products have you used?

☑ Text   ☐ Kit   ☐ i-Pass   ☐ i-Learn

During the past six months do you recall seeing/receiving any of the following?
(Tick as many boxes as are relevant)

☐ Our advertisement in *ACCA Student Accountant*

☐ Other advertisement _____

☐ Our brochure with a letter through the post

☐ Our website www.bpp.com

Which (if any) aspects of our advertising do you find useful?
(Tick as many boxes as are relevant)

☐ Prices and publication dates of new editions

☐ Information on Interactive Text content

☐ Facility to order books off-the-page

☐ None of the above

Your ratings, comments and suggestions would be appreciated on the following areas

	Very useful	Useful	Not useful
Introductory section (How to use this Interactive Text)	☐	☐	☐
Key terms	☐	☐	☐
Examples	☐	☐	☐
Activities and answers	☐	☐	☐
Key learning points	☐	☐	☐
Quick quizzes	☐	☐	☐
Exam alerts	☐	☐	☐
Question Bank	☐	☐	☐
Answer Bank	☐	☐	☐
List of key terms and index	☐	☐	☐
Structure and presentation	☐	☐	☐
Icons	☐	☐	☐

	Excellent	Good	Adequate	Poor
Overall opinion of this Interactive Text	☐	☐	☐	☐

Do you intend to continue using BPP products?   ☐ Yes   ☐ No

Please note any further comments and suggestions/errors on the reverse of this page. The BPP author of this edition can be emailed at marymaclean@bpp.com

Please return this form to: Mary Maclean, CAT Range Manager, BPP Professional Education, FREEPOST, London, W12 8BR

CAT Paper 5 – Managing People and Systems (6/04)

REVIEW FORM & FREE PRIZE DRAW (continued)

Please note any further comments and suggestions/errors below

FREE PRIZE DRAW RULES

1. Closing date for 31 January 2005 draw is 31 December 2004. Closing date for 31 July 2005 draw is 30 June 2005.

2. No purchase necessary. Entry forms are available upon request from BPP Professional Education. No more than one entry per title, per person. Draw restricted to persons aged 16 and over.

3. Winners will be notified by post and receive their cheques not later than 6 weeks after the relevant draw date.

4. The decision of the promoter in all matters is final and binding. No correspondence will be entered into.